The Most Musical Nation

The Most Musical Nation

Jews and Culture in the Late Russian Empire

James Loeffler

Yale UNIVERSITY PRESS
New Haven and London

Copyright © 2010 by Yale University.
All rights reserved.
This book may not be reproduced, in whole or in part, including illustrations, in any form (beyond that copying permitted by Sections 107 and 108 of the U.S. Copyright Law and except by reviewers for the public press), without written permission from the publishers.

Designed by James J. Johnson and set in Ehrhardt Roman type by Tseng Information Systems, Inc., Durham, North Carolina.

Library of Congress Cataloging-in-Publication Data

Loeffler, James Benjamin.
The most musical nation : Jews and culture in the late Russian empire / James Loeffler.
p. cm.
Includes bibliographical references and index.
ISBN 978-0-300-13713-2 (hardcover : alk. paper) 1. Jews—Russia—Music—History and criticism. 2. Jewish musicians—Russia—History. 3. Music—Russia—19th century—History and criticism. 4. Music—Russia—20th century—History and criticism. I. Title.
ML3776.L64 2010
780.89'924047—dc22
2009046398

A catalogue record for this book is available from the British Library.

ISBN 978-0-300-19830-0

For Rachel

Contents

Acknowledgments viii

A Note on Transliterations and Dates xii

Introduction 1

CHAPTER 1. Emancipating Sounds: Anton Rubinstein and the Rise of the Russian Jewish Musician 15

CHAPTER 2. National Voices, Imperial Echoes: Joel Engel and the Russian Jewish Musical Fin de Siècle 56

CHAPTER 3. The Most Musical Nation: The Birth of the Society for Jewish Folk Music 94

CHAPTER 4. Frozen Folk Songs: Modern Jewish Culture between Art and Commerce 134

CHAPTER 5. The Neighbors' Melodies: The Politics of Music in War and Revolution 173

Conclusion 210

Notes 221

Bibliography 245

Index 263

Acknowledgments

As a young musician coming of age in the twilight of the Cold War, I was fascinated by one of the unlikelier legacies of the Soviet Union's collapse: the sight of thousands of immigrant Jewish musicians swelling the ranks of Israeli orchestras and busking on Israeli street corners. Where had all these violinists and pianists come from? Why were there so many Jews involved in Soviet classical music? And how could they have thrived in a regime so overtly antisemitic? The search for answers to these questions led me further and further back in time to the closing decades of the tsarist era. There, alongside the klezmer fiddlers famous from Yiddish literature, I found to my surprise that Jewish classical musicians had been even more prevalent than in the Soviet period. As I sought the reasons behind this historical phenomenon, I came to realize that the stories of these musicians revealed a larger set of truths about art and identity, nationalism and empire, missing from our picture of the Russian Jewish past. What began as a casual sociological observation about the end of the Soviet Union turned into something else entirely: a cultural history of Jews and music in the late Russian Empire.

This book grew out of a doctoral dissertation written in the history department at Columbia University. There Yosef Ḥayim Yerushalmi patiently ushered me into the study of Jewish history, in the process honing my appreciation for the fine art (and flawed science) of history writing. Richard Wortman introduced me to the riches of Russian history and the paradoxes of empire, generously tolerating my early ignorance. Ezra Mendelsohn, Jeremy Dauber, and Mark von Hagen each contributed invaluable advice and feedback at both early and later stages of the writing process. Mark Slobin opened my ears to the soundscapes of eastern Europe, and Jeremy Eichler shared both his critical insights into classical music and his passion for the Russian Jewish violin tradition. Most of all, my advisor, Michael Stanislawski, taught me what it means to read the past critically, with equal parts intellectual skepticism and historical imagination. He also proved to be a model teacher, a great mentor, and a good friend.

Other colleagues have also been generous with their time, comments, and critiques along the way, including Leonid Butir, Judah Cohen, Alon Confino, Nathaniel Deutsch, Walter Zev Feldman, David Fishman, Robert Geraci, John Klier, Mark Kligman, Michael Leavitt, Klára Móricz, Benjamin Nathans, Martin Peretz, Noam Pianko, Simon Rabinovitch, Evan Rapport, Daniel Schwartz, Edwin Seroussi, Ludmila Sholokhova, Francesco Spagnolo, Shaul Stampfer, Moshik Temkin, Jeffrey Veidlinger, Theodore Weeks, and Steven Zipperstein. Paula Eisenstein Baker offered constant and enthusiastic help from start to finish. Charles and Robyn Krauthammer passionately supported the music research and provided a platform to share it with a broader public audience.

Historians depend on the immense knowledge, resourcefulness, and generosity of archivists and librarians. Rachel Becker, George Crafts, Leo Greenbaum, Sharon Horowitz, Elliot Kahn, Ellen Kastel, Erin Mayhood, Chana Mlotek, Fruma Mohrer, Peggy Pearlstein, Lewis Purifoy, Bret Werb, and the staffs of the Columbia University and University of Virginia interlibrary loan offices helped me to locate and obtain rare publications. I owe great debts as well to the Center for Jewish History; the YIVO Institute for Jewish Research; the Harvard College Library Judaica Division; the Dorot Jewish, Performing Arts, and Slavic and Baltic divisions of the New York Public Library; the African and Middle Eastern and Performing Arts reading rooms of the Library of Congress; and the Library of the Jewish Theological Seminary.

Many of the documents and images used in this book came from a host of archives in Russia, Ukraine, and Israel. I am most grateful to the staff at the Gnesin State Musical College, the State Archives of the Russian Federation, the Moscow Central Historical Archive, the Glinka Central State Museum of Musical Culture, and the Russian State Archive of Literature and Art, all in Moscow; in St. Petersburg, the Institute of Oriental Studies at the Russian Academy of Sciences, the Manuscripts Division of the St. Petersburg State Conservatory Library, the Central State Archive of Literature and Art of St. Petersburg, the Central State Historical Archive of St. Petersburg, the Peter the Great Museum of Anthropology and Ethnography (Kunstkamera) of the Russian Academy of Sciences, the Russian National Library, and the Russian Institute for the History of the Arts; Kiev's Institute of Manuscripts and Judaica Division at the V. I. Vernadsky National Library of the Ukraine, the Ukrainian Central State Archive-Museum of Literature and Art, and the Kiev City State Archives; in Jerusalem, the Jewish Music Research Centre at the Hebrew University of Jerusalem, the Central Archives for the History of the Jewish People, and the Music Department of the National

Library of Israel. I especially thank Lara Troyansky and Shelley Helfand of the American Jewish Joint Distribution Committee Archives in New York, Galina Kopytova of the Russian Institute for the History of the Arts, and Gila Flam of the National Library of Israel for permission to reproduce images from their respective collections. In Moscow, Ilya Kolmanovsky and Nikita Bezrukov provided invaluable research assistance. Will Cicola artfully translated a mass of unruly xeroxes into the neat musical examples that accompany the text.

Numerous individuals made my travels in Russia, Ukraine, and Israel an amazing experience of friendship as well as research. Thank you to Anna Abramovna Rivkina, Sam and Anna Amiel, Geoff Anisman, Lena Drozdova, Konstantin and Tanya Filiminov, Leonid Finberg, Gila Flam, Rita Flomenboim, Alexander Frenkel, J. Arch Getty, Victor Kelner, Evgeny Khazdan, Galina Kopytova, Mikhail Lukin, Larissa Miller, Maria Mikhailovna, Ludmila Milchakova, Miriam Neirick, Jascha Nemtsov, David Rozenson, Irina Sergeeva, Edwin Seroussi, and Vladimir Tropp. I am also particularly grateful to Eugene Avrutin, Michael Aylward, Ludmila Barsova, Natan Meir, and Lynn Sargeant for sharing valuable nuggets of historical and bibliographic information, including the whereabouts of specific archival materials.

Many organizations have offered generous financial assistance and intellectual encouragement to this project. The archival research was supported in part by grants and fellowships from the Center for Jewish History, Columbia University's Harriman Institute and Institute for Israel and Jewish Studies, the Foundation for Jewish Culture, the Hays-Fulbright Doctoral Dissertation Research Award of the U.S. Department of Education, the Memorial Foundation for Jewish Culture, the Wexner Graduate Foundation, and the YIVO Institute for Jewish Research. The final stages of research and writing were made possible thanks to the assistance of the University of Virginia Corcoran Department of History, Dean's Office, Office of the Vice President for Research and Graduate Studies, and Jewish Studies Program as well as the Pro Musica Hebraica Foundation. The book's publication was made possible by the support of the Columbia University Institute for Israel and Jewish Studies, the Cahnman Publication Subvention Grant, awarded by the Association for Jewish Studies, and the Sidney and Hadassah Musher Subvention Grant in Jewish Studies, awarded by the Foundation for Jewish Culture.

At Yale University Press, Jack Borrebach, Jonathan Brent, William Frucht, Keith Condon, Duke Johns, Joseph Calamia, Christina Tucker, and other staff expertly shepherded the text from unrevised dissertation to final publication. Susan Fels kindly contributed her professional expertise as an indexer. I also profited considerably from the helpful comments of Leon Botstein, Richard Taruskin, and two anonymous reviewers. Of course, it goes without saying that all errors are mine alone.

Finally, I wish to thank my family. My parents, Robert and Jane, provided great love, strength, encouragement, and valuable input throughout the entire process. My brother, Charles, was a constant sympathetic critic from the neighboring world of the social sciences. My daughter, Talia, entered at the tail end of this process, bringing love, joy, and lots of smiles with her. Her mother, my wife Rachel, was an ideal reader. Patient, honest, and insightful, she read and reread (and read again) the manuscript with a keen mind and an open heart. I dedicate this book to her.

A Note on Transliterations and Dates

Russian personal names and surnames have been transliterated according to a modified version of the Library of Congress standard guidelines, while Hebrew and Yiddish names follow the Library of Congress and YIVO Institute for Jewish Research guidelines, respectively. Exceptions to these rules are made in the case of certain names with well-established, more familiar English versions, such as Sholem Aleichem and Peter Tchaikovsky, as well as in quoted material and in the titles of some musical works, where the original spellings are retained.

Until February 1918, Russia followed the Julian calendar rather than the Western (Gregorian) calendar. As a result, in the nineteenth century, dates on the Russian calendar were twelve days behind the West, and the gap widened to thirteen in the early twentieth century. All dates in this book are given according to the Russian calendar of the time.

Introduction

Every Tuesday and Thursday afternoon in the spring of 1904, the legendary violin teacher Leopold Auer strolled through the heavy double doors to his studio on the third floor of the St. Petersburg Conservatory. There each time he found the students of his advanced violin class eagerly assembled in anticipation of his arrival. Among the young pupils clamoring for his attention were Mischa Elman, Efrem Zimbalist, Joseph Achron, and a host of other Jewish prodigies from the Pale of Settlement. Still years shy of adulthood, many of these Jewish musicians had already begun to attract wide notice as the preeminent violinists of the day. A few doors away on the same floor, the venerable composer Nikolai Rimsky-Korsakov spent many of his afternoons sitting next to the piano in his classroom, listening intently as his senior composition students presented their latest efforts. These young composers, a striking number of them Jewish as well, would soon make their impact felt across the Russian musical world. Elsewhere in the building the scene repeated itself. So many Jews entered the St. Petersburg Conservatory during the first two decades of the twentieth century that a popular joke claimed it was the only school in Russia with a quota limiting the number of *non-Jewish* students.[1]

The pictures of Russian-Jewish harmony inside the classrooms of the St. Petersburg Conservatory contrasted sharply with the scenes of deep discord outside its walls. There Russian society teetered on the brink of revolution, violent pogroms raged, and new antisemitic legislation appeared almost daily, including severe restrictions on Jewish residence in St. Petersburg. In spite of these obstacles, Jews still flocked to the very heart of Russian culture in the empire's capital. In the years before World War I, the percentage of Jews at the city's conservatory climbed well beyond 50 percent at a time when Jews constituted less than 5 percent of the total Russian population. The effects of this cultural phenomenon would be felt throughout the twentieth century, as generation after generation of Russian Jewish virtuosos soared to fame on the international concert stage.

Elman, Zimbalist, Jascha Heifetz, Serge Koussevitzky, Vladimir Horowitz, David Oistrakh, Evgeny Kissin—it is easy to compile a long list of famous Russian Jewish musicians, but much harder to say what such a catalog means. Why did Russian Jews choose music in such great numbers? And why did Russians choose Jews to create much of their music, one of the foundations of Russian national pride? Who, in the end, actually did the choosing—and what did it represent? This is a book about the enduring, perplexing links between Jews and music in late nineteenth- and early twentieth-century Russian society. To write such a history is to risk turning culture into myth. After all, any focus on Jewish overrepresentation in Europe's cultural past—as violinists, psychoanalysts, writers, or revolutionaries—can easily distort more than it reveals. And yet when properly framed, the study of Jews and music—and the myths attached to them—produces a broader picture of the interlocking complexities of modern Jewish, Russian, and European identities.

Those complexities begin with the multiple, overlapping themes contained in the dramatic history of these Russian Jewish musicians. Theirs is a story about music as a gateway to European modernity, and about music's capacity to transform individual lives and stir collective dreams of the Jewish future. It is a story of the Jewish search for a modern identity not through politics or religion but through art. And it is a story about the power of stereotypes, one in which the mere perception of Jewish predominance in Russian musical life changed the way in which both Jews and non-Jews thought about the relationship between culture and nationalism.

All these stories in turn share a common starting point in the figure of Anton Rubinstein. One of the most celebrated musicians of the nineteenth century, Rubinstein (1829–1894) was renowned as a pianist, composer, and founder of Russia's first conservatory. He was also the baptized child of Jewish converts to Christianity, a man whose Jewish past alternately generated reactions of pride, curiosity, and revulsion among his contemporaries. In turn his complicated Jewishness inspired his own musical art and cultural activity in ways both obvious and obscure. Chief among them was his effort from the 1860s to the 1890s to use the conservatory as a tool with which to reshape Russians and Jews into his vision of modern Europeans.

The next generation of Russian Jewish musicians took up Rubinstein's mission in earnest. But they also redefined the meaning of music in light of the changing nature of national identity—both Jewish and Russian—at the turn of the twentieth century. The forgotten stories of these musicians—composers and ethnographers, critics and performers—and the organizations they built challenge the simple narratives about how Jewish and European cultures developed as a whole. They range from Joel Engel (1868-1927), who began his musical career as a Russian composer and would-be disciple of Tchaikovsky and ended up the "father of Jewish music," to the Society for Jewish Folk Music, a group of St. Petersburg's leading young composers who revolted against the excesses of both Jewish politics and Russian antisemitism (as well as Russian philosemitism). In the years after 1905, they launched a broad movement to puncture the regnant Russian and European myths about Jews and music, replacing them with a cosmopolitan kind of national art music. Their voices add a new dimension to the oft told, mutually exclusive stories of Russian Jews and European modernity.

The bulk of this story takes place in the final decades of the Russian Empire. However, it neither begins nor ends there. The relationship between Jews and music runs wide and deep in modern European history. From Felix Mendelssohn down to Arnold Schoenberg, German Jewish musicians have repeatedly attracted the obsessive attentions of excitable minds eager to decipher the hidden meaning of European music and the Jewish presence within it. Jews have been credited and blamed for inventing musical modernism—and for resisting it. Antisemites from Richard Wagner onward have attacked Jewish musicians as an alien spiritual force undermining European culture. Meanwhile, Jewish advocates and their philosemitic allies have also proclaimed the fundamentally Jewish character of European musical life, often through compiling exhaustive—if not always accurate—biographical lexicons of celebrated Jewish musical figures. Even today, critics and scholars alike continue to perpetuate vast generalizations about Jewish influence in European music.[2]

Indeed, the many ways in which the history of this cultural phenomenon continues to be told—as a sentimental history of Jewish genius and artistic accomplishment, as a paean to art's spiritual victories and practical failures in the face of political crisis, or as a chapter in the broader Jewish "contribution" to modern European culture—amount to little more than oversized myths. Whatever their origins or intentions, these approaches lift Jews out of historical reality and onto the plane of ahistorical symbols. They remain interpretative allegories that confuse the high visibility of Jews in European culture with the deeper historical explanation of that presence and its meaning. The excessive focus on images of Jewish musicians ultimately tells us more about the European imagination, past and present, than it does about European Jews themselves.

For several decades now, historians have struggled to formulate a precise language to discuss the European Jewish past without resorting to mutually exclusive categories of "Jew" and "European." Recognizing the internal spectrum of identities among European Jews, they have sought to understand the minority experience in a more sophisticated manner. Historians of German Jewry, for instance, have jettisoned the opposition between "German" and "Jew" along with simplistic paradigms of "German Jewish assimilation" and the "Jewish contribution to German culture." Instead, they have highlighted the fluid, often ambiguous national and religious borders between Jews and Germans in the nineteenth and early twentieth centuries. They have also resisted the temptation to read German Jewish history backward—that is to say, as a mere prelude to the Holocaust or as a confirmation of the Zionist claim about the untenable nature of the Jewish Diaspora. The result is a richer, if thornier, picture of the German Jewish experience.[3]

At first glance, the situation in the Russian Empire appears quite different. There the border lines between Jew and Russian were drawn more starkly by the social and political character of the tsarist state and its Jewish population. Since no comprehensive Jewish political emancipation took place before 1917, Jewish difference continued to be formally enshrined in Russian law. Furthermore, in contrast to central Europe, Russia's European Jewish communities remained largely embedded within traditional Ashkenazi Jewish culture, including language, literature, and music. To take but one important example, in the 1897 Russian census, over 96 percent of Jews listed Yiddish as their mother tongue, while less than half of the remaining 3.5 percent spoke Russian as their first language. Further complicating matters, Russian national identity itself remained awkwardly poised between empire and nation, as reflected in the two terms for Russian: *Rossiiskii* (an imperial civic identity) and *Russkii* (a narrower ethnic and religious identity). All these factors had significant implications for the development of both Russian and Jewish national identities in the late nineteenth and early twentieth centuries.[4]

In spite of these differences between Russia and the rest of Europe, there were various points of intersection and blurring between Russians and Jews. This was particularly true among the two generations of Russian Jewish intelligentsia who emerged before the Russian Revolution. For these Russian Jewish elites, musicians included, their individual encounters with Russian and European culture defied easy classification in terms of "assimilation," "acculturation," or "Russification." The embrace of various languages, literatures, philosophy, art, and ideas did not necessarily come at an inevitable cost to their Jewishness. Rather it produced a Russian Jewish dual identity that combined elements of Jewish ethnicity, nationality, and cultural affiliation with Russian civic, political, national, and especially imperial identity. Likewise it generated deeper questions about the religious and national boundaries between Russians and Jews and the meaning of Jewish participation in Russian cultural life that would persist well into the Soviet period and beyond.[5]

Since the demise of the Soviet Union, there has been a flowering of new studies on this Russian-Jewish cultural encounter. Historians have pushed past the realms of tsarist imperial policies and Jewish political movements to explore the broader questions of modern Jewish culture in eastern Europe. Many of these studies have focused on the appearance of secular Jewish literature and theater in the Hebrew, Yiddish, Russian, and Polish languages. They have considerably widened the picture of Jews beyond the older stock images of a people hermetically sealed within the traditional Yiddish cultural environment of the Pale of Settlement or of a group of deracinated Bolshevik revolutionaries. They have also challenged the nationalist tendencies of Russian, Soviet, and Jewish historians alike to read Jews and Russians as fundamentally separate entities. Equally importantly, they have shifted attention away from the distinctiveness of the Russian Jewish experience to the broader comparative question of how Jews fit within the incredibly diverse tapestry of ethnic and religious minorities in the late Russian Empire.[6]

The most intriguing and controversial of these studies have taken as their starting point what literary scholar Benjamin Harshav calls the unusual "statistical density" of Jews in modern Russian and European culture. In his seminal essay, "The Modern Jewish Revolution," Harshav argues that the "massive entrance of Jews and their descendants into the general economy and into the world of culture and science" has important implications for European modernity as a whole. Modern Jewish culture and politics emerged in eastern Europe just as the larger currents of modernism swept through European culture and society. To Harshav, the coincidence of these events suggests a dual revolution of European culture and Jewish identity. In transforming themselves into a modern people, Russian Jews (joined by their other European brethren) initiated a major turning point in "the history of culture and consciousness" for Europe as a whole.[7]

Harshav's thesis has been adopted by historian Yuri Slezkine in his recent provocative book, *The Jewish Century*. Marshaling a huge array of statistics, Slezkine documents the overrepresentation of Jews in Russian and European high culture, liberal professions, politics, and economics. In his telling, all these Jewish trends together expose the fundamentally Jewish character of the modern age. Since the Jews were Europe's "model moderns," who typified and in many cases created these patterns of modernity, the story of the modern age is best understood as a tale of the rest of Europe imitating the Jews, or, in Slezkine's words, the story of "everyone becoming Jewish." Pride of place in his narrative goes to Russian Jews. Slezkine claims that, contrary to popular opinion, Russian Jews were not the most backward, least modern segment of world Jewry in the twentieth century—the ones left behind as the rest of the Jewish world chose modernism, liberalism, and nationalism in Israel and the United States. Instead, Russian Jews were the most modern by virtue of their participation in the flawed Soviet Communist experiment that they took to be the ultimate expression of universalism.[8]

Certainly the oversized presence of a marginalized minority like the Jews in modern Russian culture is striking. But for all of the novelty and rhetorical flair of both Harshav's and Slezkine's studies, they echo the same obsessive focus on the Jewish cultural function and images typical of older German Jewish historiography. Thirty years ago the historian Peter Gay warned against the trap of facile generalizations about the role of German Jews in creating cultural modernism. While the "heavy imprint" of Jews in German culture was undeniable, he explained, it remained an open question whether "that impact was 'Jewish'" in a tangible sense. To resolve this dilemma, Gay urged a closer focus on what Jewishness actually meant in the specific cases of various German Jewish artists and thinkers.[9]

Though at times his own inquiry erred too far in the opposite direction, toward insisting on the overwhelming Germanness of "Jewish Germans," Gay's larger warning about deterministic explanations of the links between Jews and European culture still applies today. Before assigning Russian Jews the role of arch-moderns, the Russian Jewish "statistical density" and the putative "Jewishness" of Russian culture must be more carefully unpacked. The new focus of scholars such as Harshav and Slezkine helps us to see that the Jews of eastern Europe were neither backward paragons of tradition nor monolithic in their identities. But the zeal for meta-arguments also risks privileging Jewish visibility in modern Russian culture over any more detailed examination of what that Jewishness actually meant across time and place in Russian society. Furthermore, in the interest of integrating Russian Jews and their culture more completely into European cultural history, these studies have the effect (intended or not) of dissolving the historical distinctiveness of the lived experience of Russian Jews themselves. They turn Russian Jews into static cultural symbols and sociological patterns, rather than diverse, dynamic identities in formation.[10]

There is another danger in relying on sweeping statistics to write cultural history. Just as not all Jews are identical in their behaviors, not all cultural genres are the same in their historical development. This is especially true in the case of Russian Jewish cultural history, where literature is often taken to be the stand-in for all intellectual and artistic life. What holds true for writers does not necessarily apply equally to musicians. Nor can we simply retrace the appearance of Russian Jewish musicians without addressing the widespread assumption among educated Russians of the nineteenth century and even some Jews that there was no such thing as Jewish music, a problem that the People of the Book never suffered from when it came to Jewish literature.

Indeed, a paradox lay at the heart of all modern Jewish musical life: the preponderance of Jewish musicians, coupled with the putative absence of Jewish music. Or, as a 1909 article in a St. Petersburg Jewish newspaper succinctly framed the issue: "They say that we Jews are the most musical nation, that the violin is our national instrument; we have given the world composers of genius; we have more professional musicians among us than any other people. . . . And at the same time, you will hardly find another nation whose national music has been so much neglected as ours." In one way or another, every Jewish classical musician who emerged in Europe from the mid-nineteenth century onward grappled with this riddle of Jewish musical predominance. But none did so more acutely or more publicly than the young composers of Rimsky-Korsakov's class. It was these Jewish musicians—with their self-conscious awareness of this paradox, their struggle to prove that a Jewish "national music" existed and to determine its proper sound, and their stubborn belief in the transcendent power of modern art—who produced some of the most interesting and heretofore overlooked expressions of Russian Jewish identity.[11]

When Catherine the Great completed the partitions of Poland in the late eighteenth century, she acquired a large Jewish population with a rich musical life. In fact, of all the Jewish communities in the premodern world, it was the Ashkenazi Jews of eastern Europe who created the most distinctive constellation of musical traditions. Like the Yiddish language, Ashkenazi Jewish music was fashioned over nearly a millennium by combining older Middle Eastern liturgical traditions with central and eastern European folk songs. That sound was also stamped with an Ashkenazi musical accent—modal patterns in place of the standard Western major-minor tonal system, pitch-bending microtones that fell between the cracks of Western scale intervals, and a variety of other stylistic features—that to many European ears lent Jewish music a particularly expressive, mournful sound. The diverse results included prayer chants and liturgical songs, Yiddish folk songs, klezmer (instrumental folk) music, and later wordless vocal compositions known as *nigunim* (Heb., melodies), associated with the Hasidic movement. All these genres shared a basic family resemblance as Ashkenazi Jewish music, even as they continued to absorb distinct influences from neighboring traditions. For a society that placed enormous value on recording and analyzing religious laws, rituals, stories, and customs, traditional Ashkenazi Jews devoted remarkably little time to documenting their own music. Up until the middle of the nineteenth century, musical notation was rarely if ever used. Instead Ashkenazim relied exclusively on oral transmission. The rabbis also favored words over music, in large part because of deep-rooted theological concerns about the power of music to inspire sexual deviance and pagan heresy. But if there was little talk of Jewish music per se, Jewish musicians were a fixture in the social landscape and cultural imagination of eastern European Jews. For centuries, the *klezmer* (Heb., instrumental musician) and the *khazn* (Heb., cantor) represented twin cultural poles in Ashkenazi society. Cantors functioned as prayer and ritual leaders in the synagogue, employed by communities as paid professionals, often performing with large choirs of men and boys. Klezmer ensembles played at weddings and other communal celebrations, as well as for non-Jewish audiences. Their music featured a dynamic, resonant combination of rhythmic folk dances and virtuosic performance pieces, particularly for violin and clarinet, along with folk songs and oral improvisations performed by their perennial musical partner, the *badkhn* (Heb., wedding jester). Both the cantor and the klezmer became iconic figures throughout Jewish eastern Europe and were frequently lionized in Yiddish folklore, the former as the voice of religious piety, the latter as the bearer of worldly passion.

While some Sephardic and Italian Jewish communities experimented with late Renaissance and Baroque styles of music for the synagogue during the seventeenth and eighteenth centuries, the vast majority of European Jews had little contact with European art music before 1800. When they did begin to seek admission to this world, they did not initially find themselves particularly welcome. In the late eighteenth century, for instance, a popular story made the rounds in Jewish Berlin of a young German Jew who was rejected from the city's Singakademie on grounds that it was "mathematically impossible that a Jew could compose music."[12]

In the years that followed, however, Jews moved steadily into the European musical mainstream. The German Jewish Enlightenment philosopher Moses Mendelssohn (1729–1786) himself considered music the greatest of the arts. He not only took piano lessons and regularly frequented concerts and the theater, but he even authored a treatise on the proper tunings for the modern keyboard. In subsequent decades, the emerging Jewish bourgeoisie attended the opera and theater in droves and sponsored chamber music performances in private salons. Soon they also began to study music formally in Europe's newly established conservatories and music academies. By the 1840s, western and central Europe were full of musical Jews, including famous composers like Mendelssohn's baptized grandson Felix, Charles-Valentin Alkan, Jacques Offenbach, Jacques Fromental Halévy, and Giacomo Meyerbeer.[13]

In eastern Europe the same pattern occurred, but much more slowly. Widespread poverty, low levels of secular education, and limited knowledge of European languages were the major factors impeding the acculturation process, to say nothing of the rabbis' overt hostility to secular gentile art and culture. While some more renowned cantors flirted with opera careers, the centripetal force of religious tradition typically held them back. Klezmer musicians proved more culturally adventurous, in some cases performing concerts for local nobility and even larger audiences in cities. In the late 1830s, for example, Yehiel Mikhl Guzikov (1806–1837), a klezmer flutist and *shtroyfidl* (wood-and-straw xylophone) player from the Russian town of Shklov (now Belarus) achieved brief fame with a series of concerts across western Europe that attracted enormous public attention. But in spite of the often romanticized reputations of self-taught folk artists such as Guzikov, klezmer musicians' extensive contacts with the gentile world generally earned them only scorn, shame, and low social status back in traditional Ashkenazi communities.[14]

Even when the Russian Jewish bourgeoisie began to embrace amateur music study at midcentury, they recoiled from music as a profession because of its klezmer taint. The Yiddish writer Sholem Rabinovich (1859–1916), better known by his pseudonym Sholem Aleichem, recalled that, in his childhood in the 1860s, "the violin played an honorable role in the program of knowledge . . . like German or French for a child of a good family." Yet his parents refused to let him take lessons, for as his father explained to him: "It's a waste of time. It smacks of being a klezmer at a wedding. Mathematics, geography, languages are something substantial. But scraping away at a fiddle—what kind of job is that?" Even as Rabinovich's father dismissed music, however, attitudes in Jewish eastern Europe were beginning to shift.[15]

The first hints of a broader new relationship between Jews and music in eastern Europe appeared in mid-nineteenth-century Odessa, the cosmopolitan port city on the Black Sea. Physically within the Pale of Settlement but culturally linked to the wider international world, Odessa was home to a famous Italian opera house that already by the 1830s had become a popular

Jewish destination. A brisk demand for music lessons for the city's Jewish children soon followed. From the second half of the nineteenth century onward, these began to bear fruit as the city produced legions of notable Jewish classical violinists, pianists, and other performers.[16]

The fabled connection between Jews and music in Odessa was solidified through decades of Russian and Yiddish popular songs and the later writings of Isaac Babel, Alexander Kuprin, and others. In song, story, and film, the Jewish musicians of Odessa came to symbolize a lost paradise of soulful and tolerant urban Russia.[17] But for all of Odessa's potent hold on the Russian imagination, then and now, the truly decisive beginnings of the Russian-Jewish musical encounter took place not in the "Little Paris" on the Black Sea, but in the two northern capitals of Russian music, St. Petersburg and Moscow. While Odessa's very newness, its ethnic diversity, and its status as a port city made it something of a cosmopolitan haven in nineteenth-century Russian society, it was the Jewish musical migration to these other two cities lying literally beyond the Pale that truly sparked the first questions about Jews, music, and Russian culture. It was there that the world of Russian classical music emerged around Russia's first two conservatories, particularly in St. Petersburg. There too the first conscious attempts to solve Russia's Jewish problem through music took place. And the two strains came together with the man most responsible for the appearance of a new kind of Russian Jewish musician: Anton Rubinstein.

Though his name is little remembered in Western musical circles today, Rubinstein was preeminent as a composer and concert artist throughout Europe for most of the second half of the nineteenth century. As a pianist he was virtually without equal, considered the sole successor to Franz Liszt. The English novelist George Eliot featured a lightly veiled portrayal of him as the symbolic centerpiece of her classic 1876 novel *Daniel Deronda*. Many German critics considered him to be the most important Russian composer of the late nineteenth century. Russians, by contrast, hailed him primarily as the founder of the country's first conservatory. The opening of the St. Petersburg Conservatory in 1862 marked the beginning of both modern musical education and the modern musical profession in Russian society. For Russian Jews, moreover, the conservatory provided an avenue of genuine though limited integration.

Rubinstein not only created the conditions for the rise of Jewish musicians in Russian society, he underwent the transformation himself. Born in a shtetl near Berdichev and converted to Christianity as an infant, he was reared in Moscow and Berlin. As a child and teenager he led the life of an international traveling virtuoso, repeatedly crisscrossing Europe. The result was a man of bifurcated national, religious, and social identities who sought refuge in music as a means of escaping the irreconcilable tensions in his own life. Yet for all the uniqueness of his story, he came to represent the typical Russian Jewish musician. As Russian antisemitism and popular nationalism grew in the 1880s, the alleged Jewishness (and lack of Russianness) of Rubinstein and his conservatory generated intense public controversy about the role of Jews in Russian culture.

Rubinstein's colorful life has inspired scores of biographies. But almost without exception, his biographers have ignored the complexities of his Russian Jewish identity, viewing him instead through a narrower musical lens in an attempt to explain why a musician of his talents and stature did not secure a more permanent place in the classical music canon. In the first chapter of this book I take a different perspective, asking not how he came to be viewed as a relatively unsuccessful composer but rather what his life and art may reveal about Jews, Russians, and music in the nineteenth century. Using his personal correspondence, archival documents, and published writings, I trace the effects of Rubinstein's own personal dilemmas of identity on his views of music and nationalism. Though he is usually ignored in discussions of the Russian Jewish Enlightenment, Rubinstein's quest to reconcile art and religion, Judaism and Christianity, and East and West reflected a novel expression of a hybrid Russian Jewish identity that deserves to be reconsidered in the context of Russian and Jewish history.

Beginning in the 1890s, even as increasing numbers of Jews followed the conservatory path laid out by Rubinstein, many of them turned to music not only to become Russian artists but also Jewish nationalists. To employ Jewish music in service of the national cause, however, they first had to create it. In the second chapter, I examine the man at the center of this endeavor: Joel (Iulii Dmitrievich) Engel (1868–1927), the "father of Jewish music." A Moscow Conservatory graduate who was prominent in both Russian and Jewish cultural life as a critic, composer, and ethnographer in the three decades before 1917, Engel pioneered the scholarly study of Jewish music and the idea of Jewish national art music.

Engel's twin search for an art and science of Jewish music fused equal parts East and West: the German "Science of Judaism" crossed with Russian "musical ethnography," the Yiddish folk heritage filtered through the aesthetics of fin de siècle Russian music. In combining these dualities, he found unlikely allies and unlikelier opponents. Sholem Aleichem, a leading advocate for folk-inspired Jewish literature, fiercely challenged his Jewish populism, while the Russian nationalist critic Vladimir Stasov enthusiastically endorsed his cause, viewing it as part of Russia's imperial cultural patrimony. Engel's greatest challenge, however, came during his most direct encounter with the folk culture he cherished. As a member of the fabled Ansky ethnographic expedition into the pre–World War I Pale of Settlement, Engel discovered that, ironically, the actual voices of the Jewish people threatened to collapse his whole folkloric model of Russian Jewish music.

The public dissemination of Engel's ideas began in 1900. But it was not until nearly a decade later that a formal movement began to coalesce around his musical vision for modern Jewish culture. During the years surrounding 1905, Russian Jews were consumed by political questions, swept up in the drama of revolution. But with the return of tsarist repression in 1907, they began to bury their intense political differences and turn collectively inward. What followed was an explosion of intellectual and artistic expression. In the musical sphere, this movement was led by a group of young musicians from the St. Petersburg Conservatory determined to renew and expand Jewish music. In the last three chapters of this book, I tell their story by examining the St. Petersburg Society for Jewish Folk Music (*Obshchestvo evreiskoi narodnoi muzyki*).

Founded in 1908, the Society for Jewish Folk Music was an organization of composers, performers, scholars, and amateur enthusiasts committed to the mission of creating modern Jewish music. It was also the most original Jewish reaction to the question of Jews and music to appear in the first half of the twentieth century. Chapter 3 traces the group's origins and its responses to the strange mixture of antisemitism and philosemitism in the Russian musical world. Theirs was an attempt to rehabilitate the image of the Jewish musician through a cosmopolitan notion of Jewish national music. Their eloquent musical arguments constituted neither a separatist rejection of European culture nor an apologetic plea for Jewish inclusion, but rather an affirmation of Jewish music as an integral yet distinct voice in modern European culture. It also derived directly from their experience as a national minority in the Russian Empire. In contrast to the multitudes of German Jews who turned to music as a path toward universalism and away from parochial identities, these Russian Jewish musicians paradoxically sought to reach the universal through the particular, to become European through asserting and emphasizing their Jewishness within the specific context of the Russian Empire.

The quest for Russian Jewish music was a delicate balancing act. But it was not just the dueling brands of nationalism and the ironies of imperialism that made the task of reconciling multiple identities so difficult. In the years before World War I, technology transformed the very meaning of all music. In chapter 4 I look at the fate of what the Yiddish writer Y. L. Peretz called "frozen folk songs"—sounds caught between art, commerce, and technology. Even as the Russian Jewish composers continued to prize folk music as the standard of national authenticity, they confronted a bewildering new world of phonograph recordings, sheet music, and other new forms of urban popular culture. These commercial products simultaneously offered the promise of tapping unlimited new audiences and the peril of eroding aesthetic distinctions between high art, low popular culture, and "pure" folk song on which their entire model of Jewish music depended.

The story of Russian Jewish culture took a radical turn after 1917, reflected most directly in the breakup of the Society for Jewish Folk Music and the dispersal of its musicians into three large emigration streams across the globe. But this rupture was less a result of the Bolshevik Revolution than is commonly thought. In this book's fifth and final chapter, I illustrate how Russian Jewish culture began to unravel from within as early as the first years of World War I, beginning with a now classic ideological debate over the very Jewishness of Jewish music. While war and revolution exacerbated the process, it was the resurgence of Jewish politics coupled with the broader aesthetic challenge of European modernism that led to the decisive breakdown of this cultural movement. In tracking the post-1917 trajectories of the central figures in the Society for Jewish Folk Music, I examine how the complicated fate of Russian Jewish culture reflected the multiple legacies and divergent experiences of Jews in interwar Soviet Russia, Mandatory Palestine, and the United States.

The post-1917 experience of Russian Jewish musicians also suggests another historical paradox: at the same time as the Society for Jewish Folk Music failed to perpetuate itself as a lasting artistic movement after 1917, its cultural ideal of a dual Russian Jewish identity continued to surface in Soviet music, even after the onset of the Stalinist terror. In the book's conclusion, I probe the implications of this broader Jewish musical legacy in one of the most important Russian-Jewish cultural encounters of the twentieth century: the post–World War II friendship of composers Dmitri Shostakovich and Mieczysław Weinberg. Their dialogue suggests how deeper patterns of cultural identity persist across even the most dramatic political rupture points in Russian Jewish history.

There is no more iconic, enduring image of Jews, Russia, and music than the fiddler on the roof. Thanks to the eponymous Broadway musical and Hollywood film adapted from Sholem Aleichem's Tevye stories, the image of the Russian Jewish violinist has taken on universal significance as the supreme expression of the Russian Jewish past. But the actual image of the fiddler on the roof comes not from Sholem Aleichem but from a series of levitating klezmer violinists painted by the Russian Jewish artist Marc Chagall as an expression of his hybrid modern Russian, Jewish, and European identity.

Despite the shared title, there is little in common between Chagall's original paintings and the Broadway and Hollywood productions that launched the image to global fame. As scholars have often noted, both the music and the characters of the American *Fiddler* are exercises in ethnic nostalgia that emphasize the Russian Jewish musician as the epitome of tradition while changing his music to effect a more American sound. The plot of the musical also presents a distorted portrait of Russian Jewish life dominated by the twin dramas of political revolution and religious crisis. The reality—reflected in Chagall's original images—is, as always, more complicated and less easily reduced to a political or religious fable.[18]

In this book, I seek to rediscover the lives of actual Russian Jewish musicians who, like the painter Chagall, looked past conventional politics and religion to culture as the foundation of modern Jewish identity. Together they pursued an artistic quest to become more authentically Jewish *and* more legitimately Russian at the same time. In the process, they turned music into a vehicle of both memory and modernity, blending past and present to forge a cultural vision at once Russian, Jewish, and European.

CHAPTER 1

Emancipating Sounds

*Anton Rubinstein and the Rise of the
Russian Jewish Musician*

To the Jews I am a Christian. To the Christians—a Jew. To the Russians I am a German, and to the Germans—a Russian. For the classicists I am a musical innovator, and for the musical innovators I am an artistic reactionary and so on. The conclusion: I am neither fish nor fowl, in essence a pitiful creature!

With these clever, ironic words, written at the end of his life, the nineteenth-century musician Anton Rubinstein fashioned his own bitter and honest epitaph.[1] But the tight symmetry of Rubinstein's phrases only begins to hint at the jumbled assortment of epithets and accolades that he earned throughout his six-decade artistic career. A prolific composer, born in the Pale of Settlement and trained in Moscow and Berlin, he published hundreds of compositions ranging from popular piano works to symphonies to operas. As the founding father of the St. Petersburg Conservatory and the Imperial Russian Music Society in the late 1850s and early 1860s, Rubinstein launched both the modern musical education system and the modern musical profession itself in Russia. During the 1870s and 1880s, his relentless performance tours of Europe and the United States made him perhaps the best-known classical music performer in the Western world. He was widely considered to be the century's greatest pianist after Franz Liszt. In fact it was Liszt who christened him "Van II," in recognition of his titanic musical abilities and his uncanny physical resemblance to nineteenth-century Europe's most revered musical hero: Ludwig van Beethoven (fig. 1).

With such a multidimensional career, a charismatic personality, and striking good looks, fame came easily to Rubinstein. In his lifetime alone he inspired thousands of newspaper accounts, personal memoirs, popular biographies, and character sketches in the Russian and Western press. But celebrity did not necessarily bring acceptance. Throughout his life, Rubinstein's complicated national and religious background left him a perpetual man apart, excluded and stigmatized by the forces of nationalism, antisemitism,

Figure 1. Anton Rubinstein. Russian Institute for the History of the Arts.

and changing artistic tastes in nineteenth-century Russian and European society. In the end, his multiple layers of identities—composer, virtuoso, German, Russian, Christian, Jew—effectively canceled one another out. In an age of modern nation building, Rubinstein remained homeless, unclaimed by any single nation as its own.

What eluded Rubinstein in life came all too easily in death. From the 1890s onward, his biographers have swept him into the widest possible range of ideological readings. His life has been claimed as part of the master narratives of Russian, German, and Jewish history. Almost without exception, these biographies have attempted to categorize him according to various national themes: he was either an anti-Russian Western cosmopolitan or a German liberal, an eastern European Jewish nationalist or an "assimilated" central European Jew, or even, finally, a Russian patriot. Few biographers have resisted the temptation to view his life through the prism of nationalism. Even fewer have ignored his external reception in favor of what Rubinstein's own writings reveal about himself.[2]

In truth, Rubinstein does not belong to merely one national or religious category. To grasp his identity and historical importance, his life must be understood within the rapidly changing context of the multiethnic nineteenth-century Russian Empire. Because he stood in an ambiguous place on the border between the emerging modern Russian and Jewish national identities, Rubinstein found himself continually frustrated by questions of religion, nationality, and socio-legal status. As an individual artist in a society transitioning from a premodern corporate social order to modern bourgeois, professional, and national identities, Rubinstein struggled to negotiate the increasingly antiquated yet stubbornly persistent Russian estate system. At the same time, as a baptized Jew disconnected from traditional Jewish religion and community, he strained to find a framework for his indistinct yet palpable sense of Jewishness.

Grappling with these dilemmas of modern identity, Rubinstein did more than seek solace in art. He carved out a distinctive new civic role for music within the larger political and cultural context of the nineteenth century. In turn his quest dovetailed naturally with broader trends in the Russian society of his day. Increasingly from the 1860s onward, Russian liberal professionals such as lawyers, doctors, and artists sought to forge partnerships with the powerful Russian state in order to help create a modern civil society.[3] They were joined by a parallel subculture of Russian Jewish elites, a small but influential group of intellectuals and wealthy merchants who shared the conviction that this new modern Russian society would logically emancipate its Jewish population. Rubinstein's musical project straddled both of these worlds. The first Russian conservatory (opened one year after the abolition of serfdom) produced not only modern, legally emancipated musicians— known literally as "Free Artists"—but emancipated individual Jews at home in Russian culture and freed from the bulk of anti-Jewish legal penalties. Ironically, however, the linkage between Jews and music ended up providing a serious test to the limits of liberal reform in the reactionary era after 1881. For his part, Rubinstein's very prominence eventually turned his own career into a symbolic battleground for a fundamental political debate concerning the legitimacy of Jewish participation in modern Russian culture as a whole. In spite of all of his uniqueness and marginality, then, Rubinstein's biography reveals a life lived very much in concert with the larger historical trajectory of the Russian and Jewish experiences in the nineteenth century. So too does it suggest a surprising linkage between the changing civic role of music and the fractured process of Jewish emancipation in nineteenth-century Russia.

Berdichev: The Birth of a Jewish Christian

Avraham ben Hirsh Rubinshteyn was born on November 16, 1829, in the village of Vikhvatinets (Wechwotinez) in the southwestern Russian province of Podolia. The small trading town was located on the left bank of the Dniester River, at the border between Russian Ukraine and Habsburg Bessarabia, in present-day Transnistria (Moldova). In July 1831, at age one and a half, he was brought to the Nikolaevskii Church in Berdichev for a dramatic baptism ceremony involving three generations and roughly thirty-five members of his family. The complicated life story of Anton Rubinstein begins with this childhood conversion to Christianity. It was an event that symbolically dominated his life, even as it remained shrouded in mystery, hovering over crucial moments to define many of his interactions with the Russian state, the Jewish community, and the conservative Russian press.

Some 30,000 Jews converted to Christianity in the Russian Empire between 1825 and 1855. Many of these conversions came about as a result of coercion during decades-long military service, particularly for child recruits. Others resulted from some murky, indeterminate combination of religious conviction and material gain. Most converts, however, hailed from the broad ranks of the "destitute and desperate," individuals who found themselves in dire financial and legal situations, owing large debts or accused of crimes, serious or petty. In these cases conversion could bring a helpful leniency or a last chance at liberty. And so it was with Reuven Rubinshteyn, Anton's grandfather.[4]

Ostensibly illiterate and barely able to speak Russian, Reuven Rubinshteyn had nevertheless successfully developed the first Jewish-owned agricultural settlement in Berdichev. In the 1820s the town had begun a rapid transformation from a typical eastern European Jewish shtetl into a large city and regional center of commerce, banking, and agricultural trade. Rubinshteyn's notable success brought him into conflict with the town's official owners, the Radziwiłł clan, one of the largest Polish noble magnate families in the Russian Empire. Facing prison and total bankruptcy on apparently trumped-up charges of smuggling, Rubinshteyn made the fateful decision to convert. To do so he traveled to St. Petersburg, where he reportedly spent several months in negotiations with church leaders, nobility, and tsarist officials before an agreement was reached, whereby the Jewish farmer Reuven Rubinshteyn would become Roman Ivanovich Rubinstein, Orthodox merchant of the first guild. As part of the arrangement, his entire family clan converted with him, a highly unusual move in those days.[5]

Generally speaking, Jewish conversion in Imperial Russia produced an ambiguous, uncertain result. In theory, converts were relieved from nearly all Jewish legal restrictions, including onerous taxes and limits on residence and travel. In reality, however, they still faced inconsistent legal treatment and skepticism from government and church officials, along with overt social hostility from Jews and Christians alike. One solution was to relocate to the larger Russian cities, where a new bourgeoisie was just beginning to emerge in the first half of the nineteenth century. Five of Roman Rubinstein's sons chose this route, moving in the early 1830s to Moscow to enter the fields of business, law, and medicine. Among them was Anton's father, Grigorii (formerly Hirsh) Romanovich Rubinstein (1807–1847).[6]

Anton's childhood coincided with the family's social and economic rise. Prior to his conversion, Grigorii had worked as a tenant farmer in Vikhvatinets. By the mid-1830s he was the owner of his own business, a successful Moscow pencil factory with seventy employees. Young and ambitious, the Rubinsteins actively pursued membership in the bourgeois culture of the Moscow merchant elite. Anton's mother, Hayyah Levenshteyn (1807–1891), came from an enlightened Jewish family across the Russian border in the Habsburg Galician town of Brody. Having converted to Christianity along with her husband's family, she now took the name Kaleriia (Klara) Khristoforovna Rubinstein. Like other middle-class Jewish women of the time, she devoted herself to a pan-European ideal of bourgeois salon life, one in which chamber music played a prominent role. An amateur pianist herself, later a music teacher by profession, she began to instruct her children in piano, the nineteenth-century bourgeois instrument par excellence.[7]

Paris—Berlin—Vienna: The Making of a European Virtuoso

By the time he was eight, Anton had begun to display extraordinary musical talent. In response, his mother promptly hired Moscow's best piano teacher to assume responsibility for his education. The young wunderkind spent the next four years in a combination of strenuous study, travel, and public exhibition across Europe that resembled the pattern of hundreds of other young eighteenth- and nineteenth-century musical prodigies. Paraded in front of audiences, Rubinstein proved to be a sensation everywhere he performed from private salons to concert halls. Thereafter he lived in a succession of European cities: the years 1840 to 1842 in Paris, Berlin from 1843 to 1846, followed by one year in Vienna before returning to Berlin in 1847. Initially Rubinstein often played together with his younger brother Nikolai (1835-1881), who had also developed into a piano prodigy. By the mid-1840s, however, he had begun to pursue his own career as an international pianist and composer.[8]

Many of Rubinstein's biographers have speculated at great length about the influence of his early years in western and central Europe and his contacts with the panoply of the day's musical masters. In Paris and Berlin Rubinstein came to know Felix Mendelssohn, Giacomo Meyerbeer, Frédéric Chopin, Clara Schumann, and Joseph Joachim, among others. Many of these musicians took an interest in the young pianist, having also begun their careers as child prodigies. He also began a decades-long relationship with Franz Liszt—part hero worship, part rivalry—that inspired his first attempts at large-scale composition and his first published music criticism. In all likelihood, though, the greatest legacy of this time was less Rubinstein's individual contacts with major musicians than his prolonged exposure to European artistic cosmopolitanism at its peak. In the salons of Berlin and Vienna, Jews, Christians, and converts, Germans and foreigners, all came together around the ideals of art and conversation, creating a powerfully neutral if transitory space in European society where religion and nationality mattered little (though the same could not be said for class). In the 1840s these grand salons, often run by haute-bourgeois women of Jewish origin, were still in their heyday, and artists, writers, scholars, musicians, and other wealthy elites pursued the new secular religion of European high culture. Under the influence of Romanticism, German art music at the time aspired to be a cosmopolitan, universal cult of art and had not yet begun to acquire the chauvinist overtones of nationalism that would emerge after 1848. Rubinstein thus imbibed a Romantic vision of art as a pan-European culture in which artists moved literally and figuratively across geographic, political, and social borders with ease.⁹

In 1847, however, Rubinstein's life took an abrupt turn. That year back in Moscow his father died unexpectedly, throwing the family's finances into question. Soon the personal tragedy yielded to political danger. When the Revolution of 1848 broke out, Rubinstein was caught in Berlin, a center of social and political upheaval. As a foreigner with no official documents or money, he found himself in a precarious position. The huge ruptures of 1847 and 1848, both personal and professional, left him with little choice but to return to Russia.

St. Petersburg: Imperial Identities in Conflict

Having left Russia nearly a decade earlier a celebrated child prodigy, Rubinstein returned in 1848 as a relatively unknown young musician with few concrete professional prospects in a bewildering and hostile society. Russia, in fact, was a country that he had never really known more than as a sheltered child. Musically, the city of St. Petersburg remained quite provincial despite its links to the European concert circuit. Most immediately, Rubinstein confronted an unanticipated array of novel legal and social pressures related to his *soslovie* (socio-legal estate), religion, and nationality. As his social status plummeted, he began to contemplate questions of music and identity in a radically new way.

Late Imperial Russia featured a complex socio-legal estate system in which individual identity was linked to legal status, education, profession, and membership in a number of overlapping, prescribed social categories. The new kinds of modern social and ethnic identities then appearing in urban sectors of Russian society did not fit easily into this hierarchical socio-legal system. This was especially true with the Jews, who by law were classified both as members of an occupational estate and a specific Jewish estate (*evreiskoe soslovie*). Russian law also ambiguously designated Jews as legal aliens (*inorodtsy*), as opposed to natives (*prirodnye*) or foreigners (*inostrantsy*). Further complicating the situation, a number of other terms were also commonly used in referring to Jews, including "people" (*narod*), "social rank" (*sostoianie*), "tribe" (*plemia*), and "confession" (*veroispovedannost*).¹⁰

With their father dead and the family business dissolved into a pile of debts, Rubinstein's family struggled to retain their membership in the merchant estate. Yet this designation brought special tax burdens and residence requirements. In response, brothers Jacob (Iakov) (1827–1863) and Nikolai each enrolled as students at Moscow University in the early 1850s to earn degrees that would stabilize their social and legal status. Having sold off her late husband's business, Kaleriia Khristoforovna supported herself and her youngest daughter, Sophia (1841–1919), by teaching music at a Moscow girls' boarding school.[11] Unlike his siblings, however, Anton was unwilling to countenance any compromises in his quest for an artistic career. As a result he found no easy solution to his legal situation and social dilemmas.

The problems began at the border with his reentry into Russia in 1848. In his memoirs, Rubinstein narrated in great detail the traumatic, "terrible" story of his arrival at the border without a passport. Having left Russia as a child registered on his mother's passport, he claimed to know nothing of the need for documents in his native country. From the moment he reached the border until his arrival in St. Petersburg, he was repeatedly challenged to produce proof of his identity. His belongings were confiscated, and he was threatened with imprisonment and deportation to Siberia. Once he reached St. Petersburg, he found himself alone in the city with no legal papers, no close contacts, and a conspicuously Jewish last name. Rather than a celebrated young artist returning home from abroad, Rubinstein was now reduced to being an anonymous, stateless, and status-less person harassed by the police and unable even to rent a hotel room.

In the end an old acquaintance finally came forward to confirm that he remembered Rubinstein from years before as a child virtuoso. But in a final, absurd humiliation, the pianist was summoned to the chief of police's office and ordered to perform a private recital for a clerk in order to prove that he was in fact a musician. This solution brought Rubinstein only a temporary reprieve. To fully verify his identity, he was required to send for a copy of his birth certificate from Berdichev, his former Jewish home, where he had not set foot in twenty-five years. Even once the immediate police matters were resolved, problems persisted. As late as 1857, nearly a decade later, he was still plagued by passport-related troubles.[12]

Beyond his legal woes, Rubinstein also struggled to integrate professionally within Russian culture. Raised on the Romantic cult of art in central and western Europe of the 1840s, he found the hierarchical, bureaucratic nature of 1850s Russian musical culture offensive and demeaning. In Vienna, Paris, and Berlin, political liberalism and the rising bourgeoisie had begun to supersede corporate estate identities. Musicians had left behind their medieval artisan status to embrace a new public role as professional artists and cultural heroes. The limited acclaim he achieved in the heavily amateur chamber music circles of St. Petersburg's salons and the occasional concert at St. Petersburg University paled in comparison to the triumphant stature of Beethoven, Mendelssohn, or Liszt.[13] Unable to secure steady work either in the Imperial Theater or as a private instructor, he spent his first two years fighting poverty and hunger. But rather than return to the itinerant existence of a touring concert soloist, Rubinstein instead made a bolder move. Between 1850 and 1854 he composed four operas, among them *Dmitrii Donskoi* (also known as *The Battle of Kulikovo*), based on the fourteenth-century Russian defeat of the Mongol Golden Horde, and three one-act works, each portraying a different nationality of the Russian Empire: Siberian natives (*Sibirskie okhotniki* [The Siberian Hunters]), Russian peasants (*Fomka Durachok* [Fomka the Fool]), and Georgians (*Mest* [Vengeance], based on Lermontov's *Hadji Abrek*).[14]

Rubinstein hoped these works would secure his artistic reputation and launch him as a major opera composer. However, the initial results were not impressive. Political intrigues and bureaucratic intransigence stymied most of his efforts to get his works performed. Those works that did make it to the stage generally encountered round rejection from public and critics alike. But they did find one sympathetic listener. The Grand Duchess Elena Pavlovna (1807–1873), Nicholas I's German-born sister-in-law and an independent-minded individual, took a strong interest in the young Rubinstein. In 1852 she invited him to join her retinue as official court pianist at her formal salon, held at the Mikhailovsky Palace throughout the 1850s and 1860s.[15]

Elena Pavlovna's salon guests represented an extremely broad cross-section of St. Petersburg society, including nobility, intelligentsia, merchants, artists, students, and the tsars themselves. The new position brought Rubinstein entrée into court and aristocratic circles and the prospects of wider exposure, further patronage, and free lodging and travel. Yet the permanent sinecure could not disguise the fact that a musician already regarded as one of the finest pianists in Europe found himself forced to perform nightly as a background accompaniment to a salon full of chattering Russian nobility. Rubinstein complained bitterly of his servantlike status, referring contemptuously to his position as the "janitor of music." Finally fed up with his struggles, in 1854 he abandoned his court position and once again left Russia. He spent most of the next four years traveling and performing in central Europe, seeking the guidance of his mentor and rival Liszt.[16]

These adult years of travel and performance coincided with the bulk of the Crimean War (1853–56). For Rubinstein the conflict awakened a new sense of national identification with Russia. In 1855, for instance, he wrote to his mother of how he had recently refused to take a concert engagement in England owing to "patriotic reasons" (*patrioticheskie prichiny*). He went on to describe his longing for his Russian "homeland" (*rodina*). Though he did not shy away from political criticism of the autocracy at times, he continued to express this instinctive concern for Russia's image abroad. It was not only a sense of Russian patriotism, though, that Rubinstein's mid-1850s sojourn abroad engendered, but also a growing awareness of his Jewishness.[17]

As the child of recent converts, Anton Rubinstein had grown up in an atmosphere of cultural contradiction and confusion. On the surface, the Rubinstein family in the 1830s and 1840s adopted the conventional religious practices of their new faith without qualms. Anton and Nikolai were raised as churchgoers and had no contact with the Jewish community; while living in Berlin they received religious lessons from a local Russian Orthodox priest. Kaleriia regularly attended church throughout her life, observed Easter Sunday with her family in Odessa each year, and received an Orthodox funeral. But if the rituals of traditional religious Judaism were quickly abandoned, the family's Jewish memories were slower to disappear. Behind the sober commitment to Christianity lurked a more complicated, ambivalent mixture of pride and guilt about the family conversion. An apocryphal family tradition held, for instance, that as part of the terms of his conversion, Rubinstein's grandfather dutifully paid for the construction of a church in Berdichev—and then proceeded to build a synagogue across the street.[18]

Whether Rubinstein himself retained Jewish memories from his early childhood is impossible to say. According to one popular tradition, until age sixteen he had no definite knowledge of his Jewish background. While this seems unlikely, Russification did have a strong impact on the family. Anton's brother Nikolai, for instance, born six years after him when the family was already firmly ensconced in Moscow, had no interest whatsoever in his Jewish background. Despite the fact that the brothers were quite close and that Nikolai eventually chose a similar musical path to that of Anton, establishing the Moscow Conservatory in 1864, he never expressed any Jewish identification. Nor, interestingly enough, did the Russian public—conservative press, Jewish community, or others—regard Nikolai as Jewish.[19]

Anton, by contrast, publicly identified himself as Jewish in a number of revealing ways. To begin with, there were the ironic and humorous remarks. He was known to refer to himself as a "wandering Jew" (*juif errant*), and once called on an artistic rival who was a known antisemite, the German pianist and conductor Hans von Bülow, with a visiting card that read "Anton Rubinstein. Slavischer Semit" (Slavic Semite). In 1888, on the occasion of receiving a medal from the tsar, he reportedly told his mother that, "for all your baptism at Berdichev, we are Jews, you and I and sister Sophie."[20]

Beyond these anecdotal comments, more intriguing evidence of Rubinstein's Jewish identity comes in the form of a long-forgotten document from one of his earliest opera projects. In February 1858, while on tour in Vienna, Rubinstein approached the noted German poet Friedrich Hebbel (1813–1863) about a possible collaboration on a new opera. As a result, the two men signed a contract for Hebbel to write a libretto about Rabbi Judah Loew of Prague (1525–1609), nicknamed the Maharal, an important rabbinic figure famously linked to the medieval legend of the Golem. Rubinstein then presented Hebbel with a strange plot scenario apparently of his own invention. In most folk versions of the Golem legend, a pious rabbi uses mystical powers to create a supernatural being who protects the town's Jews from Christian violence. In Rubinstein's telling, the rabbi suffers instead from an unrequited love for a Christian princess and dismisses the idea of the Golem as mere superstition. When a local criminal masquerading as a Jew steals a precious stone from one King Matthias, the rabbi attempts to avert a pogrom, cure his own lovesickness, and promote the cause of religious tolerance by accepting blame for the crime and sacrificing his own life. Unfortunately, we can only speculate what the final work might have been like, for Rubinstein ultimately rejected Hebbel's libretto as unusable and abandoned the project.[21]

The failure did not dissuade Rubinstein from trying again. A few months later in London he met Julius Rodenberg (1831–1914), a young German Jewish writer who had recently won acclaim for his verse translations of the Psalms. The two began a correspondence that eventually led to a number of collaborations on major works with biblical themes. Rubinstein's letters to Rodenberg are filled with sharp inquiries and mature reflections on the Bible, the Hebrew language, and various philosophical questions about modern translation and theology. But it was not only ancient Judaism that captured his imagination. Even at their first meeting, Rodenberg recalled later, he was struck by Rubinstein's proud and playful Jewish self-identification: "While we talked he played with an ivory paper knife which he laid on the table when he went into an adjoining room to dress for going out. Upon the handle of the paper folder was his name in Hebrew letters — Anton Rubinstein. He never concealed his Jewish origin; his greatest delight was anecdotes of Polish Jews, seasoned with that salt sharper than Attic salt. Ten, twenty times he would tell the same story in order to laugh over it ten, twenty times."[22]

Most striking is a story attributed to the Russian Jewish philosopher Grigorii Itelson, who recalled Rubinstein's criticism of the contemporary Jewish preoccupation with antisemitism. When in the 1880s Itelson brought him an opera libretto on the topic of the Jewish suffering during the Crusades, he later recalled, Rubinstein asked for another version with a character more along the lines of Mozart's Figaro: "It is time for us to stop whimpering and recalling the horrors of the past," he reportedly told Itelson. "After all, we have no way out, we have to live side by side with 'them.' What is the good of this eternal wailing and complaining, of constant recollection of the Inquisition and the ghettos, the pogroms and persecutions? No, give me a cheerful, joyous Jew who ridicules 'them'!"[23]

As all these artistic themes and personal gestures indicate, Rubinstein expressly identified with his Jewish heritage. Yet he could not easily fit the tangle of affinities into the social categories of midcentury Russian society. For alongside his Jewish origins, he also took deep pride in his Russian nationality, writing to his mother with excitement of the moment in the late 1860s when certain Russian newspapers began to refer to him as "our Russian composer and artist." "As a reward for all that I have done for her sake," he boasted, "I will finally be considered a Russian in Russia." In the 1860s, other Jewish elites of the day had begun to label themselves as Russian Jews (*Russkie evrei*), denoting their dual identity as Russians and Jews. Aside from one ironic reference to himself as a "Jewish-Russian composer" (*jüdisch-russiche komponist*), however, Rubinstein made no such broader rhetorical move. This was because his religious situation set him apart. Unlike other Russian Jewish intellectuals, he considered himself a practicing Orthodox Christian, and yet at the same time an atheist. As he wrote in his diary, "I live in constant contradiction with myself. That is, I think one thing and feel another. In the church-religion sense I am an atheist, but I am convinced that it would be a disaster if people had no religion, no churches, or no God." He also privately lamented that "I really cannot understand at all why people must be Christians, Jews, or Mohammedans—and least of all why Catholics, Orthodox, or Protestants," adding that people would be better off without having faith thrust on them, simply "governed not by religion but by morality."[24]

The tensions between these various inchoate ethnic, religious, and national identities—Christian, Jewish, and Russian—meant that Rubinstein was not merely a Jewish convert to Christianity or a baptized Russian Jew (both fraught identities themselves), but a modern individual thinker ensnared in a particularly inhospitable premodern-style society. He could philosophize all he wanted about the illusory nature of religion and nationality, but late Imperial Russia continued to insist on a tightly demarcated boundary between Russian and non-Russian, Jew and Christian. And more so than many others, Rubinstein had no obvious legal and social group with which to associate himself. This indeterminate status, caught between the mutually exclusive religious and national categories of the day, drove his quest to transcend them all through the invention of a wholly new social category: the musical profession of "Free Artist."

Free Artist: The Quest for Musical Emancipation

In the fall of 1858, Rubinstein returned again to Russia and resettled in St. Petersburg, where he resumed his place as court pianist for Elena Pavlovna. Status issues continued to consume him. In his memoirs, he narrates the precise incident to which he attributed his ambitious vision for a major change in the role of music and musicians in Russian society. Arriving at St. Petersburg's Kazan Cathedral on Nevsky Prospect to take the sacrament during Holy Week, he was asked by the deacon to provide his name and title (*zvanie*) for the record book. What followed was an ostensibly comic dialogue:

"Your surname? What do you do?"
"Rubinstein, an artist."
"Artist! What do you mean? Do you work in the theater?"
"No," I reply.
"Ah, perhaps you are a teacher in some institute then?"
"No," I say.
"So, you are in government service?"
"No," I repeat, "I am not in government service."

Back and forth the "cross-examination" (*dopros*) went, according to Rubinstein, as the two men struggled to find the right category in which to inscribe the young musician. Finally, the deacon asked Rubinstein who his father was. "A merchant of the Second Guild," answered Rubinstein. Relieved that he had found his answer, the church official duly registered Rubinstein as "the son of a merchant of the Second Guild."²⁵

To Rubinstein, this anecdote was proof of the invisibility and nonstatus of musicians in Russia: "It was obvious that in Russia the profession of musical artist, a profession that defined the position in society of a person who has devoted his whole life to his art and music did not exist." In his later retelling, the story became about the logic of the conservatory. As he explained, "It was to produce these sorts of people that we thought up the conservatory, out of which people would emerge with the diploma of Free Artist . . . [constituting] an entirely new division of Russian citizens." As he likely intended, biographer after biographer has relayed Rubinstein's own interpretation of the incident with little critical comment. What all have ignored is the irony that the entire incident takes place in a cathedral right before he is to receive the religious sacrament. Just as in the case of his 1848 border crossing, he once again described a situation in which he was unable to prove his identity or to locate himself within the hierarchy of Russian social and legal life. Here, however, the religious subtext suggested the deeper meaning of art as spiritual vocation (as well as the complexities of religious belonging for a baptized Jew).[26]

In fact, Rubinstein's vision of the conservatory as a mechanism for creating a Free Artist—a legally and philosophically emancipated musician— contained more than a little hint of inspired mission. It was religion that provided the passionate vocabulary and model for Rubinstein's conception of art as a spiritual, transcendent experience. Thus, writing in 1861 to a prominent lady-in-waiting in Elena Pavlovna's court, Edith F. Raden, to request that the grand duchess "liberate him" from his position as court pianist at the weekly palace soirees, he explained that he found the position "incompatible with the dignity of Art that I revere with all the fanaticism of a religion." He would later frequently invoke biblical and other religious metaphors in describing art and the role of the artist.[27]

If art was a substitute for religion, then a church was required in which to anoint the faithful and train the clergy. As early as 1852, Rubinstein had proposed the idea of a new central musical academy to Elena Pavlovna. He envisioned the school as a musical branch of the Imperial Academy of Arts, founded a century earlier. But the final years of Nicholas I's reign were an inopportune time for major public initiatives of any sort. By contrast, when he returned home in the summer of 1858, Rubinstein found a new atmosphere of liberal optimism and receptiveness to ideas of reform under Nicholas I's successor, Alexander II, "the Liberator." In July of that year, with Elena Pavlovna's help, Rubinstein received government permission to change his own legal status from "son of a merchant of the Third Guild" to "Artist of the First Rank of the Imperial Theaters." In the fall of 1859 he introduced a formal proposal for a Russian Musical Society (*Russkoe muzykalnoe obshchestvo*) authorized to present regular public concerts and offer music classes in St. Petersburg. With the support of the grand duchess and other court and noble figures, a charter was obtained. Concerts began immediately, followed soon after by free classes, some of which were held in the Mikhailovsky Palace.

As the new Russian Musical Society gathered momentum in the opening months of 1860, Rubinstein approached the Ministry of Education with plans for an "Imperial Music School." The design called for an institution basically parallel in form, function, and authority to the Imperial Academy of Arts. While the Russian Musical Society would administer the school, the government would oversee instruction, possibly subsidize its budget, and conduct certification of its pupils upon graduation, awarding them the title "Free Artist," a designation already in place for graduates of the Imperial Academy of Arts. The petition was rejected on the grounds that it was a "luxury" that would not yield useful results.[28] Frustrated by the repeated struggles with the government bureaucracy, Rubinstein sought broader public support. In January 1861 he published an article in a new St. Petersburg journal, *Vek* (Age), entitled "On Music in Russia."

Rubinstein's manifesto offered a general critique of the state of the arts in Russian society. The true artist, he wrote, was a "martyr" who selflessly sacrificed his total being to the cause of art. By contrast, he found Russia dominated by the sort of overprivileged, undereducated amateur for whom art served as "neither his main occupation nor his livelihood." Immune to psychological and financial pressures of critical and public opinion, the amateur could only pursue art for selfish purposes of "personal pleasure." There was but one solution to this problem. The government should award musicians the privileges accorded to other arts such as painting and sculpture in order to endow musicians with the "civic status of artist." The mechanism for producing suitable artists would be a new, state-sponsored national conservatory. This institution would produce "Russian music teachers, Russian orchestral musicians, and Russian singers of both sexes who will work the way a person works for whom his art is a livelihood, the key to social respect, a means of achieving fame, and a way of surrendering himself completely to his divine calling."[29]

This mixture of the economic and the spiritual marked a departure for nineteenth-century European thought. Under the influence of Romanticism, natural artistic genius was often characterized by the very *absence* of material self-interest, bureaucratic procedure, and formal education. Rubinstein now argued for these as the essential components of great art. The Russianness of Rubinstein's project also represented a novel approach to national culture. In the 1860s, the prevailing official model of Russianness continued to be defined through the Nicholaevan triple alliance of Orthodoxy, Autocracy, and Nationality (*Pravoslavie, samoderzhavie, narodnost*). In Rubinstein's eyes, Russian culture derived not from this mystical union of the church, tsar, and the loyal populace, but from a more equal partnership between the benevolent state and its active, diverse population. This rejection of conservative statist absolutism for a liberal model of imperial civic culture dovetailed perfectly with other similar public initiatives in the fields of Russian law, medicine, science, education, and the arts then appearing in the 1860s. The proponents of these new professions sought to create modern autonomous pockets in society defined by new educational institutions, formalized training, and professional differentiation. A hallmark of these projects was their shared sense of moral mission and personal independence from the ancien régime's social and legal categories. Yet without a significant European-style middle class on which to draw, Russia's would-be professionals paradoxically sought a closer public alliance with the Russian state than their European peers.[30] This was particularly true when it came to legal recognition and financial support for new organizations and educational organizations such as Rubinstein's proposed conservatory.

Rubinstein's manifesto quickly unleashed a chorus of criticism from many other musicians, including two of the most influential music critics, Vladimir Stasov (1824-1906) and Alexander Serov (1820-1871). Writing in the *Severnaia pchela* (Northern Bee) newspaper in late February 1861, Stasov offered a piercing denunciation of Rubinstein's description of art as self-sacrifice. Defining Romanticism instead through a conservative nationalist lens, he excluded the pianist from any authentic role in Russian culture: "Mr. Rubinstein is a foreigner [*inostranets*] with nothing in common either with our nationality [*narodnost*] or our art." He went on to dismiss Rubinstein's ideas of art, education, and professionalism as Western imports, unsuited to the "organic" path of Russian art. Any government involvement amounted to harmful "artificial encouragement," Stasov asserted, and creating financial and social rewards for musicians would lead only to rampant opportunism and dry scholasticism. Citing the history of Russian literature, Stasov argued that Russian culture properly developed along its own internal path beyond the bounds of state control and without need of "ranks or titles."[31]

Stasov's dismissal of Rubinstein as not truly Russian amounted to a mixture of the common anti-German prejudices of the day along with a hint of the newer anti-Jewish language then beginning to appear in the Russian conservative press. Serov, by contrast, abandoned all pretense of subtlety in his ad hominem attack on Rubinstein as the epitome of evil Jewish opportunism. In an essay also published in *Severnaia pchela*, Serov reasserted that it was the amateur who disregarded professional reward that was the true artist. By contrast, the new Jewish presence most threatened Russian music's future: "We Russians voluntarily yield to the oppression of talentless foreigners, musical Yankels. . . . Soon, with the founding of the *conservatoire* they sought for themselves as the future breeding ground for talentless musical civil servants, they will begin to throw their weight around in the province they have acquired in a thoroughly despotic manner, trying to crush any musical talent in Russia that does not spring from within their own Yankel ranks."[32]

Serov's polemic veered from the older Russian Judeophobia into a full-blown modern antisemitism. Rubinstein became "Rebenstein" in his writing (a pun on the word "rabbi"), and he nicknamed the St. Petersburg Conservatory "the synagogue." Serov's rhetorical excesses reflected both his status as the leading Russian apostle of the German antisemitic composer Richard Wagner and his own form of Jewish self-hatred. As a young man he had discovered that his grandfather, the Russian state senator Karl I. Gablits (1752–1821), was a Jewish convert. Nor did the secret remain hidden. His wife, herself the daughter of two baptized Jews, later recalled an incident in which they visited Wagner at his home in Germany on a Saturday. Greeting them, Wagner joked that their presence forced him to celebrate the Jewish Sabbath: "What are you doing to me? I write against Judaism, and you force me to observe *Shabbes*."[33]

Behind these harsh, personalized polemics lay a deeper philosophical opposition to Rubinstein's ideas. In the late 1850s and early 1860s, German Romantic ideas of national folklore and folk art coalesced with conservative Russian cultural philosophies such as Slavophilism and pan-Slavism to produce a new form of Russian musical nationalism. By 1861 this loosely defined movement of composers and critics had yet to find a name or cohesive identity for itself. Internally these musicians were divided by questions of personal rivalry and competing aesthetic philosophies. Stasov and Serov, for instance, bitterly disliked one another and repeatedly clashed publicly. Others could not decide how to reconcile their popular nationalist instincts with political loyalty to the Russian autocracy. So instead they concentrated on defining Russian music in opposition to the overtly Western, Germanic, and Judaic influences in the conservatory project, all of which were neatly encapsulated in Rubinstein's person. Stasov, Serov, and their colleagues found a useful external enemy in Rubinstein and his conservatory, against which to define their own emerging nationalist position.[34]

Rubinstein made no attempt to respond publicly to his critics. He could afford to ignore these and other subsequent assaults, for in October 1861 the Ministry of the Imperial Court issued a charter for Russia's first conservatory, together with an annual subsidy of five thousand rubles. While nominally supervised by the Ministry of the Court, the new conservatory was essentially a private school operated by the Russian Musical Society under the sponsorship of Grand Duchess Elena Pavlovna. Rubinstein's call for an inclusive and expansive definition of Russian musicians was reflected in its egalitarian admission policies. The 1861 charter allowed for the admission of both men and women "of all estates," provided they were above the age of fourteen, literate, and knew basic arithmetic and musical notation.[35]

Equally important, the Free Artist (*svobodnyi khudozhnik*) diploma, the first of which was presented to Rubinstein himself in 1863, provided the equivalent to the estate (*soslovie*) of a personal honored citizen (*lichnyi pochetnyi grazhdanin*). For most students of nonnoble backgrounds, this diploma therefore represented a considerable improvement in status. Tangible benefits included exemptions from various tax rolls and military conscription, and eligibility for positions and compensation roughly equivalent to midlevel civil servants. For Jews, the rank brought an additional crucial reward in the form of the elusive right of permanent residence (*pravo zhitelstva*) outside the Pale of Settlement. It therefore allowed individual Jews to participate in what historian Benjamin Nathans has termed "selective integration," the distinctive Russian variation on the Jewish legal emancipation elsewhere in Europe. Rather than extend blanket legal equality to its Jewish population, the Russian state proceeded in a piecemeal fashion from the late 1850s, granting individual Jews in certain qualifying groups the rights of citizenship. Jewish musicians thus joined a growing elite of retired soldiers, artisans, wealthier merchants, and graduates of Russian institutions of higher education as some of the first and only Jewish beneficiaries of this state policy.[36]

Despite the instant opportunity created for Jews, there is no evidence that Rubinstein initially viewed the conservatory as an a priori agent of Jewish sociopolitical integration and acculturation. His focus was rather the opposite, that of legitimizing his institution as suitably Russian. For this reason, the school itself was initially called a musical school (*muzykalnoe uchilishche*) and not a conservatory (*konservatoriia*), because of the latter term's foreign associations, in particular with the French *conservatoire*. Rubinstein's sensitivity to the issue of appearances was keen. Early critics had charged that the early faculty was composed primarily of foreigners, chiefly Germans and Jews. He therefore made a point of hiring ethnic Russians as instructors and insisted that the language of instruction be Russian rather than French or German, even for music theory.[37]

It was not only antisemites who saw the potential Jewish link to the conservatory. The Jews of St. Petersburg themselves, at the time in the midst of a period of communal growth and active efforts to expand Jewish rights, welcomed the new institution. In particular, the egalitarian admissions policy and Rubinstein's quest for musical emancipation immediately resonated with an important new organization of Russian Jewish liberals based in St. Petersburg, the Society for the Promotion of Enlightenment among the Jews of Russia (*Obshchestvo dlia rastropranenii prosveshcheniia mezhdu evreiami v Rossii*, hereafter OPE). Founded in 1863 in St. Petersburg, the OPE was the product of a novel alliance between two different groups of Russian Jews:

secularist urban intellectuals committed to internal religious and political reform in the Jewish community, and a new wealthy class of merchants and businessmen. Together these economic and intellectual elites promoted Jewish linguistic and cultural Russification, including participation in Russian higher education in order to hasten Jewish integration. At the head of this organization was the St. Petersburg Jewish banker Baron Evzel (Joseph) Gintsburg, a figure of enormous wealth and influence and a close personal friend of Rubinstein. Every year Rubinstein made a point of sending him a gift for the Jewish holiday of Purim. Not surprisingly, he also joined Gintsburg's new organization shortly after its founding.[38]

One of the OPE's main activities was the distribution of scholarship funds to needy Jewish students seeking to enroll at St. Petersburg universities and institutes. In his years as the organization's secretary, the historian Shaul Gintsburg recalled receiving hundreds of letters of petition from Rubinstein on behalf of Jewish conservatory students. The fruits of these efforts could be seen already in the first years of the conservatory, when several Jews from the Pale of Settlement enrolled as students. Notable among the early graduates were Borukh Leyb Rosowsky (1841–1919) and Jacob Bachmann (1846–1905), both young protégés of Rubinstein. Rosowsky, the son of a merchant from the Lithuanian shtetl of Naliboki, arrived at the conservatory in January 1865 through the sponsorship of the OPE and several individual Russian Jewish bankers. He quickly attracted attention as much for his traditional Jewish garb, strict religious observance, and unconventional family situation (he was already married with three children) as for his musical talents. Conservatory records indicate that he spent six years as a student there, studying in order to become "a Jewish cantor."[39]

Rosowsky later recalled that Rubinstein was completely bewildered by his initial appearance and the fact that he could barely speak Russian. He was even more confused when in response to his question of what the young would-be student could sing, Rosowsky answered in Yiddish, "*tefiles* and *zmires*" (prayers and Sabbath hymns). Once he heard him sing, however, Rubinstein was immediately impressed. Reportedly declaring his voice to be the best in the school, he took the unusual Jewish student under his wing, encouraging him to the point of inviting him to perform at a birthday party for Elena Pavlovna. Rosowsky also became friends with the young Peter Tchaikovsky, studying composition in the same class with him. After graduation in 1871, he briefly contemplated a performance career but went on instead to a post as the longtime chief cantor of Riga.[40]

Even more dramatic was the experience of Jacob Bachmann. Hailing from Rubinstein's ancestral home of Berdichev, Bachmann began life as a traditional synagogue chorister before moving to St. Petersburg at the age of eighteen to study composition with the conservatory director himself. Gifted with an extraordinary vocal range, he contemplated pursuing an opera career. After graduation in 1865, he even toured briefly as a concert artist with Rubinstein as his accompanist. Then, to the surprise and dismay of many, Bachmann rejected the chance to become an opera star, instead opting for the cantorate. He went on to achieve the status of a star cantor, moving from pulpit to pulpit for decades across eastern Europe as Jewish communities zealously competed for his talents. In the process, Bachmann also pioneered Western-style liturgical music for the eastern European synagogue.[41]

Rubinstein's mentoring of Rosowsky and Bachmann was but one indication of his growing personal fascination with traditional Jewish liturgical music. In the 1860s, on periodic family visits to Odessa and trips abroad, he quietly began to attend synagogues on major Jewish holidays. There he would sit in the back row as a silent observer, listening intently in order to collect melodies. This increasing interest in Jewish music was hardly compatible with the other major development of the early 1860s, Rubinstein's courtship and marriage to Vera Aleksandrovna Chekuanova (1841–1909), the daughter of a distinguished yet impoverished Russian noble. The two had met through St. Petersburg social circles in 1859. However, Chekuanova's father refused to consent to a marriage on the grounds of Rubinstein's Jewish background and his low status as a musician. After years of turmoil, the couple finally wed in the summer of 1865 in the German resort city of Baden-Baden.[42]

By all accounts, Rubinstein's marriage was not a happy one. His prodigious work ethic and travel schedule did not endear him to his wife, who preferred a more leisurely life with their three children, Iakov (Iasha) (1866–1902), Anna (Anya) (1869–1915), and Alexander (Sasha) (1872–1893). Rubinstein's extramarital dalliances and costly gambling habit only further complicated matters. On top of all this, he brought his Jewish cultural passions directly into the home. When, in November 1865, an Odessa synagogue choir performed in St. Petersburg, Rubinstein seized the opportunity to stage a private concert evening at his own home. Vera refused to attend the Jewish soiree, hiding out in her room for the duration of the event. In a letter to her mother at the time, she described her reactions: "Last week we had an 'evening' with a Jewish choir visiting from Odessa. . . . They howled, they moaned with a wild chant that is terrifying but not unoriginal. I listened from my room and it seemed to me at times that I too was about to start howling. When they had left, my maid, a fervid Catholic, sprayed all the rooms with perfume."[43]

The reactions of Rubinstein's terrified wife and maid suggested that for them, at least musically speaking, the Jews were a primeval, barbaric people belonging to Oriental rather than Western civilization. What, then, of Rubinstein's own reaction to traditional Jewish music? What did he hear in the sounds of that Odessa Jewish choir? To answer this we must turn to his own model of Jewish music.

Eastern Melody, Hebrew Song: Jewish Music between East and West

In 1855, Rubinstein published his first major work of musical criticism, an extended essay entitled "Russian Composers" in the Viennese journal *Blätter für Musik, Theater und Kunst*. The two-part survey quickly earned its author lasting scorn for his allegedly negative comments about the iconic Russian composer Mikhail Glinka. Rather than as an attack on Russian music, however, Rubinstein had intended his commentary to serve as an act of Russian patriotism by a young composer defending his homeland's cultural achievement in the midst of the Crimean War. Furthermore, the essay's true importance was completely overlooked. "Russian Composers" actually revealed less about Rubinstein's critical opinions on Russian music than his idiosyncratic ideas of nationality, civilization, and art.[44]

Rubinstein began by discussing the "innate" Russian gift for music, found everywhere in Russian society from the village to the factory. In spite of this natural musical penchant, he argued, there was no possibility of a genuinely Russian national style of art music. Owing to its "well-known monotony," "dark character," and plaintive, melancholy coloring, Russian folk song, despite its beauty, was unsuitable for the truest musical art form, opera. But the matter was not merely one of aesthetics. The larger problem, he emphasized, was a philosophical one. A universal art form such as opera could not be based on the specific colors of national folklore: "Folk music exists, but only in the sense of folk songs and dances, and folk opera, strictly speaking, does not exist. Every nuance of emotion contained in opera such as love, jealousy, homesickness, levity, gloom and so forth is found among all peoples of the world. Therefore musical representation of all of these common human feelings does not require national coloring. Its coloring must be universal (common to all mankind)."

Rubinstein's denial of the Romantic principle of national folklore as the basis for art music did not mean, as many later critics would suggest, that he rejected all cultural differences in music. Rather, he concluded that the truly essential cultural distinction lay not among nations—Russia, France, or Italy—but between two civilizations, Western and Eastern: "The only difference that does exist is between Western and Oriental music. Owing to climate, customs, and other factors, the ability to perceive sensations among Oriental peoples is much stronger than in Western peoples. And so just as no one would think to write a Persian, Malaysian, or Japanese opera, but only a general Oriental one, the same desire to write an English, French, or Russian one as opposed to a general European opera cannot seriously address this question." Clearly, from his answer, Rubinstein believed that Russian music belonged to the Western tradition. Left unanswered in this essay, though, was a related question. To which civilization did Jewish music belong: Western or Eastern?

From Glinka onward, a hallmark of Russian national musical identity was the use of exotic elements in Oriental-themed compositions. As Vladimir Stasov noted in his influential 1882 programmatic essay, "Twenty-Five Years of Russian Art," the "Oriental [*vostochnyi*] element" constituted a fundamental attribute of Russian national music, an expression of Russia's imperial national identity and enduring historic links to the East. Musically, this Russian musical Orientalism aimed to evoke various cultures of the East, including those of the Tatars, Georgians, Armenians, and other peoples in the Caucasus, central Asia, and the Near East. Along with ethnic song texts and titles, the Russian Oriental idiom often featured a number of musical stereotypes, exaggerated aesthetic devices designed to evoke the sounds of the East. These included the use of the augmented second interval, repeated syncopated rhythms, ostinato patterns, and heavy chromaticism, especially in descending melodic lines.[45]

In the minds of many Russians, there was little question that Jews ought to be included within these Eastern musical rubrics. Glinka himself began the tradition of writing songs on Jewish melodic themes, real and imagined, when he composed his "Evreiskaia pesnia" (Hebrew Song) in 1839. In the 1850s, 1860s, and 1870s, Mily Balakirev, Nikolai Rimsky-Korsakov, and Modest Mussorgsky all created works drawing on traditional eastern European Jewish musical repertoire to impart an Oriental coloring to their Russian romances, operatic arias, and cantatas. Often these compositions were titled "Evreiskaia pesnia" or "Evreiskaia melodiia" (Hebrew Melody), explicitly adapting the texts from Lord Byron's famous 1806 poetry cycle, *Hebrew Melodies*. The choice was not merely coincidental. In Mikhail Lermontov's translation, Byron's *Hebrew Melodies* had become a key text for nineteenth-century Russian writers and composers as a whole, reflecting a deep symbolic identification with ancient Israel as a prototype for Russia's own sense of national mission.[46]

Yet this common Russian identification with the ancient Hebrews did not engender sympathy for modern Jews. In fact, many of these Russian nationalist composers followed the broader nineteenth-century Russian practice of maintaining a linguistic and cultural dichotomy between a positive biblical ideal of Israelite or Hebrew (referred to as *evrei*) and the negative ideal of the modern Diaspora Jew (designated by the pejorative *zhid*). It was Mussorgsky who went the furthest in this respect. In his "Evreiskaia pesnia" (1867) and *Joshua* cantata (1877), he selected contemporary Hasidic nigunim (labeled "Israelite folk songs") and recast these melodies as ancient by stripping them of their ostensibly Ashkenazi musical features (ex. 1a). To do so, Mussorgsky avoided an overt minor key tonality in his harmonies and eliminated augmented second intervals and most grace notes in his melodies. The result was a less melismatic, more even sound intended to represent the noble, stately music of ancient Israel. Meanwhile, in his *Pictures at an Exhibition* (1874), he offered one of the most blatantly antisemitic musical depictions of Russian Jews ("'Samuel' Goldenburg and 'Schmuyle'") through a series of exaggerated musical clichés (ex. 1b). There augmented seconds, multiple grace notes, minor key tonality, and extreme chromaticism abound, producing a caricatured Oriental effect that alternates between lugubrious bass rumblings and twittering high-pitched flights of notes, both suggesting coded acoustical stereotypes of modern-day Jews.[47]

In contrast to his contemporaries, Rubinstein made no distinction between ancient Hebrews and modern Jews. For him, the question was rather how Jews differed musically from other Oriental peoples. In an 1872 letter to Julius Rodenberg he noted the similarities between his earlier opera, the Oriental fantasy *Feramors*, and a new operatic adaptation of the biblical Song of Songs, *Sulamith*, based on Rodenberg's libretto. In characters, plot, and themes, he worried, the two works were nearly identical: "What is to be done about it? Yes, even the coloring is once again Oriental, since musically it is too difficult to make Jewish distinct from Persian or Arabian."[48] Behind this confusion lay a broader struggle over his own multiple musical identities as a European, Russian, and Jew.

In fact, in his own day critics often divided Rubinstein's compositions up into two large categories, Western-style works and explicitly Oriental (*vostochnye*) pieces. Not surprisingly, however, there was little consensus as to which works belonged in the latter category. Some of these compositions, such as his 1868 romance, "Evreiskaia melodiia" (Hebrew Melody) (ex. 2), also based on Byron's lyric, and the 1874 opera, *The Maccabees*, explicitly marked themselves as Jewish. On the other hand, the *Persian Songs* (1854–55), written to the poems of the Azerbaijani poet Mirza-Shafi Vazeh (1794–1852), and the operas *Demon* (1883) and *Feramors* also evoked an Oriental

Example 1. Excerpts from Modest Mussorgsky's works on Jewish themes.

idiom musically little different from his "Jewish" music, yet without an explicit Jewish label attached. This led musicians, critics, and audiences alike to play a constant guessing game with Rubinstein's music, searching in varying degrees for the obvious melodic references attributable to his Jewish heritage. Opinions varied considerably in this respect, as did popular theories about Rubinstein's own conscious adoption of Jewish melodic materials.[49]

Example 2. Anton Rubinstein's "Evreiskaia melodiia," 1868.

There is no doubt that Rubinstein did employ traditional Jewish melodies in some of his Jewish-themed compositions. Discrete snatches of eastern European Jewish synagogue melodies appear in *The Maccabees*, for instance, as does a well-known Hasidic melody used in Leah's aria (ex. 3). Yet Rubinstein knew it only as a scrap of melody that he remembered his mother playing in his childhood.[50] This and other half-remembered musical fragments did not add up to a coherent concept of Jewish music. Without a specific model of Jewishness as a secular national category, Rubinstein simply had no philosophical language or political impulse to carve out a Jewish musical repertoire distinct from East and West. Even when secular Jewish nationalism began to appear as a movement among the Russian Jewish intelligentsia in the 1880s, he preferred instead to look backward to medieval religious models of Jewishness to explain his own identity to himself and others.

We see this most clearly in a fascinating memoir by Rubinstein's close friend, the St. Petersburg Jewish journalist Robert F. Ilish (1834–1909). In

"Beat the drums louder, beat the drums stronger, louder, stronger."
"Sing loudly to God, sing Him a song, sing loudly to God, sing Him a song."

Example 3. Leah's aria from Anton Rubinstein's *The Maccabees*, 1874. Adapted from the second edition of the Society for Jewish Folk Music *Songbook*, with Yiddish text in place of the original German and Russian.

1898 Ilish composed a posthumous literary tribute to Rubinstein in the form of a feuilleton in the Russian Jewish journal *Voskhod*, "Anton Rubinstein and Yom Kippur." Ilish's account, subtitled "Pages from My Diary," described an unusual episode that took place at an intimate soiree at the Grand Hotel Europe in the mid-1880s. Ilish arrived directly at the gathering from the closing services of the Yom Kippur holiday. Ostensibly unaware of the holiday, Rubinstein sat down at the piano and improvised a musical fantasy on the traditional Kol Nidre prayer. Ilish, surprised, informed him of the coincidence. As Ilish recalled, Rubinstein then responded: "Is today really Yom Kippur? . . . Strange, in fact! I didn't know that today was Yom Kippur, and suddenly the idea came into my head to play the Kol Nidre melody.

Some sort of childhood memories suddenly appeared in front of me and inspired me. Believe me, it is no coincidence." A discussion about the melody ensued, during which Ilish asked Rubinstein if he had ever thought to compose something in a "Jewish-national" style. Rubinstein replied:

> In my musical compositions you will find very many Jewish motives and tunes that I heard in childhood and which returned to my memory some thirty years later. I myself am sometimes surprised how these traditional tunes and melodies materialize out of nowhere and remain, haunting me, refusing to leave me in peace. . . . These childhood [musical] memories revived with a special force at the beginning of the 1880s, when the pogroms began in the Russian South. I never felt so close to Jews as I did then, when such a terrible storm burst out against us. I also felt myself oppressed and assaulted, and my heart bled when I read about these sad events. . . . In proportion to how much I grew older, my sympathy for my fellow tribe members grew even more.

Rubinstein concluded his reflections by noting his own complicated identity: "I always recall the history of the Spanish Marranos, who for many generations were officially Catholics, born that way, and in secret worshiped Judaism and at the first opportunity returned to the bosom of the synagogue. Personally I have never dreamt of returning to Judaism, but my link of blood with Jews was never cut."

Even allowing for the excesses of literary stylization and Ilish's own Jewish nationalist sympathies, this anecdote conveys the way in which music acted as a potent channel for Rubinstein's increasing emotional identification with his Jewish origins. However, as Rubinstein's reply suggested, these renewed ties did not lead him to regard himself—or his art—as Jewish in any modern sense of the term. Instead he saw himself as a musical Marrano, a former Jew inside a Christian, an Oriental mixed with a European. Furthermore, music to Rubinstein was not only a repository of nostalgia but also a potential means of personal transcendence. There was one exit from the labyrinth of memory, which he pursued vigorously for several decades, especially in the latter part of his life: a new kind of musical art known as "spiritual opera."[51]

Die geistliche Oper: Spiritual Opera between Art and Religion

In 1867, frustrated by bureaucratic politics, Rubinstein resigned the St. Petersburg Conservatory directorship to devote himself to performance and composition. From that point onward, he also began to focus in earnest on a new vision of "geistliche Oper" (spiritual opera). Traditional oratorios left him feeling "cold" and "ill-disposed" toward the biblical themes, he later wrote, given the stilted concert hall format and the performers' modern dress. To properly blend "sacred" scripture with the "profane" secular art forms of the concert hall, he proposed combining grand opera, church oratorio, medieval passion play, and modern theater into a new genre. Biblical stories would be presented in a respectful spiritual style with costumed performers in a specially constructed theater, following specific guidelines for performance style and audience behavior. The overall result would be a modern "cathedral of art" (*Kirche der kunst*), a universal kind of sacred musical theater transcending all narrow sectarian differences and exploring grand spiritual themes beyond the limits of conventional religious or artistic contexts.

From the late 1860s to the early 1890s, Rubinstein composed a number of these spiritual operas, including *The Tower of Babel*, op. 80 (1869), *Sulamith* (1883), *Moses*, op. 112 (1891), *Christ*, op. 117 (1893), and the unfinished works *Job* and *Cain*. In each case, he devoted nearly as much effort to the biblical texts as to the music itself. His letters to his principal collaborator, Rodenberg, are filled with exacting questions about the translation of particular Hebrew words and textual issues raised by modern critical biblical scholarship. Taken as a whole, these works reflected his desire to sanctify art and secularize religion until the distinction between the two collapsed. Or as he wrote elsewhere, "Art is pantheistic . . . and [its] religion is aesthetics, requiring no church religion from the artist, for he [alone] can make his forms sacred."[52]

In its broad creative fusion of music and spirituality, Old and New Testaments, and Judaism and Christianity, the spiritual opera suggested one nonconventional Russian Jewish Christian's quest for identity. But it was also a response to another bold project of cultural synthesis, one that also combined art and religion in a totalizing vision: Richard Wagner's music drama. In fact, many contemporary accounts suggest that Rubinstein conceived of his spiritual operas as a more universal, pan-European response to what he considered the aesthetically false, "supernatural" mythmaking and virulent antisemitism of the German composer. In his mind, the false "Messiah of Art" posed the same danger to culture as Otto von Bismarck's "iron ring" and German nationalism in general posed to international equilibrium: "The same falsehood which exists in a world of a million bayonets," he wrote, "reveals itself in art and in everything else as well. All of this is a lie [that means that] music is ending."[53]

Still, from its home base in Bayreuth, Wagnerism, including its antisemitic substratum, continued to spread throughout Europe and into Russian music in the late 1880s. Meanwhile, Rubinstein repeatedly sought in vain to find the large-scale support necessary to stage his own spiritual operas. In his ecumenical spirit he turned to several different quarters, including Berlin's minister of education, the dean of Westminster Abbey, the Paris Jewish community, and an American theater impresario. A variety of financial and political factors, however, stymied all of his attempts to mount full staged productions of his works. Only a smattering of scaled-down concert versions ever occurred, chiefly in Germany.[54] Meanwhile, in the late 1880s, events in Russia drew him back into a maelstrom of public controversy involving antisemitism, nationalism, and the larger political question of the Jewish place in Russian society.

The Rise of the Russian Jewish Musician

In September 1882 an official in the Moscow governor-general's office wrote a memo to the Ministry of Internal Affairs about the growing numbers of Jews entering the Moscow and St. Petersburg conservatories. Confronted with reports of police harassment of the students, he found himself sympathizing with their situation: "It is a well-known fact that Jews are distinguished by their frequently great musical talents which appear at the earliest age." Where else could they go, therefore, but to Moscow and St. Petersburg to study music on an advanced level commensurate with their ability? As a solution, he recommended that the better-performing students be allowed to remain, while others could be easily expelled back to the Pale.[55] In fact, after a short discussion, this policy was adopted at both conservatories. Those Jewish students with "exceptional musical abilities" were allowed to remain outside the Pale, in the capital cities, in order to pursue their musical educations. The resulting rise of Russian Jewish musicians defined the final phase of Rubinstein's career and changed the history of Russian music.

In the 1860s, during Rubinstein's initial tenure as director of the St. Petersburg Conservatory, critics frequently accused the institution of being a Jewish haven. Yet the actual numbers of Jews enrolled remained quite low. In 1865, for example, less than 3 percent of the students (eight out of 299) were Jewish. Even given the conservatory's egalitarian admissions policy, enrollment still required Russian literacy, considerable funds, and legal permission to travel outside the Pale. In the 1870s, however, under the directorship of Karl Davydov, himself a Riga-born convert and noted cellist, the school pursued a variety of policies that indirectly helped increase its Jewish numbers. For example, while still largely privately funded, in 1879 the conservatory initiated a comprehensive scholarship program for poorer students. Most crucially, in the late 1870s and early 1880s both St. Petersburg and its sister conservatory in Moscow actively began to support and in some cases encourage a growing Jewish enrollment. This policy was driven by many factors, including a number of sympathetic conservatory officials and government bureaucrats who shared the stereotypical Russian belief in innate Jewish musical talent. Perhaps most crucially, the Imperial Russian Music Society (IRMO), the two conservatories' parent organization, used the Jewish musical question as part of its broader strategy to secure official autonomy from the state and protect the legal privileges of its students and graduates. In a number of fascinating court battles, the IRMO argued vigorously on behalf of its Jewish students, who claimed exemptions from residence restrictions. As historian Lynn Sargeant has convincingly shown, defending the rights of Jewish musicians became a proxy means of establishing the authority and legitimacy of the Russian musical profession as a whole.[56]

As a result, in the 1880s both the pull of educational opportunity and the push of internal demographic and cultural changes within the Jewish community began to draw a whole generation of Russian Jews toward music's promise of artistic education, social advancement, and enhanced legal status. The resulting dramatic Jewish expansion in Russian conservatories took place, however, within an atmosphere of growing popular Russian nationalism, xenophobia, and antisemitism. Following the assassination of Alexander II in 1881, his successor, Alexander III, chose to employ the iron grip of reactionary authoritarian rule. The new influx of Jews into St. Petersburg and Moscow seeking educational opportunities created a highly visible target for Russian conservatives. In language that would surface repeatedly in Russian politics over the next hundred years, the conservative press assigned direct blame for all of Russia's ills—from bourgeois capitalism to revolutionary terrorism—to the Jewish population. The St. Petersburg and Moscow conservatories, with their large Jewish student minority and symbolic cultural status, quickly became lightning rods for debates about the whole question of Jewish integration.

On the last day of 1886, Karl Davydov resigned as director of the St. Petersburg Conservatory. The immediate cause was a murky combination of illness and his implication in a sex scandal with a female student. But the situation was strongly exacerbated by a huge political backlash against the perceived Jewish prevalence at the conservatory. Within days, the IRMO, seeking to control the damage, asked Rubinstein to return as director. He promptly accepted, entering a position that he had not occupied for nearly twenty years.

Rubinstein reentered the conservatory assuming that his artistic reputation would secure the institution solid footing with the authorities and the public. He was now a veteran of the international concert world, including the United States, with piles of awards and honorary titles from across Europe. In 1877 he had also been raised to the rank of hereditary noble by the tsarist authorities, finally resolving his own lingering status issues. He had recently completed a hugely popular series of historical concerts in 1886, in which he played his way through large swaths of the history of piano music, from Bach through Beethoven down to Chopin and culminating, naturally, with himself. These concerts had had an electrifying effect on audiences, especially other musicians, further accentuating Rubinstein's reputation as the preeminent pianist of the day. Yet in spite of his worldwide fame and widespread popularity in Russia, Rubinstein immediately found himself embroiled in a major political battle in which his artistic achievements mattered relatively little. His beloved institution even faced possible closure.[57]

The very day that Rubinstein assumed his new position, the conservative newspaper *Novoe vremia* (New Time) published an editorial asserting that the St. Petersburg Conservatory had declined under the impact of a "Judaization" of its student population—so much so that "one could think that the Conservatory is located in Berdichev." This deliberate swipe at Rubinstein's own ancestral home was not merely a personal taunt. So ingrained was the association between Berdichev, Jews, and musicians in the Russian mind that tsarist officials used to contemptuously refer to young Jewish military recruits as *Berdichevskie skripki* (Berdichev violins). Politically, the pressing question of Jewish overenrollment in the conservatory had already reached the level of the State Senate. Nor was the debate merely symbolic. In July 1887 the government launched a new tactic to deal with the perceived threat of Jewish overenrollment in Russian higher education: quotas. Instituted through a direct order of the minister of education, these severe new restrictions effectively ended the longstanding state policy of opening Russian schools to Jews to socially and culturally integrate them. Because they were legally constituted under the Ministry of the Court rather than the Ministry of Education, the IRMO conservatories temporarily escaped this new regulation. They were joined in this protected position by only a handful of other institutions, including the Medical-Surgical Academy under the Ministry of War and the Petrovskaia Agricultural Academy under the Ministry of State Domains. This now anomalous status, however, only exacerbated the suspicions of the government and conservative critics that the music schools had become pro-Jewish, anti-Russian enclaves.[58]

Over the course of 1887 and 1888, Rubinstein threw himself into sustained administrative and diplomatic efforts to rescue the St. Petersburg Conservatory. The most sensitive issue facing him was the charge of lax admissions that had led to the putative Jewish predominance. Private correspondence and internal conservatory documents make clear that he was aware of and concerned about this problem. However, he insisted that the real issue was a larger trend of lowered academic standards, misguided legal incentives in the admissions process, and an excessively lenient student promotion policy that had attracted the wrong kind of applicants. In Rubinstein's mind, it was not poor Jews from the Pale but the sons and daughters of the Russian urban bourgeoisie who represented the grossest kind of dilettantism and opportunism, thus swelling the conservatory ranks and undermining its reputation.[59]

To combat this problem, Rubinstein drew up an ambitious set of reform plans to tackle the interrelated questions of the internal administrative structure, the student body composition, and external relations with the government and court. He instituted stringent new admission and graduation examinations to enforce greater quality control on the students and faculty alike. For the existing student body, he introduced a full review of each individual student, expelling hundreds over the course of two years. The results were dramatic. From an all-time peak of 846 students enrolled in 1885–86, the total number dropped to 711 at the end of the 1886–87 year, then down to 584 by the 1888–89 academic year. Nearly all these reductions came from the ranks of the female pianists, some undoubtedly Jewish, but many others not. Like many of his conservative critics, Rubinstein maintained a generally dim view of females' musical abilities, associating young bourgeois women with an amateur, casual enthusiasm for music that threatened his vision of elite professional training.[60]

By the end of the 1888–89 year, only 12 percent (71 of 584) of students enrolled were Jewish. There is no evidence that Rubinstein pursued any special course of action in terms of the Jewish question. Rather, he allowed the existing anti-Jewish laws to discourage excessive Jewish enrollment. In a letter to his mother in the summer of 1889, for instance, he responded to her inquiry on behalf of a fourteen-year-old Jewish musical prodigy from Odessa who sought admission. Explaining that the *pravo zhitelstva* was required before the would-be student could even "set foot in the conservatory," he then added sarcastically, "Please pass this on to all of the Jews and Jewesses (male and female singers, piano plunkers and violin scrapers . . . of this religion) who inquire of you, thereby sparing them the travel costs and saving the musical art from a flood of genius."[61] His strict liberal vision of a neutral civil society took precedence over any preferential treatment for Jews, especially when the overall status of the musical profession was at stake.

Initially, Rubinstein's tough-minded administrative changes earned him some grudging respect from conservative critics. He was rewarded with the title of "actual state councillor" (*deistvitelnyi statskii sovetnik*), a civil service rank equivalent in military terms to a major general. However, the conservatory still faced growing competition from new private music schools such as the Imperial Theater School, which opened in St. Petersburg in the fall of 1888. Designed as an advanced dramatic training institute for opera singers, the school denied admission to Jews. Furthermore, despite his strategic attempts to reconcile with ideological opponents such as Balakirev, Stasov, and Alexander Borodin, the Russian musical nationalists remained steadfast in their attacks on both Rubinstein and the conservatory for their perceived lack of Russianness. Short-term changes could not prevent the conservatory from remaining a potent symbol within a rapidly escalating political drama.[62]

As the school year ended in the spring of 1889, preparations began for a massive jubilee celebration to mark Rubinstein's fiftieth anniversary as a performing artist. The events proved to be the catalyst for a large-scale public clash between the conservatory's critics and supporters. It was at that moment that an episode took place that forced Rubinstein into his most explicit discussion of antisemitism and Jews in Russian culture.

The Bitter Anniversary: Rubinstein's 1889 Jubilee

The actual anniversary date of Rubinstein's debut as a public performer coincided with July 11, 1889, the day on which the nine-year old pianist had given his first public recital in Moscow fifty years earlier. But the jubilee committee, a distinguished group of Moscow and St. Petersburg nobility and musicians, chose to move the celebratory events to November of that year to coincide with his sixtieth birthday. Nevertheless, on July 7, mere days before the official anniversary date, came a sudden, severe attack on Rubinstein in the pages of *Novoe vremia*. Under the title "Our Conservatories," an anonymous author took the two conservatories and their leaders to task for failing over the course of twenty-five years, even with the benefit of "generous state subsidies," to make any contribution to the military needs of the state. "There is not one regiment with a Russian military band conductor and in many cases it is necessary to use Germans and Jews, Austrian and Prussian citizens," the author charged, adding that this situation raised a threat of foreign espionage. Furthermore, the conservatories had a harmful effect on national security in other respects as well, the author argued, because they promoted dilettantism, the avoidance of military service by young men, and neurosis among young women.

In the 1860s critics had argued in similar language that the conservatory would lead to mass superficial education, opportunism, and a gross mechanization and bureaucratization of art. Now the new conservative critique emphasized not the failure to produce great artists, but rather a lack of socially useful musicians. In the new climate of post-1881 Russian conservative nationalism, the earlier Romantic focus on the individual Russian composer as creative artist had yielded to a collectivist strain of nationalist thought, in which mass production of musicians for the Russian state's military and political needs was a legitimate and necessary task—indeed the primary one—of the educational system.

Weakening national defense was not the only grave sin of the conservatories, according to the author. They had also contributed to the corruption of Russian national music as a whole by encouraging the influx of Jewish musicians, a "'talented tribe' [that] will not help the Russian character of Russian music, and not help produce great art in Russia." Beyond their alleged innate instincts for commercial opportunism, Jews were also responsible for destroying the Russianness of Russian music by their very presence. The logic of antisemitism and conservative nationalism now extended beyond composition even into the realm of performance, "In private theaters and [summer] park concerts all of the conductors are foreign, or of Russian citizenship but Germans or Jews." Even more important, the same held true for the most sacrosanct areas of Russian national culture: "Even for the court's musical choir a Russian conductor could not be found and a foreigner was hired. The same situation exists in the Imperial theaters. . . . Already Gypsy and Little Russian songs are being crooned by Jews, and if this develops any further, then in ten years the church choruses in Orthodox churches will be full of Jews and foreigners." Thus the highly symbolic core institutions of Russian national culture—the military, the tsarist court, the Orthodox Church, and the state-run Imperial Theater—were portrayed as vulnerable through music. The mere physical presence of non–ethnic Russians as performers threatened to sully these cultural bulwarks.[63]

Four days later, on July 11, the actual date of Rubinstein's jubilee arrived. Telegrams came from the tsar, tsarina, and tsarevich, respectively, along with greetings from other senior court figures. For its part, *Novoe vremia* even ran a neutral, mildly positive item about Rubinstein's jubilee that referred to him as "one of a small number of Russian artists who have achieved worldwide fame."[64] In addition, the newspaper granted a space on its front page for a letter from the laureate himself in response to the incendiary editorial earlier in the week. Such a public declaration by Rubinstein regarding music, nationalism, and politics was an extremely rare phenomenon. Though he frequently granted interviews, often peppered with colorful witticisms and ironic, aphoristic opinions about art, Rubinstein abstained from publishing any more formal, sustained remarks on Russian culture, the conservatory, or his musical and political opponents. Yet the harsh ideological attack, timed specifically to his jubilee, had gone beyond casual antisemitic innuendo or personal battles to make a direct assault on one of the central legacies of his entire career.

Rubinstein's letter was a model of diplomatic strategy, addressing the charges one by one while deftly sidestepping the underlying ideological barbs. "Having read in your newspaper the article 'Our Conservatories,'" he began, "I consider it my obligation to say a few words in their defense." He proceeded to challenge both the facts and the ideological assumptions of his accuser through a jumble of different rhetorical strategies. Overall, Rubinstein's response divided evenly into three broad points: the social usefulness of the conservatory for musical education and professional training in Russia; the Jewish question; and the issue of Russian national music. In each of these areas, he expressed his own continuing commitment to a liberal political vision of music as path of Jewish integration while still projecting a broader, explicitly patriotic mission for music in Russia.

In answer to the charge of the conservatory's failure to produce Russian musicians, Rubinstein offered a list of impressive composers and performers from among its graduates, including his own protégé Tchaikovsky, as well as Nikolai Solov'ev, Anatoly Liadov, and Anton Arensky. Rather than challenge the nationalist claims of his critics about the need for a national identity among Russian military, church, and theater musicians, he instead used a clever rhetorical technique to shift the focus away from the ethnic litmus test of the conservative nationalists to a broader definition of Russianness. *Novoe vremia* had alleged that neither St. Petersburg nor its sister conservatory in Moscow had produced any ethnic Russian military bandleaders. Rubinstein responded that he personally knew one provincial military bandleader who was a St. Petersburg Conservatory graduate, and he was certain that many other military bandleaders had also graduated. In doing so he sidestepped the issue of nationality, focusing instead on whether the conservatory had produced bandleaders for the Russian army—rather than ethnically *Russian* army bandleaders.

He found more solid ground on the topic of theater orchestras. Regarding that question, he proudly announced that over one-third of all Russian theater orchestras and the vast majority of music teachers in institutes and other advanced educational institutions consisted of conservatory graduates, along with the regent of the St. Isaac's Cathedral choir. Again, Rubinstein made no specific claims about the nationality of these musicians, implying that they were all Russian citizens rather than foreign musicians. The rhetorical strategy allowed him to leave the definition of Russianness deliberately vague.

But this subtle approach faltered when it came to the concrete question of how many Jews were enrolled at the conservatory. Here Rubinstein was hard pressed to deny that there was some numerical overrepresentation, even if it fell far short of the exaggerated figures quoted by his critics. Rather than delve into the intricate intersection of Russian law, IRMO administrative policies, and Jewish musical achievement, or directly confront the antisemitic theories of his opponents, he chose a legalistic position. Neither conservatory could be held responsible for the Jewish predomination in Russian music, he wrote, since it was the government's own laws that ultimately determined access to higher education for Jews. He then presented an ironic anecdote to explain: "During my travels abroad I have more than once had the occasion to hear from conservatory directors and voice and instrument teachers the observation, that so many *Russians* come to study with them. 'Is it really the case that in Russia there are no possibilities for musical education?' they've asked me. It turns out that a large number of these expatriate Russians are Jews. Abroad they have the naïveté to assume every Russian citizen to be Russian!"[65]

On a superficial level, this anecdote suggested that his critics were wrong; Russian conservatories were not overly accessible to Jews, the proof being that the majority of Jews were actually forced to study abroad. At the same time, Rubinstein used the innocence and ignorance of this generalized European reaction to emphasize the absurd logic of Russian conservative nationalism and antisemitism. For most Europeans, Russians were Russians, regardless of ethnicity or religion.

Following this understated challenge to Russian antisemitism, Rubinstein took up the larger theme of the national character of Russian music, "You claim that *for the national character in our music the conservatories have done nothing.* Yes, of course, for it does not concern them at all: national *performance* can hardly exist, and national *composition* depends on the individual composer." In contrast to his somewhat muted approach to the Jewish question, here Rubinstein tackled the strident, conservative nationalism of his critics head on. Reiterating and expanding his philosophy of music that he had first laid out over three decades earlier, he now defiantly wrote that nationality was encoded in music only through language rather than specific stylistic or folkloric characteristics.

Rubinstein was not deaf, however, to the political necessity of speaking the language of cultural nationalism. His own patriotic loyalty to the "fatherland" (*otechestvo*) did not preclude the idea of supporting Russian national music. He went on in his *Novoe vremia* letter to note that "the acquaintance with the fatherland's compositions is done in the Conservatory as much as necessary; students have boxes at the opera, have free entrance to rehearsals and concerts, in the classes they assign for compositions, both vocal and instrumental, the greatest of the fatherland's compositions." What Rubinstein hinted at here, in terms of the broader musical borders of the "fatherland," he made explicit elsewhere. Over the years 1887 to 1889 he repeatedly petitioned senior members of the court, including Tsar Alexander III himself, to intervene and acknowledge the valuable role of conservatories in Russian musical life by assuming official fiscal and legal responsibility for them. In these detailed proposals Rubinstein argued for a definition of Russian music based on an imperial model of Russian national identity: the definition of Russianness in music ought to be determined not exclusively by Russian nationality, but rather by Russian citizenship. In this model of "musical Russia" (*muzykalnaia Rossiia*), the corpus of Russian national music consisted of "compositions by Russian citizens, past and present." To realize this vision, Rubinstein proposed a new symphony orchestra for the IRMO devoted to the Russian national repertoire, as well as a plan for special opera houses in each major city throughout the empire to concentrate exclusively on programming Russian national repertoire.[66]

With its cultural breadth and political borders, this vision of "musical Russia" corresponded to the imperial, inclusive ideal of Russian nationality, the term known by the Russian adjective *rossiiskii*, in contrast to the more narrow word *russkii* denoting ethnic and religious Russianness. The imperial dimension was crucial, for Rubinstein continually and instinctively turned to the state to legitimize the conservatories as Russian national institutions. By providing specialized training for military, church, and state theater musicians in Russia, he hoped that the conservatories would produce musicians who were de facto recognized as Russian regardless of their individual religious and ethnic origins, rather than judged by the increasingly narrow yardstick of modern conservative ethnic nationalism. His political liberalism was therefore not inconsistent with a basic belief in the necessary power and legitimacy of a strong Russian state. Indeed, in 1889 he remarked that it was imperative that the government take fiscal responsibility and administrative control of the conservatories: "With our monarchy, a private enterprise, like a conservatory, proves impossible. The initiative was taken, and the conservatory has lasted thirty years, but now it is essential that the conservatory, like the Academy of Arts and the university, become a state institution."

Along with other Russian nineteenth-century liberals (and Russian Jewish intellectuals) Rubinstein could not envision an independent Russian culture—or a robust civil society—without the state's resources, authority, and supervision on some level.[67]

Neither Rubinstein's carefully worded public statement nor his private diplomacy managed to quell the controversy stirred up by his jubilee. Throughout the rest of 1889, the debate between Rubinstein and his critics continued in the pages of the Russian press, including newspapers such as *Novoe vremia*, *Grazhdanin* (Citizen), *Moskovskie vedomosti* (Moscow Bulletin), and *Nuvellist* and music magazines such as *Baian* (Accordion) and *Artist*. While conservative newspapers continued the pattern of broad innuendo, liberal commentators tended to characterize the whole affair as a transparent conservative plot to publicly discredit the conservatories. Indeed, there is evidence to suggest that the press campaign in the pages of *Grazhdanin* and *Novoe vremia* was orchestrated with Alexander III's complicit knowledge through his close personal ties with these newspapers' publishers, Prince Vladimir P. Meshcherskii (1839–1914) and Aleksei S. Suvorin (1834–1912), respectively.[68]

When November finally arrived, the jubilee took the form of a seven-night festival in St. Petersburg, with concerts, balls, banquets, toasts, gifts, and congratulatory messages from the length and breadth of Russia and the rest of Europe. Rubinstein received scores of honors and awards from members of the tsar's family, the IRMO, and countless musical figures, publishers, philanthropic societies, and musical organizations as well as several commemorative books. An international musical competition was begun in his honor; scholarships were endowed at the St. Petersburg Conservatory; and concerts were held in cities throughout the Russian Empire. His Jewish friends at the OPE sent an official address congratulating him on his achievements for "the fame of Russia" and for "the benefit of the rising generation for whom you are a guiding star in the field of art."[69]

Yet none of this celebration could erase the cloud of controversy that had settled over his tenure at the St. Petersburg Conservatory. During the jubilee week more articles appeared in *Grazhdanin* and elsewhere, charging that a week of celebrations devoted to one man was an indulgent waste of state funds. Another slight came from one of Rubinstein's old opponents, the composer Balakirev, who reportedly responded to his invitation to the festivities with a remark that "Rubinstein has done nothing but harm to Russian music." Undoubtedly the biggest insult, however, was delivered by Alexander III himself. Previously the tsar had displayed public respect for Rubinstein, apparently out of a political concern for international opinion regarding Russia's treatment of its own artists. Now, however, he allowed his fierce antisemitism and personal dislike of Rubinstein to dictate his reaction. Privately he mocked the jubilee events and criticized his family members and court officials for participating; publicly he conspicuously refused to attend any of the events.[70]

From the end of 1889 onward, a combination of internal power struggles, increasing public pressure, and antisemitic attacks in the press began to take their toll on Rubinstein. In the spring of 1891 he resigned from the conservatory. Now estranged from his wife, he moved first to Odessa to spend the summer with his ailing mother. In September he left Russia for what he declared to be the last time. Settling in Dresden, he spent the next two years there concentrating on his spiritual operas. But the rapid decline and death of his son Alexander, who had long suffered from asthma and heart problems, drew him back to Russia in late 1893. In June 1894 he formally rejoined his wife and family at their villa in Peterhof. But it was to be a truly final homecoming. Now plagued by illness himself, he died less than six months later, just days shy of his sixty-fifth birthday.[71]

In the fall of 1889, during the height of the jubilee controversy, Rubinstein was invited to the offices of the journal *Russkaia starina* (Russian Antiquity) to dictate his memoirs. Near the end of his remarks, he paused to ask: "How will it all end? One way or another it must resolve itself. A fusion [*slianie*]? Such a fusion would be strange. They do not want to know about me at all. They don't recognize me—neither as a Russian nor as a composer. My situation is strange: in Germany they consider me Russian, here—a German. Clearly, it was fated to be that way: either I was born too early or too late."[72]

Despite his political supporters and adoring fans, Rubinstein reacted to the conflict of 1889 with cynicism and despair. After a lifetime of struggle in the service of European art, political liberalism, and Russian culture, he felt he had earned little abiding respect for his compositions or his conservatory. His dream of musical reform had apparently collapsed from the weight of conservative nationalism and antisemitism. His vision of art as a transcendent means of breaking through the dichotomies of his own life had also begun to slip farther away. The pessimistic rejection of the possibility of *slianie*, literally "fusion" or "rapprochement," a Russian word also used to denote the idea of positive integration of Jews into Russian society, signified a loss of faith in the possibility of reconciling Russian and German, Jew and Christian. Rubinstein turned increasingly to ironic reflections on his own personal struggles of identity.

Rubinstein's final creation was not musical but literary. In the early 1880s, following the sudden death of his brother Nikolai, he began to compose a collection of thoughts, a private diary of his life reflections. Resuming work on the text after 1891, Rubinstein eventually produced a large collection of clever aphorisms and philosophical meditations. As he intended, the text was published only after his death, issued by his friend the German Jewish concert producer Hermann Wolff in 1897 under the title *Anton Rubinstein's Gedankenkorb* (Anton Rubinstein's Basket of Thoughts).[73]

The *Gedankenkorb* represents a final summation of Rubinstein's thoughts on the core questions of his life. It is also a study in paradox and contradiction. Expressions of deep spiritual longing alternate with cynical atheism. At one point in the text, Rubinstein dismisses all organized religion as sectarian intolerance that ought to be replaced by universal secular morality. Personally affected by the specter of antisemitism, he also goes so far as to endorse the proto-Zionist idea of Jewish resettlement of Palestine:

> With today's growing antisemitic movement in society, where the Jews are expelled from one land to another and not accepted anywhere, it is unclear to me why Europe is not more keen to take hold of her Jerusalem again, reward Turkey with another piece of land, and dispose of the Jews there as they please. Then they could conduct their helpful money dealings with Europe from there just as if they were in Europe itself. The insufferable agitation against a tiny people who itself has not done anything wrong other than to demonstrate its own financial superiority over other peoples is absolutely unfitting for the nineteenth century! Europe has managed to do this for the Greeks, the Romanians, Belgians, Dutch, Serbs, Bulgarians and so on, why not then for the Jews as well?

The Jewish return to Zion might solve Europe's Jewish question—and its financial needs—to everyone's satisfaction, but it would not help Rubinstein with his own individual identity. Recognized by none, "everywhere a stranger," he felt that nationalism was no solution to his personal psychological wrestling match with Jewishness and Russianness.[74]

Without any sequencing, chapters, or numbering system, the paragraphs in the *Gedankenkorb* flow in seemingly random fashion from one end of the book to the other. As such, it is difficult to determine which statement is intended to take ultimate precedence on any one theme. While Rubinstein's final thoughts on religion, nationalism, and politics contradict one another throughout the text, however, his faith in art remains supreme. The book abounds with descriptions of art's triumphant, redemptive power. Of all of these passages, one short line stands out as a personal credo. Paraphrasing the famous French aristocratic emblem, "Roi ne puis, prince ne daigne, Rohan je suis" (I cannot be king, I would not be prince, I am a Rohan), Rubinstein writes, "Dieu ne puis, roi ne daigne, artiste je suis" (I cannot be God, I would not be king, I am an artist).[75] In the final analysis, it was this abiding faith in music as a tool of personal transformation and social change that constituted Rubinstein's contribution to both Russian and Jewish modernity. Living in the age of Russian emancipation and European Romanticism, his own concept of musical emancipation operated on two levels at once, simultaneously offering a concrete mechanism of social and legal liberation for musicians and Jews, two marginalized groups in nineteenth-century Russian society, and a broader Romantic ideal of individual transcendence through the universalism of art.

If Anton Rubinstein's career represented an attempt to create a modern identity through reconciling religion, estate, and nationality in a mixture of liberal politics and Romantic art, the next generation of Russian Jews exchanged the liberalism of the 1860s for a secular Jewish nationalism heavily based on ethnicity and folklore as authentic, integral sources of modern Jewish culture. Just as Rubinstein had been drawn both to the extremes of Westernness and Easternness as a Russian (Jewish) composer, so too did these Russian Jewish musicians look both East and West for their musical models of Jewishness. However, the very sort of "self-conscious nationalism in music" that Rubinstein rejected as culturally parochial, philosophically indefensible, and aesthetically invalid emerged over the course of the 1890s and 1900s as a crucial cornerstone of modern Jewish art and identity. Although he blithely wrote that "musical nationalism" failed to garner "universal sympathy and awakens at best an ethnographic interest," it was precisely this folkloric element and nationalist character that appealed most to the next generation.[76] And if Rubinstein was neither fully Russian nor Jew yet somehow both, these younger musicians aimed not to transcend their own Russian Jewish dual identity but to express it vividly, passionately, and paradoxically, in explicitly Jewish nationalist terms. As Rubinstein's spiritual children flocked to the conservatory he built, they embraced the new nationalist spirit of the age. Likewise, in their quest to create modern Jewish music they looked less to their crypto-Jewish patriarch for inspiration than to the ideas and examples of his rivals in the Russian national school.

CHAPTER 2

National Voices, Imperial Echoes

Joel Engel and the Russian Jewish Musical Fin de Siècle

> Our brothers, the Children of Israel, look on the task of collecting folk songs as if it were a strange thing, somehow far from the needs of the moment. And even our nationalists who daily invent new ways of spreading the national idea—through meetings, speeches, newspaper articles, banquets, amulets, and "Stars of David"— the majority of them also do not understand the new idea or believe in its value. . . . Don't they know, our Lovers of Zion, that there is no such thing as nationalism without music and song?
> —Pinḥas Minkovskii, *Shirei 'Am* (1899)

> I have collected the words. You, I hope, will collect the melodies. Let them count us as "badkhns," let those who are nearsighted and pursue loud gestures and temporary success not recognize our work: the judgment belongs to those who actually understand the culture of the people more than to those who merely talk about it. And so we will work quietly, silently, and I am confident that it is our effort that will lead the people to more independence than any other practical work.
> —Letter from Peysakh Marek to Joel Engel (1900)

In 1891 the Russian Jewish historian Simon Dubnow published an essay in the St. Petersburg Jewish journal *Voskhod* (Dawn) entitled "On the Study of the History of the Russian Jews and the Creation of a Russian-Jewish Historical Society." Arguing passionately for the need for historical and ethnographic research on Russian Jewry, Dubnow called on his fellow Jewish intellectuals to collect historical and cultural documents of all kinds. Dubnow's list of potential materials, "the most essential and worthy sources for the history of Polish-Russian Jews," was detailed and exhaustive: Rabbinic writings, Russian and Polish law codes, documents from the Russian Imperial state archives, Yiddish folktales, Hebrew historical chronicles, autobiographies, synagogue prayers and elegies, Yiddish proverbs, folk customs, and even cemetery tombstone etchings. Together these legal, literary, and folkloric sources would provide the basis for the study of the Jewish past and the creation of modern Jewish culture. Missing from Dubnow's catalog was music. The omission, he explained, was deliberate: "I have not named Jewish folk *songs* in the list of sources, for the simple reason that we practically have none, at least, none with historical significance. The Jews never had *folk lyrics* in the usual sense of these words, for example, as in Ukrainian songs. The Jew never sang outside the synagogue. His songs, anguished or joyous, were always *prayers*."[1]

Dubnow was no stranger to Ashkenazi Jewish culture, having grown up in a Yiddish-speaking, traditional religious home in the Belorussian shtetl of Mstislavl. He simply assumed that music did not count as part of Jewish national culture. In his estimation, Yiddish folk songs were little more than crude translations of Ukrainian and Polish folk melodies and lyrics. Liturgical poems and prayer chants were only important for their *textual*, historical value. Judged by the standards of Jewish national content and historical significance, music failed the test of cultural relevance.

In part, Dubnow's ideas reflected his own emerging theory of Jewish nationalism, which prized historical knowledge over folklore. But his philosophical opposition to music was hardly just the idiosyncratic view of one cerebral, history-obsessed intellectual. Rather it typified a commonly held assumption of the time among the Russian Jewish intelligentsia. Even as Jewish national identity grew steadily in the 1880s, a majority of intellectuals accepted as elementary truth that Jews possessed no distinctive musical tradition of their own. Nineteenth-century Russian ethnographers and music historians likewise consistently rejected the very idea of Jewish folk music.[2]

Yet within a decade of Dubnow's 1891 dismissal of music, Jewish attitudes began to shift dramatically. From 1900 onward, music emerged quickly as one of the central tropes of modern Russian Jewish identity. In Moscow and Warsaw, Jewish writers, folklorists, and ethnographers published Yiddish folk songs collected in the Pale of Settlement. From St. Petersburg to Baku, Jewish audiences flocked to hear synagogue chants, klezmer melodies, and Hasidic nigunim performed in Russia's leading concert halls. Jewish communal organizations rushed to incorporate songbooks and singing into Jewish school curricula to foster national consciousness. By World War I there was no major Jewish political movement that had not adopted Jewish music in the form of anthems, choral groups, and public concerts as a stirring symbol and propaganda tool. In short, it had become impossible to imagine modern Jewish culture without music at its core.[3]

One way or another, nearly all of these developments can be traced to one person: Joel (Iulii Dmitrievich) Engel (1868–1927). As a distinguished composer, critic, and teacher, Engel maintained a ubiquitous presence in turn-of-the-century Russian musical life. In the two decades before 1917 he served as the music editor and chief critic for the leading Moscow daily liberal newspaper, *Russkie vedomosti* (Russian Bulletin), edited nearly every classical music reference work published in Russia, and earned an international reputation as a lecturer, pedagogue, and ethnographer. His high profile in the Russian musical world enhanced his pioneering involvement in the creation of modern Jewish culture. In his newspaper and journal writings, concerts, lectures, ethnographic fieldwork, and published compositions, Engel was the first Jewish intellectual to argue in a systematic fashion for the defining importance of music in Jewish national culture. At his death in 1927 he was acclaimed throughout the world as "the father of modern Jewish music."[4]

Just as with the case of Anton Rubinstein one generation earlier, Engel's intellectual legacy was claimed by a variety of political movements over the course of the twentieth century. Unlike with Rubinstein, however, there has been little historical disagreement over the fact of Engel's Jewishness—only its larger ideological meaning. In the immediate decades following his death, Jewish émigré intellectuals in Canada and the United States identified him as the musical apostle of secular Yiddishism and an opponent of a Hebraist Zionism. At the very same time, in Israel Engel was canonized as a Zionist hero, the "father of Hebrew music," remembered through the city of Tel Aviv's prestigious annual composition prize established in his name in 1945. Meanwhile, in the Soviet Union his posthumous reputation experienced a different and convoluted political fate. In the late 1920s the early Soviet state officially celebrated Engel as a Jewish composer through publications of his works, yet by the 1930s the ideological tide had turned against him, and he was caustically branded a "petit bourgeois liberal-populist." Then, after decades of enforced silence about his existence, the post-Stalinist Soviet musical establishment rehabilitated him on the centenary of his birth in 1968 with a published anthology of his musical criticism. The Soviet editors included just enough material to implicate him as Jewish while carefully balancing this damning gesture with documents attesting to his Bolshevik loyalties. Finally, in the post-Soviet present, contemporary Russian Jewish intellectuals have reclaimed Engel as an early Zionist forerunner of today's Russian Jewish aliyah.[5]

Each of these ideological readings captures genuine aspects of Engel's life and work. Yet they also stretch him beyond historical reality into a larger-than-life political symbol. As in the case of Rubinstein and many Russian Jews of Engel's own generation, his biography does not fit neatly into any one political affiliation or national category. For if Rubinstein was a man hopelessly caught between emerging modern categories of Russian and Jew, then in the next generation, Engel was an individual determined to embrace *both* his Russianness and Jewishness. If Rubinstein's life represents an attempt to use music as a means of escape from the irresolvable contradictions of mid-nineteenth-century Russian Jewish identity, then Engel's life reveals a quest via music for a new kind of national identity, Jewish in content and Russian in form. In his own project to create a modern style of Jewish music, he endeavored to place Jews on the early twentieth-century map of nationalities in the Russian Empire. To understand how a Russian Jewish intellectual could aspire to be at once an ardent Jewish nationalist and a Russian imperial patriot, a fervent musical populist and a sophisticated music scholar, an active composer and the foremost critic of his day, we need to peel back the layers of time and ideology to reconstruct Engel's life in the Russian fin de siècle.

Russian Composer, Jewish Musician

The man who would become synonymous with Jewish music knew little of either Jews or music in his childhood. Born in 1868 in Berdiansk (Taurida province), a small eastern Crimean port city on the Sea of Azov, Engel grew up in a Russian-speaking Jewish family with little knowledge of Hebrew or Yiddish. His father, who worked as a subcontractor, had settled the family in a coastal town at the farthest reaches of the Pale of Settlement. Engel spent his youth learning the folk songs of Italian sailors, Greek merchants, and Turkish traders. So divorced from Jewish religion or culture was he in his upbringing that friends later jokingly referred to him as a "Crimean Tatar" and a "true Jewish *Rusak* [ethnic Russian]." Like many other aspiring Russian Jewish intellectuals of his day, his first love was law. After graduating from the local gymnasium, he studied at the University of Kiev before graduating from the University of Kharkov with a law degree in 1890. It was not until his time in Kharkov that Engel first considered foregoing a legal career in favor of his newfound passion for music; he took the first music lessons of his life at age seventeen. Following military service, he spent three years tutoring children from Kharkov's wealthier Jewish families while he studied part-time at the local Imperial Russian Musical Society school. In early spring 1893 a moment of opportunity arrived. The composer Peter Tchaikovsky came to town on a visit. Impressed by Engel's talent and enthusiasm, he encouraged him to enroll at the Moscow Conservatory as a composition student. Five months later, Engel showed up in Moscow armed with a letter of recommendation from Tchaikovsky and ready to embark on a new career in music.[6]

As a student in Kharkov and Kiev, Engel had lived in two of Russia's largest Jewish student communities in cities that themselves held two of the largest Jewish populations. By the early 1890s roughly a quarter of Kiev's university students were Jewish. The figure for Kharkov was even higher. Ironically, in the heavily Jewish atmospheres of these cities in the Pale of Settlement, Engel came to consider himself more a Russian composer than a Jewish musician. The opposite quickly proved true in Moscow, a city legally closed to Jews without special residence permission. In 1891, as part of an intensification of its anti-Jewish policies, the Moscow municipality had expelled roughly two-thirds of its thirty thousand Jewish residents. Newly instituted quotas limited Jewish students to a mere 4 percent of the city's general student population. While the legal measures did not apply directly to the Moscow Conservatory, there too an informal quota system had been instituted in the late 1880s. In the 1890s this arrangement tightened into a formal quota limiting the Jewish enrollment to less than 3 percent. As a result of these measures, Engel found himself the sole Jew in the composition department for most of his student years.[7]

Even after achieving admission to the conservatory, Engel faced other practical challenges. His law degree guaranteed him the right to live in Moscow, but finding a landlord who would rent a room to a Jew was no easy prospect. Fortunately, he was not the only Jewish student left in Moscow. Late in the summer of 1893, on one of his first days in the city, he was walking along Tverskaia Boulevard in search of a place to live when he came across a cluster of young people lounging casually on the street. They turned out to be residents of a nearby boarding house popular with Jewish students on Kuznetskii Most Street. Within minutes, Engel had found an apartment, a roommate, and an entrée into the epicenter of the Moscow Jewish intelligentsia. Taking their name from their landlord, a liberal Moscow University physiology professor, Grigorii A. Zakharin (1827–1897), the Zakharinka circle, as they were known, was one of a number of informal Jewish student groups that had begun to appear in Russian universities. Promoting a loose movement of Jewish cultural nationalism rather than any explicitly ideological brand of politics, the Zakharinka circle emphasized a relaxed agenda of ethnic pride and promoted Yiddish language and folklore. The decision was deliberate. The group was led by the journalist Abram D. Idelson (1865–1921), a veteran of the Haskalah (Jewish Enlightenment) who had been involved in the late 1880s with the Moscow branch of Bnei Moshe, an early Zionist organization closely linked to the Odessa-based thinker Ahad Ha'am (Asher Gintsburg). Following the tsarist police repression of Moscow's Jewish communal and political life, Idelson reinvented himself as the charismatic apolitical elder to the city's remaining Jewish students. These would-be writers, scholars, and artists gathered together to explore Jewish cultural and intellectual affairs and debate their own emerging national identities. Regular participants included historian Peysakh Marek, pianist David Shor, conductor Serge Koussevitzky, and future political figures such as First Duma member Leon Bramson, Zionist leader Yehiel Chlenov, and Bolshevik revolutionary theoretician Mikhail Lunts.[8]

In the Zakharinka circle's vibrant, creative atmosphere, overflowing with all manner of Yiddish folktales, proverbs, and jokes, Engel discovered traditional Jewish culture of a kind that he had never experienced in his Russified upbringing on the Crimean coast. But most of all it was the music he heard that captured his imagination. Koussevitzky, for example, hailed from a large family of klezmer musicians. He had spent his childhood performing at traditional Jewish weddings before sneaking into Moscow as a fourteen-year-old with no official papers, desperate to study classical music. Idelson himself was a capable folksinger, constantly regaling the group with the Yiddish tunes he knew from his childhood in a Lithuanian shtetl. The songs stirred up vague memories of the snatches of "Jewish folk melodies" that Engel remembered his own father occasionally singing in his childhood. But these fragments of musical memory paled in comparison beside what he reverentially termed "true Jewish song."[9]

A few months after joining the group, Engel attempted to incorporate these new Jewish folk sounds in a composition of his own. The result was a short operetta, *Esther,* which the group performed on the holiday of Purim in 1894. While the work has not survived, its performance impressed one observer enough to surface a few years later in an 1899 novel by the Hebrew writer Yehiel Yosef Levontin, *Shim'on Etsyoni.* The Zionist author noted that the Zakharinka members were not "full patriots, not even ardent 'Lovers of Zion,'" but they represented something broader than political nationalism. In his estimation the performance of "Israel's melodies" to an overflowing crowd of Jewish Muscovites bore eloquent witness to the presence of a new national spirit among the heretofore "assimilated" generation of Russian Jewish students. Engel, on the other hand, dismissed his own first foray into Jewish music as mere juvenilia, with little lasting aesthetic—or communal— value. It did serve, however, to express his very personal, almost visceral awakening sense of Jewish identity. "I transcribed and studied Jewish melodies," he later recalled, "not because I was Jewish, but much more the opposite—the more I worked with them, fell in love with them, the more Jewish I became." Still, for all of this intense process of national self-discovery, Engel gave little further thought to Jewish music; "at that time," he wrote, "neither I nor anyone else had any clear thoughts on the larger world future of Jewish music." In fact his studies at the Moscow Conservatory drew him in the opposite direction, toward the cultural cosmopolitanism of turn-of-the-century Russian music.[10]

In Search of the Science of Music, East and West

The approach of the twentieth century in Russian culture ushered in the Silver Age (*Serebrianyi vek*), Russia's own term for its first modernist artistic awakening. For Russian musicians, this cultural shift translated into an increasingly cosmopolitan engagement with broader European currents of art, philosophy, religion, and even science. Today this period is remembered principally through the avant-garde experiments of Alexander Scriabin and Igor Stravinsky and other Russian composers' innumerable settings of Russian modernist poetry. Yet hand in hand with the Silver Age's internationalist modernism there appeared a new rationalist, even positivist approach to music. The influence of the newly hatched German academic discipline of musicology, with its aspirations for an objective science of music, was now reflected throughout Russian musical life: new courses in music theory and music history at the conservatories, specialized music periodicals, and a spate of translations of German and French theoretical and critical works.

All these trends were exemplified in the activities of Engel's two most influential and cherished teachers at the Moscow Conservatory: Sergei Taneev (1856–1915) and Nikolai Kashkin (1839–1920). Taneev was regarded as Russia's first important musical theorist, while Kashkin functioned as the school's resident dean of music history. Together the two men dominated turn-of-the-century Russian musical thought with a common analytical, scientific approach. Beyond his teaching, Kashkin helped launch the modern field of music criticism in Russia in his decades of writing for the *Russkie vedomosti* newspaper. After Engel's graduation in 1897, Kashkin offered him a job as the paper's junior critic. Less than a year later, the elderly professor retired. At the age of thirty, Engel suddenly found himself the chief critic and music editor for the main newspaper of the Moscow liberal intelligentsia, a position he would hold without interruption until 1918.[11]

As a journalist, Engel traveled abroad for the first time in the late 1890s to report on European music festivals and to visit his fiancée, Antonina K. Kheifits, a pianist and fellow Moscow Conservatory graduate then studying in Berlin. Engel's German sojourns solidified his fascination with European musicology and music theory. When the Internationale Musikgesellschaft opened in 1899, he joined as an early member of the new musicological society. In the following decade and a half, he went on to write, edit, or contribute to nearly all the standard reference works on music published in Russia. Many of these publications were translations of authoritative Western musicological reference books, such as the Russian version of Hugo Riemann's *Musik-Lexicon*, the definitive European musical encyclopedia for several decades. For the Russian edition, published between 1901 and 1904, Engel wrote several hundred new essays on Russian music and supervised the translation and editing of over seven thousand German entries. His other works included popular pocket music dictionaries and classical music guides.[12]

It was not only to the West that Engel looked to satisfy his growing fascination with the scientific study of music. In Russia, ethnography (*etnografiia*) had developed steadily since the 1840s, closely related to parallel fields of ethnology, folklore, and anthropology. While Western anthropological scholarship focused on broad notions of race and world history, Russian ethnography, also referred to as *narodovedeniia* (the science of nationality), concentrated more on specific questions of ethnic and national identity, particularly within the context of the Russian Empire. As a result, Russian folk song collections and related theoretical writings had appeared, beginning in the early nineteenth century. Gradually this research grew from an amateur pastime of national poets into more specialized projects by trained musicians and self-proclaimed ethnographers. In St. Petersburg in 1884, the Russian Geographic Society established a Pesennaia komissiia (Song Commission) to foster the preservation, analysis, and appreciation of folk songs of Russia, Ukraine, and the many other minority groups of the empire. In Moscow, a group of musicians began to meet in 1896 under the auspices of the newly founded Ethnographic Division (Etnograficheskii otdel) of Moscow University's Imperial Society of Lovers of Natural History, Anthropology, and Ethnography (Imperatorskoe obshchestvo liubitelei estestvoznaniia, antropologii i etnografii) (IOLEAE), an organization that dated back to the late eighteenth century. The circle, eventually formally known as the Moscow Musical-Ethnographic Commission, included a distinguished group of leading composers, music critics, and other researchers, among them Taneev, Kashkin, and Engel.[13] At meetings members presented folk songs of various nationalities acquired during fieldwork expeditions across the breadth of Russia. Given his developing sense of Jewish national identity and his strong interest in musical folklore, Engel's attention naturally turned to Jewish folk music. His shift from personal passion to national mission, however, owed its specific origins to another alumnus of the Moscow Zakharinka circle: Peysakh Marek.

Words without Songs:
Marek and Gintsburg's *Evreiskie narodnye pesni*

In the spring of 1898, a brief announcement about a new research project appeared in the various organs of the Russian Jewish press. The authors were two former lawyers, Peysakh Marek (1862–1920), now an accountant and amateur Jewish historian based in Moscow, and his friend Shaul Gintsburg (1866–1940), a St. Petersburg journalist. In Russian, Hebrew, and Yiddish, the duo echoed Dubnow's 1891 call to the Jewish intelligentsia to join in the task of researching their own history and culture. Unlike their mentor, however, they focused exclusively on what Dubnow had ignored: music. The study of Yiddish folk songs, they asserted, would lead to "the other history, alongside that which is based on official and unofficial documents." The result would be a more intimate, spontaneous oral history, "written by the people themselves as they reproduce their past in songs." Over the next two years, Marek and Gintsburg collected hundreds of Yiddish folk songs from around the Russian Empire. The eventual 1901 book, *Evreiskie narodnye pesni v Rossii* (Jewish Folk Songs in Russia), was a landmark publication, the first major collection of its kind. It served as an inspirational example for numerous early twentieth-century European Jewish intellectuals ranging from I. L. Peretz and S. Ansky to Martin Buber and Haim Nahman Bialik.[14]

In an ironic decision for a project centered on music, Marek and Gintsburg chose not to attempt to collect the songs' melodies in their efforts, only the Yiddish (and occasionally Hebrew) lyrics. One reason was practical. Unable to undertake fieldwork in the Pale of Settlement themselves, they relied instead on a widespread network of *zamlers,* volunteer collectors who mailed in folk songs from their own communities. Very few of these participants had the necessary skills to notate melodies. But on a deeper level, the project reflected the methods and models of Dubnow, as well as the older example of German Romantic thinker Johann Gottfried Herder. Even though Marek and Gintsburg intended their work to be an ethnographic corrective to Dubnow's overemphasis on written documents rather than live folk culture, they still accepted his assumption that Jewish folk culture mattered most for its "historical character." Yiddish folk songs were thus viewed as essentially textual artifacts useful for the writing of Russian Jewish history. Likewise, driven by a desire to emphasize the literary and historical nature of the Jewish experience, they chose Herder's philologically driven model of German folklore rather than the example of Russian musical ethnography closer at hand. For Herder, it was the linguistic and textual dimensions of songs rather than the melodies that ultimately most expressed national identity.[15]

Not all agreed with Marek and Gintsburg's approach when it was first announced. One of the first to object strongly was Ivan Lipaev, a Moscow music critic, a close friend of Engel, and a fellow member of the musical-ethnographic circle. Lipaev, who was not Jewish, had an intense interest in the folk music of Russian Jews and eventually published the first ethnographic study in any language of klezmer music. In a letter printed in the weekly edition of *Voskhod*, he argued emphatically that if Marek and Gintsburg truly wanted to unlock the secrets of Jewish history, they should seek them out in the "indivisible" bond between words and melodies, "like that of a loving mother and her children." Lipaev's somewhat indignant critique was echoed by a young Russian Jewish student named Leo Winz, soon to be famous as the publisher of the German Jewish journal *Ost und West*. In a long article in the monthly edition of *Voskhod*, Winz emphasized the powerful relevance of music: "[Since] the language of melody speaks much more significantly than even the simplest of words," the collection of folk melodies constituted "an undervalued source for the true understanding of the folk psyche of Jews and for the study of Jewish nationality [*narodnost*]." In addition, he noted, exposure to the traditional melodies might help counter the growing trend of cultural "assimilation" among modern Jews.[16]

For Engel, the controversy in the pages of *Voskhod* brought Jewish folk music into focus as a new potential field for ethnographic research. In the summer of 1898 he ventured briefly to the town of Tomashpol in the Vinnitsa region of the Pale (present-day Ukraine), where he transcribed roughly a dozen songs. Then, back in Moscow, he acquired a handful of other tunes from his Zakharinka friends. At the same time, Marek and Gintsburg also reconsidered their project's musical dimension. A small portion of their song texts had arrived from the provinces with musical transcriptions attached. Early in 1900, Marek approached Engel with a request that he edit these melodies for publication. The poor quality and limited quantity of material, however, made it unsuitable for the book. Instead the two agreed on a public lecture and performance in Moscow. Looking through the sixty-odd melodies that lay in front of him, Engel began to piece together his own concept of Jewish national music. But to do so also required him to grapple with the preexisting definitions of Jewish music that had emerged in Russia and the West during the late nineteenth century.[17]

Jewish Music as Apologia Judaica

The modern study of Jewish music began first in central Europe within the contexts of emancipation and the Enlightenment. Responding to these sweeping new developments, German Jewish intellectuals launched the scholarly movement of *Wissenschaft des Judentums* (Science of Judaism) in the 1820s. Philosophically, the goal of *Wissenschaft* was to generate a rational body of knowledge about the Jewish past consistent with modern European conventions of religion and secular culture. Politically, the movement sought to create a positive image of Jews as noble partners in Western civilization — not a separate nation but a religious community. In doing so, the *Wissenschaft* practitioners believed, Jews would be permitted to freely integrate within various European countries as citizens of undivided loyalties, while still preserving a coherent Jewish collective identity.

While the first generation of *Wissenschaft* researchers all but ignored music, in the second half of the nineteenth century cantor-composers such as Hirsh Weintraub, Samuel Naumbourg, and Josef Singer began to apply the same scholarly principles to the study of Jewish musical traditions. They sought to marry specifically Jewish religious aspirations — the modernization of synagogue music — to the broader cultural aim of harmonizing Jewish music with the emerging European academic discipline of musicology. These Jewish researchers likewise adopted many European Christian ideas of music. Chief among them was a basic Enlightenment division of Jewish music into two categories, liturgical and folk (or religious and secular), a distinction that had never existed in Ashkenazi musical life before. Likewise, they classified the music of the synagogue itself according to a notion of melodic prayer modes akin to the medieval church modes found in Gregorian chant. Linking Jewish liturgy in this way to the history of Christianity, they also argued implicitly — and sometimes explicitly — for the antiquity and originality of Jewish music. In addition, by positing the shared roots of Christian and Jewish liturgical music, they suggested that Jewish music — like the Jewish people — fundamentally belonged to Western civilization. Emphasizing that Jews were a religious group rather than a distinct nation naturally meant disregarding all of the Ashkenazi folk music traditions outside the synagogue. Therefore Hasidic nigunim, Yiddish folk songs, and klezmer dance melodies simply disappeared from their definitions of Jewish music.[18]

In the 1850s and 1860s, *Wissenschaft* ideas resonated eastward just as Russian Jewish intellectuals began to make some of the first tentative efforts to evaluate Jewish music. In 1861 a *maskil* and official advisor to the Russian government on Jewish affairs named Moisei Berlin (1821–1888) published his *Ocherk etnografii evreiskogo naselenia v Rossii* (Ethnographic Outline of the Jewish Population of Russia). In this work Berlin expressed both positive and negative stereotypes of Jewish musicality. On one hand he described an innate Jewish instinct for music, blithely asserting that even musically illiterate cantors and klezmer musicians could intuitively learn and instantly reproduce any piece of music they heard. Yet on the other hand, despite this "natural" endowment, Berlin also denied the existence of any kind of Jewish music beyond the liturgical sphere. Russian Jews, he wrote, expressed only moral and religious aspirations through their "synagogue songs" and lacked any "nonreligious songs" like the obscene folk ballads, coarse drinking songs, and wild folk dances of their peasant neighbors. Thus, in making his claim for Russian Jewish emancipation as a civilized people, Berlin sought to use music to dispel negative stereotypes of Jewish primitiveness and to emphasize Jewish morality. In the process, however, he ended up presenting an internalized Jewish version of the classic Russian antisemitic distinction between positive biblical Hebrew (*evrei*) and negative Diaspora Jew (*zhid*).[19]

In response to Berlin's *Wissenschaft*-like emphasis on Jewish music as a strictly religious expression, the young Jewish lawyer-turned-historian Ilia Orshanskii (1846–1875) wrote a series of articles in the Russian Jewish press in the mid-1860s arguing for the existence and value of Yiddish secular folk songs. He even went so far as to petition Jewish philanthropists in Odessa to collect and publish folk songs in order to combat Russian cultural ignorance, which he believed fueled popular anti-Jewish prejudices and Russian state policies. It was neither aesthetics nor national aims that motivated Orshanskii, but rather a Russian Jewish liberal quest to use music as an oral argument in favor of legal emancipation.[20] However, his appeal fell on deaf ears. It would be another thirty years before the idea was revived and realized in the efforts of Marek, Gintsburg, and Engel. The first concrete result was an event that would subsequently be known as "the first Jewish concert in the world."

The Ethnographic Empire

On November 30, 1900, an overflow crowd of more than 250 crammed the aisles of the Moscow Polytechnical Museum Auditorium for a joint session of the Musical-Ethnographic Commission and the IOLEAE Ethnographic Division. The first half of the evening featured a presentation on a recent research expedition to the White Sea on Russia's northwestern coast. After a short intermission, the time arrived for the "southern," Jewish portion of the program, organized by Engel. Marek spoke first. He read aloud the entire text of his recent book's introduction on the historical and cultural significance of Yiddish folk songs. Next came Engel, who had by comparison much less to say. In brief remarks, he presented a set of preliminary, tentative observations about Jewish music.

In his later recollections, Engel dismissed these first public comments about Jewish music as immature and tentative first impressions. Yet what he said that day actually reflected a surprisingly sophisticated theoretical model based on an imaginative blend of Western musicology, Russian musical ethnography, *Wissenschaft* positivism, and Russian Jewish populism. Most nineteenth-century Western scholars spoke almost obsessively of a special "Jewish scale" characterized by its distinctive augmented second tonal interval as the key distinguishing feature of Ashkenazi music. Yet Engel immediately rejected this idea, noting that the "Jewish scale" was little different than those found in the music of Gypsies, Hungarians, Persians, and other "Eastern" peoples. Furthermore, he continued, Russian Jews borrowed openly in their folk songs from "both the words and the melodies of the people[s] with whom history has fated them to live."[21]

At first blush, these denials of Jewish music's distinctiveness were counterintuitive. For if Jewish folk songs could not be isolated through their common melodies and scales and depended on external cultural influences, how could one speak of authentic Jewish national music? The answer, Engel explained to the crowd, was that cultural borrowing or shared scales were far from automatic signs of "assimilation," since both the words and melodies were often transformed, even "Judaized," with a characteristic musical imprint added to them over time. The broader identity of eastern European Jewish music emerged not from its original components but in its particular emphases: distinctive vocal intonations (the "manner of Jewish singing"), nuances of pitch, timbre, and instrumentation, and what he termed the modal harmonic system.

To illustrate this approach, Engel recounted his own attempts to transcribe Yiddish folk songs into standard Western music notation. Often he would sing back what he had recorded to his informants only to be told that his versions were wrong. They lacked the proper "Jewish" inflections that could not be captured by mere pitch patterns on the page. In place of the more conventional musicological criteria for national music, Engel emphasized a different ethnographic standard based on his Jewish cultural populism. Sung one way, a melody might be Ukrainian; with a few variations in accent, vocal style, and intonation, it became Jewish. Most of all, the final arbiter of music's Jewishness was the Jewish masses, who recognized their own style. As he later wrote, "Although some or other of its elements turn out to be more or less the same as those of other peoples, there is no doubt, however, that there exists music to which the Jewish heart responds very directly and passionately, and this music we call Jewish." The goal of musical science,

Example 4. Joel Engel's "A Ḥabadisher nigun," 1900.

he argued, should be to document how the Jewish people actively made their own national music through the subtleties of cultural expression.[22]

Aware that these theoretical abstractions might be lost on his audience at the Polytechnical Museum, Engel limited his remarks to fifteen minutes, after which he invited some fellow alumni of the Moscow Conservatory and the Zakharinka circle to join him onstage to perform several musical examples. The musicians proceeded to play arrangements of several Yiddish folk songs, klezmer instrumental tunes, and a sensitive violin-piano setting of a Hasidic nigun belonging to the Ḥabad Lubavitch tradition transcribed by Engel in 1898 (ex. 4). Like his analytical remarks, Engel's musical arrangements also reflected a careful quest to balance a reverence for tradition with a deeply self-conscious modernism.

As a conservatory-trained composer deeply versed in European and Russian music, Engel believed that Jewish music required aesthetic enhancement to qualify as true art. "Without [modern] musical culture," he later wrote, "folk songs have no future; they will die out."[23] At the same time, however, Engel feared that excessive embellishment would compromise the melodies' distinctive "national character" (*narodnyi sklad*). The solution he devised was to isolate the "original folk melody" as the primary, essential unit of folk song, to be performed by a singer or instrumental soloist with little adornment or variation. At the same time, in the instrumental accompaniment on the piano he added harmony and "improve[d]" the melody using the aesthetics of European late Romantic harmony as channeled through Taneev and his other teachers. Throughout, Engel emphasized melodic purity: "Nowhere have I actually added anything to the original melody, I did not insert one note."[24]

The results of this first musical experiment proved successful. The Polytechnical crowd, many of whom were students, roared its approval, demanding numerous encores. Critics were similarly impressed. Though the majority of the audience members were not Jewish, word of the evening spread quickly among the Jewish intelligentsia of Moscow and St. Petersburg. Soon the event was being trumpeted as "the first-ever concert of Jewish music." While it was a pathbreaking development, Engel's Jewish musical debut did more than mark a symbolic precedent for subsequent Jewish concerts in eastern Europe. It also introduced a specifically Russian imperial cultural model into the emerging lexicon of Jewish public culture: the "ethnographic concert."[25]

From its origins in the 1890s, the Musical-Ethnographic Commission had assigned itself a dual mission of "scientific" research and public education. Yet only a tiny minority of its members were university-trained musical scholars. The rest were split between composers with high artistic aspirations, populist intelligentsia committed to celebrating folk traditions, and folklorists and ethnographers with primarily academic interests. The "ethnographic concert," a term that had first been introduced in 1893, was a compromise attempt to resolve the contradictions between these various subgroups by staging formal performances of folk song in a concert hall setting. The introductory lectures and art music arrangements simultaneously elevated folk songs into an object of academic study, enlightened them as modern, civilized art, and reified folk music as authentic traditional culture. Along with workers' choruses and adult music classes, the ethnographic concerts provided a new context for the populist goal of bridging the social divides in Russian urban society. Just as the intelligentsia, middle-class professionals, and workers (and theoretically the peasants) assembled side by side in the audience, united by music, so too did folk and art music join together on the concert stage.[26]

Beyond linking together science, art, and politics in Russian culture, the ethnographic concert also functioned as a meeting point between the various national minorities and Russia's multiethnic imperial ideal. Seated behind a long green table at the foot of the stage, the distinguished panel of honorary IOLEAE members represented a symbolic jury of experts, geographers, philologists, and ethnographers who had traversed the length and breadth of the Russian Empire in order to document its majestic diversity under the vast, powerful rule of the tsar. In spite of their liberal and populist sympathies, the research of these men and women provided a semiofficial affirmation of the cultural contents of Imperial *Rossiia*. By 1900 the Moscow group had presented a huge range of both familiar and obscure folk music repertoires from across the Russian Empire, including those of Georgians, Armenians, Ossetians, Latvians, Lithuanians, Lezgians, Poles, Moldavians, Yakuts, Buriats, Tatars, and Kyrgyz. Yet before Engel proposed the idea of Jewish music, the IOLEAE researchers were not even aware of its existence. To the Russian composers, scholars, and intelligentsia present at the Polytechnical Museum concert, the encounter with Jewish folk songs came as a revelation. Engel later recalled one notable Russian musical authority's reaction: "I had always thought that the Jews, who have given so much to music of the world, ought to have their own folk music. And now I see that it exists." In this way, Engel's initial turn to the ethnographic concert format represented a de facto argument for the existence of Jewish folk music as a distinct national tradition parallel to those of the other major and minor nationalities of the Russian Empire. Or, as the critic Lipaev argued, Jewish folk music rightfully belonged inside the "treasure chest of national songs of Russia."[27]

Indeed, the song that produced the greatest audience response at the 1900 concert bore eloquent testimony to the Russian Empire's cultural diversity and social integration. "Vi zingt der khosidl, der tsigeynerl, der ivanke" (How Sings the Jew, the Gypsy, and the Russian) or "Vi er zingt" (How He Sings) was one of the first tunes transcribed by Engel in 1898. The folk song's melody and lyrics comically depict three different nationalities through miniature musical caricatures (ex. 5). In the first stanza, the Jew is symbolized by a "little Hasid" (*khosidl*), who sings a short melody of nonsense syllables in the exaggerated style of a Hasidic nigun, complete with repeated chromatic intervals and excessive augmented seconds. Next comes the Gypsy with fast, emphatic chords and a melody emphasizing open fifths, followed by the "ivanke," the Russian peasant, with a simpler melody built on a major scale with a flat sixth, hinting at a harmonic minor scale, sung in a stately adagio with minimal piano accompaniment. At the Moscow concert this song elicited such a thunderous applause, Engel recalled, that it was repeated twice. Thereafter this "masterpiece of musical ethnography" became a staple of Jewish concert performances throughout the next decade. Engel also published his arrangement three times, first as a stand-alone composi-

Example 5. Joel Engel's arrangement of "Vi er zingt," 1900.

tion, then in a 1909 Yiddish song collection, and again in 1912, at the request of the Musical-Ethnographic Commission, as one of two selections representing Jews in an anthology of folk songs of different nationalities.[28]

The 1900 concert not only brought ethnography to center stage as a tool for the study and propagation of Jewish music, it also established Engel in a new role as its prime interpreter and chief defender to both the Russian musical world and the Russian Jewish intelligentsia. This change raised a slew of new philosophical and practical questions involving both his personal identity and his public profile as a Russian musical critic and Jewish artist.

These issues were revealed in Engel's key encounter one year later with the most important turn-of-the-century Russian cultural critic, Vladimir Stasov. The meeting had multiple consequences for Engel's overall relationship to the Russian intelligentsia, his evolving theory of Jewish music, and his own Russian Jewish identity.

Easter(n) Melodies: Stasov and Engel's Theories of Jewish Music

The success of the Moscow concert led Engel, Marek, and Gintsburg to hold a similar event in St. Petersburg the following spring. In response to an outbreak of famine in the Jewish agricultural colonies of southern Russia, the editors of *Voskhod* decided to arrange a benefit concert in early April 1901 in the private art gallery of a wealthy Jewish family.[29] They invited Engel from Moscow to reprise his talk and supervise the event. Arriving in St. Petersburg on the eve of the concert, he received word that Stasov was interested in meeting him. It was a chance he could not pass up.

Since the 1860s Stasov had exerted a huge influence in the worlds of Russian music and art as an esteemed critic and fervid apostle of Russian nationalism. He had also long displayed a strong interest in Jewish culture, particularly questions of Jewish national art. In the 1870s he publicly debated the subject with poet Judah Leyb Gordon in the pages of the Russian Jewish press, urging Jews to return to an "authentic" Oriental style for the design of the new St. Petersburg Synagogue. From the 1880s onward, Stasov maintained a close friendship with the Jewish sculptor Mark Antokolskii, whom he similarly advised to pursue Jewish themes in his art. Stasov's philosemitism stemmed both from his liberal political impulses and from his imperial vision of Russian culture, according to which the empire's minorities needed to develop their own cultural traditions for the glory of Russia. As his encounters with Engel demonstrated, it was also a product of his obsession with the idea of *vostochnost*, the "Eastern" or "Oriental" theme in Russian and Jewish culture.[30]

In the April 1901 meeting at Stasov's home, the two critics talked at length about music history, folk songs, and Jewish music. Stasov outlined in rambling detail his conviction that the study of Jewish liturgical music would resolve many questions regarding the roots of Russian Orthodox and Western church music. At one point, he interrupted the conversation, gesturing out the window with his finger. Pointing in the direction of the Russian Orthodox church chants that could be heard echoing in the distance in observance of Easter, he made a bold hypothesis: "I am willing to bet my life that they sang that back then before Christ was born. They sang it in the Jerusalem Temple and from there it emerged and traveled to this day—of course, in altered form and transmitted in a different kind of scale—and it will travel onward! Listen to such a melody next to the ancient synagogue melodies—is there a resemblance? I am sure the connection will be found!"

In Stasov's rough-hewn theory, Jewish music held one of the keys to the common origins of European music as a whole. Russian Orthodox and Western church music, Russian and European folk songs—all derived in large part, he concluded, from "one and the same scale, [the] structure, character, and forms" of ancient Jewish music.[31] This reductionist theory reflected the current vogue for genealogies of Russian music that traced its roots to various ancient European and Asian traditions. It also shared a trope with European Romantic thought and *Wissenschaft* research, both of which typically held that Jewish music was a liturgical remnant of the glorious ancient music of the Bible, preserved through the long centuries of Jewish exile. Ironically, though he spoke the language of folk populism and nationalism, Stasov believed the chief value of Jewish music lay in its antiquity. In his eyes, Jewish music represented less a national tradition ripe for contemporary revival than a glorious window onto the ancient Christian past and another proof that Russia was the true heir of ancient Christendom.

Engel's deep veneration for the Russian master dated back to his early student days in Kharkov. Yet he reacted with polite skepticism to his hero's Jewish music theories, which he believed were simplistic, too fixated on liturgical music, and excessively antiquarian. After this initial meeting, the two men had no more significant contact for another three years, at which time they corresponded briefly. Even then Engel found it necessary to remind Stasov that his own research was concerned not with the history of Jewish liturgical music but with the present-day "secular" [*svetskie*] folk songs of Russian Jews. In public, however, Engel repeatedly exaggerated the depth of their relationship and the significance of the 1901 meeting. In lecture after lecture, his encounter with "the famous artistic critic and ethnographer Stasov" invariably appeared near the beginning of his talk. So frequently did Engel invoke the incident that over time it came to take on a life of its own, persisting even after his death as a grossly exaggerated, oft-repeated parable of "assimilation" and national rebirth. Typically, in this narrative, Stasov is described as the epitome of an elderly biblical patriarch, complete with flowing white beard. During the visit of the young Iulii Dmitrievich to the "prophetic" elder, Stasov chastises him for his "assimilation," telling him he should adopt his Hebrew name "Ioel" (Joel), and embrace his own people's traditions.[32]

In reality, this story was far from the truth. Engel had hardly needed the encouragement of Stasov's musical philosemitism to trigger his enthusiasm for Jewish folk song or his sense of national identification. Nor did he unreservedly embrace all of Stasov's ideas about Jewish music. Engel did little, however, to discourage the fanciful narrative. It was too useful as a clever rhetorical device, this philosemitic seal of approval. Invoking Stasov served as a device for highlighting the authoritative recognition presumably conferred on Jewish music by Russian musical nationalism. Here, after all, was irrefutable proof of Jewish music's existence and value in the form of a dramatic testimonial from Russian music's leading advocate. Ironically, this external cultural validation became a leading trope in Engel's presentation of Jewish music to the public. The endorsement was necessary because not all of the Russian intelligentsia accepted his claims. Even more troubling, the Russian Jewish intelligentsia itself was also slow to embrace his view of musical ethnography as a central part of modern Jewish culture.[33] The most explicit example of this resistance came in a public polemic between Engel, "the father of Jewish music," and Sholem Aleichem, the modern master of Jewish literature.

Sibling Rivalry: The Cultural Politics of Jewish Populism

On the same day as Engel's first Jewish concert, an advertisement appeared in *Voskhod* for a new publication entitled *Evreiskie narodnye pesni* (Jewish Folk Songs).[34] This slim volume contained Yiddish songs composed by a Kiev lawyer and amateur songwriter named Mark Warshavsky (1848–1907). At the time of the book's publication, many of these songs, including the lullaby "Oyfn pripetshik" (On the Hearth) and the wedding song "Di mezinke oysgegeben" (The Youngest Daughter Married Off), had spread so far and wide in the Pale of Settlement that they had been folklorized and refashioned as anonymous, orally transmitted songs.

The person most responsible for the success of Warshavsky's book was the Yiddish writer Sholem Rabinovich (1859–1916), better known by his pseudonym, Sholem Aleichem. Having discovered Warshavsky's songs by chance in the late 1890s, Rabinovich was amazed to learn that they had been composed by an amateur writer so limited in his knowledge of Yiddish that he was unable to write down his own songs in the Yiddish alphabet. Nor were Warshavsky's technical abilities as a musician much better. But with the help of the famous writer, himself a trained musician, Warshavsky transcribed his songs. Before long the two were performing in public at Jewish benefit dinners and literary societies in and around the city of Kiev. The 1900 publication featured an introduction full of praise by Warshavsky's new mentor. These were not mere commercial ditties or *badkhn* songs, Rabinovich wrote, for they represented "a new kind of song," beautifully "simple and genuinely Jewish, not artificial" (*prost un ekht yudish, nisht gemelkhokhet*). If they did not qualify exactly as traditional "folk songs" (*folks-lider*), he suggested in a clever word play, they were still undoubtedly "songs for the folk" (*lider far dem folk*).[35]

Engel took no notice of Warshavsky's book when it was first issued in the fall of 1900. By the spring of 1901, however, as his own reputation as an expert on Jewish folk music began to grow, he felt compelled to respond to this popular songbook that purported to contain "Jewish folk songs." In his review in *Voskhod*, he angrily condemned the songbook's unknown author and his famous literary patron. To Engel's mind, the duo was guilty of a grave musical offense against the Jewish people. The problems started with the implications of the book's title. "What do we call folk songs?" Engel asked rhetorically. "Of course, these are songs sung by the people [*narod*]. The songs can either come from unknown authors of the ancient, forgotten past (as in the case, for instance, of Russian folk songs), or these can be recently written songs that achieve a wide dispersion among the people, thanks to their folk character."

With the passage of time, Engel continued, the people would determine "what is folk and what is not." Simply to slap the label on publications in advance, however, amounted to "a deliberate forgery." Beyond highlighting this semantic distortion, Engel further accused Warshavsky of a variety of obvious musical mistakes. The worst of them, he asserted, was the blatant misrepresentation of traditional Jewish music: "Listening to Mr. Warshavsky, one might think that Jews don't sing anything except for polkas, mazurkas, and quadrilles, that all of them are in the dominant modern musical scales, major and minor, and that there is nothing distinctive or original in these songs to separate them from the contemporary repertoire of the street organ-grinder. But this would be nonsense, a colossal mistake . . . like forcing an old, distinguished Hasid in white stockings to dance a Viennese waltz or a pas d'Espagne."[36]

In published responses, both Warshavsky and Rabinovich contested Engel's narrow definition of Jewish folk song. They rejected his ethnographic approach as an overly pedantic gesture. Writing in *Voskhod*, Warshavsky challenged Engel's compulsive focus on Jewish musical "physiognomy." After all, he noted, even in Marek and Gintsburg's own collection one could find examples of polka dance rhythms. Pleading innocence in the face of Engel's artistic and intellectual elitism, Warshavsky noted that he had never claimed to be a trained composer or a musical ethnographer capable of providing a "scientific arrangement of specimens of Jewish folk music creativity." He was merely an aspiring Yiddish poet and an untutored songwriter.[37]

For his part, Rabinovich rose to his protégé's defense in an article published in *Der yid* two months later. Writing in Yiddish in full folk persona, he presented himself (as usual) as Sholem Aleichem, true Jewish populist and defender of Jewish national music. In response to Engel's charge that "folk song" (*folkslid*) was a deliberate misnomer, Rabinovich dismissed the question as one of academic hairsplitting. The term "folk songs" (*folkslider*) had emerged originally from a common printer's error in publishing early Yiddish popular song collections. Decades later any such distinction between "folk" and "popular" was practically irrelevant. As proof, he pointed precisely to the irony that a children's lullaby he himself had written, "Shloyf mayn kind," published in 1892 in his own newspaper *Kol Mevaser*, had by 1901 found its way into the published collection of Marek and Gintsburg, where it was listed as an anonymous folk song that had been mailed in by multiple correspondents from across the Pale of Settlement.[38]

But the true thrust of Rabinovich's argument was a challenge to Engel's "ethnographic" language. Such theoretical talk, he argued, was unnecessary in order for Jews to understand and appreciate their own music: "You can talk all you want about Aeolian, Dorian, Mixolydian, and other such high musical words from the 'Master's language' [*mlokhim shprakh*]. What do we simple people know from this?" By claiming that Engel's Greek-derived Western musical terminology represented merely the foreign language of the Gentile oppressors who lorded over the Jews, Rabinovich attacked both Engel's musicological pretensions and his status as a Russified Jewish intellectual. In addition, Rabinovich accused Engel of hypocrisy; Engel had publicly stated that no scale or rhythm was inherently Jewish, only to criticize Warshavsky's songs for their supposed lack of Jewish musical content. Crudely exaggerating Engel's theoretical arguments, Rabinovich even threatened to reveal a dirty little ethnic secret: "I won't even mention what the great experts . . . have found, that the character of Jewish songs in minor keys bears a strong resemblance to that of Ukrainian music."

Having skillfully deployed Engel's own sophisticated musical theory against him, Rabinovich was free to promote his own version of Jewish cultural nationalism. It was only the Yiddish language, he suggested, that could and should properly define the boundaries and contents of modern Jewish culture. This emphasis on Jewishness as a primarily linguistic phenomenon enabled Rabinovich to assert the authenticity of Jewish music while still rejecting Engel's ostensibly purist critique of Warshavsky. In other words, if the songs were in Yiddish and the Jewish people accepted them as their own, then ethnographic or musicological arguments were irrelevant. In this way he asserted a linguistic, literary model of Jewish culture against Engel's musical brand of populism. Rabinovich punctuated his retort with a folksy conclusion: "We [common people] can also talk a bit about music. Melody is after all a Jewish thing. Which Jew doesn't understand how to sing? It's one of the three things at which we, Jews, are the greatest experts in the world: wine, song, and diamonds!"

Whereas Engel had initially treated Warshavsky with condescension, he now responded to Rabinovich with unfiltered vitriol. Writing in Yiddish in the pages of *Der yid*, Engel criticized both of his opponents for disregarding the basic aesthetic dimensions of Jewish music as pseudopopulism and willful obscurantism. It was not he who was guilty of elitism, but rather Warshavsky and Rabinovich. They, after all, had attempted to bamboozle the Jewish masses by pawning off recently composed popular pieces as true "folk songs." As for the issue of linguistic exactitude, Engel argued that precisely because of the confusion and complexity involved in a "new and difficult question like 'Jewish folk music,'" musical ethnography was necessary in order "to establish as much as possible [its] specific, objective characteristics." Without scientific analysis, Engel declared, it would be impossible to define and support Jewish music: "You make fun of all of the methods and scientific names with which I have tried to show that there is very little Jewish or even general musical quality in Mr. Warshavsky's songs. . . . [However] a Jewish music does exist, completely distinct and full of original beauty. And you, instead of recognizing its beauty, enlarging it, purifying it, securing its path to future growth, instead of all this, you merely mock and debase those who devote their intellect and strength to the good of Jewish music." Moreover, Engel added, the implications of the debate went far beyond the realm of music to the broader sphere of Jewish culture:

> You must know that the spiritual life of the people is composed and constructed out of all of the phenomena which express its spirit. And if you agree that music needs to be withheld from the national spirit and one should dance to the pipe of European waltzes and polkas . . . be so good as to tell me why you do not raise the same objection with regard to Jewish literature and, more generally, to all Jewish life? Is it really possible, can it really be that you, a Jewish writer, don't realize that in this way that you yourself are cutting off the branch on which you are sitting? And it's left to me, a music critic for a Russian paper, to explain all of this to you, a Jewish "national" writer?[39]

Engel's conflict with Rabinovich and Warshavsky highlighted the tension in his own careful balancing act between positivist musical science and populist folk culture. He had positioned his musical nationalism against what he considered his opponents' cynical attempts to stretch the definition of folk culture past the point of meaningfulness. To his mind, Rabinovich's complicated cultural irony, coupled with Warshavsky's naive, simplistic attitude toward Jewish folk melody, together represented the Russian Jewish intelligentsia's great cultural distance from the world of the Jewish masses. Their Jewish "folk songs" were merely a new, stylized, and superficial form of commercial popular music—fakelore rather than folklore.

Even as the newly minted critical "expert," however, Engel could not escape the fact that the folk themselves, the Jewish masses, had recognized and embraced Warshavsky's songs as their own. Since, according to his own theory, the folk were the ultimate musical judges of Jewishness, what need was there for elite scientific research to tell the people what they already knew—let alone contradict their opinion? Still, in spite of these philosophical dilemmas, Engel remained convinced that his model of ethnographic engagement would reveal a vital distinction between what the writer I. L. Peretz called "true" and "artificial" folk songs.[40] The episode only strengthened his belief that authentic Jewish folk song faced a growing danger of cultural extinction and thus required extensive study, preservation, and cultivation. This research would lead to an accumulation of musical evidence from the Jewish masses themselves, producing an indispensable—and indisputable—body of national source material for Jewish culture. Before Engel could embark on this broader project, however, the larger drama of the Russian Revolution swept into his life.

Free Artists in Search of Freedom of Speech: 1905 and the Demands of Politics

In the later creative efforts of his Soviet biographers, Engel emerges as a Bolshevik fellow traveler, closely allied with Moscow Marxists, particularly through his friendship with the revolutionary Mikhail Lunts. Yet in reality there is little evidence that Engel engaged in politics of any kind before 1905. Newly wed and the father of two young daughters, Ada and Vera, he concentrated on his professional responsibilities and family life in these years. Whatever free time was left he devoted to his research on Jewish folk song. When the Revolution of 1905 exploded, he rallied quickly to the camp of Russian liberals. Beginning with the conservatory crisis in 1905, triggered by a student political strike at the St. Petersburg Conservatory and the subsequent dismissal of composer Nikolai Rimsky-Korsakov from the faculty for voicing his support for the strikers, Engel assumed a central role in rallying the Russian musical community to the cause of liberal political reform. In early February 1905 he authored a manifesto on behalf of twenty-nine prominent Moscow musicians, including Taneev, Sergei Rachmaninov, and Fyodor Chaliapin. The text called for a broad set of political changes, chief among them "freedom of speech and conscience." Art could not continue freely as before while life itself was held hostage to oppressive politics, the text proclaimed, adding that musicians' special privileges now meant little: "We are no longer Free Artists but rather defenseless victims of modern, abnormal socio-legal conditions just like the rest of Russian citizenry."[41]

Over the next two years, Engel emerged as a political leader of the Moscow intelligentsia. In the immediate years before 1905 he had already joined a coterie of rising Jewish editors at *Russkie vedomosti*, many of whom assumed important roles in the Moscow branch of the liberal Kadet party (the Constitutional Democrats). During the tumultuous months of 1905, he ran the paper's breaking-news section, personally manning the telephone line to St. Petersburg for the latest reports of the revolution. His growing public profile led to an invitation to serve as the newspaper's correspondent to the First Duma in 1906. He declined this offer, yet other political notoriety was less easily escaped. In October of that year antisemitic rightist political groups began to issue personal death threats against Engel, forcing him and his family into hiding. Well into the following year the situation had not improved. In March 1907 Engel and two other well-known Jewish musicians, pianist David Shor and singer Sophia Rubinstein, sister of the deceased composer Anton, together received a collective death threat addressed to the trio of *"zhids"* from the Union of Russian People. Unidentified right-wing terrorists also murdered two of Engel's Jewish colleagues from *Russkie vedomosti*, the Duma members Grigorii Iollos and Mikhail Gertsenshtein.[42]

By the fall of 1907, revolutionary chaos and liberal reform alike had been quashed by Nicholas II's reactionary policies. The Third Duma effectively marked the end of hopes for Russian constitutionalism under autocratic rule. However, in spite of the deepening crisis of repressive security measures and popular antisemitism, the Revolution of 1905 did produce some important political changes. One of these was the October Manifesto, a tsarist proclamation of the basic rights of freedom of assembly and speech as demanded by Engel and his colleagues in their own manifesto. In this new atmosphere of provisional liberty, Russian civil society expanded rapidly. Taking advantage of this opportunity, Engel joined with Taneev, Kashkin, and other colleagues from the Musical-Ethnographic Commission to launch the People's Conservatory (Narodnaia konservatoriia) in 1906. Originally conceived as a folk music department within the Moscow Conservatory, this experimental music school came to life as the music section of the newly founded People's University (Narodnyi universitet), itself a late populist response to the huge numbers of uneducated adult workers pouring into Moscow. In his speech at the school's opening, Engel spoke of how "the fundamental goal of the day" was to spread the culture of the "Russian Enlightenment, in the broadest sense of the word" to the masses. He and his colleagues took on this challenge by teaching classes in choral singing, elementary theory, and other basic musical subjects. He remained directly involved with the school over the next decade and a half as it grew into a major urban educational institution.[43]

The same period saw the rise of new forms of Jewish public culture in the larger cities of the Russian Empire, including mass-circulation newspapers, communal organizations, scholarly publications, and countless cultural societies. With the possibility of Jewish legal emancipation ostensibly sealed off by political reaction, and the urban middle class increasingly self-segregating into blocs of minorities, Russian Jews increasingly began to turn to the kind of cultural nationalism Engel had preached since the turn of the century. Music, with its powerful abilities to evoke feelings of emotional immediacy, spirituality without formal religion, and sentiment beyond language, found a special resonance in the Jewish middle class and intelligentsia. The new Jewish communal and political organizations also began to sponsor concerts to raise funds and attract supporters. In cities such as Warsaw, Lodz, Baku, and Vilnius a variety of choral groups and other musical societies emerged in the first decade of the twentieth century.[44]

With all of this new communal interest in Jewish music, Engel found a growing appreciation for his research and art. In January 1908, he presented a concert-lecture at the Moscow Conservatory's Great Hall to an audience of two thousand. Concert and lecture invitations and requests to borrow his musical arrangements also poured in from St. Petersburg, the provinces, and abroad. Articles in the press now spoke of Engel as the leader of a new national musical movement among the Jewish intelligentsia. A further milestone arrived in 1909 when Engel published his own first collection of *Evreiskie narodnye pesni* (Jewish Folk Songs). In the introduction he described the book as a continuation of the project begun almost a decade earlier with Marek and Gintsburg. This slim volume of ten songs included six of the original melodies that had been sent in by provincial correspondents, as well as three others matching texts printed in the 1901 anthology. The artist Leonid Pasternak, a close family friend, designed the book's dramatic cover imagery; in the same period Engel gave piano lessons to Leonid's son Boris, the future poet and novelist. The popularity of the first volume led to a second collection of another ten songs, issued in 1912, followed by a third edition of ten more selections arranged for piano.⁴⁵

Even as Engel found this new public success and recognition gratifying, he sensed something else missing in his life: the vital musical wellsprings of the shtetl remained tantalizingly out of reach to him in Moscow. Despite a series of brief summer visits to the Pale of Settlement in the opening years of the decade, he still considered himself an inauthentic "bad Jew," born and bred in the farthest Crimean reaches of the Pale and now a Russified Muscovite through and through. He dreamt of a more direct and personal contact with Yiddish folk culture, proposing to a fellow enthusiast in Vilnius in 1910 that they venture together into the Jewish heartland to collect more folk songs.⁴⁶ Two years later, he finally got his chance. The opportunity arrived in the form of an ethnographic expedition that catapulted music squarely into the intellectual heart of modern Jewish culture.

The Second Torah: Engel, Ansky, and the Jewish Historical-Ethnographic Expedition

If there was one other Jewish intellectual who best grasped Engel's quest to recover and elevate Jewish folk music into a national artistic treasure by means of ethnography, it was S. Ansky (1863-1920). Born Shloyme Zanvl Rappoport in Vitebsk, by 1905 Ansky had passed successively through the worlds of traditional eastern European religious Judaism, the Russian Jewish Haskalah, Russian radical populism, and Marxist socialism to emerge as a leading writer, thinker, and political leader among Russian Jewry. After spending most of the 1890s in political exile in France and Switzerland, where he helped found the Russian Social Revolutionary Party in 1901, Ansky returned to Russia under a political amnesty in 1905. Mixing populist ideas with the secular cultural nationalism of the writer I. L. Peretz, he developed a model of modern Jewish identity built on an intellectual appropriation of the traditional religious and folk culture of the Jewish masses. By 1908 this new dedication to what he called "Jewish folk creativity" (*evreiskoe narodnoe tvorchestvo*) had led him directly into the ranks of the St. Petersburg Jewish intelligentsia. Joining Dubnow and other leading scholars, that year Ansky helped launch the Jewish Historical-Ethnographic Society, itself based on the original Jewish Historical-Ethnographic Commission cofounded by Dubnow back in 1892. Ansky went on to work on a number of new Russian Jewish journals, including *Evreiskaia starina* (Jewish Antiquity), *Perezhitoe* (Experience), and *Evreiskii mir* (Jewish World), and lectured at literary events and concerts across the empire.⁴⁷

As he later outlined in his *Jewish Ethnographic Program* (1914), Ansky saw the Jews not only as a People of the Book but also as a civilization rich in folklore. He characterized this cultural heritage as a second Torah, a "book of oral tradition" comprised of all of the Jewish people's spiritual experiences in the form of stories, legends, songs, jokes, and various other customs and beliefs. Like his political colleague Dubnow, he viewed the recovery of traditional Jewish culture as the fundamental intellectual project of Jewish modernity. Both sought to salvage traditional Jewish culture in order to translate it into the building blocks of a secular national identity and a weapon in the fight against Jewish "assimilation." But where Dubnow favored a scientific approach centered on Jewish history at the expense of religion and oral tradition, Ansky envisioned a Romantic embrace of Yiddish folklore and traditional religious life through populist-inspired ethnography.[48]

Nowhere was the difference between the two attitudes more evident than in Ansky's approach to music. In fact, one of the prime inspirations for his ethnographic philosophy of Jewish folk culture—and one of the few direct sources of his knowledge of Yiddish folklore—was Marek and Gintsburg's folk song collection. In music Ansky perceived a deep, expressive bond between the rural Jewish population and the urban intelligentsia, and an affecting spiritual link across the awkward divisions of language, geography, religious belief, and culture. In his writings he repeatedly stressed the importance of authentic folk songs for Jewish national identity. Throughout the centuries, he told a St. Petersburg audience in 1911, the Jewish people had held fast to their "melodic creativity." Even though there were obvious commonalities between the music of Jews and those of other peoples, Jewish music remained distinct, distinguished by its "spirituality" and "elegiac tone," both of which reflected the inner life and soul of the Jewish people from the biblical Song of Songs down to the present.[49]

Like Engel, Ansky had long cherished the idea of a comprehensive ethnographic expedition into the Pale of Settlement to access and preserve traditional Jewish folklore. After three years of continual fund-raising and lobbying, by 1912 he had succeeded in winning the backing of the Kiev banker and philanthropist Vladimir Gintsburg and the official sponsorship of the Jewish Historical-Ethnographic Society. All that remained was to acquire the expert advice—and symbolic blessing—of the Jewish scholarly elite. To this end Ansky issued invitations to a two-day conference in St. Petersburg in late March of that year to plan the details of the expedition. The event brought together the largest and most illustrious group of Russian Jewish intellectuals ever assembled, including historians Dubnow, Gintsburg, Marek, and Maksim Vinaver, Orientalist David Maggid, anthropologist Samuel Weissenberg, and ethnographers Lev Shternberg and Engel, among others.[50]

Once assembled, the scholars proved to be less interested in Ansky's Romantic aspirations to document the vanishing world of Jewish tradition than in its potential usefulness in addressing the urgent Jewish problems of the day, including the increasing poverty and economic backwardness of the shtetl, the realities of Jewish "assimilation" among the urban middle classes and intelligentsia, and the overall threat of antisemitism. There was little debate regarding the severity of these problems. Instead differences arose over the question of the proper solution. Leading one faction was Shternberg, whose status as the senior curator of the St. Petersburg Museum of Anthropology and Ethnography lent him great intellectual authority. Shternberg's newer methodological approach to ethnography concentrated on the "hard" scientific data of physical anthropology and demography as opposed to the "soft" culture of folklore. In his eyes, Jewish statistical data and physiological measurements would provide the most objective and useful information about the true condition of the Jewish masses. Birth rates and body weights, he stressed, counted far more than old folk songs and grandmothers' tales.

Arguing against this view was Ansky himself. In a passionate oration on the conference's first day, he asserted that the documentation and preservation of Jewish national culture should take precedence over more abstract academic research, especially because of the crisis of "assimilation" at hand: "Collecting folklore is not only a scientific goal for us, but also a burning national issue. In order to raise our children in the Jewish national spirit, we must give them folktales, songs, in short, that which forms the root of children's education in other peoples." In the end, Ansky's moral exhortation prevailed over his colleague's colder sociological model.

Much of the ideological debate between Ansky and Shternberg fell squarely on the question of methodology. Should ethnographic research be conducted on location in the Pale of Settlement by members of the assembled group? Or would it suffice to deputize local people with intimate knowledge of their own communities' folk traditions to serve as surrogate researchers on behalf of the St. Petersburg and Moscow intellectuals? Not surprisingly, music figured prominently in this debate, particularly because of the earlier precedent of Marek and Gintsburg's folk song project. Reviewing their own efforts a decade later, the two men now found themselves sharply divided on the subject. Gintsburg argued that their project had convinced him that, while traveling to the locations was a necessary component, the local intelligentsia could and would also respond to appeals in the Jewish press to collect and send in useful material. Marek, on the other hand, stressed his recollection of how their reliance on correspondents had repeatedly backfired. Many people, for example, had mailed in "their own compositions passed off as folk songs." The task of resolving this impasse naturally fell to Engel, the most senior music scholar present. On the second day, he presented his thoughts in a session devoted specifically to the expedition's musical component. Ironically, chairing the session was none other than Dubnow, the man who twenty years earlier had dismissed the very idea of Jewish music as an object worthy of study.

Opening the discussion, Engel began by proudly stating that the study of folk music was no longer in question. Its value for art and science was now a given. As for the question of method, he explained, when it came to music the real challenge was not who would do the fieldwork—true research always required a partnership between specialists and knowledgeable local people—but how to properly record it. Given that the essence of Jewish music lay in its expressive subtleties beyond mere notes on a page, it was essential that the expedition use the latest technology: the phonograph (fig. 2). His interest in the device dated back to the late 1890s, when Evgeniia Lineva, a colleague in the Moscow Musical-Ethnographic Commission, had first introduced the phonograph into Russian folklore research. A former St. Petersburg opera star turned socialist radical, Lineva had spent several years in political exile in the United States, popularizing Russian folk songs. In 1893 she met the American music critic and scholar Henry Krehbiel, who demonstrated his early recordings of American Indian songs for her. Returning to Moscow in 1896, she spent the next four summers recording hundreds of Russian and Ukrainian folk songs, in the process revolutionizing the study of folk music.[51]

Engel now proposed to do the same for Jewish music. Early phonograph machines were expensive, cumbersome devices that recorded on fragile wax cylinders. Yet in spite of the logistical challenges involved, he insisted that phonograph recordings provided a superior objective method of ensuring musical precision and at the same time preserving the full richness and aural immediacy of folk music. In other words, using the phonograph to document sound would fulfill the mandates of both "hard" science and "soft" culture. By the end of his allotted time, Engel had convinced those assembled of the importance of his vision. Setting aside their differences, the positivist Shternberg and the populist Ansky both spoke in favor of his idea of using the phonograph. Even Dubnow grudgingly acknowledged the primacy of music as a main field of study in the planned expedition. With a unanimous vote, Engel was chosen to implement the phonograph plan and oversee the musical aspects of the expedition.[52]

Figure 2. Joel Engel (left) with phonograph and unknown collaborator. From the Collection of the Peter the Great Museum of Anthropology and Ethnography (Kunstkamera), Russian Academy of Sciences, MAE 2152-288.

Acting Out: Jewish Musical Ethnography Enters the Field

On the first day of July 1912, the regular morning train from Kiev pulled slowly into a provincial railroad station about three miles outside the town of Ruzhin. Onboard was a typical cross-section of the rural population of the western Ukraine: peasants and Jewish merchants returning home from business in the big city, Russian soldiers en route to border postings, and Hasidic Jews on pilgrimage to visit the former home of the legendary Hasidic rebbe, the Tsaddik of Ruzhin. Among this mixed crowd of travelers, three passengers awkwardly stood out. Descending from the train, the trio huddled self-consciously together on the platform, speaking to one another in rudimentary Yiddish. Their journey was not a homecoming. Nor was it quite a religious pilgrimage or even a business trip. And yet it was a bit of all three. For together these men, Engel, Ansky, and Solomon Yudovin, a young art student, represented the first members of the newly launched Baron Horace Gintsburg Jewish Historical-Ethnographic Expedition (fig. 3).[53]

Despite all the sober theoretical discussions back in St. Petersburg earlier that year, the ethnographic expedition turned out to be as much of a cultural adventure and nostalgic idyll as a scholarly research endeavor. From the moment of their arrival, Engel recounted later, the trio agreed to speak only in Yiddish, despite the fact that none of the men spoke it well. Their first attempts to negotiate with a local Jewish coachman led initially to comic misunderstanding. The wagon driver, named Henokh, was a traditional small-town Jew who had no idea what to make of the strangely dressed big-city intellectuals speaking a broken Yiddish. Assuming they were mocking him, Henokh refused to answer in Yiddish, instead responding to Ansky's repeated questions in Ukrainian. Eventually he decided that the travelers were actors, only to change his mind and conclude that Ansky was a cantor and Engel his choirmaster. "This idea delighted him," Engel recalled, "[for] it turned out that synagogue song was his passion." Once the musical connection was established, Henokh immediately warmed up to his passengers, especially when Engel showed him the phonograph. Soon the coachman switched back into Yiddish. As they rode slowly toward the town of Ruzhin, he regaled his curious passengers with tales of the Ruzhin Tsaddik, offering to guide them through the town's musical universe.

This initial episode, narrated in Engel's unpublished memoirs of the trip, conveys much of the three men's shared sense of spiritual journey and cultural playacting. For it was precisely their feelings of distance from the traditional Jewish shtetl that inspired their devotion to it. For Yudovin and Ansky, both born in the shtetl, the expedition was a prodigal's return to the

Figure 3. Solomon Yudovin, Joel Engel, and S. Ansky. From the Collection of the Peter the Great Museum of Anthropology and Ethnography (Kunstkamera), Russian Academy of Sciences, MAE 2152-291.

long departed world of childhood. For Engel, the effect was the opposite; he came in search of a past he had never known. Even after nearly fifteen years of serious involvement with traditional Yiddish culture, he noted, the shtetl remained terra incognita to him. The expedition, he told a St. Petersburg audience afterward, represented his first real opportunity "to immerse my head in the most remote depths of the Jewish shtetls," where Jewish cultural life remained "independent and still largely linked to the traditions of the past."[54]

For the next month, the expedition traveled from shtetl to shtetl in search of the finest and purest examples of Jewish folk tradition. Along the way, they encountered a dramatic range of responses to their effort. With his clean-shaven Muscovite physical appearance and limited knowledge of Yiddish, Engel found himself immediately marked as an outsider. Though he was the expedition's musical expert, he generally deferred to Ansky as translator and cultural mediator in dealing with informants. The curiosity and skepticism about Engel were only enhanced by the fact that he carried with him an exotic, futuristic device, the phonograph. Swarming, interested crowds assembled around him every time he set up his machine on the street. The circuslike atmosphere made it difficult to conduct careful research. In the town of Pavoloch, for example, he had intended to go visit a *shoykhet* (kosher butcher) reputed to have a great repertoire of folk songs. But a surging mass of inquisitive onlookers, both adults and children, besieged him as soon as he stepped out of the house where the trio was staying. Overwhelmed, he retreated inside. In order to escape the mob, Engel sent Yudovin, the expedition's official photographer, into the street to distract the crowd with his own newfangled contraption, the camera, while he snuck out the back door in search of his informant (fig. 4).

If the Jews of the shtetl were still technological novices, when it came to sharing their folk traditions with fellow Jews they had mastered the language of modern commerce. Fifteen years before, Gintsburg and Marek had complained about this development. "The people look at us from a calculating point of view," Marek had opined in a letter to his partner. "They do not understand at all why the intelligentsia would be interested in their songs and consider the collector to be crazy, a nutcase or a shady person." As a result, members of the fabled Jewish masses tried to negotiate with them, promising the "most folksy" melodies in exchange for more money. Ansky and Engel faced similar relentless hustling. One day in Ruzhin word spread so quickly that Engel was offering to pay five kopeks a piece for children's folk songs that, before morning had ended, the town's entire school-age

Figure 4. Joel Engel conducting fieldwork in the Pale of Settlement, 1912. From the Collection of the Peter the Great Museum of Anthropology and Ethnography (Kunstkamera), Russian Academy of Sciences, MAE 2152-289.

population had deserted their classes to come perform for the visitors. Soon they had begun to improvise new songs on the spot.[55]

Of course not everyone was so enthusiastic about sharing their music, even when money was involved. Many people, particularly women, were mistrustful of the obviously secular Jewish visitors or simply embarrassed by the prospect of singing in public for a male stranger. In some cases, recordings were made at inns or at schools after the school day's end so as to accommodate women who would not venture into the expedition's hotel rooms. Engel later recalled one male singer in the town of Skvir, "half traditional, half modern" in his appearance, who insisted that he pull down all the hotel room shades in the middle of the day and lock his door before he would surreptitiously sing into the phonograph. As it turned out, the singer, who also refused any payment, performed a deeply spiritual rendition of the song that would become famous as the "Kaddish of Rebbe Levi-Yitshok of Berdichev."

At the end of July, Engel was forced to cut short his trip because of family demands. He had visited four shtetls and accumulated forty-four recordings (on twenty-nine cylinders), as well as hundreds of hand-notated transcriptions of klezmer melodies, Hasidic nigunim, and Yiddish folk songs. Ansky now assumed responsibility for the recordings, to be joined thereafter by Engel's designated successor, a young musician from St. Petersburg named Zisman Kiselgof. Over the following two summers, the expedition continued to record music and other folklore in traditional Jewish communities throughout the Pale. By the time World War I interrupted the project's work, over five hundred cylinder recordings and a thousand transcriptions had been made. The fruits of this labor immediately began to affect Jewish communities throughout Russia. Kiselgof's involvement in itself signified one such development, for he represented a new organization in St. Petersburg, the Society for Jewish Folk Music (Obshchestvo evreiskoi narodnoi muzyki). Founded in 1908, this band of conservatory-trained composers and cultural activists immediately began to institutionalize and expand Engel's Jewish musical nationalism into an empirewide and even international movement.[56]

As for Engel himself, he returned in 1912 from his first genuine encounters with the shtetl both inspired and confused. After years of campaigning for the in-depth study of Jewish folk music, he had finally succeeded in making direct contact with the Jewish masses, only to find the experience a mixed blessing. He now possessed a rich stock of folkloric material to substantiate his theories and cultivate his artistic vision of Jewish music. Yet the closer he came to the shtetl, the more Engel sensed his own distance—

linguistic, cultural, even spiritual—from the folk itself. Even the phonograph, the device that was supposed to capture the true musical voices of the people without any bias or interference, had frequently led instead to awkward, unexpected problems. Nor was the irony lost on him of using the newest instrument of modern technology in order to save a musical tradition itself vanishing under the impact of modernity. The expedition proved so psychologically disorienting to Engel that he began to openly question his own sense of national identity.

In April 1913 his friend and colleague Andrei Rimsky-Korsakov wrote to ask if he would contribute to a book in remembrance of his father, Nikolai. In reply, Engel politely declined. Even three years earlier, he explained, he would have been more than happy to help. Now, although it pained him, he felt he could not join the memorial effort to the great Russian composer. The reason was simple. He was no longer certain of whether he considered himself Jewish or Russian:

> Earlier I spoke as a Russian, and I was right to do so, since Russia is my homeland and indeed the homeland of my beloved Russian native language and culture. Now all of that remains as it was, but something new has appeared, important and powerful, reminding me more and more that I am a Jew and that from this I must necessarily draw some conclusions. In the meantime, to speak from a Jewish perspective about many important things is impossible for me right now, and I don't know if it will ever be. For this I do not have enough spiritual experience in this life. Perhaps this will all even out, and once again I will be able to speak with a clear conscience as a Russian and a Jew, but right now this is very difficult and painful for me.[57]

At its root, Engel's dilemma was born of a conflict between an emerging Jewish national identity and a changing sense of Russian cultural identity. A decade and a half earlier, he had harmonized his Jewish national consciousness with a broader sense of Russianness. Music had provided a means for him to embrace his Jewishness without relinquishing membership in an inclusive Russian imperial civic and cultural framework. With the passage of time, the push of antisemitism, the pull of Jewish nationalism, and the collapsing social fabric of the Russian Empire, he began to feel his Jewishness growing stronger at the expense of his Russianness. Yet when confronted with the actual Jewish heartland of which he had long imagined himself part, Engel came away painfully self-conscious and disconcerted by the cultural contradictions of the early twentieth-century shtetl. Now too Jewish to count himself a legitimate Russian musician, he nevertheless also acknowledged that he could never fully become one with the Jewish tradition he sought to recover.

He was not alone, of course, in this dilemma, which defined so much of the modern dual identities of Russian Jewish artists and intellectuals of his day and afterward, forever torn between their Russian and Jewish souls. Indeed, Engel's traveling companion Ansky devoted what would become the most famous work of art to emerge from the expedition, his play *The Dybbuk*, to the theme of the Jewish soul's suspension "between two worlds." The two men had heard the original folktale of a case of spirit possession in the summer of 1912. Ansky's play both dramatized the tale and turned it into a parable for the whole tragic fate of Russian Jews, caught between religious tradition and secular modernity, Jewishness and Russianness. Years later, Engel scored the play for the Hebrew-language production at the Habimah Theater in Moscow in 1922. Fittingly, this incidental music would become Engel's best-known composition.[58]

Ultimately Engel believed that art might provide a resolution to the conundrum of Russian Jewish identity, where politics and religion failed. Even as he continued to grapple personally with questions of national and cultural allegiance throughout the 1910s, the broader mass of Russian Jews followed his lead in turning increasingly to music as an essential expression of collective identity. In the subsequent years of World War I, as the Russian and German militaries trudged back and forth across the Eastern Front, ravaging Jewish communities and displacing families by the tens of thousands, the symbolic value of Engel's Jewish folk songs only increased in the minds of the Russian Jewish public. The further the shtetl receded into the distance, the louder its music echoed in the Russian Jewish imagination.

CHAPTER 3

The Most Musical Nation
The Birth of the Society for Jewish Folk Music

The *zhidy* [kikes] leap up at the sound of their songs, handed down from generation to generation. Their eyes blaze with an honest, not a mercenary fire, and their loathsome mugs straighten out into something almost human—I've seen this happen more than once. The *zhidy* are better than the Czechs—our own Bialystok, Lutsk, and Nevel *zhidy*, who live in filth in their stinking shacks.
—Letter from Modest Mussorgsky to Mily Balakirev (St. Petersburg, 1867)

In Isaac Babel's 1931 short story, "Awakening," the narrator recalls the obsession with music among the middle-class Jewish parents in Odessa at the turn of the twentieth century: "All the folk in our circle—brokers, shopkeepers, clerks in banks and steamship offices—used to have their children taught music. Our fathers, seeing no other escape from their lot, had thought up a lottery, building it on the bones of little children. Odessa more than other towns was seized by this craze. And in fact, in the course of ten years or so our town supplied the concert platforms of the world with infant prodigies. From Odessa came Mischa Elman, Zimbalist, Gabrilowitsch. Odessa witnessed the first step of Jascha Heifetz."[1]

Babel's story describes parents dragging their children to a local music teacher, Mr. Zagursky, who runs "a factory of infant prodigies." Zagursky, an obvious pseudonym for the real-life Odessa violin pedagogue Petr Stoliarskii (1871–1944), dispatches scores of his young pupils to the great professor Leopold Auer (1845–1930) at the St. Petersburg Conservatory to become "famous virtuosi." Though the narrator displays little talent and prefers to bury his head in books by Turgenev and Dumas, his father insists that he can—and will—become a great musician: "The sounds dripped from my fiddle like iron filings, causing even me excruciating agony, but father wouldn't give in. At home there was no talk save of Mischa Elman, exempted by the Tsar himself from military service. Zimbalist, father would have us know, had been presented to the King of England and had played at Buckingham Palace. The parents of Gabrilowitsch had bought two houses in

St. Petersburg. Infant prodigies brought wealth to their parents, but though my father could have reconciled himself to poverty, fame he must have."

The "awakening" in Babel's story is literary, not musical. The narrator skips his thrice-weekly violin classes, instead sneaking off each time to the Odessa port in search of urban adventures more appealing to a budding writer. Rejecting the violin for the pen, Babel's fictional alter ego gently mocks the Russian Jewish bourgeoisie's ethnic pride and naive, optimistic faith that music lessons will secure their children's fate in the merciless modern world. Nonetheless, in his miniature self-portrait of the artist as a young man, Babel captures the sense of mythical power that music held for his contemporaries. In the Russian Jewish imagination, music represented a magical avenue of opportunity. Jascha Heifetz, Ossip Gabrilowitsch, and Efrem Zimbalist, after all, were real figures, who did soar to international fame on the concert stages of the early twentieth century. This line of famous Jewish musicians stretched back a half a century to the founding father of Russia's first conservatory, Anton Rubinstein, himself a Jewish musical prodigy from the Pale of Settlement. Even for parents more realistic about the prospects of fame than Babel's fictionalized father, a conservatory musical education offered the prestigious rank of Free Artist (*svobodnyi khudozhnik*), a bundle of tangible legal benefits including the fabled right of residence (*pravo zhitelstva*) outside the Pale, and a fairly stable, high-status professional career as a performer or teacher.

Yet there was another side to this image of music's nearly unmatched promise for Russian Jews. The thousands of Jewish boys and girls who flocked to Russia's music schools and conservatories to become individual Free Artists found themselves cast in a larger collective story of the time. As the forces of modern nationalism—both Russian and Jewish—emerged in full strength, the larger cultural meaning of Jews and music in Russian society shifted dramatically. Nowhere was this change more visible than at the St. Petersburg Conservatory. Anton Rubinstein had spent the final years of his life fighting to save his school from the escalating currents of Russian conservative nationalism and modern antisemitism. At his death in 1894 he could not have foreseen that an institution that had served as an instrument of Russian Jewish emancipation and acculturation would soon become a prime incubator for a radically new kind of relationship between Jews and Russians. For in the first decade of the twentieth century, at this supreme site of Russian-Jewish cultural symbiosis, there appeared a new organization explicitly committed to a musical doctrine of Jewish nationalism.

Founded in 1908 by a group of students and recent graduates of the St.

Petersburg Conservatory, the Society for Jewish Folk Music (Obshchestvo evreiskoi narodnoi muzyki, or Gezelshaft far yidisher folks-muzik) initiated a variety of endeavors related to the performance, study, composition, publication, and general promotion of music as a cultural expression of Jewish identity. From a small core of St. Petersburg musicians, the group grew within the space of a decade to an empirewide organization with branches in Moscow, Kiev, and Odessa and a rising international profile. By the time the society faltered during the chaos of the Russian Revolution, it had made a distinct and lasting contribution to modern Jewish identity. The group's aesthetic and intellectual legacies would endure in many different forms in the cultural life of Jewish communities in the Soviet Union, the United States, central Europe, and Palestine throughout the remainder of the twentieth century and into the twenty-first.

In many ways, the Society for Jewish Folk Music was a direct continuation and natural ideological extension of the pioneering efforts of Joel Engel to promote music as a constituent part of modern Jewish culture. Yet the new organization represented more than a mere enlargement or formal institutionalization of Engel's vision. In the transition from pre-1905 Moscow to post-1905 St. Petersburg, from individual journey to collective movement, the very concept of Jewish music underwent a series of fundamental changes. In the aftermath of the failed Revolution of 1905, the conflicting impulses of liberal integration and nationalist separatism, antisemitism and philosemitism, and cultural identification and political mobilization generated a new self-consciousness about the role of Jews in modern Russian culture. As a result, whereas Engel sought to define a nationalist conception of Jewish *music,* the musicians of St. Petersburg focused equally on the task of redefining the meaning of the Jewish *musician.* This was part of an aesthetic revolt within the broader Jewish cultural revolution, an attempt to reconstruct modern Jewish identity not through politics or religion but through art and culture. At the same time, it was an attempt by a small group of artists and intellectuals to solve one of the key paradoxes of Jewish modernity: why "the most musical nation" had no music of its own. And this paradox of Jewish musicality was never more apparent than at the St. Petersburg Conservatory in the first decade of the twentieth century.

Russian Fathers, Jewish Sons: Philosemitism and Antisemitism at the St. Petersburg Conservatory

From its founding in 1862, the St. Petersburg Conservatory was a particularly liberal, tolerant educational institution. With the support of its parent organization, the Imperial Russian Music Society (IRMO), the school managed to maintain its institutional independence from the tsarist government's Ministry of Education, skirting the wave of severe Jewish quota policies that swept through Russian higher education in the late 1880s. The conservatory and its sister schools were among a small handful of institutions of higher education (*vysshie uchebnye zavedeniia*) not placed under the direct control of the Ministry of Education, but rather the Ministry of the Imperial Court. By virtue of this quirk of bureaucratic politics and its reputation for a remarkably philosemitic faculty and administration, in the final decades of the nineteenth century the St. Petersburg Conservatory became a magnet for young Jewish musicians from all over the Russian Empire.

By the dawn of the twentieth century this influx of Jewish students had assumed even more conspicuous proportions. In 1907, for instance, Jews numbered 360 out of 1,060 students enrolled at the conservatory, or 34 percent. At the end of the same decade, this number had increased to nearly 43 percent, and by 1913 over 50 percent—1,178 students—were Jewish. Similarly striking figures could be found at many other conservatories and music schools across Russia. This was at a time when Jews formed roughly only 4 percent of the empire's total population and when the government was increasingly restricting travel and residence outside the Pale. After 1907 the government even launched a new Jewish admissions quota of 3 percent for previously exempt educational institutions. In the years that followed, there were repeated attempts to apply the same laws to music schools. But ultimately even those tsarist officials directly responsible for implementing the educational quotas generally relented when it came to music. Reviewing the situation in 1908, for instance, a Ministry of Internal Affairs (MVD) official defended the broad necessity of quotas to counter the "harmful influence that Jews exercise on our student youth," yet dismissed their suitability for music schools. In the case of conservatories, he wrote to the State Council of Ministers, there was little danger that the Jewish "pernicious tendencies" would appear. Therefore, to his mind it would be "excessive to fix any detailed *numerus clausus* for Jewish admission to music schools."[2]

As a result of this exception, the new post-1907 regulations only heightened the disparity between conservatories and the rest of the Russian education system. The entire official Jewish student enrollment in university-level schools throughout the Russian Empire never peaked beyond 12.1 percent (4,266 students) before 1907; in subsequent years, new repressive measures reduced this number to 7.3 percent (2,505 students) by 1913. This meant that on the eve of World War I the Jewish student population at the St. Petersburg Conservatory alone equaled nearly half that of those enrolled in all other Russian universities and advanced professional schools combined. Put differently, roughly one in every three university-level Jewish students in the late Russian Empire was a musician at the St. Petersburg Conservatory. This cultural anomaly gave rise to claims, only slightly exaggerated, that the conservatory was the sole Russian institution of higher education without a quota system.[3]

The atmosphere of great tolerance at the St. Petersburg Conservatory did not mean that the enormous Jewish presence went unnoticed. If outside its walls the Jewish musical question led continually to antisemitic attacks and political debates in the Duma, inside the school's corridors the theme of Jewish musicality assumed a more subtle but omnipresent form of cultural obsession. The best-known example was Leopold Auer's violin class, where the maestro took in a steady stream of gifted youngsters from the Pale. Auer frequently intervened personally with tsarist officials on behalf of his students. In the case of Heifetz, he even went so far as to enroll the nine-year-old violinist's father as a student at the conservatory in order to achieve residence rights for his family. The Auer line of Jewish violin prodigies eventually became synonymous with the Russian violin school as a whole and arguably the single most important phenomenon in the modern history of the classical violin.[4] Auer's paternal interest in his Jewish students certainly owed something to his own origins as a baptized Hungarian Jew. But he was no means atypical in his focus on Jewish musical talent. In the minds of his ethnic Russian colleagues, Jewish musicality engendered intense curiosity and a range of complicated reactions. The complex relationship between these musical "fathers and sons," characterized by shades of both antisemitism and philosemitism, in turn bred a deep self-consciousness in Jewish conservatory students. A revealing, uncensored example of these fraught interactions comes from the unpublished memoirs of musician Mikhail F. Gnesin (1883–1957) (fig. 5).

Born in the city of Rostov-on-Don, Gnesin came from a long line of Jewish musicians. His maternal grandfather, the itinerant Yiddish folksinger and synagogue chorister Shayke Fayfer (1802–1875), had been a prominent fixture in Vilnius musical life for nearly six decades. Gnesin's mother Bella (ca. 1842–1911) was a talented pianist and singer and a student of the Polish composer Stanisław Moniuszko; her three sisters were also well-known musicians, including one who graduated from the St. Petersburg Conservatory and sang at Milan's La Scala opera house. Gnesin's father Fabian (1837–1891), on the other hand, a graduate of the Vilnius State Rabbinical Seminary, was a classic Russian Jewish *maskil* of the 1860s who firmly believed that political reform and Jewish acculturation would solve the Jewish

Figure 5. Mikhail Gnesin. Russian Institute for the History of the Arts.

question in Russian society. Settling in Rostov, he worked in a bank and as a state-appointed rabbi (*kazennyi ravvin*), as well as serving on the Rostov city council.[5]

For the Gnesin family, music offered a direct means for Jews to realize the liberal promise of modern Russia. Out of nine children, seven went on to become notable musicians or music educators in Russian society. Five of Mikhail's sisters studied music in Moscow in the 1880s and 1890s, four of them at the Moscow Conservatory, before together establishing the Gnesin Musical Institute, a pioneering music school in 1895. This venerable Moscow institution not only survived the Russian Revolution but thrived during the Soviet period under the sisters' direct leadership, acquiring an international reputation as Russia's premier music preparatory school and pedagogical institute, a position it still holds today. For Mikhail and his siblings, in spite of their grandfather's legacy and their father's profession, it was their Russianness rather than their Jewishness that drew them to music. After graduating from the Rostov Realschule in 1899, Mikhail followed his older sisters to Moscow, ready to embark on a promising career as a Russian composer. At that moment, he later recalled, his status as a Jewish musician was the farthest thing from his mind.[6]

The same could not be said for the admissions committee at the Moscow Conservatory, where (unlike in St. Petersburg) anti-Jewish quotas had lately been put in place. In spite of Gnesin's obvious, considerable musical talents, the professors refused even to examine his compositions. Rebuffed by the harsh reality of antisemitism and unwilling to take the step of baptism (in contrast to his sisters), he left Moscow and returned home to Rostov. A year later he tried his luck at the St. Petersburg Conservatory. His experience could not have been more different. The admissions committee there lavished praise on his talents. After a cursory examination of his compositions, the professors admitted him directly, bypassing all the standard entrance exams. Gnesin began his studies in 1901 and remained a student there until 1909.[7]

In his memoirs Gnesin described in great detail his relationship with his professors, particularly composers Anatoly Liadov (1855–1914), Alexander Glazunov (1865–1936), and Nikolai Rimsky-Korsakov (1844–1908). These three men, he recalled, "ruled the heavens above Petersburg," and each crop of new students quickly came to revere them (fig. 6). The professors also displayed a keen interest in their Jewish students. In fact, Liadov, Rimsky-Korsakov, and Glazunov together reflected the full spectrum of larger Russian ideological attitudes toward Jewish musicians at that time, from antisemitism to philosemitism.[8]

Figure 6. Students and teachers at the St. Petersburg Conservatory. Seated in front are Nikolai Rimsky-Korsakov (left) and Alexander Glazunov (right). The back row includes Maksimilian Shteinberg (far left) and Mikhail Gnesin (second from right). Russian Institute for the History of the Arts.

Even before leaving Rostov, Gnesin had corresponded with Liadov, who had urged the young musician to give up on Moscow and switch to St. Petersburg. Once there, Gnesin met frequently with his new mentor, including at regular salon evenings at the home of the pianist Alexander Ziloti. On one such occasion, Liadov entered dramatically and, completely ignoring the other guests, walked straight toward Gnesin. After a warm greeting, he launched immediately into a disturbing monologue about Jews and music. Within earshot of all present, Liadov loudly announced that he had important matters to discuss with Gnesin:

> First of all about the Jews—I don't have the same relationship to the Jews as Alexander Konstantinovich Glazunov. He, after all, thinks they are the most talented nation in the world. I am not partial to them or to any other nation. But I've noticed something among my students. I have had a seriously large number of Jews and they're all very . . . gifted. . . . And look, as students, they shine fantastically, they perform superbly in the course, technique comes very easily to them. And yet when they leave school they immediately harden, their brains just shut down. They cannot create anything original. But I want to say that you're absolutely not like that. Still even if we take [so-and-so] . . . I am convinced that he won't develop further. In any event, in the best case his limit—hardly attainable—might be Mendelssohn.

Despite his profession of utter impartiality, Liadov's honest confession about his Jewish students reflected classical European musical antisemitism. Alleging an intrinsic Jewish pattern of empty virtuosity and a lack of artistic originality, he directly evoked the Wagnerian position on Jewish musical creativity. In his notorious essay "Judaism in Music," Richard Wagner had argued that the Jews had no national culture of their own and were therefore condemned to be cultural strangers and imitative performers in European music, rather than original, creative artists. Wagner particularly targeted the composer Felix Mendelssohn as an example of this perceived Jewish artistic deficiency.

So extreme and inflammatory were Liadov's remarks that Gnesin never discussed them publicly. His notes on the manuscript indicate that he intended this section to be published only after his death. Soviet censors duly complied and excised the passage entirely from his published memoirs. Gnesin later confessed that he simply did not know how to react to Liadov's antisemitic comments. Yet he maintained a close friendship with his mentor for years afterward. Nor was he alone in this respect. Many other Jewish musicians also had similar interactions with Liadov yet remained devoted to him.[9]

If Liadov expressed antisemitic ideas, Glazunov represented the other extreme. His ardent enthusiasm for his Jewish students was legendary. As

Liadov suggested, Glazunov, who assumed the position of conservatory director in the aftermath of the revolutionary turmoil of 1905, was singularly sympathetic toward Jewish students and vigorously proactive in defense of their rights. With a portrait of Anton Rubinstein hanging directly over his desk, Glazunov strongly resisted all efforts of the MVD to regulate Jewish student admissions. He often related how the office of Interior Minister Petr Stolypin continually telephoned to inquire about the number of Jews at the conservatory: "Yesterday they called from Stolypin. They asked how many Jews we have. I ordered them to reply that we haven't counted."[10]

Beyond these frequent rebuffs of the MVD, Glazunov went to great lengths to admit and retain individual Jewish students. In the case of underage child prodigies, this could even mean obtaining residence permits for their parents. The great violinist Nathan Milstein first arrived in St. Petersburg from Odessa in 1916 in the company of his mother to study with Professor Auer. Fearful of police harassment, the fourteen-year-old's mother appealed to Glazunov. Milstein later recalled how Glazunov immediately telephoned Prince Vladimir Volkonsky, the deputy interior minister, to ensure that they would receive good treatment. As a result of this intervention, mother and child returned home to find a police escort assigned to them for their personal protection. Such a scenario, otherwise absurdly inconceivable for Jews in tsarist Russia, proved common for the most gifted Jewish students at the conservatory. More remarkably, even students without notable musical ability could find themselves the beneficiaries of Glazunov's impassioned advocacy. Gnesin recalled that Glazunov went so far as to admit Jewish students regardless of whether they possessed significant musical talent, allowing even shrewd Jewish businessmen and merchants merely in search of temporary residence rights in the capital to take advantage of this creative loophole. His efforts earned him the sobriquet "tsar of the Jews," a pun on his own 1913 composition, *Tsar Iudeiskii* (King of the Jews), about the life of Jesus.[11]

Glazunov's commitment to his Jewish students stemmed in part from his liberal political convictions, which had also led him as a junior professor to side with the student revolutionaries in 1905. But it was not politics alone. He also held a deeper fascination with the idea of Jewish musical talent. Mischa Elman's father recalled that Glazunov did not feel the need to examine new Jewish students too closely, because he believed that "in nine cases out of ten the mere fact that the entering student was a Jew was sufficient indication of talent." Glazunov reversed Liadov's negative image of Jews as uncreative and derivative. In his mind, Jews not only shared an intrinsic aptitude for music, they deserved credit for some of the most important contributions to European musical history. Gnesin recalled Glazunov's response to Wagner's antisemitism: "Look at how Wagner and so many others after him have tried to belittle the significance of Mendelssohn, and yet how indebted to Mendelssohn was Wagner himself in terms of his music and especially in his orchestration!"[12]

Somewhere in the murky middle between Liadov's antisemitism and Glazunov's philosemitism fell the third and most important member of Gnesin's trio of composer-gods, Rimsky-Korsakov. In the aftermath of 1905, Rimsky-Korsakov's liberal politics and defiant support of the student strike earned him a reputation as the hero of all conservatory students (fig. 7). Soviet historiography echoed this trope, elevating him as a prerevolutionary patriarch of a generation of future socialist composers. Gnesin's own lifelong sense of debt to Rimsky-Korsakov was particularly large, reflected in works ranging from the 1911 introduction to his mentor's collected essays to his own 1956 book-length memoir of him.[13] Moreover, Gnesin was only one of several Jewish musicians who studied closely with Rimsky-Korsakov in the decade before his death in 1908. His classmates included the likes of Lazare Saminsky, Ilia Aisberg, Solomon Rosowsky, Moisei Milner, Peysakh Lvov, and Alexander Zhitomirsky. All would subsequently pay homage to Rimsky-Korsakov in their memoirs and compositions. Furthermore, all went on to assume prominent roles in the Society for Jewish Folk Music. Indeed, the very founding of the group hinged on a curious interaction between Rimsky-Korsakov and another one of Gnesin's Jewish classmates, Efraim Shkliar (1871–1943).

In its basic outline, Shkliar's life represents one of the two main stories of Jewish social mobility via music in late nineteenth-century Russia. Musicians such as Gnesin hailed from the urban, acculturated Jewish middle class. For this small Russified elite, talent, circumstance, and conservatory educations turned cultural passions into professional vocations. Shkliar, on the other hand, came directly out of the much broader ranks of the traditional Jewish masses. His story, by far more common in eastern Europe, was one in which music provided a concrete route "out of the ghetto," from the physical, social, and economic isolation of the shtetl into the new world of modern Russian society.

Born in the small shtetl of Timkovichi near Minsk, Shkliar had served a child apprenticeship as a *meshoyrer* (chorister) to a traveling cantor before enrolling at the Warsaw Conservatory in 1890. Four years later, the young Orthodox Jew was introduced to the composer Mily Balakirev, who was visiting Warsaw at the time. Balakirev was equally famous for his strident Russian nationalism and his very public antisemitism, much of which

Figure 7. Students and teachers at the St. Petersburg Conservatory. Seated in the middle are Alexander Glazunov (third from left) and Nikolai Rimsky-Korsakov (bearded), with Mikhail Gnesin, Solomon Rosowsky, and Iuliia Veisberg to the right. Efraim Zimbalist stands at the upper left. Russian Institute for the History of the Arts.

he directed against Anton Rubinstein. Nevertheless, he took a liking to Shkliar. With his traditional Jewish beard and sidelocks, the young musician appeared to the mystically inclined Balakirev as a divinely sent biblical Hebrew. Looking past his distaste for contemporary Jews, the composer offered to help Shkliar transfer to the St. Petersburg Conservatory. In a strange set of circumstances, Shkliar agreed, provided that his own rabbi consent and that Balakirev supply direct assistance in the form of money, a residence permit, and kosher food. Balakirev assented and even went so far as to petition the St. Petersburg Jewish philanthropist Baron Gintsburg for a scholarship. Shkliar entered Rimsky-Korsakov's class in the fall of 1895. When Gnesin met him six years later, he found the former Orthodox chorister now a fervent Zionist and a senior student in Rimsky-Korsakov's advanced composition seminar.[14]

It was there one day in 1902 that Shkliar presented an arrangement of a Jewish folk melody as a harmonization exercise. He did not explain the song's Jewish origins, apparently indicating it only to be a *vostochnaia melodiia*, an "Oriental melody." However, Rimsky-Korsakov immediately noticed its "Jewish" qualities and interrupted the performance. According to one account, the composer exclaimed, "I am very glad to see that you are writing a composition of the Jewish variety [*v evreiskom rode*]. How strange that my Jewish students occupy themselves so little with their own native music. Jewish music exists; it is wonderful music, and it awaits its Glinka."[15]

This incident has acquired iconic status as a watershed event in modern Jewish culture. As part of this canonization, Rimsky-Korsakov's comment has been frequently interpreted as an unequivocal statement of prophetic praise for the idea of Jewish music. Here, after all, was one of the great exponents of Russian national music invoking his personal cultural hero, Glinka, in order to proclaim a similar bright future for Jewish music. Rimsky-Korsakov's Jewish conservatory students idolized him for this "benevolent" endorsement, elevating him to the role of Jewish music's spiritual forefather. Even Engel, who as a Muscovite never studied with Rimsky-Korsakov, venerated the composer. In his apartment's kitchen stood a chair on which the visiting composer had once sat; no one in the family was allowed to touch it.[16]

Taken at face value, Rimsky-Korsakov's remark did evince an affirmative and encouraging view of the possibilities for a Jewish national style of music. As a classic late Romanticist, he considered "nationality" to be a natural, built-in feature of art music. True musical art, according to his line of reasoning, expressed innate national characteristics: "Music does not exist outside of nationality, and, in essence, all music that is taken for universally human, nonetheless is national. Beethoven's music is German music, Wagner's is no doubt German, Berlioz is French." This conception of music required each nation to tap its national essence as found in its native folk song. In the Russian context, Rimsky-Korsakov's vision also reflected the inclusive imperial ideal, in which all national minorities could and should pursue their own music movements, similar to the ethnographic model developed by Joel Engel and other members of the Moscow Musical-Ethnographic Commission.[17]

Yet interpreting Rimsky-Korsakov's remark as wholly positive ignores the deeper ambiguity and ambivalence in this statement that derive from the tensions at the heart of Russian philosemitism. In fact his liberal encouragement hinged precisely on a conscious nationalist distinction whereby Jews were not considered to be true Russians. As an ethnic Russian, Rimsky-Korsakov argued, he himself could not create other than Russian national music. He might compose a "Jewish song" (*evreiskaia pesnia*) as an exercise in Russian musical "Orientalism," but this was not synonymous with an authentic Jewish music. "For me, my East is rather in my head," he famously remarked, "a speculative thing." The reverse applied to his minority students. The Russian Armenian composer Alexander Spendiarov (1871–1928) recalled a similar comment from Rimsky-Korsakov about his musical potential: "You by birth are an Eastern person, for you the East, as they say, is in your blood, and precisely in this strength you may contribute something original in the field of music, something truly worthy." By the same token, Jews could not contribute to Russian music as native Russians but only as a minority people of the empire. Glinka was not their musical ancestor, Rimsky-Korsakov implied, nor did they belong by birthright to the Russian national tradition.[18]

Rimsky-Korsakov was far from an antisemite. Indeed his positive relations with Jews extended to two of his own children's spouses, the prominent young Jewish composers Iuliia L. Veisberg (1879–1942) and Maksimilian O. Shteinberg (1883–1946). Nor were his subtle statements at all comparable to the extreme ideological antisemitism then prevalent in Russian politics. But his ironic comment had a decisive if subtle impact on his Jewish pupils. Indeed, for the young Jewish musicians in St. Petersburg, the lines between paternalistic blessing and exclusivist chauvinism, between philosemitism and antisemitism, between artistic precedent and cultural colonization, were thin and elusive. Time and again the theme of mentorship, with all its complicated strains of reverence, pride, and subconscious resentment surfaced in these musicians' attitudes towards their teachers. The ongoing interplay between the "pull" of growing Jewish nationalism and the "push" of Russian antisemitism and philosemitism fed a dynamic of intense cultural self-consciousness among the young Jewish composers. They would carry this double-edged legacy directly into their collective project to create national music.[19]

The same year as the classroom episode, Efraim Shkliar took Rimsky-Korsakov's suggestion to heart and attempted to launch a new student group at the conservatory devoted to the study and performance of Jewish music. Named Kinor tsion (Heb., "Zion's Lyre"), the group produced a handful of small concerts before disbanding. A second Jewish musical organization and chorus known as Ha-tikvah (Heb., "The Hope") appeared in 1904 and lasted another two years before collapsing. Meanwhile, Shkliar, together with Baron David Gintsburg, also attempted to launch another broader Jewish artistic organization without success. Despite the growing interest in Jewish culture, the mass of St. Petersburg Jewish students and intellectuals were much more focused on the larger Russian political drama unfolding during these years. Early in the spring of 1905 the revolutionary protests sweeping Russian society reached the doors of the conservatory. Students there joined their fellow university students in staging a major strike, leading to mass arrests and a paralyzing political showdown inside the school. Among the student revolutionaries were several Jewish students of Rimsky-Korsakov, among them Mikhail Gnesin. The government response was swift and unforgiving. Gnesin and his coconspirators were expelled from the school, albeit temporarily; the Jews among them were also forced to leave the city and return to their hometowns in the Pale of Settlement.[20]

From Russian Politics to Jewish Culture

The decade before 1905 had witnessed the rise of modern Jewish political movements in the Russian Empire, as nationalist and socialist organizations began to compete vigorously for the support of the Jewish masses. The Revolution of 1905 only intensified this chaotic, dynamic process of Jewish political mobilization. Over the course of 1905 and 1906, Zionists, Bundists, Jewish Diaspora nationalists (Simon Dubnow's Folks-Partey), and Jewish liberals (the Evreiskaia narodnaia gruppa) traded increasingly intense polemical blows, attacking one another's leaders and political platforms from every conceivable angle. Spurring this conflict was the fierce pursuit for seats in the state elections to the Russian Duma. The promise of full Jewish civil emancipation and political integration into Russian society loomed tantalizingly close, generating an almost messianic sense of expectation among the Jewish intelligentsia.[21]

As quickly as they came, however, hopes for groundbreaking political change vanished. In the run-up to the Third Duma in the fall of 1907, the tsarist government manipulated the electoral requirements to undermine any possibility of real parliamentary politics or reform. The Jewish parties were outmaneuvered by a desperate autocratic regime willing to embrace reactionary nationalist and antisemitic measures in an attempt to pacify its riotous population. Zionists and Bundists now found themselves the targets of direct government attacks, while the broader promise of Jewish emancipation disappeared.

In place of politics, Russian Jews switched rapidly instead to questions of culture. From debates about political representation, national autonomy, and self-defense, Jewish organizations from across the ideological spectrum began to concentrate on creating Jewish national culture. As part of this dramatic turn, the political leadership—nationalists, socialists, and liberals alike—began to cooperate in a new fashion. Collective energies were now devoted to a new focus on Jewish "organic work." The rise of this new trend was evident beginning in late 1907, when work began immediately on a number of new or restructured Jewish cultural societies. Over the course of the next year a host of organizations were launched in St. Petersburg, including the Jewish Literary Society, the Society for Lovers of the Hebrew Language, the Jewish Historical-Ethnographic Society, the Betsalel Society for Jewish Art, and the Society for Jewish Folk Music. By the end of the decade, some seventy such new cultural societies had emerged in St. Petersburg.[22]

What explains this sudden shift from politics to culture? On the simplest level, the state allowed it. New government regulations instituted in 1905 and 1906 simplified the Russian legal process and expanded the possibility for cultural societies, public voluntary activity, and public assembly. Partly a strategic concession to revolutionists' political demands, partly a tactic to placate various restive minorities, the expanded legalization of civil society resulted in a huge flowering of cultural, social, and artistic groups across the entirety of Russia. But the broad facts of sweeping social and legal change do not answer the question of how profound internal political divisions and bitter personal rivalries subsided within a matter of months. Did "culture" simply substitute for stifled Jewish political aspirations in the post-1905 period? Or did it serve as a more conscious rejection of politics in favor of art and identity?[23]

For the contemporary observer Dubnow, the post-1905 cultural renaissance was neither. Rather he saw the explosion of new Jewish cultural life as a natural result of the general "advance of national self-consciousness" within Russian Jewry that dated back to the 1880s. Recent scholars have argued similarly that the embrace of Jewish national culture reflected a gradual, decades-long phenomenon, partially stifled by tsarist censorship policies and then released—and exacerbated—by the 1905 revolution. But this does not go quite far enough. For to appreciate the meaning of this cultural renaissance we have to see both precisely how the idea of Jewish national culture bridged recently hostile Jewish political camps and why it resonated no less strongly among the acculturated and heretofore Russified Jewish intelligentsia.[24]

Towards the end of 1907, a small circle of friends led by Gnesin, Shkliar, composer Solomon B. Rosowsky (1878–1962), and pianist Lev (Aryeh) Nesvizhskii (1885–1985) began to plan a new Jewish musical organization. Rosowsky knew Gnesin from Rimsky-Korsakov's composition class and had joined him as a student protest leader in 1905. He also had the distinction of being the son of the early conservatory graduate Cantor Borukh-Leyb Rosowsky. Raised in Riga, Rosowsky had grown up in a musically cosmopolitan home, where the music of Wagner and Strauss was popular and the composer Jean Sibelius was a frequent guest. Initially he followed his two older brothers into law by enrolling at the University of Kiev, later switching to music in St. Petersburg. Shkliar had graduated in 1904 but remained in the city as choral director of the St. Petersburg Main Synagogue. The fourth member of the circle, Nesvizhskii, also the son of a cantor, was nicknamed "Little Herzl" for his passionate Zionist beliefs. He had also recently graduated and begun to develop a strong reputation as an impressive concert soloist.[25]

The immediate initiative for the group's organization came from Shkliar and Nesvizhskii, both of whom aspired to create a more successful version of the failed Kinor tsion and Ha-tikvah groups. The duo received active encouragement from the St. Petersburg Zionist establishment, including the newspaper *Razsvet* (Dawn), whose editor, Abram Idelson, had supported Engel's musical efforts a decade earlier in Moscow. But Zionism alone would not attract the kind of broad base necessary to sustain a major cultural organization. The group knew, Gnesin recalled later, that the pre-1905 attempts to organize St. Petersburg's Jewish musicians along national lines had failed precisely because Zionism was viewed by most Jewish conservatory students as too chauvinist and ideologically rigid. He himself had been one of those who earlier rebuffed overtures from the "extreme nationalists." As an active socialist revolutionary, he simply could not stomach the way the Zionists rejected "everything in a person not formally related to Judaism, everything that didn't bear the mark of Palestinophilism." So the proponents of the new Jewish cultural nationalism reached out to a diverse group of fellow Jewish musicians with an inclusive ethos designed to accommodate the complicated, evolving Jewish national identities of their peers—and themselves.[26] One such individual recruited by Gnesin in the early planning stages was Lazare Iosifovich Saminsky (1882–1959) (fig. 8). Born into a family of longstanding Odessa Jewish merchants, he early displayed a prodigious intellect, studying multiple European languages, philosophy, and advanced mathematics. By age sixteen he had written a commentary on Spinoza's *Ethics* and translated Descartes' *Meditations* from Latin into Russian. After graduating from a commercial lyceum in Odessa, Saminsky moved to Moscow to study composition at the Moscow Philharmonic Music School. Then in 1905 he was expelled for socialist political activities. Relocating to St. Petersburg, he enrolled simultaneously as a mathematics and philosophy major at the university and a composition and conducting major at the conservatory.

Saminsky later recalled the contradictions in his identity and politics at that point. He readily denounced his fellow Jewish musicians for their sin of national "assimilation." Yet he also resisted the overt Zionism of his friends Rosowsky and Nesvizhskii, and he recoiled openly from the "fanatically Jewish" nationalism of Shkliar. At the same time Saminsky, despite his revolutionary politics, felt a proud sense of Russian patriotism in connection with the recently ended Russo-Japanese War: "With all the protest that arose in my young self, with all my sense of injured justice, with all the Jewish nationalist or Zionist emotions new to me, with all my loathing of the tzarist police rule, I still remained a son of Russia—full of worries for her honor, well being, [and] place in the world."[27]

Saminsky's complex tangle of political affiliations and cultural attachments was typical of many of the early leaders of the group. David A. Chernomordikov (1869–1947), for instance, was a Baku-born graduate in composition from the St. Petersburg Conservatory and a music critic and editor at a number of well-known St. Petersburg journals. He was also an open member of the Bolshevik faction in the Russian Social Democrats. Chernomordikov's political activity even extended to music. In 1906 he produced the *Pervyi sbornik revoliutsionnykh pesen* (First Collection of Revolutionary Songs), a book that featured the first Russian-language version of the "Internationale" to be published in Russia. Yet Bolshevik ideology did not prevent him from embracing the idea of Jewish national music, as well as writing and editing the music section of the monumental Russian-language *Evreiskaia entsyklopediia* (Jewish Encyclopedia) issued between 1906 and 1911.[28]

Saminsky and Chernomordikov were but two of a broad cross-section of St. Petersburg Jews drawn into the ranks of the Society for Jewish Folk

Figure 8. Lazare Saminsky. From Albert Weisser, *The Modern Renaissance of Jewish Music* (1954), courtesy of the Bloch Publishing Company.

Music's early leadership. Liberals, Zionists, Bundists, Social Democrats, Diaspora nationalists, and other political variants were all comfortably represented. Moreover, the technical and legal framework for the group was provided by a representative of the oldest Russian Jewish communal organization, the Society for the Promotion of Enlightenment among the Jews of Russia (Obshchestvo dlia rastropranenii prosveshcheniia mezhdu evreiami v Rossii, or OPE). The OPE's St. Petersburg leadership had long been dominated by a coterie of Jewish bankers, merchants, and lawyers, all staunch advocates of political integration and acculturation as the solution to the Jewish question in Russia. In the first decade of the twentieth century, however, the OPE leadership had begun to take a more active interest in the idea of Jewish national culture. At the center of this institutional transformation was one of the most important prerevolutionary Jewish political leaders: lawyer and political activist Genrikh B. Sliozberg (1863–1937). Beyond his work in Jewish communal affairs as the right-hand man of the OPE's leader, Baron Horace Gintsburg, Sliozberg was also the principal architect of the entire post-1881 Jewish political strategy centered on the Russian legal system. He and his cohort of liberal elites pursued political integration and fought against discriminatory government legislation and antisemitic violence through lawsuits, trials, and propaganda based on Russia's own laws. In the years of the first Russian Revolution he had channeled many of his political energies into the liberal Constitutional Democratic Party (the Kadets). From 1907 onward he played a defining role in establishing the majority of the new Jewish cultural societies in St. Petersburg. More than simply a pragmatic leader drawn to a political platform of national unity, he was also an enthusiastic proponent of Jewish culture. When it came to music, there was a specific reason for his strong cultural identification. Sliozberg had spent his childhood in the 1860s in the Lithuanian shtetl of Naliboki listening to Solomon Rosowsky's own grandfather, a Hasid, sing *zmires* (Sabbath table songs) and Hasidic nigunim. So closely were the Rosowskys and the Sliozbergs connected in the shtetl, and so strong was the impression that the music made on the future Kadet leader, that nearly seventy years later he could still vividly recall the sounds of the songs he had heard as a child.[29]

Wagner's Ghost: Redefining the Jewish Musician

In November 1909 an article appeared in the pages of *Razsvet* discussing the paradox of Jews and music. "They say that we Jews are the most musical nation, that the violin is our national instrument; we have given the world composers of genius; we have more professional musicians among us than any other people," the author, writing under the pseudonym M. Nagen (a pun on the Hebrew word *ha-menagen*, or musician) noted proudly, before lamenting, "And at the same time, you will hardly find another nation whose national music has been so much neglected as ours." While other nations had created symphonies and operas out of their native musical traditions, he continued, Jewish composers had barely touched their own treasure trove of folk song. Instead, enticed by the folk sounds of other traditions, the younger generation of Jews had readily succumbed to musical "assimilation." The "most musical nation," it turned out, had no "national music" of its own. Undeterred by this diagnosis, Nagen's article ended on a note of hope. With the appearance of the Society for Jewish Folk Music, he claimed, it was now finally possible to create a Jewish national music. All Jewish musicians in Russia should therefore join in its efforts.[30]

In many respects, the idea of a Jewish organization devoted to music simply paralleled the other Jewish cultural organizations then in the process of formation in St. Petersburg. How different, after all, was music from literature or visual art when it came to modern Jewish culture? The same general ingredients of secular ethnicity and Romantic nationalism could be found mixed together in the various attempts to generate Jewish literature, Jewish art, Jewish scholarship, and so forth. On the other hand, the particular dilemmas of Jewish musicians in confronting Russian antisemitism and philosemitism burdened the group with a larger philosophical mission. As Nagen's article suggested, Russian Jews looked to the Society for Jewish Folk Music to do more than simply promote Jewish music. It was expected to shoulder the responsibility for normalizing the entire relationship between Jews and music in Russia and European society more broadly.

As a result, right from the start in 1907, difficult questions about Jews and music dominated the group's planning discussions. Was Jewish music best defined as music composed by Jews? Or did the composer's identity matter less than the use of Jewish folkloric material in the composition? What role did liturgical music play in a modern secular national culture? This last question nearly split the group. Some favored a focus on "liturgical" (*dukhovnaia*) music, others "secular" (*svetskaia*) folk song. The issue was initially resolved, Gnesin later recalled, by pragmatically defining Jewish music in broad, inclusive terms. Henceforth "Jewish national music" (*evreiskaia narodnaia muzkya*) would be taken to include both the liturgical and secular repertoires.[31]

Behind the thorny questions of how to define Jewish music lay the much deeper, vexing problem of Jewish musicianship itself. To begin with, were Jewish musicians the only artists capable of creating Jewish music? This was not merely an exercise in abstract theory. For the idea of art music on Jewish national themes had also captured the imagination of non-Jewish musicians. One such person was Vasilii A. Zolotarev (1873–1964), a fellow Rimsky-Korsakov classmate. Shortly after graduating in 1900, he had composed an *Evreiskaia rapsodiia* (Jewish Rhapsody), a one-movement orchestral work based on Jewish folk melodies transcribed from klezmer musicians during a summer visit to the Pale of Settlement. Zolotarev's piece even premiered at an IRMO concert in St. Petersburg in 1901. Wildly popular, the work went on to a 1906 premiere in New York City and a featured performance at the Society for Jewish Folk Music's own first major public concert in St. Petersburg in 1909.[32]

The popularity of Zolotarev's composition led writers in both the Russian and Jewish press to note the irony that "the only Jewish symphony" in existence had been written not by a Jew but by a young Russian "bureaucrat." Implied in this observation was a question: Why hadn't the Jews themselves taken the lead in creating their own national art music? One answer was supplied by the Russian opera soprano Maria Olenina-d'Alheim (1869–1970), another non-Jewish musician who in the first decade of the twentieth century publicly trumpeted a complicated philosemitic musical philosophy similar to Rimsky-Korsakov's. Year after year, in her popular lecture-concerts held at the Dom Pesni (House of Song) that she founded in Moscow, Olenina-d'Alheim performed folk songs of various nationalities. She lavished particular attention on the Jewish repertoire, openly promoting her own candidate as the father of Jewish national music: the late Russian composer Modest Mussorgsky. In fact, she explained in her lectures, Mussorgsky had accomplished for Jewish music something no previous Jewish composer (Meyerbeer, Mendelssohn, or Rubinstein) had succeeded in doing:

> Once in the countryside Mussorgsky had some Jewish neighbors. In the course of their daily burden of life's troubles, these poor people had lost the artistic sense of their nation. Sometimes they sang. But their melodies, with the halting rhythms that resemble a fearful babble, with vague outlines, lost their simple, supreme beauty. . . . In these degenerate songs, Mussorgsky succeeded in discovering their original beauty and relaying it to us. I believe very strongly that the day is near when the Jews will finally renounce their "conquest" . . . of the established forms of commercial art, the art of the Grand Operas and Music Halls, and will search for their own national spirit.[33]

There was no doubt that Olenina-d'Alheim regarded the prospect of Jewish folk music returning to its national splendor as a positive development. Elsewhere she even remarked that, "thanks to Mussorgsky, I have even come to feel myself a little bit of a Jewess." But interwoven with her philosemitism was a darker, more negative image of Jewish music and musicians. Incoherent, degenerate, misshapen, savage—Olenina-d'Alheim's depiction of Jewish folk song resembled the kind of crude attacks on the language and physical appearance of Jews that had been common in central Europe since the early nineteenth century. In part, her imagery borrowed directly from Mussorgsky's own curious form of antisemitism, which combined positive perceptions of ancient Hebrew music with harshly negative representations of contemporary Jews themselves. Likewise, her image of Jewish musicians as capitalist peddlers of cheap, worthless entertainment music echoed aspects of Richard Wagner's own antisemitic thesis.[34]

In fact Wagner's ideas were gaining new ground in Russian musical circles in the first decade of the twentieth century. While references to his writings could be found in the Russian musical press continually from the late 1880s onwards, the dawn of the twentieth century witnessed a new level of interest in his cultural theories among the artistic intelligentsia, occasioned in part by the rise of Russian modernism. The chief Russian advocate of Wagnerian antisemitism at the time was Emil Medtner (1872–1936), a figure well known as the principal music critic of the Russian symbolist movement. Over the course of 1907 and 1908, Medtner published a series of articles in the symbolist art journal *Zolotoe runo* (Golden Fleece), extending Wagner's nineteenth-century diagnosis of the Jewish onslaught on German culture to twentieth-century Russia. He described a plague of "little Jew boys from Lodz" ruining Russian and German music with their "Asiatic" and "barbarous" ways. Under the influence of the leading European antisemitic propagandist of the day, Houston Stewart Chamberlain, Medtner injected a new kind of modern racialist language into Russian musical discourse. Once present, it proved extremely hard to avoid. Similarly, the *Novoe vremia* critic Mikhail M. Ivanov identified visiting musicians from abroad by their Jewish nationality. When Gustav Mahler's Fifth Symphony was premiered in St. Petersburg in 1913, Ivanov attacked the work as "decadent" foreign "rubbish" by a "Viennese Jew."[35]

Even those who explicitly denounced Medtner's antisemitic ideas internalized much of the same racialist thinking. The composer Alexander Scriabin, for example, publicly condemned Medtner's writings yet still had no trouble casually remarking to a student that "among Jews there were hardly any composers," only performers. In his opinion they embodied the essence of a noncreative, mercantilist, "physiological," and finally "materialistic approach to art." Unlike Medtner, however, Scriabin viewed the notion that Jews were racially predisposed to be performers as a net positive result for music. "Without them," he once confided to the young Russian musicologist Leonid Sabaneev, "music would die out." Furthermore, he had no trouble specifying a Jewish reverse *numerus clausus* for proper symphonic music: "For an orchestra to sound right, it must have no less than 15 percent Jews in the string and horn sections."[36]

The hostile ghost of Wagner thus loomed large for the early leaders of the Society of Jewish Folk Music, in both subtle and explicit ways. From 1907 onward, the *Ring* cycle was staged each year at the Mariinsky Theater, accompanied by a steady stream of articles, books, and translations of Wagner's writings. The year 1908 saw the publication in St. Petersburg of the first Russian translation of "Judaism in Music." The blunt force of European musical antisemitism and the discomfiting phenomenon of Russian musical philosemitism only reinforced the ethnic logic of Jewish nationalism, which demanded that Jewish musicians devote themselves to producing their own national art.[37]

The St. Petersburg group did not shy from acknowledging the spur of antisemitism in their work. Gnesin noted the irony that the Russian "special style of antisemitism" deserved partial credit for bringing Jewish national music into existence. The composer Mikhail (Moisei) A. Milner (1886–1953) kept a portrait of Wagner prominently displayed in his room to remind himself that "We are surrounded by enemies." Saminsky went even further in his published writings of the time, invoking Wagner to denounce "assimilated" Jewish musicians, past and present, as little more than cultural parasites, incapable of producing authentic music. He differed from Wagner, he explained, only in that he saw a solution to the Jewish artistic dilemma. By embracing Jewish "national melody," the contemporary Jewish composer could thereby redeem himself and rebut the antisemitic critique.[38]

The new Jewish musical society these men began in 1908 represented a nationalist answer to the problem of Jews and music in Russian and European society. It was, in Saminsky's words, less a new "page in the history of Jewish music" than in the history of "Jewish musicians," the result of "a movement that drove Jewish musicians [*evrei-muzykanty*] to turn to their own native art." The word *evrei-muzykant*, literally translated as "Jew-musician," was the result of a common Russian locution in which two nouns were linked together to denote a compound identity, as in *evrei-kupets* (Jew-merchant) or *evrei-vrach* (Jew-doctor). In the case of music, it suggested something stronger than a mere musician who happened to be Jewish, but instead a fixed social character. The term carried an especially heavy negative connotation within the early twentieth-century atmosphere of Russian antisemitism. The Society for Jewish Folk Music's leaders aimed to transform *evrei-*

muzykanty (Jew-musicians) into *evreiskie kompozitory* (Jewish composers). From an ethnically linked professional, they hoped, the Jewish musician would come to symbolize a national artist.[39]

The semantic and philosophical complexities of this process were reflected in vigorous early debates over how to define the group's goals and membership. One of the thorniest questions centered on whether to include non-Jews in their mission. The final, published version of the group's charter stated that "the Society for Jewish Folk Music aims consist of the active pursuit of the study and development of Jewish folk music (religious and secular), by means of collecting examples of folk creativity, their artistic arrangement, and their propagation in society, as well as supporting Jewish composers and other musical activists." Yet in the planning meetings some insisted on excluding these "other musical activists," that is, non-Jews, in favor of musicians of "Jewish nationality" (*evreiskaia natsionalnost*), while others called for including all active friends of Jewish music "without regard to nationality." Even screening out the question of nationality could not resolve the problem of Jewish converts to Christianity. Many Russian Jewish musicians had converted to advance their careers yet still lent their personal support to Jewish cultural causes, including such well-known contemporary figures as Leopold Auer, Simeon Bellison, David Krein, and Serge Koussevitzky. In the post-1905 years, the ambiguous legal status of these converts remained a subject of controversy and political debate in the Duma. Attitudes among the leaders of the Jewish cultural renaissance were often less equivocal and less forgiving. In preparing his ethnographic expedition, for instance, S. Ansky wrote to his fellow writer Haim Nahman Bialik that he would consider inviting any and all kinds of Jews to participate, even if they had never previously associated with Jewish communal and cultural life in any way, except for "apostates."[40]

The society's final official charter chose the language of awkward and inconsistent compromise. On one hand, no nationality or religion requirement was specified. Consequently, theoretically both Jewish and non-Jewish musicians could become members and beneficiaries. On the other hand, the charter also announced a prize competition limited to "Jewish composers." Moreover, although never officially codified, the group adopted an informal, tacit policy of refusing to publish or perform compositions by Jewish converts.[41]

The sensitivity to language was not only a response to the delicate questions about the religious and national boundaries of Russian Jewry. It was also a natural reaction to the imperial government's strict regulation of all public cultural activities of any kind, especially those associated with national minorities. Such was the case with the group's choice of name. Originally the musicians had considered calling themselves either the "Jewish Musical Society" (Evreiskoe muzykalnoe obshchestvo) or the "Society for Jewish Music" (Obshchestvo evreiskoi muzyki). However, on March 4, 1908, the day on which Solomon Rosowsky led a small delegation to present the charter to the St. Petersburg city governor, Major General Daniil V. Drachevskii, for registration, he found himself forced to defend both the group's name and its raison d'être. Drachevskii, a member of the ultraconservative, antisemitic Union of Russian People, demanded of the group, "Jewish music? Does Jewish music exist?" In a deft reply, Rosowsky drew on his legal training to deliver an impromptu *apologia pro vita sua* for Jewish music. He argued that Jewish music had been written both by Jewish composers such as Rubinstein, Halévy, and Meyerbeer and also by the great Russian composers—Glinka, Balakirev, Rimsky-Korsakov, and Mussorgsky. The latter had even chosen to have the Jewish folk melody he used in his "Joshua" cantata (*Iisus Navin*) engraved on his own tombstone. Was there no better proof for the existence of Jewish music?

Rosowsky's comments stressed that Jewish music was not limited to the output of insular political nationalists akin to the Baltic, Ukrainian, and Polish choral societies that had emerged as part of their respective nationalist movements. Rather, this was a musical tradition with deep roots and a legitimate place in the grand imperial tradition of Russian culture. Ironically, though, the city governor's Jewish musical associations were far more parochial and prosaic. Halfway through Rosowsky's speech, the official interrupted him: "Yes, yes. I also recall now a Jewish melody, which I heard once at a Jewish wedding in Odessa. But that was a folk melody. I think that your society should be called the 'Society for Jewish Folk Music.'" Crossing out the name and quickly substituting the Russian official's "suggestion," Rosowsky handed back the document. Approval was granted on the spot.[42] In the 1850s a young Anton Rubinstein had been challenged by a St. Petersburg government official to prove that he was a Russian citizen through his music. Now, sixty years later, a second-generation Jewish graduate of the St. Petersburg Conservatory found himself turning to another city bureaucrat to prove the existence of Jewish music.

Building National Community through Culture

The first general meeting of the society was held on November 30, 1908, at the St. Petersburg OPE community school building on Offitserskaia Street (later known as Dekabristov), the de facto physical center of the St.

Petersburg Jewish establishment. For the next several years, this location also served as the site for administrative meetings and small concert performances. Appropriately enough, given the location, the presiding chair of the meeting was the OPE representative, Sliozberg, now officially designated as the group's legal counsel. After a slate of speeches on the group's genesis and goals, one hundred new members were registered and a board was elected. The leadership reflected the diversity of the St. Petersburg Jewish musical elite. Not surprisingly, the core segment came almost exclusively from the ranks of recent graduates of Rimsky-Korsakov's class. Along with organizers Saminsky, Gnesin, Rosowsky, Shkliar, and Chernomordikov, these included Milner, Alexander M. Zhitomirsky (1881–1937), and Peysakh (Pavel) R. Lvov (1880–1913). Nearly all these individuals shared a background in the world of synagogue music as sons or grandsons of cantors and *ba'alei tefillah* (lay prayer leaders) or as childhood *meshoyrim* (choristers) themselves.[43]

These young musicians were joined by more senior members of the St. Petersburg musical establishment. One such individual was the society's first president, Joseph (Iosif) S. Tomars (1867–1934), a leading star of the Russian opera stage and a voice professor at the conservatory. The son of a retired Jewish soldier who had settled in St. Petersburg in the 1860s, Tomars had grown up with little contact with Jewish community. Indeed his first music teacher had been his father's close friend, a Russian Orthodox choir director. As a student at the St. Petersburg Conservatory during the politically tumultuous years of the late 1880s, he had found a mentor in Anton Rubinstein. Despite years of success on the Russian and European opera stages, Tomars continued to face humiliating legal obstacles to his career. As a Jew, he was at various times denied roles at St. Petersburg's Mariinsky Theater and Moscow's Bolshoi Theater. By 1908, when he joined Nesvizhskii and Rosowsky in registering with the new society, he had become an eager advocate of Jewish national music. Other important local musical figures included the critic and publisher Isai Knorozovskii and the Imperial Opera artist Alexander M. Davydov (né Levinson, 1872–1944). Many nonmusical Jewish cultural figures also played active roles in the early leadership, including the writers S. Ansky and Mark Rivesman, and the engineer Israel S. Okun (1877–1941), who was also a prominent member of the Bund's executive leadership. Okun's political radicalism did not prevent him from serving dutifully as the longtime secretary of both the Society for Jewish Folk Music and the Jewish Historical-Ethnographic Society.[44]

One of the most striking demographic facts regarding the pre–World War I Russian conservatory was that well over half of the Jewish students were female. In St. Petersburg in the 1909–10 school year, for instance, there were 413 female Jewish students and 342 males enrolled (out of a total of 1,762). With a policy of open enrollment to men and women alike in place from the St. Petersburg Conservatory's founding, the IRMO music schools and conservatories were among the few Russian institutions of higher education consistently accessible to women from the 1860s through World War I. The Jewish female presence was overwhelmingly composed of piano and voice students (in a roughly three-to-one ratio). These women tended to hail not from cantorial or klezmer families but from the ranks of the urban Jewish middle class. Compared with their male counterparts, Jewish female music students were nearly twice as likely to have acquired advanced educations and the coveted residence rights (because of parental legal status) before entering the conservatory. Inspired by pan-European (especially German) notions of education and art as tools for moral edification and embourgeoisement, they turned to the study of music.[45]

As a result of these social differences, Jewish women often applied their musical educations to Jewish-related philanthropic and cultural activities. Several such women served on the society's board: Fania Vaisenberg, a trained vocalist and wife of a St. Petersburg attorney, served as the group's early liaison to the city's newspapers; Elizaveta (Leah) Babus, wife of a First Guild merchant from Kharkov and an active organizer of local Zionist cultural activities, provided her Sezzhinskaia Street apartment as the group's official legal address for several years from 1910 onward. They were joined by one of the wealthiest and best-known Jewish women of St. Petersburg, Sophie Benenson, wife of the leading tycoon Grigorii Benenson. Prominent in her own right for her Wednesday afternoon salons ("the talk of Jewish Petersburg"), held at the family's home on the upper floors of the Volkonsky Palace on the Moika, she served for a number of years as a board member and treasurer.[46]

Given the diverse class backgrounds and professional paths of the leadership and membership, the more elite artistic aims of the composers naturally clashed with the broader cultural mission of public education and communal engagement. At the outset, for instance, the society announced a wide and ambitious range of activities involving publishing (sheet music, "theoretical works," and a journal), public performances (concerts, lectures, operas, school programs), along with a choir and orchestra, music library, and prize competition for Jewish composers. Not all of these programs came to pass. One reason was that the leaders decided to form a specific membership subgroup comprised principally of its composers. Known as the "musical committee," this cohort dominated programming decisions. They also shifted the focus in the organization's opening years from enlightening the masses to educating themselves. An internal educational circle (*kruzhok*) was started, and lectures on "the history and theory of Jewish song and music" quickly became a staple of meetings.[47]

The same orientation inward prevailed in the semiprivate concerts known as "musical meetings" (*muzykalnye sobraniia*). The first event took place on January 21, 1909, at the city's Hall of the Society of Civil Engineers. Following opening remarks, a small ad hoc chorus conducted by Shkliar performed his arrangements of Yiddish folk songs, and Saminsky played a piano arrangement of Jewish folk melodies written by Ilia Aisberg. Attendance at this event, like most other subsequent musical meetings, was primarily limited to the society's members or invited guests. One reason for this policy was the contemporary legal situation, which required official government permission to host any "public" gatherings. Beyond the technical reasons, however, these private musical events were evidently intended to serve as an elite, intimate artistic studio at which the composers could comfortably discuss and experiment with their ideas of Jewish art music.[48]

Even with their elite orientation, the society's composers still subscribed to the stated mission of taking their message to the broader Jewish public—and as artists they craved an audience. Winning the backing of the city's Jewish intelligentsia and upper classes and recruiting members from among the huge community of university and conservatory students therefore still represented important immediate goals. But it was not merely a question of staging open concerts for a willing public. In order to ensure the success of its national cultural mission, the society found itself charged with creating that public—a new kind of Jewish musical audience—among St. Petersburg Jewry.

National Music in Search of an Audience

In December 1906 the St. Petersburg Conservatory played host to a highly unusual holiday concert. Rather than Tchaikovsky's *Nutcracker Suite* or an evening of Russian Christmas carols, the concert hall was filled with the sounds of Warsaw star cantor Gershon Sirota (1874–1943), the "King of Cantors" and the "Jewish Caruso," backed by the St. Petersburg Main Synagogue choir. The event was a Hanukkah concert sponsored by the St. Petersburg Jewish community. A reviewer for the *Russkaia muzykalnaia gazeta* (Russian Musical Gazette) noted the odd contrast between the yarmulke-clad performers solemnly intoning "a spiritual program imbued with a heavy mood of prayer" and the eager, cheering audience, which "applauded, stamped their feet, and prayed (!) for an encore."[49] The audience's excited reaction was but a hint of what was soon to come.

St. Petersburg's wealthy Jewish elite had long played an active role in the capital's musical life as concertgoers, amateur musicians, and arts patrons. Families such as the Gintsburgs held chamber music evenings in their homes and provided financial support to talented young Jewish musicians. Then, at the turn of the century, new kinds of public Jewish cultural events began to appear. The growing St. Petersburg Jewish middle class and intelligentsia now flocked to Jewish "concert balls" and "literary-musical evenings" that included Jewish opera soloists and readings by writers such as Shimon Frug and S. Ansky, along with tableaux vivants and dancing.[50]

This new Jewish public formed a natural audience for the society's concerts. The general membership rolls suggest the presence of these groups. Among the early members to join were leading Jewish businessmen such as Grigorii Benenson, Mark Varshavskii, and Miron Kreinin and Jewish Duma members Leon Bramson, Maksim Vinaver, and Mikhail Sheftel. The long list of Jewish intellectuals featured scholar-activists Mikhail Mysh and Isaak Markon, historian and bibliographer David Maggid, and Ilia Efron, the founder of the Brockhaus and Efron publishing house. Membership grew steadily over the first few years, from just over two hundred in 1911 to roughly four hundred by 1912.[51]

To be sure, some factions initially offered resistance to the very idea of public concert performances of Jewish art music. Solomon Rosowsky recalled bitterly that opposition came from various quarters: "The assimilated Jewish intelligentsia with its arrogant contempt of the primitive forms of folk art, sneered at our delight in the simple little songs in which we discovered ever new fascination." At the same time, the Orthodox religious establishment initially opposed the "injury" to Jewish music that would come from mixing folk songs and liturgical melodies with "Russian" arrangements. Even the famous Odessa cantor Pinḥas Minkovskii, who had earlier called for the study of Jewish folk song, initially chided Rosowsky: "Are you not ashamed of yourself, a university man like you, to take an interest in those kitchen maid songs?"[52] Still, on the whole, the St. Petersburg public's reactions were intensely positive, as evidenced from the first major concert event hosted by the society on April 12, 1909, at the Malyi Zal (Small Hall) of the St. Petersburg Conservatory (fig. 9).

To stage the event, billed as an "Evening of Jewish Song," the St. Petersburg musicians imported the ethnographic concert format of Joel Engel, along with the man himself, from Moscow. By 1909 Engel had presented

Figure 9. Program cover for a 1909 Society for Jewish Folk Music concert. Russian Institute for the History of the Arts.

concert hall lecture-performances of Jewish music across the length and breadth of Russia. His opening remarks, now honed to an engaging stock speech about the dramatic origins and importance of modern Jewish music, were a near verbatim repetition of his last major speech in St. Petersburg, eight years earlier. Nevertheless, his talk proved a hit with the audience at the inaugural concert. Since none of the St. Petersburg composers were ready to unveil their compositions to the larger public, Nesvizhskii and several other musicians performed a set comprised exclusively of Engel's music. The fourteen numbers, all premieres, were new arrangements of Yiddish folk songs and Hasidic nigunim. While the Moscow composer was once again careful to note that all his harmonizations had been achieved "without altering the [folk] melodies," he now gave himself license to expand his creative palette in terms of the instrumentation. Moving beyond his standard violin-piano or voice-piano pairings, Engel offered unusual new combinations, such as the familiar Yiddish lullaby "Shloyf, mayn kind" (Sleep, My Child) arranged for four-voice choir, string quartet, and piano and "A Habadisher nigun" (A Habad Melody), scored for violin, cello, organ, and piano.[53]

The concert was an overwhelming success, easily surpassing the society's expectations both in terms of attendance and performance quality. Detailed accounts of the event appeared in newspapers ranging from the Yiddish daily *Der fraynd* (The Friend) to the Russian liberal organ *Rech* (Speech) and specialized music journals such as the *Russkaia muzykalnaia gazeta*. While most press coverage focused on the celebrity of Engel and the "curious" phenomenon of seeing and hearing Jewish folk music transformed into European-style art music on a concert stage, it was the pseudonymous *Razsvet* critic M. Nagen who noted an equally important drama taking place offstage: "You should have seen these Petersburg businessmen, doctors, writers, and student dandies. You should have seen how they listened with such attention to these familiar, long-forgotten sounds to which their native mother perhaps rocked them long ago somewhere in a remote shtetl in the Pale and which yielded their places to new sounds and words, to understand what strength and power still lurks in our national creativity, how it is strong enough in one instant to wrest the lost sons of the people from foreign embraces and return them to their native breast."[54]

There was no doubt an element of exaggeration in the critic's passionate account, perhaps explained by his paper's sometime Zionist persuasion. If, however, his psychosexual claim that Jewish national music could return "lost sons" to their mother's milk was overstated, his basic characterization of the concert's deep effect on audiences was not. Other newspaper accounts described a "holiday" atmosphere with roaring, "stormy applause" for both the lecture and the musical performances. In countless subsequent descriptions of the society's public concerts, critics repeatedly referenced the emotional intensity and extreme enthusiasm of the audience reactions. The January 1910 concert was a case in point. Roughly three thousand attended the event at the St. Petersburg Hall of the Nobility, the city's largest and most ornate concert space. With hundreds more turned away, it was reportedly the largest Jewish cultural gathering the city had ever witnessed. The event drew such wild applause that, according to one account, "the fervent mood of the public sometimes threatened to spill out of control." At one point the ovations were so great that the electric house lights had to be lowered to signal the crowds to silence. "Festive, raucous applause" and endless requests for encores proved standard. Soon the society would speak casually of the "typical ecstasy" that its concerts produced among audiences.[55]

What were the feelings behind these powerful audience reactions to the music? M. Nagen himself suggested one answer in another review, this time of a 1910 concert. Music, he argued, could penetrate emotional spaces that other forms of culture could not, adding that the "compelling, spontaneous folk spirit was irresistible even to the half-assimilated soul of the Petersburg Jew, who typically responds so little to anything Jewish."[56] He was only half correct. The music did indeed generate strong feelings. But mixed with national pride, cultural curiosity, and a range of other more inchoate emotions was another distinctive phenomenon: nostalgia.

In a world of rapid, massive change, music's qualities of immediacy, intimacy, and expressiveness made it a perfect vehicle for vivid Jewish recollection and longing for the vanishing world of tradition. For some, this meant memories of childhoods spent in the synagogue. Saminsky wrote in a 1909 review of a concert of liturgical music that the cantorial solos stirred up the "most tender and wonderful . . . memories of naive childhood faith and childhood joy" in an educated Jewish adult of lapsed Orthodox faith such as himself. For others, the music was associated less with beliefs left behind than with childhoods spent in shtetls. As one member wrote of the composer Peysakh Lvov's folk song arrangements, "Listening to his pieces, or even playing them myself, I fell strongly under the influence of the sounds of these chords, which carried me gently back to the good old times. It seemed that I was in an old Jewish place, where peace, tranquility and quiet reigned."[57]

Such music-induced memories hinged on a strong sense of cultural distance and estrangement from traditional Judaism. Yet given the high degree of acculturation in the Russified Jewish middle class and intelligentsia of St. Petersburg, for many in the audience the concerts represented their first direct exposure to traditional Jewish music. After all, the average Petersburg

Jew, wrote Shaul Gintsburg at the time, had "never even heard Jewish jargon or song" before in his or her life. What cultural nostalgia could audiences feel in listening to such music for the first time? Perhaps paradoxically, however, precisely those Jews furthest removed from the traditional culture of Ashkenazi Jewish music had the strongest emotional reaction to the performances. Just as in the case of Engel, the further the distance—real or imagined—from the shtetl and synagogue, the greater the emotional hold of folk-based music on modern Russian Jews. For the young Jewish composers and new Jewish audiences in early twentieth-century St. Petersburg, music provided a route back to a past they had not necessarily ever known themselves.[58]

Although the music transported listeners to faraway places of the imagination, the Society for Jewish Folk Music remained concerned that they not forget where they were in the present. In fact, the choice of venues figured prominently in defining the aesthetic image of Jewish music as modern high art. To create a true Jewish public meant more than recruiting to Jewish-themed events acculturated Jews who might otherwise frequent Russian concerts. Nor was it simply a question of tapping a ready-made, receptive audience that would recognize and applaud its own national folk songs in their new more formal, elaborate guise. What was really at stake was a reinvention of the aesthetics of Jewish listening. Through performing Jewish music on the modern concert stage, the society's leaders aspired to cultivate a new kind of Jewish cultural space as well as a new modern Jewish audience to fill it. In hearing their own folk songs recast as European-style concert music, the musicians believed, Jewish audiences would come to revalue their cultural heritage as simultaneously vigorous national expression and cosmopolitan, modern art. The concerts were designed to emphasize the highest levels of both "the artistic and national" dimensions of Jewish music, as the society proudly asserted in one of its annual reports. For this reason, its major public performances, typically held once a year, were staged in one of the two main concert halls of the St. Petersburg Conservatory. The choice of site was clearly intended to lead audiences to associate Jewish music with the grandest traditions of Russian and Western classical music in Russia's "temple of art." The conservatory also appealed because of its legacy as a place in which Jews had long contributed to broader Russian cultural life.

In turn, other city venues proved more fraught with contemporary cultural politics. The January 1910 concert at the Hall of the Nobility, for example, produced a minor controversy because of the Jewish presence at that venerable shrine of the Russian nobility. Before and after the concert, the press was filled with strongly antisemitic denunciations from the conservative St. Petersburg nobility, who attacked the musicians for their "*zhid* desecration" of the august symbol of Russia's national heritage (on a holy Sunday, no less). Vladimir Purishkevich, one of the principal leaders of the Russian Far Right, issued a public statement calling on the government to intervene to prevent the "nobles' nest" from being turned into a "part of the Pale of Settlement." From that point on, the large events were primarily restricted to the St. Petersburg Conservatory.[59]

It was not merely the symbolic associations of place that the society sought to impress on its audiences, but also the European conventions of bourgeois decorum that accompanied the concert hall. While audience enthusiasm and frequent demands for encores were read as encouraging signs of positive "national" success, the dictates of art music also required that order and correct behavior be maintained in the concert hall out of respect for the music's seriousness and high cultural level. Back in the 1840s, St. Petersburg's Imperial Theater Directorate had taken the step of banning applause during opera performances as part of a process of instilling "civilized" Western values. For many middle-class Jews, attendance at the society's concerts represented their first introduction to the formal conventions of the grand public concert hall. For this reason, the society adopted the practice of publishing a printed concert program, which often included explicit instructions prohibiting entrance and exit from the hall during performance as well as proscribing unnecessary requests for "superfluous repetitions" of individual musical numbers.[60]

The concert programs also emphasized a correct understanding of the music's meaning. They frequently included detailed explanatory notes on the selections chosen and booklets with a mixture of song lyrics in the original Hebrew and Yiddish, accompanied by romanized transliterations and occasional Russian translations. They also featured statements of the society's aims, sometimes in the form of mini-manifestos, as well as advertisements for membership and publications. As time went on, the increasingly elaborate programs included commissioned artwork from young Jewish artists, often with ornate images evoking Jewish music's ancient past (fig. 10). Finally, the society made it common practice to open the concerts with a short introductory lecture (*vstupitelnoe slovo*) on a literary, cultural, or historical theme related to Jewish music. The preconcert talk provided another way to introduce the musicians of the society to the public as well as to tie the evening back to broader themes in Jewish culture through the inclusion of writers such as Frug, Ansky, Rivesman, and Peretz.[61]

Controlling the meaning of Jewish music naturally also meant defining the limits of the repertoire in a way that balanced the national and the cosmopolitan aesthetic impulses. In this respect a survey of the concert pro-

Figure 10. Program cover for a 1919 Society for Jewish Folk Music concert. Russian Institute for the History of the Arts.

grams reveals an interesting trend of shifting strategies. Judging from the nearly twenty large-scale public concerts presented in St. Petersburg between 1908 and 1919, initially the Society for Jewish Folk Music adopted a notably flexible approach to musical sources. Yiddish- and Hebrew-language folk songs, Hasidic nigunim, instrumental klezmer selections, and liturgical prayers all appeared. Before 1913 the only musical sources explicitly excluded were compositions based on "pseudo-folk music, fragments of *badkhn* song, wretched fragments of foul Jewish operettas and so forth." These genres were simply deemed illegitimate because of their cultural impurities and lower-class and popular associations with Yiddish vaudeville and theater; their origins conflicted with the ideological goal of elevating authentic Jewish folk songs into modern concert hall art songs. But the quest for national folk purity did not prevent the inclusion of Yiddish theater songs by Avrom Goldfaden and Peretz Sandler, as well as liturgical works by central European Jewish composers Louis Lewandowski and Salomon Sulzer and other Jewish-themed works by Russian and European non-Jewish composers.[62]

To compensate for the looseness of repertoire, the arrangements of the first several years veered conspicuously toward the conventional and conservative. Compositions took the form of simple, unadorned melodic harmonizations, following the same late nineteenth-century Romantic aesthetic model as did Engel, scored for two or three instruments, often voice or violin with piano accompaniment. This did change after 1913, when concerts began to include more original compositions (*svobodnoe tvorchestvo*), often with greater harmonic and melodic abstraction and mild formal experiments characteristic of Russian musical modernism. At the same time, however, these new aesthetic liberties arrived hand in hand with a tightening of nationalist standards for the melodic source material, or a "more strict selection of folk melodies chosen for arrangement." In the mid-1910s, the society's concert programs proudly noted the presence of more "advanced" and "modern" compositions, coupled with a richer trove of genuine Jewish melodic scales and freshly transcribed folk melodies. There were undoubtedly many reasons for these aesthetic shifts. But the changes were less striking than the overarching continuities. Faced with a diverse set of audiences in St. Petersburg, ranging from politically active Jewish nationalists to avowedly antinationalist Jewish liberals to non-Jewish Russian intellectuals, the society continually sought to carefully balance conservative and liberal aesthetic impulses in its programming. Concert booklets and published advertisements made this strategic blend of particular and universal explicit, emphasizing both the authenticity of Jewish music and its general appeal beyond the parochial boundaries of nationality. The advertisements for the

March 10, 1912, concert, for instance, argued that the performance would appeal not only to those who look to "folk songs as an example of [Jewish] national genius" but also to all serious musicians interested in how the music of various nations can serve as "a source for the general enrichment of musical language."[63]

The close care paid to marketing Jewish music was not for the benefit of St. Petersburg audiences alone. For through the advertisements and reviews in the Jewish and Russian press, word of the society's concerts quickly began to spread well beyond the confines of the capital to cities across Russia and to eastern and central Europe. By 1909 the society was receiving letters from individuals and organizations filled with requests for advice, assistance, and musical performers and teachers in a wide range of communities. Some letter writers sought to advance explicit political goals, such as a Zionist film collective in Odessa looking for music for a propaganda film or a Russian Jewish immigrant in Palestine who wrote to propose that the society establish a national conservatory there. Yet many others were simply local Jewish charitable organizations, student groups, and even small-town rabbis from across the Pale of Settlement looking for Jewish musicians to perform at charitable benefits or holiday celebrations such as Purim and Simḥat Torah. Linking all of these writers was a growing sense that Jewish public life—be it cultural, religious, or political—required explicitly Jewish music. In the words of one correspondent from the shtetl of Tetiev, it was "sad and terribly embarrassing" that, at Jewish community meetings and celebrations in his town, "when our soulful mood wants to break out into song ... we have no suitable Jewish national songs and must sing instead foreign ones ... belonging to other nations." To remedy this problem, this range of individuals, groups, and institutions looked increasingly to St. Petersburg as the central authority and national source for Jewish music.[64]

In response to these appeals, the society considered expanding its activities through opening provincial branches and establishing its own publishing imprint. More immediately, however, the group decided to engage the provinces directly by sending its own musicians to perform on concert tours. In the summer of 1910 the first such group of four musicians spent two months traveling between ten cities across the northwest of the Pale of Settlement and Congress Poland. Encouraged by the extremely positive audience reactions, the society expanded the project. By 1912 the group had staged concerts in over two hundred cities and towns across the Pale and the interior of Russia, including Siberia. The same year, musicians representing the society concertized throughout Germany and the Austro-Hungarian Empire in cities such as Budapest, Vienna, Kolomyia, Lviv, Czernowitz,

Cologne, and Leipzig. In 1913 and 1914 the tenor Alexander Medvedev even journeyed to France, England, and the United States, where he performed as a semiofficial representative of the group. Eventually, over the course of ten years, the society produced a total of over twelve hundred such concerts throughout the Russian Empire and Europe.[65]

The society's concerts effectively created a new Jewish public space in Russian culture for a broad range of musicians, intellectuals, middle-class professionals, and business elites. Beyond the confines of the synagogue, the political club, or the formal communal meeting, the concert hall setting offered a neutral public forum for national community, a place in which, at least in theory, all Jews could gather to consume and hence affirm Jewish culture without a requirement of ideological commitment, either in religious or political terms. Though the very concept of Jewish cultural nationalism represented an implicit political statement about Jewish collective identity, the society repeatedly emphasized the cosmopolitan and open nature of the Jewish musical project.

Indeed, the very site of this Jewish music making, the urban Russian concert hall, was itself marked as a repository of Russian music and European high culture. This was especially so in the concert halls of the Moscow and St. Petersburg conservatories. In these "temples of art," the elaborate physical decoration and heavy ornamentation, featuring portraits of the tsars, other Romanovs, and leading Russian and European composers, told an unspoken story of concert music as the embodiment of both Western civilization and aristocratic Russian pride. This temporary Jewish cultural space therefore hovered inside a larger Russian imperial framework, which in turn was itself positioned within a complex relationship with Europe. In spite of the society's leaders' protestations about Russification and Jewish "assimilation," their Jewish audiences in St. Petersburg and elsewhere clearly flocked to the concerts in part because they afforded simultaneous access to both Jewish music and Russian culture. Even as concert hall performances of Jewish art music helped to prove that Jewish music and Jewish national creativity existed, they could not erase the ironies—and anxieties— of the Russian and European influences in modern Jewish culture. In this sense, the quest for modern Jewish music echoed the contradictory, dynamic modern identities of Russian Jewry and of Russia itself.[66]

Perhaps the best proof of this lies in the very name of the society. Beyond its Russian version, the society dutifully translated its own name into both Yiddish (Gezelshaft far yidisher folks-muzik) and Hebrew (Ḥevrat musikah 'ivrit 'amamit) in much of its published correspondence. Yet above all it favored the Russian version. The dictates of Russian law aside, the choice reflected not so much the linguistic "assimilation" of the society's leaders as their sense of shared, parallel common purpose with the Russian intelligentsia as a whole. From at least the mid-nineteenth century, Russian writers, artists, and musicians had been consumed with questions regarding the relationship between art and society. In a country in which formal politics had been withheld from the public's reach and the monarchy had promoted itself as synonymous with the state, excluding the people from a role as body politic, the Russian intelligentsia focused relentless attention on debates over the proper role of art, whether as escape from otherwise meaningless reality or as sharp-edged instrument with which to critique and reform society.

The Russian Jewish cultural movement of the early twentieth century resonated with similar weighty questions of national mission, political responsibility, and the ultimate role of art in society. After 1905, cut off from the possibility of direct involvement in the transformation, political or otherwise, of Jewish and Russian society, despairing of an immediate secular redemption, Jews from across the political and religious spectrum found common cause in the project of modern Jewish culture. Like Russian music, literature, and art, however, modern Jewish culture ultimately took as its target not the challenges of political reconstruction but the enigmas of identity itself. Music appealed to Russian Jewish intellectuals as a doubly resonant path to national self-discovery and a proud parallel movement alongside Russia's own distinguished musical voices. This is why Rimsky-Korsakov's fateful comment that Jewish music awaited its Glinka, probably made without much forethought or afterthought, became such an iconic, prophetic utterance for the Jewish musicians of St. Petersburg. It suggested that the Jewish and Russian fates in the modern world were somehow intertwined and redeemable through aesthetics. It was not Babel's fame that the young Jewish musicians of St. Petersburg sought in music as much as a coherent cultural identity as modern Russians, Jews, and Europeans.

CHAPTER 4

Frozen Folk Songs
Modern Jewish Culture between Art and Commerce

If you read my songs in a book,
And the melody has not been passed on to you,
It is like a photograph, beloved brothers,
Everything is completely correct,
Only it lacks life.
—Eliokum Zunser, *Ha-menageyn* (1873)

In 1871 a music collection entitled *Kanaf renanim oder zeks folkslider* (Songbird, or Six Folk Songs) appeared in print for the first time in Vilnius. Its author, a veteran Jewish folk artist named Peysakh-Eliyahu Badkhn, took the unusual tack of opening his work with a dialogue between himself and his creations. In the book's preface, Badkhn speaks directly to his creations, encouraging them to leave their nest: "Many years have already passed since you were born. You've been well-liked, and now the time has come to go be seen by the masses. Get thee out into the world!" The personified songs in turn fret about finding an audience in the larger world: "We are afraid to travel with our business out into the world. We've lived here a long time and do not know the road. . . . [Moreover,] the world does not want us, and we know exactly why. We have too little piety for the *Hasid*, and too much Yiddish for the *Maskil*. Both would like to shove us under the table."[1] The nervousness ascribed by the author to his songs was of course his own. For Badkhn was fully aware that he himself represented a new phenomenon in the history of Jewish culture: the modern popular musician.

We are accustomed to remembering eastern European Jewish folk musicians as timeless paragons of tradition. But nineteenth-century Yiddish folksingers, *badkhns*, and klezmers were often conscious agents of cultural change, actively shaping the emerging musical contours of Jewish life by dramatically reimagining their own roles and repertoires from the mid-century onward. Beginning in the 1850s and 1860s, as the forces of industrialization, urbanization, and secularization quickened their pace, the street corners of the larger cities in the Pale of Settlement and the inns, coffeehouses, and wine gardens of smaller towns along the Austro-Hungarian border played host to a new class of troubadours pioneering a secular Jewish popular music centered on Yiddish-language songs. Peysakh-Eliyahu Badkhn was one such transitional figure. Like his anxious songs, he had left behind the familiar world of shtetl weddings, where, as his last name suggests, he was known widely as the *Gaon Badkhonim* (Genius of Jesters), to travel the roads of the Pale and perform for anonymous crowds in Vilnius and Minsk.

Despite the new opportunities, Badkhn hesitated to fully embrace his destiny. As he explained in his book, he had written most of his songs back in the 1850s but resisted publishing them because "I know very well the fate of these authors in the modern world." It was only when he learned of others peddling his songs under their own names that he decided to proceed with publication. It was not the prospect of selling his music that disturbed Badkhn. He was, after all, a professional musician, who effectively sold his compositions every time he performed them in public for money. Rather he sensed a loss of control as he observed music changing into a form of modern commodity, a segment of popular culture that dispensed with the artist himself. This acute self-awareness and ambivalence about the new intersection of art and commerce was one of the first hallmarks of modernity itself in Jewish eastern Europe.

A generation later, the Russian-speaking, conservatory-trained composers of early twentieth-century St. Petersburg faced a situation not that different from that of Badkhn and his contemporaries. They too detected both powerful opportunities and risks in music publishing. For the leaders of the Society for Jewish Folk Music, the printing press represented the most obvious way of fulfilling their vision of spreading national culture and consciousness to the broadest possible segment of the Jewish public. It afforded a small cadre of intellectuals a potent tool for moving beyond the elite realm of ethnographic studies and concert hall performances to reach directly into other Jewish communal organizations, cultural societies, and schools across Russia, Europe, and far beyond.

But in a time of rapidly shifting conceptions of art, commerce, and Jewishness in Europe as a whole, the very technology that provided unprecedented new access to mass audiences also threatened to subvert Jewish music's meaning. As the dichotomy between high art and low popular culture crystallized in Jewish eastern Europe, these musicians struggled to determine whether the commercial medium for their music was truly friend or foe. Amplifying art in this way brought to the surface philosophical tensions and cultural conundrums the likes of which Badkhn and his nineteenth-century contemporaries could scarcely have imagined. For Jews in eastern Europe, modernity was not only about the secularist tendencies of the Haskalah, the rise of mass politics, and the transformation of Jewish economic life. It was also about an ongoing experiment with culture and technology that forever changed the way Jews thought about—and experienced—their own cultural traditions.

We can see this clearly by examining three ambitious projects that the Jewish musicians of St. Petersburg undertook in the years before World War I: sheet music publishing, commercial sound recordings, and a Jewish national songbook for use in schools, homes, and other cultural venues. The first and last of these projects came to fruition; the second did not. Taken together they reveal how, in the shift from idea to reality, modern Jewish music both reflected and shaped the larger struggle to chart a cultural path into European modernity on distinctively Jewish terms.

Birth of a Genre: Publishing Jewish Music

It is only a slight exaggeration to say that Jewish modernity in eastern Europe began with the modern printing press. Of course, eastern European Jews were far from newcomers to the printed word. Published Jewish books from central Europe and the Ottoman Empire had been distributed across the region from the sixteenth century onward. But it was the emergence of new printing technology in the middle of the nineteenth century that enabled Jewish publishers in eastern Europe, particularly in cities such as Warsaw, Vilnius, and Lviv, to begin issuing all sorts of inexpensive publications in large quantities. The result was an explosion of printed Yiddish popular culture, ranging from novels and newspapers to chapbooks and broadsheets. Suddenly it became possible for a mass audience of Jewish readers to experience their day-to-day lives described and analyzed in their own language of Yiddish. Literature and newspapers both opened a new window onto broader Russian and European society for Jews and provided them with a new reflective mirror onto their own condition.[2]

As part of this printing revolution, music also began to circulate within communities and beyond borders in a fundamentally new way. During the 1870s and 1880s, scores of printed pamphlets and booklets of Yiddish song lyrics appeared. Although clearly intended to be used for singing, these publications did not yet include musical notation because of the technical limitations involved. Instead, their authors relied on oral transmission for the melodies. By the 1890s, though, the spread of cheaper mass printing techniques and the growing Jewish urban population led printers in cities such as Vilnius and Minsk to begin issuing individual music pieces with musical notation. In the years between the first mid-century efforts of musicians such as Eliokum Zunser and Peysakh-Eliyahu Badkhn and the founding of the Society for Jewish Folk Music in 1908, an entire industry of Jewish music publishing arose.

As the former *badkhn*'s plaint suggested, the audience for this published music was neither the intellectual Hebrew readers of the Haskalah literature (*maskilim*) nor the religious traditionalists (*Hasidim*). Instead it was the urban, secularized Jewish bourgeoisie and working class then developing in eastern Europe. These were Jews hungry for entertainment beyond the confines of the synagogue but uncomfortable with Polish- and Russian-language theater, newspapers, and literature. For them, simple ditties that mixed the familiar musical cadences of Yiddish folk songs with clever lyrics to sketch sentimental portraits, ironic parodies, and sharp-witted social commentaries on stock characters from traditional Jewish life proved hugely popular. By century's end, the rise of the Yiddish theater throughout eastern Europe and the United States, along with the growing Jewish embrace of the piano, extended this process by launching a new market for published sheet music editions of popular songs.[3]

One of the most striking characteristics of these compositions was the increasingly common use of titles such as *Yidishe lider* (Jewish Songs), *Yidishe folkslider* (Jewish Folk Songs), and *Yidishe musik* (Jewish Music). These terms were all neologisms, heretofore unknown in Yiddish, again reflecting the unmistakable stamp of modernity. Previous generations of eastern European Jews simply took their own folk songs for granted and saw no need to qualify them with the adjective "Jewish." Now, as Jewish popular musicians found themselves living as a minority population within the urban multiethnic and multilingual cultural stew of Russians, Ukrainians, Poles, Lithuanians, and others, they increasingly chose to mark — and market — their music as "Jewish." The term revealed their new, self-conscious understanding of a different social reality. In a sense, then, the very concept of Jewish music — like Jewish culture in eastern Europe as a whole — owed its existence to the evolution of modern Russian Jewish publishing.[4]

In Russia, however, the government was never far behind the scenes. The twin impulses of national pride and niche marketing faced an obvious challenge from the tsarist state's repressive legal policies toward Yiddish culture in the late nineteenth century. The most famous example of this was the 1883 ban on Yiddish theater performances after their auspicious start in the 1870s. In the case of music publishing, the greatest challenge came from official censors, who often rejected artistic publishing projects by the Jewish intelligentsia as unacceptably political expression. In the late 1890s, for instance, the Yiddish writer Isaac Leybush Peretz repeatedly tried to publish a collection of Yiddish folk songs only to be rebuffed by the Warsaw Jewish censor. Shaul Gintsburg likewise recalled that before he was allowed to publish his 1901 *Voskhod* collection of Yiddish folk songs, the St. Petersburg censor, himself a baptized Jew, demanded that several *treyf* (unfit) texts that referred negatively to Jesus Christ and Tsar Nicholas I be omitted.[5]

After 1905 new laws on freedom of expression and freedom of the press, as well as less stringent government censorship, gave Jews greater latitude in publishing, particularly in St. Petersburg. A sudden upsurge in Jewish journalism, literature, and other published popular culture promptly ensued. Along with Yiddish theater and popular songs, more "highbrow" forms of sheet music compositions also began to materialize. Some of the earliest efforts came from the large Russian music publishing houses Bessel in St. Petersburg and Jurgenson in Moscow, the latter of which published early original compositions by Joel Engel and stylized arrangements of klezmer melodies by Moscow Art Theater composer Ilia Sats (1875–1912). In 1909 Engel took the further step of self-publishing a collection of his music, *Evreiskie narodnye pesni* (Jewish Folk Songs) for voice and piano.[6]

That same year, discussion began in the Jewish press concerning the idea of a national publishing house for Jewish music. Writing in the Warsaw paper *Der fraynd*, one critic (identified only as "A. L.") put the matter succinctly: "Without Jewish songs there is no Jewish music," he wrote, "and the few songs and musical pieces that we have are scattered here and there, [such that] we seldom learn of them." Despite the appearance of active choral societies in Warsaw, Lodz, and Riga, and the Society for Jewish Folk Music in St. Petersburg, he complained, most such groups had only a handful of Jewish compositions to perform in their repertoire. Echoing this idea in *Razsvet*, the pseudonymous critic M. Nagen called on existing Jewish musical societies to pool their funds under the auspices of the St. Petersburg group for a massive music publishing project. The best way to combat the Jewish public's ignorance of its own culture, he wrote, was to place Jewish music directly into schools, homes, and youth groups across Russia. The following year, the Society for Jewish Folk Music responded to these calls by establishing its own publishing imprint. It quickly emerged as the premier publisher of Jewish music in Russia and Europe as a whole.[7]

The St. Petersburg musicians had examined the idea of music publishing during the society's founding discussions in 1907. Philosophically, they identified it as a means of projecting a broad nationalist message to the Jewish public, as well as improving the masses' appreciation of the kind of "serious musical compositions" being created by Jewish composers. From a practical point of view, publishing also afforded a new, national minority organization lacking institutional or state support a means of providing a steady income for itself and its core constituency of composers. Given the large issues at stake, the group devoted meeting after meeting in its first two years to debating the various aesthetic, technical, and financial aspects of music publishing.[8]

First and foremost, this bold cultural project raised the question of what Jewish art music should sound like. All were in agreement that the basic aesthetic template had already been established by Engel. He had culled folk melodies from his own collection of melodic transcriptions, carefully adding "modern musical culture" (*sovremennaia muzykalnaia kultura*) in piano accompaniments harmonized in conventional late Romantic style. His broader goal, unstated but obvious, was to blend the musical language of the Russian national school, with its predilection for minor modes, metric flexibility (often within regular meters), and heavy chromaticism with traditional Ashkenazi Jewish melodies. In his estimation, the greater the portion of unadulterated folk melos, the greater Jewish music's aesthetic achievement.[9]

A similar ethnographic impulse prevailed in the works of the St. Petersburg musicians during their first decade. It is most easily seen in the very ways in which the composers themselves labeled their own music. In sixty of the eighty-one compositions issued by the society between 1910 and 1918, the music is credited to "arrangers" rather than "composers." Furthermore, the melodies were frequently identified as folk music transcriptions, labeled with the subtitles "folk-song," "folk-melody," or "fantasy on a folk-melody." In some cases the name and place of the original informant was also included.

Ironically, in spite of this conservative ethic of composition, the melodies selected as sources reflected a highly elastic definition of "folklore." This was especially true in the society's early years, when few composers were able to undertake fieldwork themselves. The first such batch of fifteen compositions, issued in 1910, included three broad categories of songs. First were several arrangements of well-known Yiddish-language folk songs such as Efraim Shkliar's piano-vocal versions of "Di gildene pave" (The Golden Peacock) and "Di alte kashe" (The Old Question), and Lazare Saminsky's "Unter Soreles vigele" (Under Little Sarah's Cradle) for voice and string quartet. A second genre consisted of Yiddish theater hits such as Shkliar's arrangements of the popular Avrom Goldfaden songs "Feryomert, ferklogt" (In Grief, In Despair) and "Shtey oyf, mayn folk" (Arise, My People) for choir and piano. But the boundary between these two categories was porous, reflecting the problems inherent in the search for unadulterated, "authentic" folk material.

Such was the case with one of the final pieces in the first series, Mordechai Shalyt's "Eili, Eili" (My God, My God) for voice and piano. Despite its designation as a traditional Yiddish folk song, "Eili, Eili" had been composed in 1896 for the New York Yiddish theater by the immigrant choral conductor Peretz Sandler. The song quickly came to be featured in several different shows. Sandler's work was first recorded in 1906, published in 1907, and by the end of the decade had traveled across the Atlantic, where it circulated in guise of a local folk song. Even as the St. Petersburg composers published and performed Shalyt's 1910 arrangement as an authentic anonymous Yiddish folk song, it continued to be performed repeatedly in the United States as a Yiddish theater and vaudeville hit. By the end of World War I, Shalyt's published arrangement of the tune had recrossed the Atlantic, and in 1917 New York's Schola Cantorum Chorus performed it as a "traditional Yiddish melody of Russia and Poland." Further complicating its trajectory, that same year Mischa Elman recorded the song as a "Zionist hymn" for RCA Records, which in turn led Henry Ford's antisemitic newspaper *The Dearborn Independent* to denounce the tune's nationwide popularity as part of an international Jewish conspiracy. At the same time, Sandler launched a major lawsuit to reclaim the copyright to his song from various American publishers. In order to do so, he had to prove that the song was his own composition and not a work of traditional eastern European Jewish folk music. The case progressed to the U.S. Federal Court of the Southern District of New York, which ultimately recognized his authorship but rejected his legal ownership because of his "fatal acquiescence," establishing a landmark precedent in American copyright law.[10]

While the perils of the international Yiddish popular music market undermined the folk populism of the St. Petersburg intellectuals, the politics of European musical nationalism proved no less of a thorny challenge as reflected in a third category: the modern political song. This genre was best represented by Shkliar's treatment of the Zionist national anthem, "Ha-tikvah." First published as a poem in 1878 by the itinerant Galician *maskil* Naftali Herts Imber, the song emerged as a favorite of Zionist pioneers in Palestine and their European supporters, typically sung to a melody of unknown origin. At the 1907 Zionist Congress at The Hague, the movement officially selected "Ha-tikvah" as its anthem. But the obscure provenance of the song's melody remained a source of controversy and political embarrassment. It was sometimes identified as a Moldavian folk tune brought by a Jewish immigrant to Palestine. Yet a similar melody also appeared in the

Example 6. Efraim Shkliar's arrangement of "Ha-tikvah," 1910.

Czech composer Bedřich Smetana's *The Moldau* symphonic poem. In response to charges that the melody of "Ha-tikvah" was not Jewish but Czech or possibly Moldavian, some Jewish musicians argued that the melody derived from an ancient Sephardic melody used in the Hallel holiday liturgy. Others, such as musicologist Avraham Tsvi Idelsohn, held that the melody belonged to a category of pan-European "wandering melodies" with no specific geographic or national source. A third group proposed jettisoning the melody altogether in favor of a newly composed one.[11]

Shkliar took a different approach (ex. 6). His arrangement preserves the well-known melody but deemphasizes its minor-key, eastern European aspects. It opens with a solo voice singing the first stanza, with a very soft (*pianissimo*) piano accompaniment. In the second stanza, labeled "Coro," all four voices (soprano, alto, tenor, and bass) sing in harmony; this is followed by a repetition of the opening stanza, again for solo voice, then a repeat of the second stanza. With its ascending and descending chromatic voices, extensive use of passing tones, and awkward shifts to a major key (C major) in the piano accompaniment, the arrangement resembles less an eastern European folk song, Jewish or otherwise, than a typical nineteenth-century central European synagogue chorale in the German Protestant tradition. The cumulative effect was to create further distance between the song and

Smetana's *Moldau*. But Shkliar's creative approach earned poor marks from his fellow composers. In a review, Engel dismissed Shkliar's efforts as ineffectual. The broader problem, he wrote, was that the melody was "entirely unsuitable for a national anthem" because of its lack of typical Jewish elements, its resemblance to a popular Ukrainian folk song, and its overall minor, pessimistic character. Mikhail Gnesin, on the other hand, criticized Shkliar on substantially different grounds. He objected more generally to a so-called Western aesthetic approach to eastern European Jewish melodies. In Gnesin's eyes and ears, monophonic Jewish songs, which in their traditional forms lacked harmonization, could not and should not be casually adapted to the four-part harmony typical of Western music.[12]

The enduring question of the Western-style harmonization of Jewish melodies represented a larger, long-standing theoretical problem of how to situate Jewish music within the tonal hierarchy of Western art music. The so-called common practice of European music as it had developed since the Renaissance relied on a system of specific tonalities and underlying chordal harmonic patterns. It remained an open question, however, as to whether Jewish melodies could or should be categorized in this way. The presence of microtones, the lack of fixed scalar conventions akin to Western modes, and the absence of harmony in traditional Jewish folk and liturgical music all suggested a closer congruence with non-Western musical traditions. But if Jewish music were classified as Asian or Middle Eastern in its origins, this would have major implications for Jews seeking cultural integration within European culture. Identifying Jews as musical "Orientals" would only bolster the antisemitic arguments of Wagner and others regarding the putatively foreign Jewish presence in Western music. At the same time, to treat Jewish music as Western raised another vexing question: How far could Jewish composers venture into mainstream Russian and German musical models without losing the original Jewish character of their traditional folkloric sources?[13]

Not all of the St. Petersburg composers struggled as much as Shkliar in their initial efforts. One of the most successful was the violinist and composer Joseph (Iosif Iulevich, Yoyzel-Dovid) Achron (1886–1943) (fig. 11). Born in the shtetl of Lodzey in the Suvalki province (present-day Lithuania), the son of a *ba'al tefillah* (lay prayer leader) and amateur violinist, Achron displayed an early talent for music. His father moved him to Warsaw to begin formal musical studies at the age of eight. Two years later, in 1893, he made his concert debut and soon embarked on a career as a child prodigy acclaimed throughout Russia. A concert tour of several major cities in 1897 brought

Figure 11. Joseph Achron. Music Department, National Library of Israel.

him to St. Petersburg, where he delivered a command performance at a birthday party at the Gatchina Palace for the Tsarevich Grand Duke Georgii Aleksandrovich, in the presence of Nicholas II. The gold watch he received that day from Nicholas's mother, Tsarina Maria Fedorovna, was a memento that he treasured for the rest of his life.

Achron studied at the St. Petersburg Conservatory with Leopold Auer, who considered him one of his greatest students. After graduating in 1904 with the conservatory's famed gold medal and the Mikhailovsky Palace prize of 1,200 rubles, Achron soon began a career as a touring concert soloist in Europe. Given his success on the concert stage, he easily could have continued along this well-trod professional path. But he longed to become a composer rather than just another Russian Jewish violinist. Inspired by the Society for Jewish Folk Music, he began to try his hand at writing Jewish music. In December 1911 he penned his most famous work, the "Evreiskaia melodiia" (Hebrew Melody). When Achron premiered the piece as an encore at a court concert ball in 1912, it caused an immediate sensation.[14]

Like Shkliar and Engel, Achron strove to preserve the folkloric ethos of the melody on which his composition was based. In his case, this meant a novel ethnographic approach. At the top of the published score was a transcription of the "original folk melody" with a note explaining that the composer had recorded it himself (fig. 12). The tune was a nigun (wordless melody) that he had heard in a Warsaw synagogue on Nalevki Street. At the same time, he pushed past simple arrangement to a more creative interpretation of the folk material, recasting his tune as a "fantasy" for violin with piano accompaniment. The resulting work reflected his conviction that the search for a Jewish compositional aesthetic should grow organically out of the traditional Jewish elements of the melodies themselves. As he later observed, Jewish composers needed to recognize three crucial fundamentals: the distinctive Jewish melos, the characteristic melodic ornamentation and recitative style of Ashkenazi vocal and instrumental music, and the absence of harmony in traditional Jewish music.[15]

Achron's concern with all three of these elements is apparent from the very beginning of the piece (ex. 7). Slowing down the original melody's tempo from a moderate, loping triple meter (3/8) to a more dramatic rubato, he opens with a six-measure piano introduction. Descending the scale in parallel octaves in the bass clef, the piano part announces the *Mi shebeyrakh* synagogue prayer mode, on which the melody is based. This liturgical mode (also known as "altered Dorian") featured a raised fourth degree on the minor scale, the tonality in which the piece remains throughout. While the melody itself follows a series of familiar patterns that alternate clearly between the

Figure 12. First page of sheet music edition of Joseph Achron's "Evreiskaia melodiia." Music Department, National Library of Israel.

Example 7. Joseph Achron's "Evreiskaia melodiia," 1911.

dominant and tonic in the key of A minor, the piano's flowing accompaniment reflects Achron's attempt to create an authentic "Jewish harmony." His goal, he wrote later, was not so much to replace European-style harmony as to shift the emphasis from the standard harmonic chordal progressions to the less conventional and more modal nature of Jewish melody. He pursues this effect by avoiding any resolution to the tonic in the piano chords. Instead, for most of the work, the piano's left hand maintains a steady pedal point on the

tonic, while the right-hand chords stretch beyond the conventional harmonic system. At key cadence points in the melody, when the phrase resolves to the tonic, the chords instead favor the dominant or the subdominant over the tonic pedal point in the bass clef. The shifting harmonies, punctuated with descending chromatic passing chords, create a harmonic tension resembling Chopin or Brahms mixed with Achron's putative Jewish modal effects. At other points he introduces arpeggiated diminished and tonic minor chords with sharpened leading tones juxtaposed against the violin's simpler melodic patterns. The work concludes with a long violin cadenza that features a fiery storm of sextuplet and septuplet thirty-second notes. The cadenza incorporates the expressive ornamental tradition of Jewish violin and cantorial chant, combined with the concert virtuoso style. At the end the violin restates the opening chordal run of the *Mi shebeyrakh* mode, ending with a stronger resolution on the A-minor tonic.[16]

Achron's "Hebrew Melody" was published by the Society for Jewish Folk Music in 1914 to great public and critical acclaim as a "masterpiece." In the same year it had its American debut at New York's Carnegie Hall. Through subsequent performances by other Russian Jewish virtuosos such as Elman, Auer, Jascha Heifetz, Efrem Zimbalist, and Nathan Milstein, the piece quickly became known as a popular encore throughout the classical world. Multiple recordings and published arrangements also followed, including an entire 1935 film inspired by the piece, *Schir Iwri*, recorded in Berlin and Jerusalem with the German Jewish Kulturbund Orchestra. Eventually "Hebrew Melody" became easily the best-known composition to emerge from the entire Russian Jewish musical oeuvre. What appealed most to early listeners seems to have been the lyrical melancholy of Achron's arrangement, perhaps because it matched preexisting expectations of what Jewish art music should sound like given the influential clichés of Mussorgsky and other Russian composers. The American Jewish critic Isadore Lhevinne, for instance, noted in 1926 that the original traditional melody, "much livelier in tempo," had undergone a "transformation akin to that undergone by Hollinshead's chronicles crystallized into a Shakespearean tragedy." In his estimation, Achron's composition represented the "eternal spirit of Judaism . . . [with a] morbid sweetness that tugs at your heart."[17]

As the folk melodies reprinted above the main score of Achron's "Hebrew Melody" suggested, the creation of Jewish art music meant more than simply a search for a national sound. Indeed, the works of Achron, Shkliar, and others also represented Jewishness through other forms of visual iconography, chief among them the sheet music cover. Initially the Society for Jewish Folk Music opted for a simple text-heavy cover, with the full series of compositions listed inside an art nouveau frame, dominated by the society's name printed in Yiddish at the top. By 1913 the group had turned to the Jewish artist Moses Maimon for a sophisticated design of a lion and deer that became a hallmark of both its sheet music covers and concert programs. Maimon's design drew on traditional Jewish folk art motifs arranged in a modernist style, a visual evocation of the blend of old and new, European and Jewish (fig. 13).[18]

Beyond music's aural and visual dimensions, the other core aesthetic questions lay in the realm of language. The international Czernowitz Conference in 1908 had marked the official beginning of a culture war between the advocates of Yiddish and those of Hebrew, each side arguing that theirs should be considered the primary national language for eastern European Jewry. At the same time, many Russian Jewish intellectuals continued to promote Russian as the only viable language option for modern Jewish culture. Given this trilingual split, publishing vocal music intended for use by eastern European Jews presented the Society for Jewish Folk Music with a number of difficult choices. Should Hebrew- and Yiddish-language texts be published with accompanying Russian (or German) translations, or only in the original language? If the text appeared in Hebrew and Yiddish, should a romanized transliteration be included as well? Was it necessary to print the original Yiddish or Hebrew text below the musical staves? If so, should it run from left to right (in keeping with the direction of the Hebrew and Yiddish alphabets), or from right to left? These questions went straight to the heart of the cultural and political tensions within Russian Jewish identity. After extended debate, the group instituted a policy of performing and publishing folk song arrangements exclusively in Yiddish, "religious compositions" in Hebrew, and original works in their respective European languages. As a concession to the practical exigencies of typesetting, transliterations of Hebrew and Yiddish texts were included in the musical scores, while the original Hebrew-character texts were printed on separate pages.[19]

Reviewing the society's publications in *Razsvet* in 1910, Engel praised both their form and content, which he considered the logical "next, future stage of work" in the field of Jewish national music.[20] He had only one criticism: at a cover price of five rubles and twenty-five kopecks for a set of fifteen works, how could the society hope to reach the Jewish masses? Engel's observation pointed to a larger challenge confronting the creators of modern Jewish music. The very mechanics of the nationalist project to distribute this music required that the society embrace a role as a private entrepreneur in the Russian (and increasingly international) cultural marketplace. This raised yet another question: could the communal mission of national art

Figure 13. Title page of Joseph Achron's "Evreiskaia melodiia." Music Department, National Library of Israel.

be separated from the pragmatic—and profit-driven—demands of modern commerce?

Between Communal Mission and Commercial Culture: Distributing Jewish Music

As a small, still largely unknown, and minimally staffed cultural organization based exclusively in St. Petersburg, the society was not in a position to handle its own distribution throughout the entire Russian Empire. Some kind of commercial intermediary was necessary to sell the music to the public. But the society's leaders repeatedly expressed ambivalence and uneasiness about the prospect of a private commercial firm assuming responsibility for the distribution of the national music of the Jewish people. Such a move, they feared, would compromise the lofty ideals of Jewish cultural nationalism by substituting the baser economic imperatives of the marketplace. In board meetings, some members urged selling the publications at cost to reach the maximum possible audience. The leading advocate for a strictly noncommercial approach to distribution was the individual perhaps most sensitive to the issues of art and capitalism, the society's second president, Isai Knorozovskii (1858–1914), himself a publisher in the Russian music and theater world.

The son of a Grodno *maskil*, Knorozovskii had graduated from both the gymnasium and university in St. Petersburg with a law degree. He first settled comfortably into the career of a wealthy, Russified St. Petersburg lawyer, working on behalf of foreign companies seeking to invest in Russia. In the late 1890s his life took a dramatic turn. Famously ill-tempered, he grew so angry in the course of a court proceeding that he physically attacked the opposing counsel, tearing part of the man's suit off of him. After ignoring his subsequent censure by the court and continuing to denounce his opponent publicly, he was formally disbarred. At that point Knorozovskii simply retired from the law and turned exclusively to his passion for music and theater. After a brief period of private musical study, he embarked on a second career as a writer, editor, and publisher of several journals, including the satirical weekly *Strely* (Arrows) and the music and theater magazines *Teatr i iskusstvo* (Theater and Art) and *Teatralnaia Rossiia* (Theatrical Russia), the latter of which was billed as "the first journal devoted to the Russian theater." Not until late in his life did he turn to Jewish cultural affairs, assuming the presidency of the Society for Jewish Folk Music in 1911.[21]

Knorozovskii's professional experience had provided him with ample knowledge of how to launch cultural publications. But he was also no stranger to the common antisemitic tropes of the time, many of which accused capitalist Jewish entrepreneurs of commercializing and corrupting the art of music. In late nineteenth- and early twentieth-century Russia, Jewish entrepreneurs such as Knorozovskii and Serge Koussevitzky played prominent roles as founders and managers of circus troupes, musical theater revues, orchestras, and music publications. Others served as agents and producers in the business of concert promotion. But rather than viewing these entrepreneurs as pioneering contributors to modern Russian culture, antisemites and reactionary Russian conservatives often blamed them for a perceived decline in the quality of Russian and European musical life. The link between Jewish cultural entrepreneurship and the perceived commodification of culture in Russia and elsewhere in Europe was regarded as both a symptom and a cause of the general malaise of modernity.[22]

Such antisemitic rhetoric reinforced the Society for Jewish Folk Music's own sense of itself as a public organization committed to the high-minded pursuit of Jewish national art. In an impassioned speech during a 1910 board meeting, Knorozovskii argued for the group's special responsibility when it came to publishing. "The Society for Jewish Folk Music is an intermediary between the composers and the public," he explained, and therefore "ought to stand in equal relation to Jewish composers and to the Jewish public." Selling its own publications, he declared, "would be like cutting its own living roots."[23]

Most of the board shared Knorozovskii's view that avoiding the profit motive was an important point of Jewish national pride. But the realities of the marketplace demanded some commercial distribution apparatus. In the end, the group decided to partner with the local branches of several cultural and philanthropic organizations, such as the Jewish Literary Society and the Society for the Promotion of Enlightenment among the Jews of Russia, to sell sheet music at a substantial discount, with additional price reductions for members of these groups and other selected Jewish communal organizations. A limited number of stores in St. Petersburg were also authorized to sell the publications on commission. It was the provinces, however, that emerged quickly as the society's main market, due in part to its advertisements in Russian and Jewish newspapers and mailed circulars.[24]

Starting in 1911, publishing became the society's chief focus. While public lectures and performances in St. Petersburg occurred at most once a month, and the large concerts only twice a year, publishing was an ongoing, intensive pursuit. Because of publishing's effectiveness as a means of interacting with the larger Jewish public, the society searched constantly for new ways to expand the operation's reach. In 1912 a second series of nineteen compositions was published in Berlin through a partnership with Leo Winz, the Russian-born publisher of the Jewish journal *Ost und West*, and distributed in both Germany and Russia. This series included several more arrangements of well-known folk songs such as "Zog zhe rebeynu" (Tell Me, Rebbe) and "Shloyf, mayn kind" (Sleep, My Child); other compositions based on folkloric material, such as Leo Zeitlin's string quintet "Reb Naḥmans nigun" (Reb Naḥman's Melody); and the first treatment of a Hebrew poem, I. Kaplan's arrangement of A. D. Lifshits's "Numo Feraḥ" (Sleep, Flower). From that point on, the group increasingly devoted the bulk of its financial resources and time to music publishing.[25]

The Message in the Medium: Contemplating Sound Recording

Despite its importance, sheet music publishing was not the only way to spread the gospel of Jewish music to the masses, for early twentieth-century Russia was also in the grip of a new mania: commercial sound recording. After 1900, record companies had sprung up in cities such as St. Petersburg, Riga, Warsaw, and Vilnius. Catering to the huge new urban populations, Russian and European companies issued recordings of all sorts of folk music, classical works, and popular songs. By 1915, according to one estimate, roughly twenty-five million records were being sold each year in the Russian Empire. Along with Armenian, Tatar, Ukrainian, and other groups, Jewish commercial recordings found a serious ethnic niche market. The earliest of them were made in Lviv in 1902, Vilnius in 1903, and St. Petersburg in 1904 and promptly resulted in special catalogues devoted to Jewish music and aimed at the Jewish urban middle class. One discographer has estimated that at least fourteen thousand different recordings of Jewish music were made in pre-Holocaust eastern Europe, the vast majority prior to the First World War. To no one's surprise, these recordings sold well, especially in the Pale of Settlement.[26]

Most Jewish commercial recordings were Yiddish folk and theater songs and cantorial selections. But more formally arranged choral works and art music settings of folk songs also appeared in record company catalogues, and by 1912 the industry had discovered the Society for Jewish Folk Music. That year an article in the magazine *Grammofonaia zhizn* (Recording Life) featured the society's published works, noting that "the high artistic value and deep ethnographic interest of these songs present[ed] a great opportunity for gramophone recordings" waiting to be realized.[27] Soon the society's board began negotiations with various record companies. Just as with sheet music publishing, however, aesthetic, commercial, and communal impulses collided in the effort to turn technology into an instrument of national art.

A case in point was the society's interaction with the Vilnius Jewish record merchant Wolf Isserlin. A prominent businessman and active member of Vilnius's Jewish community, Isserlin ran a successful pharmacy business before he and his brother entered the record industry in 1902. By a decade later he had become the epitome of a commercial entrepreneur, owning the Russian Empire's central agency for phonographic record distribution and grossing hundreds of thousands of rubles in sales each year. Isserlin's success generated much antisemitic feeling regarding the perceived Jewish domination and exploitation of Russian music. Extremist Russian nationalists such as Vladimir Purishkevich demanded that the Ministry of Internal Affairs take action against the "Judaization" of the gramophone industry. The government itself kept a watchful eye on the situation, restricting the sales of recordings of Orthodox Church music by Jews and other persons "of non-Orthodox faiths."[28]

In the spring of 1914 Isserlin was locked in a fierce, controversial battle to create an industrywide syndicate of Russian record companies. Yet he still found time to dispatch a series of letters to the society, portraying himself as a loyal devotee of the Jewish national cause. Like others before him, he proposed that the group partner with him to issue recordings of the St. Petersburg Jewish composers' works. While the existing market for Jewish records catered to the "primitive tastes of the so-called mass public" in the form of Yiddish theater, vaudeville, and other "Jewish *shund* songs" (popular hits), Isserlin wrote, the phonograph represented "one of the best means of transmitting . . . the splendid Jewish repertoire" of the composers to the masses. Acknowledging that there was little likelihood of commercial success with this kind of Jewish music, Isserlin nevertheless asserted that his commitment to the project stemmed not from any "mercantile" profit motives but out of a simple desire to "enrich the Jewish recorded repertoire."[29]

For their part, the St. Petersburg musicians displayed cautious enthusiasm for commercial recording. There was no question that the phonograph could be a useful tool both for capturing melodies in the shtetl and demonstrating them to urban audiences. But there were other issues to consider. In evaluating the potential benefits and pitfalls of the opportunity, they drew on the personal experience of an active member, Alexander Davydov, who had played a prominent role in Russian Jewish musical life and the early Russian recording industry. A renowned opera soloist at St. Petersburg's Mariinsky Theater, he had launched a second career in the 1910s as one of the most popular recording artists of the day. He recorded about a hundred selections of everything from opera arias to Russian and Gypsy folk songs, an experience that led him to undertake a public campaign for the legal and economic rights of performing artists in the new industry. With Davydov on its board, the society was keenly aware of both the rewards and the risks involved in entering the commercial recording industry. From 1910 onward, each piece of sheet music published by the group bore a printed warning: "Reproduction by means of phonograph without the permission of the publisher is forbidden."[30]

In addition to the concerns of Jewish artists and the political attacks of the Russian Far Right, there were other prominent Jewish musicians who had taken aggressive stances against the very idea of recording Jewish music in any form. In Odessa, Cantor Pinḥas Minkovskii published a book-length diatribe in 1910 to denounce the "gramophone epidemic" sweeping Russian society. In his estimation, the recent traumas of the Russo-Japanese War and the Revolution of 1905 had produced two great "pornographic tendencies": erotic cinema and the gramophone (which he called the "lust machine"). The immoral, sexual associations of the new device with saloons, bars, and theaters made it inappropriate for the sacred melodies of the Jewish synagogue, he argued. Furthermore, he stressed that the mixing of *shund* with authentic Jewish melodies was a betrayal of both the religious and the national elements of Jewish music. Having himself spent a decade refusing recording contract offers, Minkovskii singled out other star cantors such as Gershon Sirota and Zavel Kvartin for their "debasement" of Jewish liturgical music.[31]

With all these concerns in mind, the society's secretary, Israel Okun, responded to Isserlin's 1914 overture by stipulating a number of conditions that would have to be met before a partnership could move forward. To ensure the quality of the performances and preserve its own "exclusively artistic-national goals" as a "cultural-national organization" rather than a "private, purely commercial [firm]," Okun wrote, the society would allow Isserlin to record and sell the music, but it would retain final approval over which musicians were used as well as its own independent distribution rights in Russia and abroad. Most crucially, Okun insisted on a clear distinction between the society's Jewish art music and the other kinds of Jewish popular music marketed by Isserlin's company: "In terms of distribution of the recordings we would want the catalogue of our songs to be completely separate and not mixed together with the '*shund*' songs." Contact with this Jewish popular music, not to mention comedy sketches and musical parodies, would threaten the society's purer "cultural-aesthetic" aspirations for Jewish music.[32]

Though Isserlin responded with assurances, the outbreak of World War I in the late summer of 1914 ended this prospective collaboration between the St. Petersburg artists and the Vilnius businessman. In all likelihood, though, it was less the practical exigencies of the day than the society's underlying ideology that explains the failure to reach an agreement with Isserlin or any other record company. For the St. Petersburg musicians, quality control was not the chief concern; it was the specter of commercialism. The powerful, aesthetically neutral forces of the market represented a danger to the delicate balance they strove to maintain between an elite form of national art and a populist mission. Equally important, the technology of the phonograph did not allow the society sufficient power to determine how, where, and what the Jewish masses would experience as Jewish music. In their eyes, Jewish music needed to be consumed and appreciated not merely as popular entertainment but also as an aural entry ticket into national community. This was reflected in their final major project begun before 1914, the Jewish national songbook.

Musical Canon and National Community: The Songbook Project

In December 1913 newspaper announcements appeared in the Russian-, Hebrew-, and Yiddish-language Jewish press throughout Europe announcing an international musical competition. To mark its fifth anniversary, the Society for Jewish Folk Music in St. Petersburg would award a prize of three thousand rubles to the composer of the "best Jewish opera." Immediately the group began to receive submissions from across the Russian Empire. Reading through the letters that accompanied the entries offers vivid snapshots of the different places in Russian society to which music had transported Jews. Jewish bandleaders in Russian army units scattered across the empire wrote in with their compositions. So did theater musicians, café orchestra conductors, big-city synagogue choir directors, and small-town music store owners.[33]

Even more striking was the response from the Russian Jewish diaspora that had materialized far beyond Russia's borders. From London came a letter from a British cantor and liturgical composer named Samuel Alman (1878–1947). Originally from the shtetl of Sobolevka in the Podolia province, Alman had studied in the IRMO school in Odessa and served in a Russian army band unit before immigrating to England. There he had achieved fame as a composer for the Yiddish theater and the synagogue. In fact, his letter announced, this Russian Jewish musician already held the distinction of having composed the first Jewish grand opera, *King Aḥaz*. It had premiered in 1912 at the opening of the Feinman Yiddish People's Theatre in London's Jewish East End. His letter boasted of the "huge praise" lavished on his Yiddish-language work by both the Jewish and the mainstream British press. If the society were interested, Alman generously allowed, he would consider permitting the St. Petersburg group to publish it.[34]

At the other end of the Jewish musical spectrum was Aaron Avshalomov (1894–1965), then a nineteen-year-old university student in Zurich. In his letter, Avshalomov apologized for the poor national quality of the composition he was submitting. By way of explanation, he gave the basic facts of his biography. Born and raised in the Russian Far East, the grandson of a Juhuru (Mountain Jew) from the Caucasus exiled to eastern Siberia, he had grown up in a wealthy family and was raised with the help of a Japanese nursemaid and a Chinese manservant. Now, at the insistence of his parents, he had arrived in Switzerland to prepare for a career in medicine. But his true wish was to become a Jewish composer. Along with his submission to the contest, an overture entitled *Esther*, he enclosed a disclaimer: "This is my first composition, which I wrote last year in Siberia. . . . It is altogether possible that there is very little Jewish element in it. I was in Nikolaevsk, where there are very few of us Jews. . . . I want very much to familiarize myself with the form of Jewish melody and I would be very grateful if you would point out to me what there is written on this subject in Russian as, unfortunately, I don't know any Jewish languages. . . . My soul sings with Jewish melodies. I hear so many songs—but I just cannot manage to capture them on paper."[35]

That a Ukrainian-born cantor turned Yiddish opera composer in England and a Siberian-born medical student in Switzerland would both look to the Jewish musicians of St. Petersburg for advice and opportunity illustrates the broad appeal and centralizing force of Jewish culture in the years before World War I. But it also neatly encapsulates the dilemma of the Society for Jewish Folk Music. On one hand, commercialized efforts at Yiddish theater such as Alman's, with its popular connotations, were precisely what the group had hoped to avoid. On the other hand, Avshalomov's appeal suggested a more basic need for educating a broader Jewish artistic public, on an international stage, about its own cultural heritage.

In search of an answer, the musicians of the society turned, like other Jewish nationalist writers and folklorists of the time, to an entirely new cultural form, one which would enable them to disseminate their combined educational and artistic vision of Jewish music in a tangible, inclusive, influential manner: the musical anthology. Zionist intellectuals such as Aḥad Ha'am in Odessa and Joseph Klausner in Warsaw had already pioneered the idea of a literary anthology that would collect the essential Jewish religious legacy for modern secular Jews. Other nationalist activists such as S. Ansky and Martin Buber had promoted the idea of documenting Jewish visual art and folk literature through similar publication projects.[36] In the years immediately prior to World War I, the St. Petersburg musicians realized their version of this idea: the *Songbook for the Jewish School and Family* (*Sbornik pesen dlia evreiskoi shkoly i semi; Lider-zamelbukh far der yidishe shul un familye*).

The genesis of this first major Jewish musical anthology reflected both the broad impulses of Jewish cultural nationalism and a more particular set of organizational and communal priorities for St. Petersburg Jewry. From its inception, the society had seen itself as a far-ranging national organization, with eventual branches in provincial cities and towns across the Russian Empire. Expansion was both an ideological imperative and a practical means of generating much-needed revenue (in the form of membership dues) to fund large-scale research, performance, and publishing. Unfortunately, in 1911 a new crackdown on minority organizations by Prime Minister Petr Stolypin forced the group to put these plans on hold. That year the government closed more than a hundred branches of the widespread Jewish Literary Society. Perhaps because of its smaller size, the Society for Jewish Folk Music survived intact.[37]

By 1912 the political climate had improved enough for the society to begin official efforts to organize branches in the provinces. At the beginning of the year they printed thirty thousand copies of a brochure outlining their history, philosophy, and activities. After summarizing the group's mission and listing its artistic accomplishments, the brochure explained that the goal of collecting Jewish folk melodies would depend on the work of its creative partners in the provinces. There followed an appeal to provincial activists to join the society, form new branches, and help cultivate the "richness" of Jewish "folk poetry."[38]

Over the remainder of 1912 the society undertook three crucial, interrelated tasks at once. First, it officially opened its membership rolls to individuals living outside St. Petersburg, adding almost four hundred new people to its list by the end of the year. Second, it began the process of establishing official branches in Moscow, Kharkov, and Odessa, all of which would begin to function in 1913. Finally, it published the first edition of the *Songbook for the Jewish School and Family*. The close links between increased membership, organizational expansion, and music publishing can be seen clearly in the history of that volume. During the next few years, the *Songbook* played a vital role in the group's evolution from a small St. Petersburg cultural organization to a broad voice of authority and creative force in Russia and beyond.

The immediate origins of the *Songbook* lay in the partnership between the society and the long-established Society for the Promotion of Enlightenment among the Jews of Russia (OPE). In the first decade of the twentieth century, the OPE had grown from a liberal, integrationist communal organization into a new forum for Jewish intellectuals of various political backgrounds, united by a commitment to developing Jewish national identity. While previously the OPE had primarily supported the Russian-language culture of Russified Jewish elites, in the aftermath of 1905 it turned its attention to the Jewish component of primary schools and children's education. Hence the need for suitable textbooks and other resources for the proper study of Jewish history, religion, and culture emerged as a major focus.[39]

Soon after its founding, the society had begun informal discussions with the OPE about Jewish musical education. Among the individuals leading this effort were board members Mark Rivesman (1868–1924) and Zisman Kiselgof (1878–1939), both of whom taught in the OPE's St. Petersburg Jewish school. The case for a Jewish songbook for use in schools was not a difficult one to make. In the years after Marek and Gintsburg published their 1901 collection of Yiddish folk songs, other popular songbooks had appeared throughout eastern Europe. These publications had found wide audiences in Jewish schools, choral groups, and other communal venues. But they varied considerably in both contents and quality. In 1910 an empire-wide conference on Jewish educational reform was held in St. Petersburg. Out of this meeting emerged an organizing committee assigned to publish a new Jewish songbook. While several individuals made significant editorial contributions to the project, it was Kiselgof who played the most important role as principal editor and visionary of the *Songbook*.[40]

Zisman Kiselgof and the Creation of Jewish National Song

Born in the town of Velizh in the Vitebsk province, Zisman (Zinovii Aronovich) Kiselgof had grown up in a highly traditional Jewish environment (fig. 14). The son of a local *melamed* (elementary religious schoolteacher), he had no secular education or knowledge of the Russian language until the age of eleven. By 1898, however, Kiselgof, then twenty, had graduated from the state-run Vilnius Jewish Teachers' Institute. For the next several years he taught in both Orthodox Jewish schools and state-run Jewish schools. At the same time, he entered the ranks of the Bund, then an illegal organi-

Figure 14. Zisman Kiselgof conducting fieldwork in the Pale of Settlement. From *The Historical Collection of Jewish Musical Folklore 1912–1947*, vol. 3 (2004), courtesy of Irina Sergeeva.

zation, and served a year in prison in 1900 for possession of revolutionary literature. Undeterred, Kiselgof continued to pursue teaching and politics in equal measure. In 1906 he arrived in St. Petersburg and joined the local branch of the Bund and the faculty of the newly founded OPE Jewish primary school.

Kiselgof's only formal training in music consisted of brief childhood study with his town's klezmer violinist. Nevertheless, even as a young teenager he had given music lessons to other children. In the late 1890s he had toured professionally as a concertina player, performing in summertime concerts throughout Russia. As the circle of Gnesin, Saminsky, and others gathered in 1907 to plan the Society for Jewish Folk Music, Kiselgof immediately assumed a central leadership role, personally recruiting several composers to the group. He also served on its music committee and frequently lectured and performed at concerts. But his most important niche was as the group's resident musical ethnographer. In 1907 he made the first of what would become annual trips to cities and shtetls in the Pale of Settlement to collect Jewish folk songs. Eventually his collection amounted to some two thousand melodic transcriptions, including Yiddish folk and liturgical songs, klezmer melodies, *badkhn* chants, and Hasidic nigunim.[41]

Following closely in Engel's footsteps, Kiselgof viewed ethnography as a populist mission to recover and promote Jewish national music. His introduction to the *Songbook*, written in June 1911, outlined the project's guiding philosophy: "School should be a place national both in its general form and in the content of the studies taught within it." Along with such subjects as language, geography, and history, music formed an essential part of any solid "national curriculum." Songs sung in the school, and in the home and synagogue, would forge deep bonds between the individual child and the Jewish nation's "true folk soul." Kiselgof went on to discuss the increased psychological effect of folk songs on children's "national consciousness." In particular, he singled out the lullabies sung by mothers to their children as a valuable source of cultural imprinting and emphasized that the melodies learned as children remained firmly lodged in adult memories.[42]

Along with music's emotional resonance and psychological impact on identity formation, Kiselgof explained, folk songs also represented a valuable resource for exposing children to the historical experiences that had shaped the Jewish nation. This nationalist interpretation of Jewish music as a tool for teaching spiritual history comes across clearly in the structure and contents of the *Songbook*, which offers a complete Jewish aural universe, encompassing the full range of Jewish music, past and present: Yiddish folk songs,

Hasidic nigunim, melodies for biblical chant, and even modern Western-style art songs.

The Jewish musical canon presented in the *Songbook* consists of eighty-nine selections. Arranged principally by two recent conservatory graduates and members of the society's music committee, Peysakh Lvov and Alexander Zhitomirsky, the three-voice vocal parts (soprano and two altos) are designed to be sung either in harmonized arrangement or in unison, by one person or a chorus, and at home, school, or in synagogue. A simple accompaniment, suitable for a trained amateur pianist, is included, in some cases with foot-pumped harmonium parts instead. All the texts are printed on separate pages in the original language (Hebrew or Yiddish) along with romanized transliterations. The *Songbook* was issued in two versions: one with lyrics only, the other with both lyrics and music, the words printed left to right under the musical staves in the original Yiddish or Hebrew, except in the case of the art songs, for which both Yiddish and Hebrew translations and original German and Russian texts were included.

The eighty-nine musical selections are divided into five categories:

1. *Skarbove folks-nigunim—Narodno-sinagogalnye pesni* (1–12) [sacred folk melodies]
2. *Veltlikhe folks-lider—Svetskie narodnye pesni* (13–57) [secular folk songs]
3. *Lider on verter—Pesni bez slov* (58–62) [songs without words]
4. *Kintslerishe lider—Khudozhestvennye pesni* (63–82) [art songs]
5. *Trop (tamey ha-negines)* (83–89) [melodic chant patterns]

The most striking aspect of Kiselgof's classification system is the departure from earlier models of Marek, Gintsburg, and Engel. In their work, they emphasized secular Yiddish folk song as the main genre of Jewish national music, defining it in principal opposition to the Hebrew-language liturgical melodies of the synagogue. Kiselgof, however, resisted making strict theoretical distinctions between genres or styles of Jewish national music on the basis of language and the religious-secular divide. Instead, he repeatedly stressed the unity of "Jewish song" (*evreiskaia pesnia*) as one large category, emphasizing that biblical chant, Sabbath hymns, Yiddish folk songs, and Hasidic nigunim all belonged to the overarching class of "folk song" (*narodnaia pesnia*) linked by a shared Jewish "folk-soul."

This rhetorical move was reflected in the subtle but distinctive manner in which Kiselgof named and populated the first two categories of the *Songbook: skarbove folks-nigunim* and *veltlikhe folks-lider.* The twelve selections in the first category were Hebrew-language liturgical songs clearly associated with the synagogue and the Sabbath. Yet in labeling this group, Kiselgof referred to them with the neologism *skarbove folks-nigunim*, literally "sacred folk melodies." *Skarbove*, often thought to derive from the medieval Latin *sacra*, referred to the most revered, traditional liturgical melodies in the Ashkenazi Jewish religious tradition (often known as *Misinai* melodies). The appellation *folks* implied a more folkloric, national dimension, not necessarily secular but broader than the purely religious sphere of the synagogue. The forty-five "secular folk songs" (*veltlikhe folks-lider*), which comprised the *Songbook*'s largest category, included not only Yiddish-language "secular" folk songs but also mixed-language Hebrew-Yiddish paraliturgical songs such as "Omar Adonai li-Ya'akov" (God Spoke to Jacob), traditional Yiddish religious songs such as "Helf uns gottenyu" (Help Us, God), and even Rivesman's newly composed Yiddish-language songs on religious themes such as "Oy, khanike" (Oh, Hanukkah) and "Zint on likhtlekh" (Light the Candles). The "secular folk songs" section ends with a Yiddish-language Sabbath Havdalah song, "A gute vokh" (A Good Week).

Kiselgof was not the first researcher to observe that language and religion were not always neatly correlated in the Ashkenazi Jewish experience. But his choices went beyond merely descriptive decisions to a conscious, prescriptive blurring of religious and national elements into a generic Jewish "folk melody." Though he was an avowedly secular Bundist, he still had no trouble making statements such as that "Jewish song is sung about God and Torah: on Him hopes and aspirations, to Him entreaties and petitions, in Him comfort and peace." The cumulative effect of these sections was to emphasize a secularized national spirituality that transcended conventional religious categories.[43]

It was not only the lines between religious and secular that were blurred in the *veltlekhe* category, but also the distinction between songs for children and adults. Kiselgof took pains to exclude any songs on explicitly adult themes such as history, politics, work, marriage, sex, or crime. Instead, the selections favored children's play songs and lullabies, suggesting that children were largely the intended audience for the book. But the three-part vocal harmonies far exceed the technical abilities of most schoolchildren, implying that arrangers Zhitomirsky and Lvov had in mind trained choruses of adults rather than elementary school music classes. Even the lyrics of certain songs, including lullabies, suggest an adult audience. In fact, the first song in the "secular folk songs" section of the *Songbook* is one of the ultimate exercises in adult nostalgia for childhood—real or imagined: Mark Warshavsky's iconic anthem "Der alef beys" (The Alphabet) (ex. 8).

"On the hearth burns a flame, and the room is hot. And the rabbi teaches the little children the alphabet."

Example 8. Mark Warshavsky's "Oyfn pripetshik" ("Der alef beys"), 1900. Adapted from the second edition of the Society for Jewish Folk Music *Songbook*, arrangement by Peysakh Lvov.

Better known by its opening words, "Oyfn pripetshik" (On the Hearth), this was one of the most popular Yiddish songs in turn-of-the-century eastern Europe. The text, which presents a classic image of young children in *kheyder* learning the Hebrew alphabet for the first time, is accompanied by a simple, lilting melody that favors a natural minor scale (Aeolian mode). The song's staying power and emotional resonance have persisted to the present day, making it perhaps the most famous Yiddish folk song in the world. But despite its popularity and air of antiquity, "Oyfn pripetshik" was composed less than a decade and a half before its appearance in the *Songbook* and first published in *Der yid*, a Zionist newspaper, in 1899. In addition, in contrast to traditional children's Yiddish alphabet and rhyming songs, Warshavsky's text is clearly written from the viewpoint of an adult, narrating the experience of learning from the outside:

Oyfn pripetshik brent a fayerl,	On the hearth burns a flame,
Un in shtub iz heys.	And the room is hot.
Un der rebe lernt kleyne kinderlekh	And the rabbi teaches the little children
Dem alef-beys.	The alphabet.

Zet zhe, kinderlekh, gedenkt zhe, tayere,	See here, children, remember, dear ones,
Vos ir lernt do.	What you are learning here.
Zogt zhe nokh a mol un take nokh a mol:	Repeat it again and again:
Komets-alef: o!	Komets-alef is pronounced "o"!
Az ir vet, kinder, elter vern,	When you grow older, children,
Vet ir aleyn farshteyn,	You will understand yourselves,
Vifl in di oysyes lign trern,	How many tears lie in the alphabet,
Un vi fil geveyn.	And how much pain.[44]

Despite its idyllic tone, the self-conscious shift from external narrator to the *melamed*'s own voice, the heavy theme of Jewish suffering symbolized by the alphabet, and the imperative address to the children all demonstrate the song's adult perspective. In reality, Warshavsky's own sacralization of the *kheyder* and the Yiddish language derived directly from his own middle-aged sense of distance and nostalgia as a Russified Jew with a poor command of Yiddish. As literary scholar David Roskies has observed, "The Jewish alphabet loomed so large in Warshawski's [sic] imagination because he himself had forgotten how to use it." More than mere calculated imitations of children's music, songs such as "Oyfn pripetshik" functioned as mediating devices between past and present, conjuring up musical reveries in which a lost place (the traditional shtetl) was conflated with a lost time (the early years of childhood). As the years went on, Warshavsky's song itself received further creative interpretations. In the 1930s it was recast both as a Soviet Yiddish revolutionary song and as Revisionist Zionist anthem (the latter by Russian Jewish politician Vladimir Jabotinsky), then as a hymn of ghetto resistance in the 1940s, followed by a Soviet Refusenik anthem in the 1960s. Most recently, "Oyfn pripetshik" surfaced as a Holocaust dirge in the 1993 film *Schindler's List,* evoking the entire vanished world of Jewish eastern Europe.[45]

Jewish Art Music between Universalism and Particularism

If the sophisticated musical arrangements and overtly nostalgic material were two signs that the *Songbook* was intended as much for adults as for children, another indication was the presence of *kintslerishe lider,* or "art songs." Here the universalist aspirations of Jewish artists collided with the particularist demands of Jewish nationalism. In his introduction, Kiselgof explained that the art song section comprised pieces either "composed by Jewish composers or those that have at their root a national melody." Twenty-one art songs were included, all with Russian lyrics and Yiddish and Hebrew translations provided by Rivesman and the Hebrew poet Saul Tchernichowsky, respectively. Kiselgof's statement that art songs possessed a national soul when "a folk melody lies at their core" implied that non-Jewish composers who employed Jewish folkloric material could effectively produce music worthy of being called Jewish national art.[46] Ironically, though, the composers and selections chosen for the art songs section represented a potpourri of names and themes that stretched the meaning of Jewish music in still more disparate new directions.

In fact, the "Jewish Art Songs" section opens with two selections from Beethoven, including his iconic "Ode to Joy" from the Ninth Symphony. Obviously, there was nothing in Beethoven's music that suggested any Jewish "national melody." But translating the lyrics into Yiddish and Hebrew, Kiselgof and his colleagues apparently reasoned, stamped the music with a sufficient Jewish imprimatur. The German poet Friedrich Schiller's paean to international brotherhood was therefore refashioned in Rivesman's Yiddish as "Di freyd," and in Tchernichowsky's Hebrew as "Ha-simḥah."

In justifying this decision, Kiselgof again focused on children, the purported users of the volume: "Even when the melody is not Jewish, a song in the native [*narodnyi*] language is much closer and more accessible to children, both in terms of its words and its melody." The awkward, paradoxical wording of the explanation suggested that linguistic translation could even Judaize the musical character of a song's melody. These conceptual acrobatics allowed Kiselgof to define the Beethoven selections as simultaneously Jewish and universal. A similar notion of synthesis drove the logic behind the translations of Schiller's original German text. Both Tchernichowsky and Rivesman replaced the pantheistic poetic imagery of the German original with more classically Jewish and less theologically problematic images.

Original German:

> Freude, schöner Götterfunken,
> Tochter aus Elysium,
> Wir betreten feuertrunken,
> Himmlische, dein Heiligtum!

> Joy, fair spark of the Gods,
> Daughter of Elysium,
> We approach, drunk with fiery rapture,
> Goddess, your holy shrine!

Rivesman's Yiddish translation:

> Vi a shtral, a gots-matone
> Oft kumst tsu undz, du freyd!
> Un a palats ful mit vunder
> Hostu frayndlikh ongegreyt.

> Like a ray, a gift from God,
> You come to us often, Joy!
> And a palace full of wonders
> You have joyfully prepared.

Tchernichowsky's Hebrew translation:

Simḥah, at notsart ba-'eden,	Joy, you were created in Eden,
Zik el ḥay laykum hayit,	A spark from the living God you were to the universe.
Mil'e gil she'arayikh navo,	Full of delight we will enter your gates
Hekhal-kesem laḥ ivit.	To the magical sanctuary, desiring you.

In the hands of his conscientious translators, Schiller's polytheistic Romantic imagery of Greek gods and goddesses was refashioned as a tamer, monotheistic creed.[47]

The Beethoven selections and a lullaby attributed to Mozart ("Shirat ha-erev") in this section of the volume represented one extreme of the Jewish national canon. While none of these pieces featured Jewish themes in their melodies or lyrics, it was assumed that the creative Hebrew and Yiddish translations of their texts and their supranational cultural associations partially neutralized their obvious foreignness. At the other cultural pole were selections such as Mussorsgky's "Joshua ben Nun" aria from his "Joshua" cantata (*Iisus Navin*) and Glinka's "Persian Chorus" from the opera *Ruslan and Lyudmila*. In these works it was not the texts but the Jewish "national elements" in their melodies that qualified them as Jewish. Regardless of the composers' identities, Kiselgof wrote, these pieces warranted inclusion in an anthology of national music because of their Jewish musical roots.[48] Here the philosemitic seal of approval resurfaced as an external validation of Jewish music's intrinsic artistic value.

If explicitly non-Jewish composers could be accommodated in this way, the logic of Jewish nationalism took an even more tortuous turn in the cases of more ambiguously Jewish composers such as Anton Rubinstein and Felix Mendelssohn. Technically, Kiselgof explained, Mendelssohn and Rubinstein belonged to the Jewish tradition as *yidn-kompozitoren* (composers who are Jews) or, in the Russian version, *evrei-kompozitory*. Claiming kinship to these recent historical figures had an obvious appeal, since it allowed for a legitimate, usable past of great nineteenth-century Jewish composers. Yet mere national pride or cultural utility could not erase the obvious facts of their Christian faith and putative assimilation.

The various strategies adopted by Kiselgof to justify the inclusion of works by these composers reflected the two contrasting images of the Jewish musician in Russian and European music: the ultimate exotic Easterner and the ultracosmopolitan Westerner. Rubinstein, who was represented by excerpts from his opera *The Demon* (1883) and the oratorio *The Tower of Babel* (1872), had long been known for the *vostochnyi* (Oriental) coloring found in much of his music. Increasingly in the 1880s and 1890s, Russian Jewish listeners had begun to identify this Eastern style as specifically Jewish. Rubinstein's 1894 obituary in the Russian Jewish newspaper *Voskhod*, for instance, referred to the "many Jewish melodies [that] entered into the compositions of Anton Grigorevich, distinguished by their Oriental coloring." In the decades after the composer's death, Kiselgof and others took this process of reclaiming one step further. They pointed to Rubinstein's extensive use of the distinctive augmented second, an interval traditionally associated with Jewish folk song and liturgical music in eastern Europe, as indelible quasi-scientific proof of his musical Jewishness. Thus, in spite of his Christian baptism and cultural distance from traditional Jewish life, Rubinstein belonged in a national anthology of Jewish music.[49]

Mendelssohn represented an even greater challenge to Jewish musical nationalists. None of his music contained the same musical markers of ethnicity found in the work of Rubinstein. Even Mendelssohn's thematic interest in the Bible and religion, evident in his famous oratorios *Paul* and *Elijah*, bore witness to a theologically and culturally problematic relationship to Christian sacred composition through their identifiably antisemitic elements. Perhaps in acknowledgment of this issue, Kiselgof avoided Mendelssohn's works on religious themes, offering instead a selection of the composer's lieder on texts by various German poets. Of course, with their stately classical melodies and bucolic imagery, Mendelssohn's songs hardly resembled the Yiddish folk songs so prized by Kiselgof and others. In fact, Mendelssohn's songs implied an image of the Jew as a Westernized cosmopolitan or, worse, as an imitator of German music.[50] But the composer's illustrious lineage as the grandson of the icon of the Haskalah, Moses Mendelssohn, made him a desirable candidate for inclusion.

Ultimately, grouping Rubinstein and Mendelssohn along with Beethoven and (ersatz) Mozart in a Jewish national anthology enabled Kiselgof and the editors to make a double-edged symbolic statement about the universalism of European art and the integral Jewish presence within it. On one hand, as Rosowsky had argued in front of the St. Petersburg governor general in 1908, Jewish music was a cosmopolitan form of national art to which all musicians could contribute creatively (and presumably equally). At the same time, constructing the genre of Jewish music in terms of two overlapping criteria as Kiselgof did (the composer's Jewish background or the music's Jewish content) implied a moral claim about the impossibility of Jewish "assimilation." Regardless of their respective religious conversions or cultural "assimilation," the book suggested, both Rubinstein and Mendelssohn retained an inexorable Jewish essence.[51]

Perhaps to compensate for his problematic excursion into the ideological thickets of the European Jewish musical past, Kiselgof chose to bracket the art song section with the two categories of Jewish melodies he evidently considered the most traditional. Immediately before the art songs he placed a set of five Hasidic nigunim. Though the heading *lider on verter* (songs without words) ironically evoked Mendelssohn's *Songs without Words*, the tunes had in fact been recently transcribed in the Pale of Settlement. To close the *Songbook*, Kiselgof turned back to the quintessence of Jewish national music: *trop* (biblical chant). This section included the melodic patterns used for the recitation of the regular and holiday biblical portions, the Scroll of Esther, Song of Songs, Lamentations, and the Shavuoth hymn, "'Akdamot." During the planning discussions for the volume, the OPE educational committee had vigorously debated the suitability of including this sort of religious music in an anthology intended for use in secular schools. Some went so far as to claim that the nonmetrical nature of traditional *trop* chants would "impair the proper musical development of children." As if to compensate, Kiselgof's preface highlighted the melodies' historicity rather than their religious associations. These melodies had "great significance for national education," he wrote, because they constituted the "most ancient Jewish national music, passed on from generation to generation and today retaining its original melodic form."[52]

Music on the Road, 1912–1914

Work on the *Songbook* was completed in the fall of 1911. The following year the text was copublished in St. Petersburg by the society and in Berlin by Leo Winz. As the society conceived of the *Songbook* as a tool for membership expansion, the volume was sold at great discounts and every new member of the group was entitled to a free copy. The success of this strategy was confirmed almost immediately. New members joined in dramatic numbers. Within the first year after the *Songbook*'s publication, roughly five hundred individuals joined the organization's ranks from places as diverse as Baltimore, Irkutsk, and Tel Aviv. During the same period, Jewish communities in the Pale of Settlement, the Russian Caucasus, western Europe, and elsewhere adopted the *Songbook* for use in amateur choral and chamber music groups, Jewish schools, and other communal venues. By 1913 the society had sold or distributed nearly eight thousand copies.[53]

The demand for the book led quickly to a second edition, which was published in April 1914. In his introduction to the new version, Kiselgof described how the *Songbook* had already begun to transform the nature of Jewish music. In Jewish schools, he wrote, the anthology had helped drive out alien "non-Jewish song" from the mouths of Jewish children. At home, he declared, a similar "de-assimilation" process was taking place among Jewish parents. Soon, he predicted, "parents will sing with tears in their eyes the same little tune that their parents once upon a time sang over their own cribs."

Kiselgof noted with pride that he had taken the criticisms of reviewers into account in preparing the second edition. While the Russian Jewish press was generally positive in its response to the *Songbook,* some reviewers had noted the awkwardness and inappropriateness of the complicated "Germanic" multipart harmonizations of monophonic Jewish melodies, especially given the stated audience of schoolchildren. In response, several songs had been reharmonized to simplify them and to emphasize a "more national style." The other main change, Kiselgof explained, was the expansion of the art song section to include three new selections: the "Sabbath" and "Leah's Song" arias from Rubinstein's popular opera *The Maccabees* (1874) and Glinka's "Evreiskaia Pesnia" (Hebrew Song) (1840).[54]

The second edition of the *Songbook* also proved to be a strong commercial success. As a source for both composers and music teachers, the publication remained unmatched for decades in its scope and breadth. Eventually it would go through four editions, the final one published in Berlin in 1923. More immediately, it resulted in a new level of cultural visibility for Jewish music and an entrée into the world of Jewish cultural life beyond St. Petersburg. The success of the *Songbook* also encouraged the society to move ahead aggressively with other publishing projects. In April 1914 it issued a third series of works, twenty-five compositions published in Leipzig by Breitkopf and Härtel, and republished selected items from the first series. Work began immediately on a fourth series and an edition of liturgical works. That same year the society also published its first full-length book, a collection of articles by Lazare Saminsky entitled *Ob evreiskoi muzyke* (On Jewish Music).[55]

This increasingly ambitious variety and scale of publishing began to take a toll on the society's finances. The annual publishing budget rose from three thousand rubles in 1913 to four thousand in 1914, far outstripping revenues from concert tickets and member dues. At the same time, the leadership was loathe to eliminate the substantial publication price discounts and giveaways. To do so would violate their fiercely anticommercial mandate. Once again, commerce, art, and national mission clashed. Faced with this challenge, they refocused their funding hopes on the growing provincial branches.[56]

Over the course of 1913 and 1914, the society opened branches in Moscow, Kiev, Riga, and Kharkov. These groups grew quickly in numbers and activity. By the end of 1913, for instance, both the Kiev and Moscow branches had achieved membership rolls of over 150 people and presented an array of concerts and lectures.[57] Together the emerging branches represented a major potential source of much-needed revenue for St. Petersburg. But before these resources could be tapped, the First World War broke out in early August 1914, bringing with it a sweeping set of changes for Jewish culture.

Frozen Folk Songs

One day in the fall of 1910 the famous Warsaw Yiddish writer Isaac Leybush Peretz arrived in St. Petersburg to participate in an event hosted by the Jewish Literary Society. The composers of the Society for Jewish Folk Music eagerly sought him out for his blessing on their collective artistic experiments. In addition to his own inspiring act of transforming Yiddish folklore into modern Jewish literature, Peretz held special significance for the composers as himself an avid collector of Jewish folk songs. But instead of voicing his support, the visiting legend surprised the group's members with a sharp, sardonic response. Solomon Rosowsky later described his recollection of the exchange: "'Jewish music in Petersburg?' Peretz said ironically, 'You want to create Jewish art? Come to us, here, stand next to the cradle of Jewish music and create art!' And when we told him that every year we would make a pilgrimage to the cradle of the Jewish folk song, and we sought out the most remote shtetls and the yeshivas and wrote down all the nigunim and melodies straight from the people's mouths, he replied, 'Yes, yes, I understand you. But on the long road to cold Petersburg the songs will freeze a little bit.'"[58]

Recalling the episode, Rosowsky hastened to add that Peretz's playful barb was soon replaced with a positive appreciation and encouragement of the society's artistic efforts. Read this way, it was simply an ironic quip from a writer who considered "Jewish Warsaw" a better place for Jewish national culture than "*goyishe* [Gentile] St. Petersburg," as it was known among Yiddish writers. In fact, a whole school of Polish Jewish musical folklorists had emerged in Warsaw under Peretz's patronage.[59] On another level, though, Peretz's reference to "frozen folk songs" was also a hint of a more general philosophical problem lurking at the heart of Jewish national culture. To make Jewish music "modern" required plucking folkloric musical elements from their natural habitat in the Pale of Settlement and converting them into a new genre of European art music. Yet to do so, Peretz suggested, was to commit the sin of destroying traditional Jewish culture in the very name of preserving it. For how could these Russified Jewish musicians, fluent in the forms and sounds of German and Russian music, prevent the folk songs from ossifying in their modern classical arrangements? The danger, Peretz's witty remark implied, was that the Jewish music they cherished would turn into "frozen folk songs"—museum relics rather than a living tradition.

Throughout the 1910s, the Society for Jewish Folk Music wrestled with precisely this dilemma as it attempted to spread its vision of Jewish national music. Music publishing enabled the society to expand rapidly from a local musical circle into a broad communal organization and leading exponent of Jewish cultural nationalism. The thousands of copies of individual sheet music compositions and anthologies carried the ideal of Jewish national music along the roads leading from St. Petersburg back to the Pale and well beyond. But publishing also represented a complicated artistic endeavor rife with issues of commercialism and competing cultural aesthetics. If Jewish art music became just another version of the *shund* songs sold as phonograph records or in cheap sheet music editions on the streets of Warsaw and Kiev, then the Jewish national artistic mission would remain unfulfilled. At the same time, even if Jewish performers brought the society's sheet music editions into Russian concert halls, the risk remained that the performances themselves would fail to articulate the Jewish national spirit residing in Jewish folk music. How could one teach the Jewish folk spirit in music to those Jews who knew little of it?

In spite of these philosophical quandaries, the society pressed on with publishing even as World War I broke out. While the war's Eastern Front ravaged the shtetl communities of the Pale, Jewish folk songs—frozen or not—only grew in symbolic importance for the Russian Jewish intelligentsia. If it was not possible to control the new contexts into which Jewish music would flow, at least the national musical message would continue to go forth. For this reason, even in the face of censorship and other financial and logistical difficulties during the tumultuous years of World War I, the Society for Jewish Folk Music poured nearly all of its remaining resources into publishing. Even after the Russian Revolution had dispersed St. Petersburg's Jewish musicians to the four corners of the earth, they remained steadfastly committed to their publishing efforts, reissuing each other's works in new editions long after they had lost direct contact with one another. Of course, technology proved to be, as always, a double-edged sword. The message of Jewish music continued to live on in sheet music, recordings, and songbooks for decades—but neither as sonic time capsules nor as frozen folk songs. Instead the very meaning of modern Jewish music grew increasingly contested and ambiguous as nationalist politics, Marxist ideology, and high art collided in the post-1917 era of war and revolution.

CHAPTER 5

The Neighbors' Melodies

The Politics of Music in War and Revolution

> Where do our melodies come from? Perhaps we inherited them, perhaps they are from our neighbors.
> —I. L. Peretz, "The Transmigration of a Melody" (1901)

> Jewish music is the face of a frozen Sphinx only just awakening to life after thousands of years. . . . Up until now European music sounded its sweet siren's song for Jewish composers, luring musical youth away from their national ambitions and drowning them in waves of European art, where the bewitched would lose their national consciousness. . . . Now we will establish our national genius by realizing its melos inside ourselves, forging songs in the crucible of the unique Jewish spirit, not only for ourselves and for our own people, but for the entire world.
> —Alexander Krein, "Problems of Jewish Music" (1918)

It is rare for an academic scholar to retract his work, rarer still for him to apologize publicly for a mistake. Yet this is precisely what occurred in April 1914 at the annual meeting of the Society for Jewish Folk Music in St. Petersburg. After the standard slate of introductory speeches and a concert performance of new works, the remainder of the evening was devoted to an unprecedented spectacle: a public mea culpa from the leading Russian music historian of the day, Liberio Sacchetti (1852–1916) of the St. Petersburg Conservatory.

In his talk Sacchetti acknowledged what everyone present undoubtedly already knew: he had spent his entire career denying the very existence of Jewish music. In his Russian-language *Lectures on the History of Music*, first published in 1882, he had claimed that the Jews lacked a true national music of their own. As a people with an "exclusively moral—religious character" rather than an aesthetic one, their synagogue melodies (he ignored folk music altogether) "reflect[ed] the musical influences of those peoples among whom the Jews have lived." By the time of his 1914 speech, the volume had gone through multiple academic and popular editions to become the best known and most widely read book of its kind in Russian music schools, conservatories, and beyond.

Addressing Jewish St. Petersburg, the senior scholar now contritely admitted his error. What had changed his mind, he explained, was the discovery of a vibrant Jewish musical tradition alive and well within the halls of his own beloved conservatory. Some months earlier, he had sat in the audience in the same auditorium when the Society for Jewish Folk Music held its fifth anniversary concert. To his astonishment, Sacchetti reported, he had heard music that he had previously not known existed. Congratulating the Jews on their fine musical history, he also lavished particular praise on the new school of Russian Jewish composers. Jewish art music, in his eyes, constituted a wonderful surprise for European music as a whole. Recalling the speech a few days later, the society's new president, liberal politician Benjamin Mandel, boasted that what Sacchetti had heard was the rising sound of a "new national school of music, one that would contribute one of the most interesting new chapters in world art."[1]

Sacchetti's belated stamp of approval was one unmistakable sign that the debate in Russian culture about the existence of Jewish music was officially over. It also marked the arrival of the Jewish "national school" in music. The cadre of young Russian Jewish musicians now associated with the group extended far beyond Rimsky-Korsakov's former pupils to include performers with rising international profiles such as pianist Maria Yudina (1899–1970), violinists Jascha Heifetz and Miron Poliakin (1895–1941), and pianist and conductor Issay Dobroven (1891–1953). Equally impressive was the list of composers with growing reputations in Russian music, such as Liubov Shtreikher (1888–1958), Iuliia Veisberg, Jacob Veinberg (1875–1956), and Alexander Krein (1883–1951).

Commenting on this phenomenon, one critic noted that it was not merely these Jewish composers' mainstream success that was striking. Even more telling was the fact that "the prestige of nearly all of these representatives of young Russian composition is based in no small part on their involvement in the field of Jewish folk music." These were Russian Jewish composers who had achieved widespread recognition as creators of both Jewish *and* Russian music. Indeed, by 1914 Jewish music symbolized a movement toward the artistic universal through the particular. In other words, in making Jewish music, Russian Jews were becoming not only more Jewish, but also more Russian—and more European.[2]

This idyllic vision proved short-lived. By 1918, the tenth anniversary of the Society for Jewish Folk Music, the musicians who had come together so enthusiastically had begun to split apart. Their separation took the most visible and literal of forms: emigration. During the 1920s, the mass of Russian Jewish musicians spread out across the world. Though select members of the society tried in various ways to continue their activities for almost another decade under Soviet rule, their colleagues now launched a Russian Jewish musical diaspora stretching from Tel Aviv and Jerusalem to Berlin, Vienna, Paris, New York, and Los Angeles. If the project of Jewish music had not quite disappeared, it had certainly departed radically from its pre–World War I form.

The most obvious explanation for the collapse of this Jewish cultural movement is the combination of World War I and the Russian Revolution. The sheer physical violence visited on the Jews of eastern Europe in the years between 1914 and 1921 uprooted millions of people, cost hundreds of thousands their lives, and destroyed thousands of communities. The Russian Civil War and the new Bolshevik regime swept away numerous Jewish political, communal, and religious institutions and radically transformed Jewish social and economic life. But while there is no denying the large-scale effects of war and revolution, the reality of the changes to Russian Jewish culture in this period was subtler and more complicated. The post-1917 cultural emigration reflected more than the vicissitudes of individual lives and displaced communities in the vortex of wartime and revolutionary eastern Europe. Nor, despite the persistent narrative of Jewish collective memory, did it result from a blanket attack on Jewishness and Jewish culture by the Bolsheviks. Rather, the crisis of Russian Jewish culture and the massive exodus derived from the convergence of two more specific trends: the resurgence of politics in the Jewish cultural world and the broader shift in modern European aesthetics.

In the years after 1917, the new artistic currents of European modernism and the rekindled political ideologies of Jewish socialism and nationalism shattered the loose consensus about the delicate balance between universal aspirations and particularist commitments in Russian Jewish culture. Beyond the destructive forces of war and revolution, it was these modernist ideologies—political and aesthetic—that called into question the meaning and purpose of Jewish national art and culture as a whole. In the musical world, this crisis was reflected in a fundamental way: the musicians simply could no longer agree on how to define Jewish music—and where it should live.

The first hint of these ideological conflicts arrived in the early years of World War I when a dramatic public rift emerged between two dominant intellectual figures: Joel Engel and Lazare Saminsky. This episode, crucial to modern Jewish cultural history yet often grossly misunderstood, was soon followed after 1917 by a broader series of confrontations, personal and collective, with the new political forces and artistic currents emerging in Russian society. As the Russian Jewish intelligentsia began to fray under the pressure of various old and new ideological allegiances, its musicians spun off in multiple directions in search of new homes for modern Jewish music. As we shall see, their attempts to transplant themselves and their movement to fresh soil in postwar Soviet Russia, Palestine, and the United States ultimately proved unsuccessful. In each case, though the reasons vary, these failures reveal just how rooted the project of modern Jewish music was to its original Imperial Russian context. The various afterlives of Russian Jewish culture in the post-1917 period highlight in final, stark relief the distinctive features of Russian Jewish identity itself.

Jewish Culture at War

The outbreak of World War I had an immediate, deleterious effect on Jews in the Pale of Settlement, a region now transformed into the war's Eastern Front. Hundreds of thousands of Jews were physically uprooted. Their cultural lives were also deeply impacted, particularly because of Russian military censorship. In Moscow and St. Petersburg (newly renamed Petrograd), however, the war actually had the opposite effect on Jewish cultural life. There a host of new Jewish communal relief organizations embraced musical and literary events as instruments of philanthropy. The Society for Jewish Folk Music's concerts began to serve as fund-raisers on behalf of organizations such as the Society for the Preservation of the Health of the Jewish Population in Russia (Obshchestvo okhraneniia zdorovia evreiskogo naseleniia v Rossii) and the Jewish Committee for the Aid of War Victims (Evreiskii komitet pomoshchii zhertvam voiny). The society itself also proceeded in determined fashion with its plans, opening new branches in provincial cities such as Simferopol, Ekaterinoslav, and Rostov-on-Don and organizing large-scale summertime outdoor orchestral concerts in Odessa, Kiev, and elsewhere. Back in Petrograd, the local membership ranks rose to over 750 by 1917 with an average of three hundred people in attendance at each musical meeting.[3]

Along with fund-raising, the Petrograd musicians dramatically increased their publishing output. In 1914 the group sold eight hundred publications of all kinds. The following year the number had leapt to well over 2,600. This included a second *Songbook* edition, two more series of composers' new works, a two-volume collection of synagogue music, a book of thirty-four children's songs, and a lithograph edition of folk song transcriptions. In spite of rising costs, paper shortages, communications difficulties, and military censorship, the Petrograd group committed itself to publishing as its single most important activity, an obvious means of cultural preservation in the face of the massive destruction in the Yiddish cultural heartland.[4] To realize this growing challenge, it began to lean more heavily on its newly established branches for support. The most obvious partner was in Moscow, where Engel had established the group's first regional branch in 1913. Engel's Moscow cohort was heavily drawn from the ranks of the Moscow Conservatory, including David Shor (1867–1942), a piano professor and prominent local Zionist activist, and recent graduates Jacob (Iakov V.) Veinberg and Alexander Krein, both emerging young composers. Quickly the group launched a full roster of concerts and lectures, along with its own chamber music ensemble. In 1915 it accepted the invitation of the main branch to enter into a joint publishing partnership. An intercity committee of composers was established and charged with selecting the works for publication.[5] On the surface, the growing collaboration between Moscow and Petrograd was a sign of unity in the face of external adversity. War provided a common focal point for collective action; the challenges of the day only enhanced the sense of common purpose. But the publishing partnership between the two cities also brought to light deepening political and aesthetic ideological fissures regarding the very question of what constituted authentic Jewish national music.

Defining the Future through the Past: The Polemics of National Music, 1915–17

By 1915 Engel had emerged as the undisputed elder statesman of Jewish music. The Petrograd musicians had symbolically confirmed this status three years earlier by electing him their first and only honorary member. Yet his authority was to be severely tested that year by a brash, younger representative of the Petrograd group, Lazare Saminsky. The challenge began innocuously enough, in the form of an article by Saminsky in *Razsvet* in February entitled, "Artistic Achievement in the Recent Work of the Society for Jewish Folk Music." On the surface, Saminsky's commentary was simply a critical appraisal of the first five years' worth of compositions by his fellow Jewish composers. But his other agenda involved a new definition of Jewish music quite at odds with Engel's well-established theory. The ensuing debate between the two men eventually became one of the most important chapters in the history of modern Jewish culture. Yet its precise meaning has proven consistently elusive. The Engel-Saminsky polemic has been alternately characterized as a repetition of the contemporary Hebrew-Yiddish language wars, a reflection of the religious-secular divide in Jewish music, or a political argument about Zionism. However, the debate was ultimately about the changing nature of Jewish art and culture as a whole in modern eastern Europe.

Following his graduation from the St. Petersburg Conservatory in 1910, Saminsky had departed for the Caucasus to perform his military service in the Imperial Grenadiers. There he became fascinated by the cultural distinctiveness and ostensible antiquity of the Jewish communities of Georgia, Dagestan, and Azerbaijan. He began to spend increasing amounts of time in the region, imbibing the sounds of their "exotic" Asian Jewish music. By 1915 Saminsky had relocated permanently to Tiflis (Tbilisi) to become a professor at the city's new conservatory.

From his first encounters with the Caucasus, Saminsky began to construct an elaborate theory of Jewish musical history. In his 1914 book, *Ob evreiskoi muzyke* (On Jewish Music), published and distributed by the Petrograd branch, he proposed that Jewish music might be defined on the basis of the common musical traits that linked the global Jewish nation together and protected them from the pressures of thousands of years of assimilation in the Diaspora. His 1915 *Razsvet* article now offered a more detailed iteration of this theory, centered on the primacy of "ancient religious melodies" in modern Jewish art music.[6]

After five years of careful ethnographic research and artistic experimentation, he wrote, Jewish composers had finally begun to tap "the rich seams of our ancient religious melodies." This distinction between "religious" (*religioznaia*) or liturgical Jewish music and "domestic" (*bytovaia*) or secular Jewish music was well established in both central European and Russian Jewish musical thought. Engel himself had earlier invoked it in his work. But Saminsky now took the unprecedented step of explicitly ranking the two categories in a nationalist hierarchy. The "true foundations of Jewish music," he argued, were the "religious melodies" of the synagogue. They constituted the purest segment of Jewish music, dating from the time of the First Temple. By contrast, all other forms of Diaspora Jewish music were less Jewish, both by virtue of their more recent vintage and the heavy external cultural influences on them. Accordingly, the bulk of eastern European Jewish music, including secular Yiddish folk songs, instrumental klezmer tunes, and even Hasidic nigunim all failed Saminsky's test of national distinctiveness; he dismissed them as little more than "Polish folk dances," "altered versions of German and Ukrainian folk songs," and borrowings from "Oriental music." As recent, foreign grafts onto the central corpus of Jewish melody, they were nationally illegitimate and unsuitable for the current musical renaissance.[7]

Saminsky's article prompted an immediate, angry response from Engel.

In an "An Open Letter to L. I. Saminsky," published in *Razsvet* two weeks later, Engel attacked Saminsky's "true foundations" as a "superficial, nearly mechanical definition" of Jewish music. While he acknowledged that Jewish composers had previously exploited synagogue melody less, Engel rebuked Saminsky for his "scornful," "severe" dismissal of "secular Jewish music." Despite a more recent provenance, he wrote, Yiddish folk songs and other nonliturgical eastern European Jewish music also counted as legitimate, authentic expressions of the "Jewish soul." Why did Saminsky unfairly malign these genres of Jewish music regarding their "national" value?[8]

Saminsky's reply was uncompromising. The solemn task of creating modern national music required the Jewish composer to employ only the most verifiably Jewish sources: "No matter how Jewish melody is developed, masterfully cultivated, and imbued with individual creativity," he wrote, "the value of the work, both in national and general cultural terms, depends on which of these melodic patterns is used as its foundation." With the modern tools of ethnographic transcription and musicological analysis, Saminsky explained, the music of the Jews could be broken down into its most essential melodic units, the unpolluted musical genes: "No foreign musical growths have ever grown on the core of our traditional synagogue music. . . . You will not confuse a cantillation fragment of *Song of Songs* with an opera aria that has entered into the synagogue. . . . It is quite different with our domestic melody. Even its specimens that are valuable in purely musical terms present such an obvious, distinctive knot of foreign influences that to isolate the pure specimens is a project of enormous difficulty and importance."[9]

In presenting this musical genealogy, Saminsky leaned heavily on the modal theory of Jewish music then prevalent among both central European cantors and Russian ethnographers. According to this theory, the national identity of a given piece of music, regardless of its complexity, could be reduced to the basic underlying modal or scalar structure of its melody. One mode that had attracted considerable attention from earlier researchers was the so-called altered Phrygian mode (often known as *freygish* or *ahavah rabbah*), characterized by an extra step appearing between the second and third degrees of the Western Phrygian scale (created by raising the third degree a half step to create the augmented second). This was the very mode that Zisman Kiselgof and his colleagues had identified as a unique marker of Jewish musical distinctiveness, a common link between Polish Hasidic nigunim, Moldavian klezmer melodies, Lithuanian Sabbath chants, and the operas of Anton Rubinstein.[10]

Yet Saminsky now dismissed the very Jewishness of this "Jewish" mode. Referring to it contemptuously as "pan-Oriental" (*obshchevostochnyi*), he

Example 9. Ascending and descending scales in the altered Phrygian ("pan-Oriental") and Aeolian modes.

explained that it was equally common to many other peoples of the eastern Mediterranean, including the Turks and the Greeks. Rather than an authentic national marker, it was therefore better understood as a sign of cultural contamination. He even invoked a biological metaphor to describe this mode's presumably pernicious effects on Jewish musical purity. Folk melodies that possessed the "generic, hackneyed, and pan-Oriental structure," he wrote, "cannot become the embryos for the growth of national-musical organisms."

To bolster his case, Saminsky referred both to the ethnographic evidence gathered by Engel and Kiselgof during the recent Ansky expeditions in the Pale of Settlement and to his own fieldwork in Georgia, where he claimed to have found another ancient melodic mode, one unique to the Jewish people. The purest part of Jewish music, the part least touched by "assimilation" and external cultural influence, Saminsky argued, was the set of traditional melodies used for biblical and liturgical chant, particularly those in what he called the Jewish Aeolian mode (see ex. 9). As proof, he pointed to the underlying similarities in Jewish liturgical chant between two vastly different and geographically distant Jewish communities: the Ashkenazi Jews of eastern Europe and the Asian Jews of the Caucasus.

The Engel-Saminsky polemic was interrupted by the tsarist authorities' shutdown of *Razsvet* in July 1915. By that time, however, the conflict had begun to spread beyond the pages of the press. In April, Saminsky wrote to Alexander Krein, Engel's close friend and colleague, to reprimand him for using "vulgar wedding melodies . . . [that are] in essence not Jewish but Romanian, Hungarian, etc" in his compositions. That fall Engel and Saminsky each took their arguments directly to the Petrograd branch, campaigning for their theories in the form of dueling lectures. Meanwhile, within the Petrograd musical committee, the composers had collectively begun to shift toward Saminsky's camp in their work, embracing a conscious "reorientation in the direction of religious melodies" in their newest orchestral works.[11]

The following January the two theorists resumed their argument in print. In a long article entitled "Jewish Domestic Folk Song" in the newspaper *Evreiskaia nedelia* (Jewish Week), Engel recapped his and Saminsky's arguments at length. He then turned to the science of music to defend the national integrity of Yiddish folk song and the rest of eastern European Jewish music. To disprove the charges of a preponderance of foreign melodic modes and rhythms, Engel referred readers to the Society's own *Songbook* as an authoritative academic collection of Jewish music. Comparing the folk songs included in that collection with those in Polish, Ukrainian, and Romanian folk music anthologies, he asserted that Jewish secular folk music comprised far more than just the "Oriental" mode Saminsky had claimed. As evidence, he noted that of sixty-two secular folk songs in the *Songbook*, only twenty-two featured the problematic "Oriental" mode and interval of the augmented second. And even in these twenty-two, this musical feature "appears only sporadically and does not dominate."[12]

But Engel was not content to stake his entire intellectual claim on a positivist statistical argument. He also added a more basic criticism of Saminsky's model of monolithic national purity: "A mode by itself still only means very little," he wrote. "It is merely an outline, a scaffold against which it is possible to create a melody, deeply varied in form and spirit. After all, the very same 'pan-Oriental' mode is characteristic of many Hungarian, Romanian, Armenian, Persian and other melodies. So is it really possible to conclude from this that in the case of Hungarians, Romanians and Armenians their music 'as such does not exist, that it is simply a part of Oriental music'?!" Going further, he attacked Saminsky's favored "ancient Jewish synagogue melodies and biblical *trop.*" These were "by no means the exclusive private property of the Jews," he noted archly, for the Aeolian mode could be found in medieval chants of the Catholic and Orthodox churches and even in the folk songs of various peoples. Turning the argument around, Engel asked, "Is it therefore truly possible to deny the unique musical physiognomy of any old Russian, Norwegian, or Finnish song or of any Gregorian or Slavonic Church melody or to call an old synagogue chant less authentic because all of them are built on a 'hackneyed' Aeolian mode?"

By demonstrating with simple logic that no one-to-one correspondence existed between nations and their chosen musical modes, Engel effectively accused Saminsky of requiring a higher standard for Jewish music, thus creating an impossible myth of purity and cultural exceptionalism. "Modes are few, peoples many," he explained further, "and from these same building blocks each people in its own way constructs its own edifice, its own type of melody." Why hold Jews to an absurd standard of cultural purity, far beyond what was expected of any other religion or nation? In place of Saminsky's model, Engel restated his earlier model of Jewish music as an open but distinctive cultural system. Instead of the nationalist idée fixe of cultural borrowing, he proposed a concept of cultural adaptation or "Judaization." At the end of the day, he explained, the cultural paternity or "musical physiognomy" of Jewish folk song was created and confirmed by the Jewish masses. Modal analysis mattered little when compared with the power of the Jewish people to imprint their national style on their folk music.[13]

In reply, Saminsky unabashedly mocked this sophisticated strain of Jewish cultural populism as a dangerous folly for scholars and composers alike. He lambasted Engel for his "pious belief in the most supreme holiness of what the people produce as folk song." The "fondness of the Jewish heart," he wrote, had produced only naive amateur versions of Jewish music, as evidenced by all the Yiddish theater ditties, bawdy wedding couplets, and Ukrainian folk songs masquerading as Jewish children's songs in the *Songbook*. The impulse toward musical populism was no substitute for the modern Jewish composer's obligation to create truly national music. He therefore repeated his appeal to Jewish composers to reject the "commonplace, borrowed element of our songs, characterless in terms of nationality, dull and decrepit," in favor of pure Jewish ingredients suitable for the "organic" growth of Jewish "national-musical organisms."[14]

At the end of 1916 Engel and Saminsky ceased their public arguments by mutual agreement. The inability of Jewish newspapers to print notated musical examples and the lack of sufficient source materials given the wartime disruptions made it pointless to continue the debate. Meanwhile, the final salvos came from neither man but an altogether different interlocutor, S. Ansky. Writing under the pseudonym "Unicus," he entered the fray with a series of short letters published in the fall of 1916 and early 1917. While Ansky sympathized with Saminsky's fears about the debasement of Jewish musical taste, he wrote, he sided ultimately with Engel in his belief in the authenticity and national genius of Ashkenazi music. Ansky pointed out that Jewish music's origins mattered less than its transformation by the spirit of the people. Jews stamped music with their unmistakable folk ethos just as they did with other parts of their religion and culture: "Just try to return the monotheism we borrowed from the Egyptians to them after its transformation in the crucible of our national spirit," wrote Ansky. "Just try to return our mysticism to the Persians and Babylonians. Just try to return the Hasidic 'nigun' to its original owners, the Ukrainian or Hungarian—would he recognize it? Would he recognize his offspring in it? In song just as in philosophy, it is not the lifeless building material, but the animating spiritual force that defines its owner."[15]

The poetic intervention of a political figure like Ansky was one clue to the broader ideological argument hovering behind the questions of taste and theory. Ansky was the leading Jewish populist of the day, with deep links to the Bund and the Socialist Revolutionary movement, and a firm opponent of Zionist politics. More recently he had become a leader in the Folks-Partey efforts to build a twin cultural and political framework of Jewish Diaspora nationalism to legitimate and represent Jewish national communities in eastern Europe. Indeed, if Engel's musical populism reverberated with overtones of the Diasporist political ideologies of Ansky, Dubnow, and others, Saminsky's strident differentiation between Yiddish music of the "assimilated" Diaspora and the "true Hebrew music" associated with ancient Zion smacked of the Hebraist cultural Zionism of the 1910s. The elevation of the ancient Jewish biblical homeland over the Jewish Diaspora's national assimilationism and the privileging of the Hebrew language over the Yiddish vernacular implied a musical transposition of the political theories of the Zionist thinker Ahad Ha'am.[16]

In fact, a nearly identical theory had been propounded at the very same time by an explicitly Zionist musician, Avraham Tsvi Idelsohn (1882–1938). Born in Russia's Kurland province (present-day Latvia), he received a traditional cantorial education in Lithuania and conservatory training in Germany before settling in Jerusalem in 1907. There he launched a massive research project to collect all of the musical traditions represented in the various communities of the Yishuv in order to isolate the ancient, authentic Hebrew musical heritage uncorrupted by the Diaspora. Idelsohn's goal, openly influenced by the ideas of Ahad Ha'am, was to build a new Hebrew national music in the homeland. While there is no evidence that he and Saminsky knew of one another's ideas in this period, they nevertheless shared many tropes: a conscious denunciation of the futility of European Jewish "assimilation," an explicit embrace of key components of Richard Wagner's musical antisemitism, and an explicit aesthetic of musical Hebraism. Idelsohn would go on to have enormous influence on Zionist musical circles throughout the world in the 1920s and 1930s through his scholarly monographs, songbooks, and his ten-volume musical source collection, the *Thesaurus of Hebrew-Oriental Melodies* (1914–33).[17]

Reading Saminsky against Idelsohn's Zionism and Engel against Ansky's Jewish Diaspora nationalism, it is easy to see the resurgent force of political ideology in wartime Russian Jewish culture. But this is only part of the story. Even with the implied similarities, it would be a mistake to reduce the Engel-Saminsky argument to a direct cultural reflection of competing Jewish political movements, as many writers have sought to do.[18] In reality, each man's musical thought also reflected the deeper Russian and European sensibilities built into modern Jewish culture.

In Saminsky's case, for all of his radical rejection of the Jewish Diaspora past coupled with an overpowering vision of a modern Hebraic culture, his choice of vocabulary, imagery, and aesthetic sensibilities all bore equally strong, if jumbled traces of the core precepts of the Russian Silver Age. Born in 1882, he had come of age just as the Russian musical world was turning swiftly toward Europe in search of new cultural and philosophical ideas. The Silver Age, Russia's version of the European fin de siècle, was characterized by a renewed interest in European Romanticism, myth, religion, and mysticism, and the new aesthetics of modernism.

Saminsky's Wagnerism was one clear reflection of these trends. His thinking about Jews and Jewish culture hinged on a set of binary polarities that derived from a Russian variant on Wagner's antisemitic formula: the opposition between the good ancient Jew (*evrei*), with his positive biblical qualities of manliness, courage, forthrightness, nobility, and physicality, and the bad modern Jew (*zhid*), a paradigm of femininity, weakness, duplicity, immorality, and rootlessness. Saminsky later recalled how the pre-1905 revolutionary events in Russia had left him with two contradictory images of the Jew: the positive heroic ideal of Grigorii Gershuni (1870–1908), a young Jewish Bolshevik leader known to have masterminded political assassinations of tsarist officials, contrasted with the negative figure of Evno Azeff (1869–1918), also a Jewish radical but at the same time a tsarist double agent who infiltrated revolutionary circles only to betray both his government masters and his comrades. The contrast led Saminsky to his own "favorite theory" of Jews as a perpetually "neurotic people" of contrasting extremes, "capable of giving mankind a Jesus of Nazareth or a Spinoza but also of inflicting upon it the most foul [of] criminals."[19]

In addition to Wagnerism, Nietzschean aesthetic ideas echo repeatedly through Saminsky's writing, most notably in his notion of the individual artist as an elite vanguard and a prophet of modernity. For Saminsky, this translated into a revolution in Jewish musical aesthetics predicated on "merciless" rejection of all that was old, "doubtful" and "foreign-born." Thus for him the Jewish religious melos evoked not a return to a pious past of eternal tradition but a radical revival of "ancient Hebraic paganism."[20] These sorts of European modernist and antisemitic cultural currents mixed together with analogous Zionist philosophical impulses in Saminsky's cultural model. But his goal of national cultural renaissance was not Zionist in the conventional political sense of his Russian Jewish contemporaries. Even on a symbolic cultural level, his imaginary geography of Jewish national music centered not on a romance with Zion but on Russia's own grand empire.

In his unpublished memoirs, Saminsky evoked a childhood obsession with the Eastern peoples and places of the Russian Empire, particularly the Tatars, Georgians, and Karaites who dominated his vision of the Caucasus. "I dreamed of the splendid race of Tartar conquerors, of their endurance, horsemanship, contempt for death," he recalled later, "of that real life depicted by Pushkin, Lermontov, and Tolstoy in their immortal Caucasian stories, of the merry Circassian *auls* drowning the vineyards. . . . There was nothing on earth I wanted so much as to live in the Caucasus; [to] drink of its life and be a brother amidst its people."[21]

Saminsky's autobiography overflows with similar images of the "ancient races, creeds, and cultures" of the Caucasus. Some of these impressions are clearly derived from Russian literature, but others stem from his own experiences in the region, such as the intense delight he felt at his honorary adoption by fellow composer Liubov Shtreikher's Georgian Jewish family. In fact, taken as a whole, his pronouncements in lectures, articles, and memoirs suggest an obsession not so much with ancient Jerusalem as with nineteenth-century Tiflis. In other words, it was from the comparison of the East and West within the particular context of the late Russian Empire that Saminsky derived his passionate nationalist vision of Jewish music. Even as he celebrated the Revolution of 1905 as a popular uprising against a tyrannical tsarist regime and urged his fellow Jews to embrace the true Oriental component of their shared national identity, Saminsky situated his dense mixture of Hebraic Zionism and German antisemitism within an Imperial Russian framework. And the glue holding together these diverse intellectual commitments was an overarching commitment not to Jewish politics but to European aesthetics.

In the years before World War I, the Russian avant-garde had begun to take an active role in the currents of musical modernism then appearing in France and Germany. Composers such as Stravinsky and Scriabin stretched the fabric of conventional tonality, harmony, and rhythm to the outermost limits in search of a new kind of sound. But for many Russian Jewish composers, European modernism raised an obvious dilemma about the parochial character of national art, especially of a minority culture, in an age of internationalism. Saminsky's response was to idealize ancient Jewish music as the key to a renewed, modernist European culture as a whole. Extending this integrationist vision a step further, he argued that Christian liturgical music—the roots of Western art music—hailed from ancient Jewish sources.

By turning to their Hebraic roots, Jews would lead all of musical Europe to a rejuvenating source for human culture in the modern era. Saminsky's revolt against the commonplace was thus a search for a Jewish musical space within European culture. As he wrote in the introduction to his 1914 book, "By returning to its pure origins, Jewish composition will add a new, beautiful culture, of previously unknown harmony and colors, to European art."[22]

In contrast to Saminsky's enthusiastic ethnic modernism, Engel, fifteen years his senior, felt a deeper attachment to the nineteenth-century Romantic populism of his youth. Engel's East was neither Zion nor the Caucasus but eastern Europe and—within it—the Pale of Settlement. This was less a function of his populist political sympathies than of his populist aesthetics. While Engel spoke of modern harmonies for Jewish musical folklore, he still envisioned an essentially nineteenth-century ideal of folkloric realism: art should depict reality or risk losing its stylistic coherence and cultural raison d'être. On some level, Engel believed that Jewish art music needed to sound like the folk songs upon which it was based. Or, as he often said, quoting his teacher Sergei Taneev, when it came to art, "only that which is rooted in the folk is solid." Saminsky, on the other hand, as an adherent of the modernist mandate of aesthetic abstraction, considered it sufficient to use the national essence for a freer form of composition. Art, in his view, need not represent reality directly, provided its sources were culturally authentic.[23]

Above all, both Engel and Saminsky each resisted casting their cultural work as political because "Jewish music" and "Jewish national culture" amounted to sufficient ideological ends in and of themselves. Thus, while Saminsky's rhetoric may have smacked of Zionism, he himself maintained an avowedly apolitical stance. Engel meanwhile took pains to downplay the conflict, even as it took a toll on his relations with Petrograd. At the end of 1916, frustrated by the slow pace of the publishing partnership with the Society for Jewish Folk Music and likely piqued by the rift with Saminsky, Engel took steps to establish his own publishing imprint under the auspices of the Moscow branch. Yet in lectures that he delivered in various cities and towns across Russia that year and the next, he deemphasized the broader significance of the disagreement. Any potential political differences among advocates of Jewish culture were overshadowed by a deeper sense of national unity. All the Jewish political parties shared this sentiment, he repeatedly claimed, citing a popular Jewish song lyric: "What we may be, we'll be, but we are all still Jews."[24]

Other leaders of the society adopted similar attitudes. Even as ideological conflicts surged again among Russian Jewry during the war years, they strove to avoid any overt politicization of their mission. This endeavor did not always prove easy, especially when it came to the growing political conflicts initiated by Zionists over language. When, for instance, the newly opened Kharkov branch wrote to Petrograd in 1916 about the society's language policy, the group's secretary, Israel Okun, himself still an active Bundist, responded with exasperation: "Our society has and will continue to occupy itself solely with questions of Jewish music, and not language. In order to achieve purely musical goals, we resort to all available means including with regards to language. Contact us and correspond with us in whatever language you please." Going further, he struck a pragmatic tone: "If there is a wide circle of people in Poland, Galicia, America, England, and so on, interested in buying our sheet music, we are necessarily required to print prospectuses in Yiddish, the language most accessible to them. If there turn out to be a substantial contingent of people needing the prospectus in Hebrew, then we would of course also print that." Language does not matter, he concluded, "as long as the music is Jewish."[25]

Of course a protest against politics is one of the surest signs of politics. The proponents of Jewish music certainly were not immune to the growing ideological tensions of the day. But they were also determined not to reduce national art to a single political platform. The ideologies of Zionism and Folkist Diaspora nationalism were only vague presences in the project of Jewish music in the decade before 1917. Despite the claims of subsequent memoirists and scholars, Jewish cultural nationalism did not automatically equate art with politics by other means for the Russian Jewish intelligentsia of the time. Indeed, the kind of nationalism espoused by Engel, Saminsky, and their colleagues reflected a shared perception that Jewish particularism facilitated—and even required—a greater engagement with mainstream Russian and European cultural life.[26]

If modern Jewish culture allowed some Jews to become more Russian and European, so too did it have the opposite effect on others, renewing a palpable sense of Jewishness among otherwise Russified Jewish elites. The Europeanization of Jewish culture attracted a broad cross-section of this group to a cosmopolitan concept of Jewish national unity. This was because beyond all politics—Jewish or Russian—post-1905 Jewish cultural nationalism continued the work of the Haskalah in its quest to modernize, civilize, and emancipate Jews. Within the ostensibly politically neutral realm of culture, the two sides of the Russian Jew could meet as one. The breakdown in the consensus about the Jewishness of Jewish music was one sign that the Russian Jewish nineteenth century was now finally ending. The resistance to politics revealed that a renewed process of politicization had already begun, and that its challenge was a wholly new one. The meanings of Jewish culture and Jewish nationalism were beginning to morph once again. The final catalyst was the Bolshevik seizure of power in October 1917, which threw all of Russian society into the maelstrom of revolution and civil war.

1917: The Revenge of Politics

The February Revolution of 1917 initially brought optimism, tempered by caution, to Russian Jewry. Among its first steps, the Provisional Government formally abolished the Pale of Settlement and legally emancipated Russian Jewry. That April, Engel led a Moscow Jewish musical delegation on a monthlong concert tour of fourteen cities and towns across Russia. At each stop he delivered a rousing speech, voicing his hope for a new democratic Russia in which the Jews, having attained full civil liberties, would also be granted cultural autonomy or "freedom of national self-definition." As equal citizens, Engel declared, Jews should embrace their collective Jewish "national identity" within the multiethnic liberal Russian state. In the process, Jewish artists would contribute as individuals to their Jewish nation, and the collective "river of Jewish art" would run into the "endless ocean of all humanity's art."[27]

Engel's tour met with an overwhelming positive response. In nearly every city, he noted, he found audiences that had never experienced this kind of "serious" Jewish cultural event and hungered for more. They cheered excitedly for encores, showered the performers with flowers, and clamored for copies of the sheet music. It was a moment of triumph for Jewish national music and the Society for Jewish Folk Music alike, he recalled immediately afterward. The organization and its mission now stood to be embraced passionately by "all sectors and parties of the Jewish population," including the full political spectrum of Zionists, Bundists, Poalei Zion (Marxist Zionists), and all others who came together to celebrate Jewish national culture. Again and again, Engel noted with pride and satisfaction, an audience member would approach him during a concert intermission to confess, "I am a Social Democrat, but I now feel that they [the nationalists] are right!" In his judgment, a spirit of "unity and joy for all Israel" prevailed among Russian Jewry. Here was proof of the ability of art to transcend conventional party politics in the name of national unity.[28]

At every concert on the spring tour, Engel repeated his claim that modern Jewish culture would finally be able to realize its full promise in post-tsarist liberal Russia. At the same time, however, the political battles of 1905 began to reemerge into full public view with a new intensity. Over the spring and summer of 1917, representatives from the full spectrum of Jewish political parties and cultural organizations began to prepare for elections to an All-Russian Jewish Congress, intended as a Jewish national parliament. Nearly all these groups voiced support for the ideal of Jewish national culture in the abstract. Huge differences, however, had begun to surface regarding the more specific questions of language, religion, and politics. The events of October 1917 rendered many of these debates moot. With the eruption of the Bolshevik Revolution, Jewish national unity and culture now faced an unprecedented kind of political test.[29]

From the very beginning of the October Revolution, the Bolsheviks assigned art and culture fundamental roles in the creation of a radically new kind of society. One of the regime's first moves was to establish the People's Commissariat for Enlightenment (Narodnyi kommissariat prosveshcheniia, abbreviated as Narkompros). Founded as a mechanism to employ education and culture in the revolutionary reconstruction of Russian society, Narkompros eventually became a powerful, if not uncontested, political force in early Soviet cultural life. But despite the ideological decrees and radical legal measures, change did not happen overnight. Instead, Russia entered a dreamlike state of internal contradiction as elements of the old and new regimes jostled incongruously against one another.

The chaotic absurdities of the moment were readily apparent in Petrograd. There, as the conservatory student and future musicologist Nicholas Slonimsky later recalled, the former tsarist capital had become "a city of death," slowly collapsing from starvation and illness. Yet months after the Bolsheviks took power, Slonimsky still found himself providing piano lessons to the son and stepdaughter of Grand Duke Mikhail Aleksandrovich, the tsar's brother. They lived on in prerevolutionary luxury in a suburban palace to which he was delivered by a horse-drawn imperial coach once a week. For the city's other inhabitants, life was no less extreme and absurd. Even as dogs, cats, and horses became a principal source of food for people of all classes, symphony concerts, chamber recitals, and choral performances continued unabated. By one count, there were as many as five to six such musical events per day in 1919. As the composer Arthur Lourié recalled, "There was no bread, and art took its place. At no time and in no place have I seen people, not listening to, but devouring music with such trembling eagerness, such feeling as in Russia during those years."[30]

Petrograd's Jewish culture displayed similar schizophrenic tendencies. While civil war raged in the south and many Jews fled the city in droves, concerts, plays, and literary events continued unimpeded. But the most dramatic change was the nearly instant politicization of the city's Jewish cultural life. At the first meeting of the Society for Jewish Folk Music after the Bolshevik Revolution, arguments broke out between newly identified Liberals, Bundists, and Socialist Zionists, as party affiliations sprang into the open.[31] Surprisingly, to judge from the society's internal minutes, this was the first time in ten years that political parties had ever even been mentioned at a board meeting. It augured greater challenges soon to come.

By early 1918 Petrograd's economy had broken down completely, owing to the Bolshevik nationalization of banks, elimination of private property, and currency devaluation. Meanwhile Narkompros gradually seized control of musical life, including concert venues, publishing houses, conservatories, and private music institutions. Even the music of deceased composers was declared technically state property. Like their Russian counterparts, Jewish intellectuals and artists overwhelmingly sought to retain cultural autonomy from the rapidly growing Bolshevik state apparatus. But their initial attempts at political independence soon yielded to a practical recognition of the shifting balance of power. For the musicians' remaining leaders, all decisions boiled down to one question: where should they turn in search of immediate financial support?[32]

The answer was not readily apparent. In the early revolutionary years, Bolsheviks, Zionists, Bundists, the Folks-Partey and other political movements campaigned openly for Jewish loyalties. The Bolsheviks had long been ideologically hostile to any concept of a separate Jewish nationality or Jewish national culture. Yet they could ill afford to ignore the ostensible mobilizing power of the Jewish intelligentsia and Jewish political movements on "the Jewish street." They also faced the constraints of their own revolutionary rhetoric, which had promised representation and in some cases autonomy to Russia's many minority populations. As a result, before the Bolshevik consolidation of power in 1922, their Jewish policy was guided by a two-pronged strategy. Generally speaking, Jewish political parties and cultural organizations were allowed to operate freely. At the same time, the Bolsheviks worked steadily to undermine Jewish autonomy through various administrative and legal measures and to co-opt their membership into Communist organizations. In 1918 they also created two new institutional frameworks for Jews: the Jewish Sections (Evsektsii) of the Party's Central Committee and the Jewish Commissariat (Evkom) of the Commissariat for Nationality Affairs (Narkomnats). Though both the Evsektsii and Evkom launched direct attacks against Jewish religious and communal organizations and rival political groups, at least initially they accepted the principle of Jewish nationality and by extension Jewish national culture.[33]

More important, when it came to Jewish art and culture, Narkompros made a key decision to support Jewish cultural activities alongside those of other minorities. The Petrograd Jewish community further benefited from the fact that one of the principal Narkompros officials was Zerach (Zakharii) Grinberg (1889–1949), a former Bundist and avowed devotee of Jewish culture. Grinberg made a point of funding a series of public concerts of the Society for Jewish Folk Music, as well as a Jewish national art theater in which many composers participated.[34]

Even with its power of the purse, Narkompros faced a serious challenge for control over the Society for Jewish Folk Music from the Petrograd Central Zionist Council, which cosponsored a series of benefit concerts in 1918. The first such event, held January 21, also marked the debut of a new chamber music sextet, the society's Zimro Ensemble, led by clarinetist Simeon Bellison (1881–1953), an alumnus of the Moscow branch. Later that year the Zimro group left Russia on a world tour to raise funds for a national opera house and conservatory in Palestine. The second such concert took place in late April and featured the Russian opera star Fyodor Chaliapin singing Hebrew psalms, Engel's Yiddish songs, and "Ha-tikvah."[35]

The Zionists and the Bolsheviks were not the only political groups who sought to win the Petrograd Jewish musicians to their side. From Kiev came a series of entreaties from the Kultur-Lige (League for Culture), a new, avowedly nonpartisan Jewish cultural organization. Founded in 1918, the organization represented Jewish intellectuals of various political stripes linked by a goal of creating an eastern European–wide network of Yiddish-language cultural institutions under a platform of national unity quite similar to that of the Society for Jewish Folk Music. In fact, the first head of its music department was Abraham I. Dzimitrovsky (1873–1943), a former conductor at the Brodsky Synagogue in Kiev, a fellow student of Arnold Schoenberg in Vienna, and a member of the society's Kiev branch.[36]

Eager to effect a merger with the society, the Kultur-Lige offered small subsidies and proposed a plan to integrate the musicians into its membership and help publish the massive backlog of manuscripts. While the society had issued its fourth series of compositions, some twenty-two works, over the course of 1917 and 1918, more than a thousand pages of music remained unpublished, including children's songs, orchestral works, and a new edition of the popular *Songbook*. Private publishing was technically still possible, but increasingly difficult because of continuing scarcities of paper and functioning presses. Despite serious discussions, however, no formal program ever resulted. Instead, over the course of 1919 the society turned to the more powerful Narkompros for direct assistance in its publication efforts.[37]

Emboldened by this clamor for its attentions, the society celebrated its tenth anniversary in March 1919 with a jubilee concert at the Petrograd

Conservatory. But the event proved to be less of a milestone than an informal ending. Regular contacts with the other branches had long since been broken due to political pressures and wartime chaos. Ambitious projects such as a jubilee volume, a reprint series, and a massive four-month ethnographic expedition to the former Pale all failed to materialize. When Grinberg and the Bolshevik cultural establishment relocated to the new capital in Moscow later that year, Narkompros funding dried up. Equally crucially, the musicians themselves began to disappear from the city. Letters from the period describe desperate attempts to locate missing colleagues. Throughout 1919 and early 1920 only a handful of members continued to meet in Petrograd, primarily Solomon Rosowsky, Joseph Tomars, and Kiselgof, along with journalist M. G. Syrkin and politician Leon Bramson.[38]

Fittingly, one of the society's final creative acts was a new Yiddish translation of Anton Rubinstein's opera *The Maccabees*, an unintentional requiem for the vanishing world of Russian Jewish culture. But in place of the planned Yiddish production, instead a Russian-language version was mounted in 1921, complete with actors costumed in Jewish prayer shawls, provoking controversy about a religiously themed production in the new atheist state. By that time few of the Petrograd musicians were there to see it. Throughout 1920 and 1921, even the core leadership disintegrated as, one by one, they fled the city for Moscow, Riga, Berlin, New York, and Tel Aviv. In correspondence over the next few years, the far-flung musicians attempted to continue the organization from afar by deputizing Kiselgof as their representative. But the loss of leadership and the increasing repression of non-Communist Jewish cultural organizations from 1921 on proved too great. When these efforts failed, they focused their energies on saving the music itself through publishing the society's remaining compositions abroad. But to do so meant turning to the Russian Jewish musical diaspora. The Petrograd chapter had drawn to a close.[39]

The Triple Diaspora

The 1917 October Revolution and the Balfour Declaration jointly ushered in a fundamentally new set of practical choices for and philosophical challenges to Russian Jewry. For Jewish artists and intellectuals, these two events sparked a series of elemental questions about the relationship between art and politics in Russian society. Was Jewish national art still viable within a revolutionary regime that insisted on a universal and rigorously secular transformation of society? Were the modernist aesthetics of the Russian avant-garde—which demanded a disregard for the ideological content of art and culture—a radical, proletarian act? Or were they a reckless dodge of political responsibility in a socialist society? Was Palestine the only legitimate place in which to build Jewish national culture? Or would the international character of the growing Jewish national movement obviate the need for one exclusive Jewish cultural center?

Before the dust had settled on the 1920s, the Russian Jewish musical intelligentsia had begun to vote on these questions with its feet. The result was a new diaspora split three ways: Sensing the fundamental tension between Jewish nationalism and Bolshevik communism, many opted to head east to Zion. A second stream headed west in pursuit of another liberal, multiethnic home for Jewish culture. Passing through the Russian expatriate colony in Berlin, these intellectuals often eventually landed on the shores of the United States. The third population, by far the largest, remained to build new lives in the emerging Soviet Union. They too typically migrated, however, following the Bolshevik government to the new capital in Moscow.

For those musicians who chose Palestine, Zionism offered the tantalizing prospect of a Jewish homeland in which music was already regarded as a key component of national rebirth. Several arrived in the early and mid-1920s to assume prominent roles in Tel Aviv's musical life as scholars, performers, and teachers, including Lev Nesvizhskii (now known as Arieh Abileah), Solomon Rosowsky, and David Shor. Others, including Mikhail Gnesin and Jacob Veinberg, came on more temporary sojourns. Undoubtedly, though, the most interesting and least likely musical immigrant was none other than Joel Engel.[40]

Engel had greeted the October Revolution with no less enthusiasm than he had the February Revolution. Though the coup cost him his main livelihood, he responded positively, telling Rosowsky, "I bless the Russian Revolution . . . because the Bolsheviks have shut down all of the newspapers and I have, thank God, nowhere left to write." Freed of his journalistic obligations, he turned to a renewed focus on his own music and teaching. One of the immediate results was Engel's most important composition, the incidental music to Ansky's play *The Dybbuk*, which premiered in a Hebrew-language version by the Moscow Habimah Theater in January 1922. *The Dybbuk* was an immediate success, eventually becoming perhaps the most famous Jewish play in the world. Engel's music not only represented his boldest stylistic foray yet into modernism, but also created a haunting sound that reportedly left audiences weeping from its pure expressive power. In the 1920s and 1930s, his *Dybbuk Suite* (ex. 10), adapted from the play's score, saw performances everywhere from Europe to Latin America to India and publication in Tel Aviv and Berlin in 1926 and in the Soviet Union in 1929–30.[41]

Example 10. Joel Engel's "Mipnei Ma" theme from the *Dybbuk Suite*, 1922. Adapted from the published piano reduction of the score.

Another major consequence of the Bolshevik Revolution was Engel's final break with his Petrograd colleagues. In 1917, even as the two groups collaborated on his spring concert tour, Engel began to transform the Moscow group from a satellite branch into its own autonomous organization. Two months after the October Revolution, the Moscow group renamed itself the Society for Jewish Music (Obshchestvo evreiskoi muzyki). The new name was chosen, as a concert program noted in May 1918, to highlight their broadened focus on "all types of folk song as well as the more complex forms produced by modern music." Their initial success was reflected in a series of some eighty works published over the course of 1918 and 1919, largely comprised of reissues of earlier compositions by Engel with a handful of new works by Alexander Krein.[42]

Beyond his Jewish creative activities, Engel joined the larger Bolshevik musical world as lecturer and musical advisor. Though not a Bolshevik, his populist musical credentials certified him as politically acceptable. Consequently he was invited to lecture at various theaters, concert halls, and factories around Moscow, and he taught a training course on aesthetics to music teachers at the Moscow Conservatory. He also served in the Moscow Union of Composers and the Musical Division of Narkompros. Among the latter organization's first publications were Engel's arrangements of revolutionary songs like the "Internationale" and "Awake and Rise Up, Working People."[43]

Despite this promising start, however, the civil war's material effects soon took their toll on Engel. At the beginning of 1920 he fled the cold and hunger of the Moscow winter for the town of Malakhovka, roughly twenty miles southeast of the city. There he joined several other Jewish artistic luminaries including Marc Chagall and Yiddish writers Dovid Hofshteyn and Der Nister (Pinḥas Kahanovich) on the faculty of a Jewish children's colony for war refugees (fig. 15). By 1922, however, Engel had grown increasingly disillusioned with the larger prospects for Jewish culture in the Soviet Union. The following year he relocated to Berlin on the pretext of helping to establish the new Soviet state's music publishing links to Germany. Once there Engel relaunched his music publishing efforts with the Yuval imprint and performed two concerts in the name of the Moscow Society for Jewish Music. But by the end of 1924 the reports of the growing Jewish musical world in Palestine, and particularly plans for a new conservatory, had captured his imagination. That December he and his family left Berlin for Tel Aviv.[44]

Even before his arrival, Engel explained in a letter to the Zionist musical committee sponsoring his immigration that his move was hardly a political conversion: "I am no Zionist, but I regard the national element in general and in human creation in particular as of supreme importance, and this brings me closer to Zionism." Regardless of his disclaimer, Engel came to Palestine with high hopes for a Jewish musical renaissance. Yet he quickly found it quite difficult to adjust to the cultural realities of his new homeland. While the Zionist immigration provided a climate of artistic freedom and national enthusiasm, the fractious cultural politics of the Yishuv produced ideological debates about the meaning of Jewish music that echoed the tensions present in wartime Russia. In spite of the respectful status and central symbolic role accorded Engel as the "father of Jewish music," Zionist critics, composers, and scholars often identified explicitly with an "Oriental" musical sound, in direct opposition to the Yiddish folk culture of eastern Europe. To their ears the latter carried too many echoes of Jewish cultural "assimilation" and the negative influences of the Diaspora. This even led to a linguistic distinction between Diasporic "Jewish music" (*musikah yehudit*) and Zionist "Hebrew music" (*musikah 'ivrit*), extending the distinction that Saminsky had proposed a decade earlier in Russia. The multiethnic soundscape of Palestine also proved challenging to Engel's aesthetics. In spite of their zeal for authenticity, the early Zionists pioneered a genre of Hebrew song that borrowed freely from a diverse array of musical traditions—Yemenite Jewish prayers, Arabic folk songs, Russian popular songs, and Hasidic nigunim. These demographic and social realities eroded the logic of choosing Yiddish

Figure 15. Joel Engel (seated on stoop at left) at the Malakhovka Colony. American Jewish Joint Distribution Committee (JDC) Archives in New York.

folk song as the defining marker of Jewish musical identity, as Engel had done within the context of the Russian Empire.[45]

Nevertheless, Engel readily embraced the new Hebrew style. He wrote arrangements of Sephardic and Yemenite folk songs and composed children's songs, some of which later became staples of the Israeli national song repertoire. He also collaborated with the prestigious Ohel Theater group on productions of the work of I. L. Peretz. What explained his about-face? In 1901 he had taken a stand as an artist and intellectual against the purveyors of a faux populism, empowering himself to make his own ethnographic definition of Jewish music. During World War I he had allied himself with the folk against Saminsky's modernist elitism, defending the national character of Jewish music through recourse to a Yiddish-tinged ethnographic populism. A decade later, in his encounter with the new Zionist musical world of Palestine, he found a compelling new site for his populist artistic instincts. If the cultural reality had changed dramatically, he wrote to Mikhail Gnesin in 1925, it nevertheless represented a truly "Jewish atmosphere" in which to create national music. It was impossible to determine what constituted "Hebrew music" as "objective fact," he noted in 1926, in his final statement before his death the following year, given that "music is not logic." But there was one solution: "The people, only the people.... Final judgment in such matters may be reached only by life itself, by the daily toil of the Hebrew masses."[46]

For all the irony of Diaspora Jewish music's greatest advocate now offering his blessing to Hebrew music, Engel's late-in-life transition to musical Zionism was less a political endorsement or a calculated renunciation of his earlier populism than a reflexive recasting of his Russian Jewish cultural nationalism, given the new post-1917 realities of the Jewish world. Political ideology aside, the overwhelming Zionist commitment to a nationalist aesthetic similar to Engel's prior model proved compelling to the composer. Shorn of its European and Imperial Russian framework, Engel's cultural philosophy turned out to be quite malleable. The key factor was the Zionist musical establishment's dedication in creed, if not in deed, to a populist, folkloric ideal of national music. In the secular Palestinian homeland, Engel believed that Hebrew song had assumed the role of *bytovoi* or secular folk song, and he the "Hebrew composer."

Of course this ideological volte-face did not guarantee Engel an easy personal fate. He was frustrated both by his difficulties in learning spoken Hebrew and by the local musical politics that prevented him from assuming a prominent position at one of the new conservatories. Privately he complained that, unlike in Moscow or Berlin, in Tel Aviv his fame felt superficial and irrelevant. He was treated like a national hero, but his music and ideas were largely ignored. At the end of his life, Engel remained both a struggling immigrant and a misunderstood icon. Nor was Zionism able to neatly resolve the competing aesthetic and political conceptions present at its birth. For the problematic competing relationships between the cultural ideals of Diaspora and Zion, East and West, and religious and secular traditions continued to occupy a central place in the musical identity of the Yishuv and Israeli composers for decades to come.[47]

While Engel found Zion in his final years, his Hebraist rival Saminsky traded his own romance with the East for a career in the West. Early in 1919 he left Russia via Odessa for Istanbul and from there to Palestine. He spent three months touring and lecturing and was impressed to pronounce the Zionist Yishuv as the new "national-cultural center of the Jewish people." However, the Jewish homeland, in all its provinciality, could not compete with the allure of the West for a cosmopolitan composer and conductor aspiring to international fame. In mid-1919 he embarked for western Europe, and by 1920 he had arrived in the United States to serve as guest conductor of the Boston and Detroit symphony orchestras.[48]

In coming to the United States, Saminsky saw himself as a distinguished artistic émigré, fleeing the uncertainty of Russia for a more comfortable Western perch. But he was also very much an immigrant joining a stream of Russian Jews that had stretched back four decades. And like many earlier Russian Jewish intellectuals, Saminsky found himself stymied by the social and political character of American society, in which Jews were rapidly repositioning themselves as a religious community rather than a national or ethnic minority. The shift would have major consequences for the fate of Jewish music, as evidenced by Saminsky's experience.

In America Saminsky discovered to his surprise that Jewish music was primarily defined as a religious repertoire. In 1921 he noted in a letter to Solomon Rosowsky that "my Jewish choral works . . . are becoming Christian music." Ironically, it was American Christian religious choirs who expressed the strongest interest in performing his work. American Jews, on the other hand, rejected his racially tinged model of Jewish music. Though he gained a position as music director of the citadel of American Reform Judaism, New York's Temple Emanu-El, his efforts to expand the repertoire by adding classical sacred works by non-Jewish composers led to angry charges that he was adding Christian music to a Jewish religious service. His response was defiant. There was "no such thing as Christian versus Jewish music," he argued, since it only made sense "to speak of Jewish music versus German or Italian or Russian music" in national terms. But the conflict suggested just how out of sync his cosmopolitan Jewish nationalism was with mainstream American Jewish culture.[49]

Saminsky faced similar challenges to his broader ambitions as a mainstream composer. He quickly assumed a prominent role in New York's modern music circles, cofounding the League of Composers in 1923. Over the next several decades, he produced a roster of symphonies, chamber works, and choral pieces. Given this productivity and the notable successes of his other Jewish colleagues such as Ernest Bloch, George Gershwin, and Aaron Copland, it would have been logical for him to earn a place in an American musical world that was itself largely a culture of outsiders, immigrants, and émigrés. But instead, critics frequently disparaged his music, tagging him a poor man's Stravinsky who had failed to transcend his Russian roots to become a "Western composer." In his own eyes, by contrast, he saw himself as a "Eurasian: Asiatic through the demand of flesh, Western through a craving for clarity." The crude self-characterization reflected his Russian Jewish quest for a musical symbiosis of East and West, folklore and modernism. But these were cultural subtleties lost on American audiences.[50]

As his reputation declined, Saminsky blamed the excesses of capitalist society and the vulgarities of the new modernist masters, particularly Igor Stravinsky. In a 1932 book-length screed, *Music of Our Day: Essentials and Prophecies*, he lamented that "the yoke of the market and its conquest have transformed the composer into a musical pyrotechnician, into a master of fireworks storing up unceasingly new entertainment for the modern barbarian." He also lashed out at the formalist dictates of 1920s modernism, which brooked no sympathy for his more folkloric, nationalist style. But he reserved his harshest words for his more successful Jewish colleague Arnold Schoenberg. As Saminsky wrote in his 1934 book, *Music of the Ghetto and Bible*, an expanded and revised version of his 1914 essay collection, Schoenberg's brand of internationalist modernism amounted to another form of musical "assimilation" of the kind Saminsky had denounced back in the 1910s: "The mimicry of modernism is a sort of Jewishness that hides its passport and screens its physiognomy. Like internationalism, modernism in music plays for the Jewish composer the part of a civic religion . . . a strange kind of substitution for Jewishness in music, a sort of escape from an anticipated and feared course." He later extended this line of attack to Gershwin, Copland, and other Jewish contemporaries. The satisfactions of such literary polemics, however, could not make up for an American musical career marked by bitter disappointments.[51]

Saminsky was not alone in his struggle to find a niche for Jewish music in American life. Other alumni of the Society for Jewish Folk Music also emigrated to the United States, including Joseph Achron, Leo Zeitlin, Jacob Veinberg, and Solomon Rosowsky. Like Saminsky, they discovered that fame as composers eluded them despite their attempts to integrate. Achron, for instance, morphed into a musical jack-of-all-trades in New York, composing for the synagogue, theater, and concert hall. He then relocated to Los Angeles to try his hand at Hollywood's film score industry. Ultimately, he failed to find his musical niche in the American scene, prompting none other than Schoenberg to remark that Achron was "the most underestimated musician of our time." His fellow composers' stories were similar. None ascended to the ranks of composers with significant national reputations. Instead, they generally remained within the New York Jewish community as educators and cultural activists or entered the more anonymous worlds of American radio, vaudeville, and musical theater.[52]

Not all Russian Jewish musicians floundered in twentieth-century America. But those who flourished earned their fame and fortune not as composers of Jewish music but as performers of Russian music. Many alumni of Leopold Auer's violin class, including Nathan Milstein, Jascha Heifetz, Efrem Zimbalist, and Mischa Elman, achieved extraordinary American careers as prime exponents of Russian classical music. Auer himself ended his career in the United States, feted in 1925 at age eighty by his many former pupils at New York's Carnegie Hall. From the 1920s on, a steady stream of Russian Jewish musicians (typically referred to as simply "Russian") became popular fixtures on the American concert stage. Ironically, it was in the careers of these Russian Jewish instrumental soloists, not composers, poised somewhere between immigrants and exiles, that the prerevolutionary Russian Jewish cultural ideal reached one of its fullest expressions. Relieved of their Jewish labels and valorized as a link to Russia's pre-Soviet cultural past, Russian Jewish musicians — particularly violinists — came to symbolize Russianness in its most magnanimous and illustrious cultural form. Years later, the Russian-born violinist Isaac Stern summarized this phenomenon by joking that Soviet-American cultural exchange consisted of a simple pattern: "They send us their Jews from Odessa and we send them our Jews from Odessa."[53]

As Stern's quip suggested, in the Soviet Union, just as in the United States, a dramatic influx of Jews into the conservatories, orchestras, and other areas of Russian musical life continued unabated after 1917. Indeed, many of the greatest twentieth-century Soviet concert soloists, who attracted huge international fame and media attention as premier exponents of Russian national music, were Jews, including David Oistrakh, Leonid Kogan, and Emil Gilels. But while Russian Jewish musicians in American society came to symbolize the grandeur, elegance, and nostalgia of the Old World, the Jewish presence in Soviet musical life took on a considerably different set of sensitive political meanings. Indeed, the high level of Jewish cultural visibility in Soviet music remained a complicated political phenomenon. On one hand, the Soviet regime was keenly sensitive to issues of international cultural prestige and allegations of antisemitism, given its professed political progressivism. On the other hand, the ideological dictates of communist universalism, Marxist antisemitism, and Russian ethnic nationalism repeatedly led authorities to attempt to reduce the Jewish demographic presence in Soviet culture. The phenomenon of Jewish overrepresentation in Soviet music remained an awkward reality that produced a variety of contradictory attitudes and tacit policies regarding Jewish participation in Soviet music.[54]

If the Jewish concert artist remained a half-submerged icon in Soviet culture, the Soviet Jewish composer proved to be an even more culturally ambiguous and politically fraught category. As part of its early policy of "indigenization" (*korenizatsiia*), the Soviet state actively promoted the national cultures of minority groups, including the Jews. The Bolshevik policy of deliberately supporting Yiddish-language Jewish culture therefore generated arguably the strongest opportunity for modern Jewish culture in the interwar period. The opening years of Bolshevik rule generated a roster of official state-sponsored Jewish artistic ensembles, theaters, publishing projects, and other related musical endeavors unparalleled even in the Zionist Yishuv.

Indeed, the initial signs were promising. Throughout the 1920s, Narkompros issued Jewish-themed works as part of its general series of modern art music. State-sponsored "evenings of modern music" at the Moscow Conservatory and Bolshoi Theater in the 1920s included Krein's settings of Ḥayyim Naḥman Bialik's poetry and similar works by Gnesin and Alexander Veprik, among others, alongside premieres by Prokofiev, Stravinsky, and Nikolai Myaskovsky. Official Soviet klezmer and Yiddish vocal ensembles also appeared, as did at least fourteen Yiddish theater companies in Moscow, Minsk, Kharkov, and elsewhere.[55] From the late 1920s to the late 1940s, the Soviet Jewish ethnomusicologist Moisei (Moyshe) Ia. Beregovskii (1892–1961), a disciple of Engel, ran the Department of Musical Folklore at the Kiev Institute for Jewish Proletarian Culture, an official division of the Ukrainian Academy of Sciences in Kiev. There he conducted the most extensive Jewish scholarly project of any kind in the Soviet Union, assembling a massive musical archive with hundreds of phonograph recordings and thousands of musical transcriptions based on his own fieldwork and the materials of Ansky, Kiselgof, and Engel.

Yet this promotion of secular Jewish culture and the classification of Jews as a nationality coexisted uneasily with the Soviet aspirations for socialist universalism and deep-rooted Marxist-Leninist ideological animus toward Jewish peoplehood. Thus the Bolshevik invitation to forge Jewish national music proved to be a double-edged sword. Signs of this tension appeared even in the earliest years of the regime. In 1923 the composer Moisei Milner, a veteran of the original Society for Jewish Folk Music, witnessed his opera, *Di himlen brenen* (The Heavens Are Burning), purportedly the first full-length Yiddish-language opera, banned after only three performances in Petrograd on grounds of Jewish nationalism and aesthetic violations of revolutionary ideals. Beregovskii paid a steeper personal price as a later victim of a Stalinist purge. He spent five years in the Gulag and died a broken man, his life's work consigned to near oblivion until decades after his death.[56]

The examples of Milner and Beregovskii notwithstanding, the majority of Jewish composers survived and even prospered in the Soviet Union. Even those who had overt associations with Jewish culture did not necessarily face repression on the scale of their fellow Soviet Jewish writers and theater professionals.[57] The complex dynamics of Jewish visibility and vulnerability were best reflected in the twists and turns in the life of one of the Society for Jewish Folk Music's original founders: Mikhail Gnesin.

In the years before World War I, Gnesin had developed a strong reputation as a true modern iconoclast for his outspoken Jewishness, brazen Marxism, and European avant-gardism. He passionately maintained that the Russian masses could be taught to embrace modern art. "I waited and yearned for the Revolution," he later recalled. "I thirsted for action. I wanted to see how the artistic life of the people would change. Where there had previously been coarseness and boredom, now life would blossom and art would bloom." In the 1910s he had begun to compose music for the famed experimental theater productions of avant-garde Marxist director Vsevolod Meyerhold. But despite his revolutionary enthusiasm, Gnesin also flirted with another messianic dream, Zionism. He spent 1913–14 living in Palestine, immersing himself in the new Jewish musical life of the Yishuv, which he duly reported on to the Odessa Zionist Committee.[58]

In the immediate aftermath of the October Revolution, Gnesin likewise flitted between avant-garde Marxist musical circles, the prerevolutionary Russian conservatory milieu, and the reconstituted elements of Jewish national culture. In 1918 he was named professor at the Rostov Conservatory and then soon thereafter dean. In 1921, however, he returned to Petrograd to rejoin Meyerhold, who by that time was a prominent Bolshevik government cultural official engaged in a daring reformulation of Russian theater aesthetics along modernist European lines.

Yet even as he was drawn deeper into the Bolshevik artistic world, Gnesin remained involved with a Zionist musical circle led by David Shor, and he developed a plan to republish the music of the Society for Jewish Folk Music along with new Jewish works. At the end of 1921, he left Russia for a second extended visit to Palestine. For the first six months of 1922, he lived in Bab-el-Wad, midway between Jerusalem and Tel Aviv, where he worked on a major Hebrew-language opera, *Iunost Avraama* ("Abram's Youth"). He also taught at the Shulamit Tel Aviv Conservatory and continued work on his republication venture, now known as the Jibneh Press. The appeal of life in the Jewish homeland was strong, and Gnesin contemplated settling in Palestine permanently. He even went so far as to request visas for his wife, his son Fabian, and his mother-in-law from the British authorities. But the pull of Russia and revolution eventually proved stronger. He returned home by way of Berlin and, once back in Moscow, in 1923 joined the faculty of the Gnesin Musical Institute. That same year Gnesin Krein, Shor, and others reorganized the remnants of the Moscow and Petrograd branches of the Society for Jewish Folk Music into a new state-approved private organization known as the Society for Jewish Music (Obshchestvo evreiskoi muzyki). The group gave small-scale concerts in Moscow and published selected compositions throughout the 1920s.[59]

What allowed Gnesin to pursue these Jewish national musical activities was not only the official Soviet cultural policy but also the ideological disorder in the early Soviet musical world of the 1920s. The Soviet regime did not immediately strangle all art in a death grip of ideology and censorship. Although music quickly became politicized, an ideological consensus about what the revolution required of Soviet musicians was slow to emerge. As a result, the 1920s were a period of radical experimentation and intense competition as three major factions fought to advance their musical visions for the new communist state. The modernists of Petrograd (renamed Leningrad in 1924) and Moscow favored an overt embrace of the most radical notions of art, in keeping with transnational European modernism: to move forward into the future, music should shed all its national characteristics and realist tendencies in a formal revolution of avant-garde aesthetics. Their natural opponents were the "classicist" composers clustered around the reorganized conservatories, a cohort of musicians who viewed the heroic prerevolutionary Romantic tradition of Russian composers, particularly such icons as Rimsky-Korsakov and Glazunov (who remained director of the Leningrad Conservatory until 1930), as compatible with the socialist politics of the day. They found the Bolsheviks somewhat receptive to the Russian prerevolutionary musical heritage as an element of their program for the cultural regeneration of Russian society. A third group, the "proletarians," was much smaller in numbers but grew increasingly vocal throughout the 1920s in its attacks against both the traditionalists and the modernists. These musicians, led initially by none other than the early Society for Jewish Folk Music leader David Chernomordikov, insisted on the primacy of Marxist aesthetics, political ideology, and explicit populism in Soviet musical life. In some cases, this meant a rejection of both nineteenth-century Russian symphonies and new avant-garde tonal experiments in favor of radically simplified music for the socialist masses, based on easily digestible folk songs and popular melodies.[60]

As with his politics, Gnesin's musical affiliations were complex. The abstract harmonies and flirtations with atonality heard in early works such as his settings of poems by Russian symbolists Viacheslav Ivanov, Alexander Blok, and Konstantin Balmont had put him at the forefront of the prewar Russian modernist avant-garde. But in spite of these modernist sympathies, his use of Jewish folkloric material set him apart from his more radical contemporaries. His close prewar relationship with Rimsky-Korsakov and his involvement with the prerevolutionary Gnesin Musical Institute linked him to the classicist faction. He was also the first Soviet composer to take the Bolshevik Revolution as a programmatic theme, in the form of his 1925 work *Symphonic Monument to 1905–1917*, based on texts by the poet Sergei A. Yesenin, for chorus and orchestra. To further complicate matters, his interest in Yiddish folk songs allied him with some of the populist aspirations of the proletarian musical agitators and the Yiddish cultural establishment. Yet in 1924 he was one of seven Jewish intellectuals to call for the return of Hebrew to Soviet Jewish cultural life.[61]

In spite of these contradictions—or perhaps because of them—Gnesin continued to rise in the musical world. Appointed professor at the Moscow Conservatory in 1925, he became dean the following year and in 1927 was awarded the title "Honored Artist" of the Russian Soviet Federation of Socialist Republics. By the late 1920s he had become one of the most respected members of the Soviet musical establishment. At the same time he continued to compose on Jewish themes and actively participate in Jewish cultural initiatives under the auspices of the Society for Jewish Music, of which he emerged as the principal leader.[62]

Triply committed to Marxism, modernism, and Jewish cultural nationalism, Gnesin and his cohorts walked a fine line in the unpredictable ideological climate of 1920s Soviet music. Alexander Krein composed a *Funeral Ode in Memory of Lenin* (1926) and other ideologically correct works, such as his 1932 symphonic oratorio, *The USSR—Shock Brigade of the World Proletariat*, but he also produced a series of works on Jewish themes and some twenty theater scores for modernist productions of the Habimah Hebrew-language theater and various Yiddish theater companies. By the late 1920s, however, treading the tightrope had become increasingly difficult. The Soviet regime began to roll back much of its support for Jewish national culture. After 1927, following a spate of Stalinist directives, Soviet society lurched toward a new radical phase of cultural revolution. In the music world, the Marxist proletarians began to win the upper hand. In practical terms, this meant a growing campaign against Westernized aesthetics associated with both the Russian avant-garde and the classical conservatory traditions.

By 1931 direct state control of cultural life had begun, and all private organizations were officially disbanded. The experiments with artistic freedom were over. The new Stalinist orders increasingly denounced musical "formalism" and modernist aesthetics as bourgeois imports in direct violation of the imperatives of the revolution. That year, after a number of increasingly savage battles with various ideological groups, the Moscow Society for Jewish Music officially closed down. Soon individual members of the artistic intelligentsia began to be targeted for political crimes. Gnesin's close colleagues Meyerhold, Kiselgof, and his own brother, Grigorii (1884–1938), were eventually arrested and secretly executed. Gnesin himself felt the pressure when the Russian Association of Proletarian Musicians publicly denounced him as a reactionary threat to Soviet music.[63]

In response, Gnesin took the drastic step of composing a letter to Stalin himself. "Dear Comrade Stalin," he began, "over the course of several years I have striven to speak out on the critical questions regarding our situation in the field of music." Though he had achieved a solid "reputation as one who struggles on behalf of proletarian musical art," Gnesin explained, he had now come under public attack as a "class enemy" and "counterrevolutionary." Hoping for Stalin's intervention, he presented a long list of theoretical questions and ideas about art, politics, and society for the leader's consideration. Gnesin never sent the letter. Indeed, his own survival in the Stalinist period was due, at least in part, to a wise policy of strategic silence.[64]

The same judicious approach was reflected in the curtailment of his participation in any overtly Jewish cultural activity from that point onward. Instead, Gnesin switched his focus, as did other Jewish composers, to the folk music of other Soviet minorities: Azerbaijani, Armenian, Circassian, Chuvash, and others. And even though he did occasionally return to Jewish themes in his music, he adopted a heavy cloak of abstract modernism in his compositions so that they could not be readily identified with folkloristic motifs or other Jewish ethnic markers.[65]

This was the case with one of Gnesin's final and most important compositions, the 1943 Piano Trio, op. 63, "In Memory of Our Murdered Children"

Example 11. Opening of Mikhail Gnesin's Piano Trio, op. 63, 1943.

(ex. 11). The work, a veiled musical remembrance of the Jewish children murdered by the Nazis, was one of the first artistic treatments of the Holocaust to appear anywhere. It was also as close as Gnesin would come to a Jewish reference in his titles in the post-1931 period. Premiered in Tashkent in 1943 during the wartime evacuation from Leningrad and published in 1947 by the Soviet state music publishing house, the work makes no explicit reference to the Jewishness of the children. Nor does it quote from recognizable Jewish folk or liturgical themes. Indeed, on the surface it commemorates a more personal tragedy, the death from illness of Gnesin's own son Fabian (1907–1942). But the oblique musical style and stark autobiographical link did not disguise the broader Jewish valence to its Jewish listeners. In June 1948, for instance, the Central Committee of Jews in Poland wrote to Gnesin to inform him proudly that his Piano Trio, "dedicated to the murdered Jewish children," had been performed on Polish radio on April 19, 1948, in recognition of the fifth anniversary of the Warsaw Ghetto Uprising.[66]

The timing of the letter from Polish Jewry to Gnesin was ironic. For that same year Gnesin again had come under intense political scrutiny. Between 1948 and 1953, as part of Stalin's "anticosmopolitanism" campaign, he found himself repeatedly accused of the political crime of supporting Jewish nationalism, tainted by his earlier involvement in Soviet Zionist circles, his two sojourns in Palestine, and his previous Jewish musical works. In 1950 Soviet authorities attempted to close down the composition department of the Gnesin Institute, of which he was the head. To save the department, Gnesin agreed to accept forced retirement, handing his position over to one of his leading students, Aram Khachaturian. In fact, Gnesin's later fate during this period was intimately linked both with Khachaturian and with his other prize student, the composer Tikhon Khrennikov. Together the two composers played key roles in the drama of Jews and music in the Soviet Union as successive heads of the powerful Union of Composers (Soiuz kompozitorov). Established in 1932, the union operated with a considerable degree of professional autonomy from the rest of the Soviet cultural world. While not immune to broader currents of antisemitism and state pressure, the organization resisted the periodic calls for anti-Jewish quotas or political purges in Soviet music, partially shielding its Jewish members (and mentors) such as Gnesin from the brunt of Stalin's postwar purge of the Soviet Jewish intelligentsia. While many of his former friends and colleagues in the Yiddish literary and theater intelligentsia were arrested and secretly executed, Gnesin escaped their fate. Instead, his career ended on an ambiguous note characteristic of the entire postwar Soviet Jewish experience: physical survival accompanied by enforced silence. For the last ten years of his life, he all but ceased to compose.[67]

In 1934, on the fortieth anniversary of Anton Rubinstein's death, Gnesin delivered a lecture on the composer's legacy and his contemporary significance. Noting Rubinstein's famous epitaph ("To the Jews I am a Christian, to the Christians a Jew . . ."), he explained that in this long list of contradictions one was missing: class. In tsarist court circles Rubinstein always remained "the son of a third-guild merchant" from the Jewish Pale of Settlement. But to the liberal intelligentsia, the "Yankel" was permanently tainted by his cozy associations with the imperial court and high nobility. For both, Rubinstein's social and economic status (and the taint of his Jewish parvenu origins) set him apart, along with the other national, religious, and artistic factors. Comparing the situation in Rubinstein's own day with the present state of Soviet music, Gnesin concluded that there were many similarities. In the 1930s the demand was for "art that was national in form, socialist in content, and realist in its method of expression." Back in the 1860s Rubinstein had faced essentially the same requirement of "art that was national in form, collectivist in content, and once again realist in its means of expression."[68]

Gnesin intended his remarks as a broad sociological comment on the continuities in the relationship between art and society in prerevolutionary and Soviet Russia. Yet his evaluation of Rubinstein was not wholly accurate in its depiction of the class conflicts and political ideologies of the 1860s. Nor did the socialist realism of his day match the spirit or techniques of the nineteenth-century Russian Romantic realist composers. Instead, the tribute to Rubinstein neatly captured his own dilemma as a Russian Jewish musician facing a bewildering array of cultural conflicts and political pressures. The implicit comparison between Rubinstein and himself served as an ironic comment on Gnesin's own fate as a Jewish artist seeking to balance multiple identities and affinities in the face of a Russian society that demanded a rigid political, aesthetic, and nationalist definition of art.

War and revolution did not destroy the project of modern Jewish music. What they did do, however, was impose a new burden of ideologies—political and aesthetic—that altered the basic meaning of modern Jewish culture as a whole. Geography further sealed that fate. Distributed around the globe, Engel, Saminsky, Gnesin, and their colleagues continued to argue for decades in person, in correspondence, and in their works about the future of Jewish music. As late as 1934, Saminsky could be found shadowboxing against the long-departed Engel, reprinting their dialectic in a self-serving, expurgated English translation of his 1914 book on Jewish music. In Israel and the United States, well into the 1950s, composers and musicologists continued to rehash the question of what the Society for Jewish Folk Music had achieved. In the Soviet Union, party-line denunciations of Saminsky's bourgeois nationalism commingled with subtler tributes to the cultural achievements of Engel, Gnesin, and others. Ultimately, however, in all three places it was primarily the memories, the memoirs, and the reflections on the past that took the place of the music itself. In different ways, the legacies of the Society for Jewish Folk Music still persisted within Soviet Russia and beyond. But the surging ideologies of modernism, socialism, and Zionism had unalterably transformed the meaning of Russian Jewish culture.

Conclusion

At the height of World War I, Mikhail Gnesin published an editorial entitled "Antisemitism and Music" in a Rostov-on-Don newspaper. In this 1916 commentary, he discussed a recent flare-up of the perennial question, why were there so many Jews in Russian music? Antisemites continued to denounce Jewish musicians as a crude swarm of "Asiatic" opportunists subverting European music with their artless commercial virtuosity and Eastern "exoticism." Meanwhile, philosemites reached opposite yet still disturbing conclusions. The critic Leonid Sabaneev, for instance, had written that modern musical history proved no race to be more musically gifted than the Jews. Far from being cultural Easterners, in his words, Jewish musicians had "always and everywhere" epitomized Western classicism, championing the conservative ideal in European music.[1]

Reading the opponents and defenders of Jewish musicians side by side, Gnesin judged both equally problematic. Despite their differences, antisemites and philosemites offered mirror images of the Jews as "a nation apart," a migrant race, at once artistically deficient and culturally foreign. Collectively, he explained, these conflicting images of the Jewish musician as primitive Oriental and cosmopolitan Westerner were based on the most facile and vast of generalizations. Both substituted ahistorical fantasy for honest social inquiry. In reality, the statistical overrepresentation of Jewish musicians in Russian music reflected neither an innate racial talent nor a malign plot. When state-sponsored prejudice kept other professions and educational institutions closed to them, Gnesin pointed out, Russian Jews simply turned to music in search of tangible opportunity.

Furthermore, ascribing some biological musical gift or essential cultural role to the Jews—positive or negative—made little sense when Jewishness itself was in such a state of flux. After all, Gnesin asked, who could say for certain whether an Anton Rubinstein or a Felix Mendelssohn should be considered Jewish simply by virtue of his lineage? By this standard, Richard Wagner himself might even count as a Jewish composer given the persistent rumors about his own ancestry. In the face of these modern dilemmas, it was impossible to reduce all Jewish musicians to some particular essence. He concluded his argument with a prescient warning to Russians who would invoke "race" to explain modern music: "In comparison with the 'pure' race of 'Germans' living in central Europe, it would seem that not even the Russians would pass the test of authentic 'Aryan' art. We therefore see how dangerous this path is."[2]

Beyond exposing the persistent similarities between philosemitism and antisemitism, Gnesin's article also suggested a deep ideological continuity running through modern Russian culture. From the mid-nineteenth century onward, the figure of the Jewish musician functioned as a virtual screen onto which Russians projected a larger set of elemental questions about art, nation, and identity. As a minority concentrated on the empire's Western border yet with cultural origins in the East, the Jews were perfectly suited to stand in for modern Russia's own dualistic identity as a civilization caught between Europe and Asia, East and West. The Jewish musician proved particularly irresistible as a useful symbolic double for the Russian intelligentsia.

But rather than remain voiceless symbols, many Jewish musicians consciously rebelled against this modern musical myth, in the process fashioning their own multivalent identities as Russians, Jews, and Europeans. In fact this trend had begun with Rubinstein, the baptized, Germanized "rabbi" of Russia's first conservatory. Even as he struggled to extricate himself from an assigned role in the musical imaginations of his contemporaries, Rubinstein became much more than a Jewish "assimilationist" or a failed Russian composer. He turned music into a means of emancipation, both for himself—technically speaking, he was the St. Petersburg Conservatory's first graduate—and for Russian Jews and Russians as a whole. Eschewing religious and ethnic bases for modern Russian identity, Rubinstein argued for a liberal definition of national culture broad enough to include Jews and other minorities in a neutral civic society. So too did his artistic experiments fuse the exotic East and the classical West into an original vision, albeit a less critically successful one.

For all of the overlapping associations among Rubinstein, Jewishness, and music in the 1860s, it was not until the 1880s that the Jewish musical myth appeared in full relief in Russian society. It was then that Jews entered the St. Petersburg and Moscow conservatories in numbers large enough to attract the attention of government officials, public opinion, and the press. This demographic shift coincided with the emergence of new popular forms of conservative Russian nationalism and antisemitism. The proponents of these two ideologies quickly seized upon the high visibility of Jewish musicians as a pretext for elaborate conspiracy theories. In the worst of these attacks, the distinctions between Rubinstein, the masses of Jewish musicians, and the conservatory all collapsed into one sweeping critique of the "Judaization" of Russian culture.

But despite the high volume of verbal assaults on Rubinstein and the conservatory, and the repeated demands for government intervention, the conservative, antisemitic backlash did little to stem the flow of Jews into the Russian musical world. In fact for Jewish musicians the social and economic consequences of the new post-1881 antisemitism were fairly minimal. The sweeping legislation designed to limit all Jewish access to higher education in the 1880s and 1890s did not prevent Jews from entering the conservatories in numbers wildly disproportionate to their size in the empire's population. Though professional discrimination certainly existed, Jewish graduates still found ample employment as orchestral musicians, provincial music teachers, theater performers, and military musicians. Jewish movement along this musical path continued virtually without exception through 1917 and afterward.

However, while the Russian musical profession remained open to Jews, Russian music in the broader sense did not. The thousands of Jewish violinists, pianists, and singers who passed through the doors of the conservatories in St. Petersburg, Moscow, or Odessa before 1917 hoping to become Russian artists instead found themselves cast in the role of Jewish musicians. There were, of course, stopgap solutions — a name change here, a conversion there — but these applied only to individuals, and selectively at that. This dilemma was felt most acutely among the composers in the generation of 1905. The disciples of Rimsky-Korsakov, Glazunov, Taneev, Liadov, and Balakirev who came of age in the revolutionary years struggled to reconcile a dilemma at once internal (a newfound sense of Jewish national identity coupled with a strong attachment to Russian high culture) and external (the exaggerated imaginings of both antisemites and philosemites).

Joel Engel was the first prominent figure to propose a solution to these challenges. His ethnographic explorations revealed the way in which he believed music could produce a distinctive Russian-Jewish cultural synthesis. This did not mean a disappearing borderline between the two categories, as in the vaunted German-Jewish symbiosis. Rather his synthesis was premised on a vision of Russia as a multiethnic empire that could accommodate creative national minorities within an expansive definition of modern Russian culture. And for Jews this made their national identity compatible with Russian citizenship, a path to a modern dual identity as Jews and Russians. As one man's informal program, Engel's musical vision could remain both a Russian and a Jewish enterprise. But the St. Petersburg musicians who institutionalized his ideas faced an increasingly complicated balancing act. The Society for Jewish Folk Music was founded in support of Engel's twin objectives: to affirm a multifaceted Russian Jewish cultural identity and at the same time to recast folk music as an integral part of Jewish national identity. But even in its muted, depoliticized form, this sort of Jewish cultural nationalism still contained within it two competing identities. The uneasy if fruitful marriage of two aims into one organization—Russian acculturation and Jewish self-assertion—amplified the tension at the heart of all Russian Jewish culture.

Given this built-in tension, it is little wonder that even after the society's demise, its leaders continued to argue over which cultural strain took precedence. In 1924 Solomon Rosowsky published a short memoir in a Riga newspaper on what would have been the fifteenth anniversary of the group's founding. He stressed the musicians' guiding passion for Jewish national folk song as the society's primary raison d'être. From Berlin, Engel wrote to Rosowsky to protest. "The Society for Jewish Music [sic] in Petersburg was *actually* initially conceived not for [Jewish] folk music," he noted, "but for Rubinstein, Meyerbeer, Bruch, and so forth as well as to support Jewish musicians."[3] While Jewish national aims were certainly part of its mission, he explained, this was secondary and only at the suggestion, ironically enough, of the St. Petersburg city governor. In reality, Engel's letter suggested, with a hint of reproach, the society had tended too much toward an overly broad, deracinated Jewish art music. Its cosmopolitan definition had stretched the national boundaries wide enough to include "assimilated" European Jewish composers such as Rubinstein, Giacomo Meyerbeer, and even Max Bruch, a German Protestant who had famously arranged the Yom Kippur Kol Nidre prayer into a popular work of chamber music. This minor historical spat between Rosowsky and Engel testified to the fact that the Society for Jewish Folk Music had failed to clarify the ambiguous, problematic relationship between Jewish musicians and Jewish music.

Yet somewhat paradoxically, it was this very lack of clarity that explained the terrific success of Jewish music in the first two decades of the twentieth century. No doubt its wide resonance was partly due to larger trends of education, embourgeoisement, and commercial publishing coupled with the spread of national consciousness among Russian Jews. But a key factor in

Jewish music's particularly broad appeal was its very cultural neutrality—or interpretive ambiguity. In the hands of skillful composers, Jewish music could expressively evoke spirituality beyond the formal strictures of religious Judaism, the sound of Yiddish without the Yiddish language, and, more generally, a recognizably Jewish aesthetic in a form of high culture associated with modern European and Russian art. The strength of this musical project was that it served simultaneously as a clarion call to Russified intellectuals to embrace their own Jewish national identity and as a sophisticated rejection of Jewish ethnic parochialism and political separatism. Endowed with these features, Jewish music offered a unifying bridge that spanned the otherwise divisive political, religious, and social fissures of early twentieth-century Russian Jewry.

By the time of World War I, this musical bridge had begun to crack under the weight of external pressures and the renewed political and aesthetic debates inside the Jewish world. Of the many resurgent political ideologies, it was Jewish nationalism, particularly in its Zionist form, that most strongly demanded a new clarity about the lines between Jews, Russians, and Europeans. After 1917, as the Zionists in Palestine and their allies abroad transitioned from a global nationalism into a more targeted movement of political self-determination, they brooked less and less sympathy for the vagaries of the Russian-Jewish synthesis.

The same pursuit of clarity—and simplicity—marked the post-1917 Russian Jewish experience in the United States. There Jewish national identity proved to be an increasingly untenable halfway position for Jewish intellectuals confronting the starker poles of religion and race in a liberal society. In the early Soviet Union, by contrast, an uneasy mixture of socialism, nationalism, and Soviet empire building did create a space for Jewish music to continue in a public form. The price of Soviet Jewish culture, however, was the ongoing burden and insecurity of Soviet politics. Jewish national culture could exist, provided it did not become a vehicle for Jewish nationalism. In practice, the distinction proved hard to make, especially given that the Soviet regime itself took steps to define Jews as a separate nationality and increasingly encouraged strains of Russian nationalism and antisemitism. At the same time, the ideological dictates of Marxist cultural policies emphasized the utopian ideal of a deracinated universalism. When it came to the Jews, Soviet culture was thus torn between two conflicting tendencies—the impulse to erase Jewish difference and the desire to affirm it.

Stalin's "silent pogrom" of the late 1940s and early 1950s dealt a final, crushing blow to the various Jewish cultural projects that traced their origins to the prerevolutionary period, music among them. So too did it seek to reassert the essential Russianness of Soviet culture in every respect. At the Leningrad Conservatory, Rubinstein's complex Russian Jewish legacy was largely effaced. In March 1944, less than two months after the wartime siege of Leningrad had ended, the Soviet authorities announced with great fanfare that the school would henceforth be named in honor of Rimsky-Korsakov. Despite the fact that it was Rubinstein who had founded the conservatory, the ethnic Russian composer proved a more ideologically correct choice. The decision reflected both a resurgent Russian national pride and an early indication of the coming Stalinist attack on the Jewish presence in Soviet Russian musical life. Not only were present-day Jewish musicians increasingly in peril, but the regime had begun to wipe away the last traces of the Russian Jewish musical past itself.[4]

Over the next decade, the Soviet government mounted a sweeping campaign of repression against all forms of Jewish cultural life. As part of this process, Jewish music officially ceased to exist in Soviet culture. Similar efforts began to reduce the Jewish "domination" across the Soviet music world. Internal party memos now offered detailed "exposés" of the prevalence of Jews on the faculties and in administrative positions at the Leningrad and Moscow conservatories. But despite the purges, the "anticosmopolitanism" campaign failed to fully disentangle Russians and Jews in Soviet music. Simply put, the lines between the two had become too blurred.[5]

The best evidence for this enduring intimacy came in the political thaw that followed Stalin's death in 1953. In the opening years of the 1960s, a pair of closely linked composers, Dmitri Shostakovich (1906–1975) and Mieczysław (Moisei) Weinberg (1919–1996), introduced two new symphonies. Remarkably similar in form and theme, their parallel portraits of the intertwined history of Russians and Jews revealed how resilient and entrenched Jewish musicality remained—as cultural symbol and social reality—in Soviet culture. Their shared story offers a fitting conclusion for this book.

The friendship between these two men dated to 1943, two years after Weinberg arrived in the Soviet Union from Poland, fleeing the Nazi invasion. The son of a Yiddish theater musician, he had trained as a pianist and composer first in Warsaw, then in Minsk. Weinberg was eventually evacuated to Tashkent, and it was from there that he sent Shostakovich a copy of his first symphony. Impressed by his junior colleague's potential, Shostakovich immediately secured an invitation for him to relocate with his family to Moscow, thereby launching a relationship with profound consequences for both men's professional and personal lives.

In many respects, the connection between Weinberg and Shostakovich echoed earlier encounters between musicians such as Gnesin, Engel, and

Rosowsky and their Russian mentors. Born and raised in newly independent Poland, Weinberg came to Shostakovich as a young composer from the former western borderlands of the Russian Empire, the periphery of Russian culture, in search of the reigning Russian musical master's approval. He quickly adopted some key features of Shostakovich's musical style as his own, particularly the distinctive admixture of modernist textures and folk idioms. At the same time, Shostakovich found in Weinberg's Jewish background a captivating source of inspiration. From the mid-1940s onward, elements of Yiddish musical folklore began to surface dramatically in Shostakovich's work. Over the next few years, both men produced a body of Jewish-themed music, including strikingly similar settings of Yiddish poetry, folk songs, and klezmer tunes.[6]

In February 1953 Stalin's campaign of terror reached Weinberg directly. Five years earlier, his father-in-law Solomon Mikhoels, the Moscow State Jewish Theater director and de facto leader of Soviet Jewry, had been assassinated in the first purge of the Soviet Jewish intelligentsia. Year by year after that, he watched as friends and colleagues vanished into Soviet prisons and gulags. Now Weinberg himself stood accused of plotting with a Jewish "terrorist group" and the American Jewish Joint Distribution Committee to launch a separatist Jewish national republic in the Crimea. The two volumes of synagogue music in his possession were taken as conclusive proof of his intention to build the putative Jewish republic's conservatory. Faced with the prospect of a death sentence for his friend, Shostakovich wrote a letter to Lavrenty Beria, head of the Soviet secret police, pleading for Weinberg's release. Anticipating the worst, he also began formal steps to adopt Weinberg's daughter. The latter gesture proved unnecessary; after the death of Stalin in March 1953, Weinberg was quickly freed.[7]

The symphony premieres in 1962 and 1963 marked the culmination of the composers' musical dialogue. Shostakovich's Thirteenth Symphony, subtitled "Babi Yar," was debuted by the Moscow Philharmonic in December 1962. The work, scored for bass soloist, male chorus, and orchestra, took its subtitle from a poem by non-Jewish poet Yevgeny Yevtushenko about the notorious 1941 Nazi massacre of 33,000 Jews over two days in Ukraine. Shostakovich built the symphony's first movement, an Adagio also titled "Babi Yar," around Yevtushenko's text. In a time when discussion of Holocaust-era Jewish victimhood and antisemitism were forbidden topics, the work's premiere generated enormous public controversy. Despite the cancellation of a planned television broadcast and other attempts at intimidation and censorship, the performance was a major success, marking a turning point in the Soviet Union's public reckoning with its own antisemitism.[8]

Given the stature of Shostakovich as the Soviet Union's greatest composer, critics have endlessly scrutinized his "Babi Yar" for political meanings. Many have viewed it as a clear moral indictment of Soviet totalitarianism and antisemitism. Others have noted that, in spite of its controversial subject matter, the work arrived after Shostakovich had made a basic and unnecessary moral compromise by joining the Communist Party in 1960. In addition, after the work's premiere Shostakovich and Yevtushenko agreed to changes in the symphony's text (though not the printed score) that deemphasized the uniqueness of Jewish suffering at Babi Yar, noting the deaths of ethnic Russians and Ukrainians as well.[9]

But beyond the questions of the composer's political convictions and the precise ideological meaning of his symphony, Shostakovich's "Babi Yar" revealed a fundamental deeper truth about Russian culture. Four decades after the Society for Jewish Folk Music had vanished, and ten years after Jewish music in its entirety had officially ceased to exist, Jewishness resounded through the work of Soviet music's leading composer. Moreover, Shostakovich's channeling of Jewishness in "Babi Yar" was not simply a potent if ambiguous political statement about *Jews* but an undeniable expression of *Russian* identity. Indeed, one of the ironies of Shostakovich's most overtly "Jewish" work is that, unlike his other works in this vein, it bears no trace of any Jewish folk melodies or other discernible Jewish musical style. Its Jewishness is entirely in its programmatic theme, its text, which in turn constantly emphasizes not the particularity of the Russian Jewish historical experience but its universality. In fact, the symphony's four other movements deal with the experiences of average Soviet citizens confronting censorship, long bread lines, perpetual fear, and the broader struggle between greatness and conformity throughout history. In other words, the ultimate power of the symphony lies precisely in its collapse of the historical distinction between Russian and Jew. This fusion is captured best in the closing lines of the first movement's text—which remained unchanged even after the later revisions—where the narrator declares: "No Jewish blood runs through my veins, but I feel the corrosive hatred of the antisemites as if I were a Jew, and that is why I am a true Russian!"[10]

If Shostakovich's Thirteenth Symphony symbolically invokes Jewishness to emphasize its own Russianness, Weinberg's Sixth Symphony takes a similarly complex path reflective of his own blend of Russian, Polish, and Jewish cultural roots. In his work, Weinberg employs texts by three Soviet writers—Mikhail Lukonin, Shmuel Halkin, and Leyb Kvitko—the latter two of whom were also noted Yiddish poets. The poems cycle through a range of interrelated themes: the magic of childhood and music, the terrors of war, the suffering of Jewish children during the Holocaust, and dreams for world peace. Again, the particular Jewish historical experience is linked to the universal subjects of children's innocence and man's inhumanity.

Weinberg's musical framework for these texts is also remarkably similar to that of Shostakovich. Both are five-movement choral symphonies in the key of A minor, with the last three movements performed without interruption. The coincidence was likely deliberate, as Weinberg had heard Shostakovich's symphony as a work in progress while working on his own. At the same time, behind the screen of Weinberg's Soviet modernist idiom, the starkly evocative sonorities of Jewish folk music are still audible. A similar dynamic surfaces in the texts themselves, many of which were originally written in Yiddish and then translated into Russian.[11]

The interplay of Russian and Jewish is evident throughout the symphony, but particularly so in the second movement. There Weinberg's music and Kvitko's text produce an image of the Russian Jewish violinist—as Russian classical virtuoso and klezmer fiddler—in an ode to the transformative power of music. The text of the 1928 poem "Dos fidele" (The Little Violin, "Skripka" in its Russian translation), speaks of a young boy who fashions a fiddle from a plywood box to enchant his audience of birds and animals. This idyll gives way seamlessly to a dynamic third movement, completely instrumental, with surging rhythms and violin effects that summon up both the klezmer tradition and the somewhat similar scherzo movement in Shostakovich's First Violin Concerto.[12]

Because of its distinctive second movement, the Sixth Symphony acquired the unofficial nickname of "the Jewish Violin." But even with its heavy Jewish overtones and deeply felt valence of Jewish tragedy—Weinberg's parents and sister had perished in a Nazi concentration camp, and Kvitko had been executed during the infamous Night of the Murdered Poets in 1952—neither the musical language nor the translated Yiddish poets' words ever fully assert their own Jewishness. Indeed, the violin image reappears in the fifth and final movement in the non-Jewish poet Lukonin's "Sleep, People" (*Spite, liudi*), a secular prayer that speaks of a day when "violins will sing of peace on earth." At that point "the Jewish violin" has left behind any hints of its cultural paternity to join a larger chorus of violins praying for peace as stars shine over the Volga, Mississippi, and Mekong rivers. The move is deliberate, for Weinberg's symphony aspires to a blend of particular and the universal. The composer simultaneously celebrates Russian culture, quietly but unmistakably asserts the Jewish presence within it, and points to music itself as a force that transcends all nations and religions.[13]

No storm of controversy greeted "the Jewish Violin" at its debut. The

Moscow Philharmonic premiered Weinberg's symphony in November 1963. The work went on to a respectable role in the Soviet repertoire, earning a chapter in a 1967 published survey of the top seventy-five Soviet symphonies and a 1970 recording on the state-run Melodiya label.[14] The Jewish presence in Russian music had once again become an accepted and undeniable part of broader Soviet culture. Shorn of its more nationalist assertiveness and overt romanticist folklorism, the musical ideal of the earlier Russian Jewish composers continued to operate in the music of Weinberg.

In their personal musical dialogue writ large, Shostakovich and Weinberg encapsulated the entire gamut of the Russian-Jewish cultural encounter. Both sides of this equation—the Russian mythologization of the Jew and the Russian Jewish search for a multilayered modern identity—were woven together in a tight, mutually dependent embrace. For over a hundred years, Russians had defined themselves as Russian partly through their selective embrace of Jewish folk music; Jews in turn created Jewish art music in order to become both more Jewish *and* more Russian. In that sense, Weinberg's symphony hinted at a larger truth: for all the official repression of Jewish cultural life in the later Soviet Union and the differences between the tsarist past and the Soviet present, Russian Jewish music continued to reflect a hybrid ideal of intertwined Russian and Jewish cultures. In spite of the political ruptures of key dates such as 1881, 1917, and 1948, music pointed to the deeper continuity of Russian Jewish identity and cultural experience throughout the nineteenth and twentieth centuries.

Arriving as they did in 1962 and 1963, the symphonies of Shostakovich and Weinberg together offered an unintentional tribute to one more feature of the Russian-Jewish historical encounter: the one hundredth anniversary of the St. Petersburg Conservatory. In 1862 Anton Rubinstein had struggled against the myths of nationalism in his quest to fuse Russian, Jew, and European into one culture. One hundred years later, the myths continued unabated, and his legacy at the conservatory had been substantially suppressed. But the broader contours of Rubinstein's legacy remained visible in surprising ways. For in the intervening century, the Russian-Jewish musical encounter had dramatically shaped the nature of what it meant to be Russian, Jewish, and European in modern times.

Notes

Abbreviations

AV IV RAN	Archive of Oriental Studies, Institute of Oriental Studies, Russian Academy of Sciences, St. Petersburg Branch
CAHJP	Central Archives for the History of the Jewish People (Jerusalem)
d.	*delo* (Rus.) file
GARF	State Archive of the Russian Federation (Moscow)
IR NBUV	Institute of Manuscripts, V. I. Vernadsky National Library of the Ukraine
JTSA	Archives of the Jewish Theological Seminary of America (New York)
LN	Anton Rubinstein, *Literaturnoe nasledie v trekh tomakh* (Moscow, 3 vols., 1983-86)
ll.	*listy* (Rus.) pages (sing. *list*)
OR SPbGK	Manuscripts Division, St. Petersburg State Conservatory Library
razd.	*razdel* (Rus.) file folder
RGALI	Russian State Archive of Literature and Art (Moscow)
RIII	Russian Institute for the History of the Arts (St. Petersburg)
RMG	*Russkaia muzykalnaia gazeta*
RNB	Russian National Library (St. Petersburg)
TsGALI SPb	Central State Archive of Literature and Art of St. Petersburg
TsGIA SPb	Central State Historical Archive of St. Petersburg
TsGMMK	Glinka Central State Museum of Musical Culture (Moscow)
v	verso
YIVO	YIVO Institute for Jewish Research (New York)

Introduction

1. Solomon Rosowsky, "Great Musicians I Have Known," *Day Jewish Journal*, May 18, 1958, 4.

2. For the most recent philosemitic variant on the biographical lexicon of musical Jews, see Stevens, *Composers*. Wagner's work has recently been reissued in a Russian translation with an appendix listing, sometimes incorrectly, Jews in Russian and Soviet music. See Wagner, *Evreistvo v muzyke* (2003).

3. See, for instance, Ascheim, *In Times of Crisis;* Botstein and Hanak, *Vienna: Jews and the City of Music;* Mendes-Flohr, *German Jews;* Mosse, *German Jews;* and Steinberg, *Judaism.* For a useful critical survey of these trends, see Samuel Moyn, "German Jewry and

the Question of Identity: Historiography and Theory," *Leo Baeck Institute Yearbook* 41 (1996), 291–308.

4. On the tensions between imperial and national identities in Russian history, see Hosking, *Russia*. The links between Jewish political integration and Russian Jewish identity are best analyzed in Nathans, *Beyond the Pale*.

5. On the concept of Russian Jewish dual identity, see Eli Lederhendler, "Did Russian Jewry Exist Prior to 1917?" in Ro'i, *Jews and Jewish Life*, 23–25, and Benjamin Nathans, "Jews, Law, and the Legal Profession in Late Imperial Russia," in Eliashevich, *Evrei v Rossii* (1998), 101–27.

6. A recent sampling of publications focused on the Russian-Jewish cultural encounter includes Fishman, *Rise of Modern Yiddish Culture*; Ivanov, *Russkie sezony*; Litvak, *Conscription and the Search for Modern Russian Jewry*; Moss, *Jewish Renaissance*; Safran, *Rewriting the Jew*; Safran and Zipperstein, *Worlds of S. An-sky*; Stanislawski, *Zionism and the Fin de Siècle*; and Veidlinger, *Jewish Public Culture*. For a good introduction to the new historiography of religion, nationality, and empire in tsarist Russia, see Geraci and Khodarkovsky, *Of Religion and Empire*; Gerasimov et al., *Novaia imperskaia istoriia*; and David-Fox, Holquist, and Martin, *Orientalism*.

7. Harshav, *Language in Time of Revolution*, 42.

8. Slezkine, *Jewish Century*, 1.

9. Gay, *Freud, Jews, and Other Germans*, 174, vii. For an extension of Gay's argument, see Michael P. Steinberg, "Jewish Identity and Intellectuality in Fin-de-Siècle Austria: Suggestions for a Historical Discourse," *New German Critique* no. 48 (Winter 1988), 3–33.

10. For an important critique of Gay, see George Mosse, review of *Freud, Jews, and Other Germans*, *New Republic* (Nov. 26, 1977), 40–41.

11. M. Nagen, "O evreiskoi muzyke," *Razsvet* 44 (Nov. 1, 1909), 6–7. For suggestive reflections on Jewish musicians and modern European culture, see Eric Hobsbawm, "Benefits of Diaspora," *London Review of Books* 27:20 (Oct. 20, 2005), 16–19; Sander Gilman, "Einstein's Violin: Jews and the Performance of Identity," *Modern Judaism* 25 (2005), 219–36; Yehudi Menuhin, "The Violinist," in Villiers, *Next Year in Jerusalem*, 329–38; and David Schoenbaum, "Fiddlers on the Roof: Some Thoughts on a Special Relationship," in Tewes and Wright, *Liberalism, Anti-Semitism, and Democracy*, 273–87.

12. Elon, *Pity of It All*, 63. On Jews and European art music, see James Loeffler, "Concert Music," in Hundert, *YIVO Encyclopedia*, vol. 1, 1228–33, and Ezra Mendelsohn, "On the Jewish Presence in Nineteenth-Century European Musical Life," *Studies in Contemporary Jewry* 9 (1993), 3–16.

13. Altmann, *Moses Mendelssohn*, 66–67. On the overall attraction of German Jews to music, see Botstein, *Judentum und Modernität*, 126–48, and Ruth Katz, "Why Music? Jews and the Commitment to Modernity," in Volkov, *Deutsche Juden und die Moderne*, 31–38.

14. Guzikov's biography is recounted in Ottens and Rubin, *Klezmer-Musik*, 157–70, while the subject of klezmer musicians more generally is surveyed in Beregovskii, *Jewish Instrumental Folk Music*, 21–35.

15. Sholem Aleichem, *From the Fair*, 168.

16. Zipperstein, *Jews of Odessa*, 65–66; Patricia Herlihy, "Odessa Memories," in Iljine, *Odessa Memories*, 14–22.

17. See, for instance, Babel's *Odessa Tales* (written from the 1910s onward) in N. Babel, *Complete Works*, 129–96, and Kuprin's story "Gambrinus" (written in 1906) in Kuprin, *Gambrinus*, 11–73. See also Robert Rothstein, "How It Was Sung in Odessa: At the Intersection of Russian and Yiddish Folk Culture," *Slavic Review* 60 (2001), 781–801.

18. Slobin, *Tenement Songs*, 195–97; Seth L. Wolitz, "The Americanization of Tevye or Boarding the Jewish Mayflower," *American Quarterly* 40 (1988), 514–36; Stephen J. Whitfield, "Fiddling with Sholem Aleichem: A History of *Fiddler on the Roof*," in Kugelmass, *Key Texts*, 105–25.

Chapter 1. Emancipating Sounds

1. The phrase is from Rubinstein's *Gedankenkorb*, 95–96, reprinted in Russian translation in Rubinstein, *Korob myslei*, 200.

2. For the most significant biographies, see the two classics, Findeizen, *A. G. Rubinshtein*, and Barenboim, *Anton Grigorevich Rubinshtein*, along with the two recent English-language works: Sitsky, *Anton Rubinstein* and Taylor, *Anton Rubinstein*.

3. On the emergence of professional groups and nineteenth-century Russian civil society, see Balzer, "Conclusion: The Missing Middle Class," in Balzer, *Russia's Missing Middle Class*, 301–303; Kassow, West, and Clowes, *Between Tsar and Society;* and Joseph Bradley, "Subjects into Citizens: Societies, Civil Society, and Autocracy in Tsarist Russia," *American Historical Review* 107:4 (Oct. 2002), 1094–1123.

4. Stanislawski, "Jewish Apostasy in Russia: A Tentative Typology," in Endelman, *Jewish Apostasy*, 195–200. On Jewish conversion in this era more broadly, see Stanislawski, *Tsar Nicholas I*, 141–48; John D. Klier, "State Policies and the Conversion of Jews in Imperial Russia," in Geraci and Khodarkovsky, *Religion and Empire*, 92–112; and Avrutin, "Legible People," 197–237.

5. Jacob Letshishinky, "Barditshever yidisher kehile fun 1789 biz 1917," *Bleter far idishe demografye, statistik un ekonomik* 1:2 (1923), 37. The exact details of the Rubinshteyn family conversion remain obscure and disputed. Important accounts include N. G. Findeizen, "K biografii A. G. Rubinshteina (iz neizdannykh materialov)," *RMG* 45 (Nov. 8, 1909), 1021; Menkov, *Zapiski*, vol. 2, 79–83; Gintsburg, *Meshumodim*, 279–308; Barenboim, *Anton Grigorevich*, 1:13–18 and 2: 202; Bowen, *Free Artist*, 3–14; and Semen Melnik, "Novyi vzgliad na fakty biografii Rubinshteina," in Khoprova, *Anton Grigorevich*, 194–95.

6. On the postconversion identity of the Rubinstein family in Berdichev, see "Sankt-Peterburgskaia letopis'," *Nedelnaia khronika voskhoda* 46 (Nov. 19, 1889), 1162–63.

7. V. N. Storozhev, "Bratia Rubinshteiny (Istoricheskaia spravka k piatideiatiletiiu Moskovskoi konservatorii)," *Golos minushego* 4:9 (1916), 246–47; M. B. Rosenberg, "Anton Grigorevich Rubinshtein: Zametki k ego biografii, doktora M. B. R-ga," *Russkaia starina* 64:11 (Nov. 1889), 579; Dov Sadan, "Li-motsa'o shel A. Rubinshteyn," *Tatzlil* 4 (1964), 53-53; Kaplan, *Making of the Jewish Middle Class*, 121; Beregovskii, *Jewish Instrumental Folk Music*, 35–36, 59–60.

8. A. G. Rubinstein, "Avtobiograficheskie rasskazy," in *LN* 1:65–71.

9. On the role of salons and music in German Jewish life, see Leon Botstein, "Music, Femininity, and Jewish Identity: The Tradition and Legacy of the Salon," in Bilski and Braun, *Jewish Women and Their Salons*, 159–69.

10. On the concept of social identity and the evolving estate system in Imperial Russia, see Wirtschafter, *Social Identity*, and Gregory Freeze, "The *Soslovie* (Estate) Paradigm and Russian Social History," *American Historical Review* 91:1 (Feb. 1986), 11–36. On the problem of Jewish classification in this social system, see Nathans, *Beyond the Pale*, 72–73, and Klier, *Imperial Russia's Jewish Question*, 66–83.

11. Anton's other sister, Liubov (1833–1903), married a baptized Jewish lawyer named Jacob (Iakov) Veinberg. Rubinstein's mother also made efforts to change the family's estate

status to relieve them of financial obligations. For archival information on the evolving family status, see Storozhev, "Bratia Rubinshteiny," 246–51.

12. *LN* 2:83–84 (A. G. Rubinstein to K. Kh. Rubinstein, Feb. 4 and 21, 1857). On the problem of Jewish-sounding names for baptized Jews, see Iu. Avrutin, "Kreshchenye evrei, etnicheskii konflikt i politika povsednevnoi zhizni v Rossii vo vremiia pervoi mirovoi voiny," in Budnitskii et al., *Mirovoi kriziz*, 101–6.

13. Rubinstein, "Avtobiograficheskie rasskazy," 69 and 74.

14. *LN* 2:22–25, 33 (A. G. Rubinstein to K. Kh. Rubinstein, June 12, 1850, Nov. 1 and Dec. 28, 1850, and Sept. 27, 1851); Rosenberg, "Anton Grigorevich," 584.

15. *LN* 2:25, 27, 30–33, 36–39, and 86 (A. G. Rubinstein to K. Kh. Rubinstein, Dec. 28, 1850; Jan. 12, Mar. 14, Mar. 26, Apr. 16, Aug. 18, and Sept. 27, 1851; Apr. 21, May [undated], June 4, and Aug. 19, 1852; Dec. 7, 1857).

16. W. Bruce Lincoln, "The Circle of the Grand Duchess Yelena Pavlovna, 1847–1861," *Slavonic and East European Review* 48:3 (July 1970), 373–87; Tiutcheva, *Pri dvore dvukh imperatorov*, 166–69. On the relations between Rubinstein and Liszt, see "Perepiska Fr. Lista s A. G. Rubinshteinom," *RMG* 8 (Aug. 1896), 829–66, and Hermann Ritter, "Personliche Erinnerungen an Anton Rubinstein: Nebst Briefen," *Signale für die Musikalische Welt* 59:16 (Feb. 20, 1901), 241–44.

17. *LN* 2:71–72 (A. G. Rubinstein to K. Kh. Rubinstein, July 9, 1855); Barenboim, *Anton Grigorevich*, 2:231–35; Bowen, *Free Artist*, 73, 222.

18. Rosenberg, "Anton Grigorevich," 581; Menkov, *Zapiski*, 2:81; TsGMMK, fond 50, d. 235, l. 1 (manuscript memoir about K. Kh. Rubinstein); Melnik, "Novyi vzgliad," 194–95.

19. On Nikolai Rubinstein, see Barenboim, *Nikolai Grigorevich*.

20. Barenboim, *Anton Grigorevich*, 1:17; Bowen, *Free Artist*, 309; Storozhev, "Bratia Rubinshteiny," 246; Julius Rodenberg, "Meine personlichen Erinnerungen an Anton Rubinstein: Nebst Briefen," *Deutsche rundschau* 21:6 (1895), 244. See also Yitshok Pirozshnikov, "Anton Rubinshteyn," *Tsukunft* 19:11 (Nov. 1914), 1157, and Kogut, *Znamenitye evrei*, vol. 4, 87–88. On questions of identity among nineteenth-century European Jewish converts in general, see Todd Endelman, "Memories of Jewishness: Jewish Converts and Their Jewish Pasts," in Carlebach, Efron, and Myers, *Jewish History*, 311–29.

21. RNB, fond 654, op. 478a, d. 2, ll. 1–2 (contract with Friedrich Hebbel); *LN* 2:89–90 (A. G. Rubinstein to K. Kh. Rubinstein, Apr. 12, 1858). See also Paul Bornstein, "Friedrich Hebbel in seinen Beziehungen zu Musik und Musikern," *Die Musik* 23 (1908–9), 269–70; Heinz Stolte, "Ein Steinwurf oder Opfer um Opfer: Zur Interpretation von Friedrich Hebbels Operntext," *Hebbel-Jahrbuch* 34 (1979), 12–38; and Nagler, *Hebbel*, 59–65. On the Golem legend, see Hillel Kieval, "Pursuing the Golem of Prague: Jewish Culture and the Invention of a Tradition," *Modern Judaism* 17 (1997), 1–20.

22. Rodenberg, "Meine personlichen Erinnerungen," 249.

23. Gershon Swet, "Russian Jews in Music," in Frumkin et al., *Russian Jewry*, 306.

24. T. Z. Skvirskaia, "Iz neizdannoi perepiski Antona Rubinshteina, khraniashcheisia v biblioteke Peterburgskoi konservatorii," in Khoprova, *Anton Grigorevich*, 177; Rodenberg, "Meine personlichen Erinnerungen," 256; *LN* 2:161–62 (A. G. Rubinstein to K. Kh. Rubinstein, Apr. 2, 1868); Rubinstein, *Gedankenkorb*, 16–17, 106, and 117.

25. Rubinstein, "Avtobiograficheskie rasskazy," 86–87. Curiously, Rubinstein's retelling of the incident includes an obvious mistake; in reality, his *soslovie* was that of a son of a merchant of the Third Guild, not the Second. See Storozhev, "Bratia Rubinshteiny," 246–47, and RNB, fond 654, op. 478a, d. 1, ll. 1–2 (copy of baptismal certificate from July 25, 1831 [1856]).

26. Rubinstein, "Avtobiograficheskie rasskazy," 86–87.
27. GARF, fond 698, op. 1, d. 221, l. 5 (A. G. Rubinstein to E. D. Raden, Mar. 21, 1861).
28. Findeizen, "K biografii A. G. Rubinshteina," 1043–44; I. F. Abaza, "Iz vospominanii Iu. F. Abaza," *Russkaia starina* 40:140 (Nov. 1909), 332–34; "Pismo (A. G. Rubinshteina) adresovannoe Ministru narodnago prosveshcheniia russkim muzykalnym obshchestvom," *RMG* 45 (Nov. 8, 1909), 1012–20; A. G. Rubinstein, "Dokladnaia zapiska Ministru narodnogo prosveshcheniia," repr. in *LN* 1:43–53. For a comprehensive study of the Imperial Russian Music Society, see Sargeant, "Middle Class Culture."
29. A. G. Rubinstein, "O muzyke v Rossii," *Vek* 1 (1861), 33–37, repr. in *LN* 1:46–53. For a complete English translation, see Campbell, *Russians*, 64–73.
30. Harley Balzer, "Introduction," in Balzer, *Russia's Missing Middle Class*, 3–38, and Ruane, *Gender, Class, and the Professionalization*, 5–20.
31. V. V. Stasov, "Konservatorii v Rossii (Zamechannia na statiu g. Rubinshteina)," *Severnaia pchela* 45 (Feb. 24, 1861), repr. in Stasov, *Stati o muzyke* 2:5, 8–9. On Stasov's musical thought, see Taruskin, *Defining Russia*, 152–54.
32. A. N. Serov, "Zalogi istinnogo muzykalnogo obrazovaniia v S.-Peterburge," *Severnaia pchela* 124 (May 9, 1862), repr. in Serov, *Kriticheskie statii* 3:1426–32. Serov's career is analyzed at length in Taruskin's *Opera and Drama*.
33. Lazare Saminsky, "Pamiatnik Antona Rubinshteina (K 20 letiiu so dnia konchiny)," *Novyi voskhod* 5:47 (Nov. 27, 1914), 36; Bazunov, *A. N. Serov*, 6–7; Serova, *Serovy*, 10, 131.
34. Taruskin, *Defining Russia*, 123–24. For further discussion of these themes, see George G. Weickhardt, "Music and Society in Russia, 1860s–1890s," *Canadian-American Slavic Studies* 30 (1996), 45–68; Ridenour, *Nationalism*, 27–28; and Marina Frolova-Walker, "The Disowning of Anton Rubinstein," in Kuhn, Nemtsov, and Wehrmeyer, *"Samuel" Goldenberg*, 19–60.
35. Puzyrevskii and Sakketti, *Ocherk*, 1–31; Kremlev, *Leningradskaia*, 1–25.
36. *Ustav muzykalnogo uchilishcha* (1861), quoted in Vulfius, *Iz istorii*, 13; Glebov, *Anton Grigorevich*, 101; Lynn Sargeant, "A New Class of People: The Conservatory and Musical Professionalization in Russia, 1861–1917," *Music and Letters* 84:1 (Feb. 2004), 41–61; Nathans, *Beyond the Pale*, 45–79. For the history of this issue in the conservatories, see TsGIA SPb, fond 361, op. 11, d. 161, ll. 1–18; TsGIA SPb, fond 361, op. 11, d. 577, ll. 8–16; and GARF, fond 102, op. 76a, del. 2, d. 185, ll. 1–57 (IRMO correspondence on Jewish legal rights).
37. Kavos-Dekhtereva, *A. G. Rubinshtein*, 45; *LN* 2:123 (A. G. Rubinstein to V. A. Kologrivov, July 9, 1862); Rubinstein, "Avtobiograficheskie rasskazy," 91.
38. "Anton Grigorevich Rubinshtein," *Evreiskaia entsyklopediia*, vol. 13, cols. 706–10; Gintsburg, "Anton Rubinshteyn," 307–9. For an example of the OPE's attitude toward Rubinstein, see "Sankt-Peterburgskaia letopis," *Nedelnaia khronika voskhoda* 46 (Nov. 13, 1894), 1222, and 47 (Nov. 20, 1894), 1245. On the OPE's general history, see Horowitz, *Jewish Philanthropy*.
39. Nathans, *Beyond the Pale*, 225–30; Gintsburg, "Anton Rubinshteyn," 307; TsGIA SPb, fond 361, op. 1, #3462, ll. 1–15 (student records of Borukh Rozovskii).
40. M. Gerts, "Di Lebens-Geshikhte fun B. L. Rosovski," *Di khazonim-velt* 10 (Aug. 1934), 2–3; JTSA, Solomon Rosowsky Collection, box 2, folder 50, 1–8 (memoirs of Solomon Rosowsky); Friedman, *Lebensbilder*, 3:28.
41. James Loeffler, "Jacob Bachmann," in Hundert, *YIVO Encyclopedia*, 1:107–108; Kruk, "Voices of Odessa," 23–27.
42. Barenboim, *Anton Grigorevich*, 1:232–34; Friedman, *Lebensbilder*, 1:191–92.
43. Barenboim, *Anton Grigorevich*, 2:110–11; RNB, fond 654, op. 478a, d. 93, l. 1

(V. A. Rubinstein to A. F. Chekuanova, Nov. 29, 1865). For more lurid accounts of Rubinstein's marriage, see Héritte-Viardot, *Memories,* 59–110, and Melnik, "Novyi vzgliad," 189–94.

44. Anton Rubinstein, "Russiche Kompositoren," *Blätter für musik, theater und kunst* nos. 29, 33, and 37 (May 1855), republished in Russian translation in Glebov, *Anton Grigorevich,* 56–61, along with derogatory comments in response, including those of Glinka himself.

45. V. V. Stasov, "Dvadtsat piat let Russkogo iskusstvo: Nasha muzyka," *Vestnik evropy* (1882–83), repr. in Stasov, *Izbrannye sochineniia,* 2:525–29. For a general musicological discussion of Russian musical Orientalism, see Taruskin, *Defining Russia,* 194–217.

46. On the popularity of Russian translations of Byron's "Hebrew Melodies," see S. S-si, "Lord Bairon i ego 'Evreiskie melodii,'" in *Evreiskie melodii v perevodakh Russkikh pisatelei* (Ekaterinoslav, 1898), 1–19, and A. Finkel, "Lermontov i drugie perevodchiki 'Evreiskaia melodiia' Bairony," *Masterstvo perevoda* 6 (1969–70), 169–200.

47. The segment "'Samuel' Goldenburg and 'Schmuyle'" in *Pictures at an Exhibition* is more commonly known as "Two Jews, One Rich and One Poor." Richard Taruskin has noted, however, that the original score contains no such heading and actually suggests that the two portraits refer to one and the same Jew. See Taruskin, *Musorgsky,* 379–83, and Taruskin, *On Russian Music,* 190–201. The phenomenon of Jewish musical Orientalism among Russian composers is discussed in Móricz, *Jewish Identities,* 55–91, and Ilia Kheifets, "Evreiskaia muzykalnaia idioma i kompozitsionnaia tekhnika (na primere dvukh proizvedenii M. I. Glinki i M. P. Musorgskogo)," *Vestnik evreiskogo universiteta v Moskve* 5:23 (2001), 49–76. On Mussorgsky in particular, see Boris Schwarz, "Musorgsky's Interest in Judaica," in Brown, *Musorgsky,* 85–94, and Weiner, *Richard Wagner,* 144–47.

48. Rodenberg, "Meine personlichen Erinnerungen," 255.

49. See, for instance, P. Minkovskii, "*Shirei 'Am,*" *Ha-shiloaḥ* 5 (1899), pt. 3, 206; O. Ia. Levenson, "Anton Grigorevich Rubinshtein," *Artist* 3 (1889), 76–82; Barenboim, *Anton Grigorevich,* 1:188–96; V. V. Bessel, "Moi vospominaniia ob Antone Grigoreviche Rubinshteine (1829–1894)," *Russkaia starina* 94:5 (May 1898), 374; Kavos-Dekhtereva, *A. G. Rubinshtein,* 98–99; "Anton Grigorevich Rubinshtein," in Riemann, *Muzykalnyi slovar,* 1142; and "Za nedeliu," *Novyi voskhod* 6:9 (Mar. 6, 1915), 34. The Russian music critic Nikolai Findeizen even invoked the *evrei-zhid* dichotomy in his 1907 biography of Rubinstein, suggesting that his subject's personality and music typified "the descendant of the ancient, biblical Hebrew type—generous, noble, possessed of a wonderfully rich and truthful nature"—rather than the other negative features of his people. See Findeizen, *A. G. Rubinshtein,* 3.

50. *LN* 3:32 (A. G. Rubinstein to K. Kh. Rubinstein, Oct. 14, 1875).

51. R. Ilish, "A. G. Rubinshteyn i Iom-Kipur (Listia iz moego dnevnika)," *Khronika voskhoda* 18:10 (Oct. 1898), 42–45; *LN* 2:181 and 3:32 (A. G. Rubinstein to K. Kh. Rubinstein, Apr. 18, 1871, and Oct. 14, 1875).

52. Rodenberg, "Meine personlichen Erinnerungen," 243–62; Rubinstein, "Die geistliche Oper," quoted in translation in Lisovskii, *Anton Grigorevich,* appendices, 27–34; Stargardt-Wolff, *Wegbereiter,* 42; Rubinstein, *Gedankenkorb,* 149.

53. Rubinstein, *Gedankenkorb,* 15. See, for example, Ritter, "Personliche Erinnerungen," 243–44; Bessel, "Moi vospominaniia," 371–72; Barenboim, *Anton Grigorevich* 2:56–58; GARF, fond 698, op. 1, l. 24v (A. G. Rubinstein to E. K. Raden, Mar. 29, 1869); and Rubinstein, "Avtobiograficheskie rasskazy," 95. Rubinstein's aesthetic critique of Wagner can be found in its fullest form in Rubinstein, *Muzyka i ee predstaviteli,* repr. in *LN* 1:143–46.

54. "Anton Grigorevich Rubinshtein," *Evreiskaia entsyklopediia,* col. 710. A thorough analysis of Rubinstein's spiritual operas appears in Täuschel, *Anton Rubinstein,* 138–49.

55. GARF, fond 102, del. 2, op. 1, d. 66, ll. 1-2v (Office of the Moscow Governor-General to Ministry of Internal Affairs, Sept. 7, 1882).
56. Kremlev, *Leningradskaia*, 16 and 20-21; Ginzburg, *K. Iu. Davydov*, 77; TsGIA SPb, fond 361, op. 11, d. 161, ll. 1-27; GARF, fond 102, del. 2, op. 1, d. 66, ll. 1-105, d. 185, ll. 1-57, and d. 1018, ll. 1-167; Sargeant, "A New Class of People."
57. Bowen, *Free Artist*, 304-5, and Kremlev, *Leningradskaia*, 53-54.
58. Mark Slobin, "Klezmer Music: An American Ethnic Genre," *Yearbook for Traditional Music* 16 (1984), 39; M. Ivanov, "Muzykalnye nabroski," *Novoe vremia* 4800 (Jan. 11, 1887), quoted in Ginzburg, *K. Iu. Davydov*, 82.
59. *LN* 3:103-4 (A. G. Rubinstein to K. Kh. Rubinstein, July 20, 1888); Rubinstein, "Avtobiograficheskie rasskazy," 99-100.
60. Kavos-Dekhtereva, *A. G. Rubinshtein*, 49-50, 115-17; Barenboim, *Anton Grigorevich* 2:325-26; Iastrebtsev, *Reminscences*, 74; Bessel, "Moi vospominaniia," 366-67; M'Arthur, *Anton Rubinstein*, 142-43; Puzyrevskii and Sakketti, *Ocherk*, 173-74; Rubinstein, *Muzyka*, in *LN* 1:152-53.
61. OR SPbGK, #5342 (A. G. Rubinstein to K. Kh. Rubinstein, Aug. 11, 1889).
62. TsGIA SPb, fond 361, op. 12, d. 20, ll. 1-150 (Conservatory records, 1888-1889); "Teatr i muzyka: S-Peterburgskaia konservatoriia," *Grazhdanin* 136 (May 15, 1888), 3, and 240 (Aug. 29, 1888), 4; Liapunova, *Perepiska*, 2:24, 104-105, and 406-409; Liapunova and Lazovitskaia, *Milii Alekseievich Balakirev*, 302, 311; Kremlev, *Leningradskaia*, 53-54.
63. "Nashi konservatorii," *Novoe vremia* 4796 (July 7, 1889), 1.
64. Lisovskii, *Anton Grigorevich*, appendices, 43-44; "A. G. Rubinshtein," *Novoe vremia* 4800 (July 11, 1889), 1.
65. A. G. Rubinstein, "Eshche o konservatoriakh (Pismo v redaktsiiu)," *Novoe vremia* 4800 (July 11, 1889), 1. Emphasis in the original.
66. Ibid., 4. Emphasis in the original. A. G. Rubinstein, "Dokladnaia zapiska v direktsiiu S.-Peterburgksogo otdeleniia Russkogo muzykalnogo obshchestva," repr. in *LN* 1:64-65. For the full text of the three crucial proposals from the years 1887 to 1889, see *LN* 1:62-65, 104-7.
67. Stanislawski, *Autobiographical Jews*, 123-25; Weeks, *Nation and State*, 27-28; Rubinstein, "Avtobiograficheskie rasskazy," 102. It should be noted, however, that at times Rubinstein would elide the difference between the terms *russkii* and *rossiiskii*, referring to Russian citizens as *russkie podannye*.
68. See, for example, V. Baskin, "A. G. Rubinshtein: K 50-letiiu ego articheskoi deiatelnosti," *Trud* 3:14 (1889), 149-69; "Kureznaia polemika," *Nuvellist* 5 (Sept. 1889), 3-5; "K voprosu ob obrazovatelnom znachenii nashikh konservatorii," *Baian* 22-23 (Sept. 11, 17, 1889), 177-88, 185-86; Barenboim, *Anton Grigorevich*, 2:358-60; and Chaikovskii, *Zhizn Petra Ilicha*, 3:325-26.
69. RIII, fond 24, op. 3, d. 38, ll. 1-2 (OPE to A. G. Rubinstein, Nov. 18, 1889).
70. Lisovskii, *Anton Grigorevich*, appendices, 51-54; "Iskusstvo, filantropiia i 'Grazhdanin,'" *Moskovskie vedomosti* 319 (Nov. 18, 1889), 2-3; "Literaturno-kriticheskii feleton," *Grazhdanin* 311 (Nov. 9, 1889); "Slovo o kniaze Vladimir Meshcherskom i ob Antone Rubinshteine," *Moskovskie vedomosti* 306 (Nov. 5, 1889), 2-3; Lamzdorf, *Dnevnik*, 237-38; Wallace, *Century*, 26. On the possible international diplomatic calculus in the tsarist regime's treatment of Rubinstein, see Pobedonostsev, *K. P. Pobedonostsev*, 1:557-58, and Dudakov, *Paradoksy*, 237-39.
71. On Rubinstein's final months, see Barenboim, *Anton Grigorevich*, 2:401-4.
72. Rubinstein, "Avtobiograficheskie rasskazy," in *LN* 1:102.

73. An uncensored Russian translation was not published until 1999. On the publication history, see *LN* 1:35–41, and Barenboim, *Anton Grigorevich*, 2:231–36.

74. Rubinstein, *Gedankenkorb*, 39. Rubinstein's reference to himself as "everywhere a stranger" comes from an unpublished memoir quoted in Barenboim, *Anton Grigorevich*, 2:251–52, "Sad is my fate. Nowhere do they recognize me as their own. In my homeland I am a *'zhid,'* in Germany I am a Russian, in England 'Herr Rubinstein.' Everywhere I am a stranger."

75. Rubinstein, *Gedankenkorb*, 7.

76. Rubinstein, *Muzyka*, in *LN* 1:162.

Chapter 2. National Voices, Imperial Echoes

1. The second of the two opening epigraphs is inscribed on the first printed copy of the folk song collection, *Evreiskie narodnye pesni v Rossii*, sent by Marek to Engel after their concert debut in Moscow and now in the Vernadsky Library in Kiev, IR NBUV, fond 190, d. 281, l. 132. Dubnov, *Ob izuchenii istorii russkikh evreev*, 47, 70–75 (emphasis in the original).

2. On Dubnow's intellectual model, see Robert M. Seltzer, "Coming Home: The Personal Basis of Simon Dubnow's Ideology," *AJS Review* 1 (1976), 283–301; Jeffrey Veidlinger, "Simon Dubnow Recontextualized: The Sociological Conception of Jewish History and the Russian Intellectual Legacy," *Jahrbuch des Simon-Dubnow-Instituts* 3 (2004), 411–27; and Rabinovitch, "Alternative to Zion," 22–64. For examples of the Russian denial of the existence of any Jewish folk music across the nineteenth century, see "Polskie evrei," *Biblioteka dlia chtenia* 28 (1838), 63–64, 75; "O khramovoi muzyki u iudeev," *Moskvitianin* 17:5 (August 1852), 23–30; and Sakketti, *Ocherk vseobshchei istorii muzyki*, 30.

3. For discussions of music's role in the Bundist and Zionist movements, respectively, see Litvak, *Vos geven*, 226–44, and Philip Bohlman, "Before Hebrew Song," in M. Berkowitz, *Nationalism, Zionism and Ethnic Mobilization*, 25–59.

4. G. Svet, "Di faryesomte yidishe muzik (Etlekhe verter tsum toyt fun Yoyel Engel)," *Der moment* 18:42 (Feb. 18, 1927), 7.

5. For attempts to recast Engel as the proponent of a Yiddishist cultural-political agenda, see Rabinovitsh, *Muzik bay yidn*, 159–73; Saminsky, *Music of the Ghetto and Bible*, 227–52; and Izaly Zemtsovsky, "Muzykalnyi idishizm: K istorii unikalnogo fenomena," in Guralnik, *Iz istorii evreiskoi muzyki*, 119–24. Engel's Zionist hagiography was achieved through Menashe Ravina's three publications, *Yo'el 'Engel, ḥayyav ve-yetsirato*, *Mikhtavim 'al ha-musikah ha-yehudit*, and *Yo'el Engel ve-hamusikah ha-yehudit*, and in Moshe Braunzaft's *Yo'el Engel*. Later sources continued to credit Engel as the founder of "Israeli folk music." See, for instance, Keren, *Contemporary Israeli Music*, 55. The Soviet image of Engel is reflected in Beregovskii, *Evreiskii muzykalnyi folklor*, 6; I. Kunin, "Muzykalno-kriticheskaia deiatelnost Iu. D. Engelia," in Engel, *Glazami sovremennika*, 5–28; and Viktor Lenzon, "Yuli Engel—Der kritiker, folklorist un kompozitor," *Sovetish heymland* 12 (1986), 134–41, while the post-Soviet Zionist interpretation is evident in Yakov Soroker, "Govoriat, est takaia strana (Ioel Engel)," in Parkhomovskii, *Evrei v kulture russkogo zarubezhia*, 2:374–91.

6. IR NBUV, fond 190, d. 262, ll. 4–5 (autobiographical sketch by Engel), and TsGMMK, fond 93, d. 534, l. 1 (autobiographical sketch by Engel); Iu. D. Engel, "V Zakharinke (vospominaniia ob A. D. Idelsone)," in *Sbornik pamiati*, 58; Ada Engel-Roginskaia, "Iu. Engel (Vospominaniia docheri)," in Engel, *Glazami*, 493; TsGMMK, fond 93, d. 539, l. 1 (Iu. D. Engel to P. I. Chaikovskii, June 1, 1893).

7. Halevy, *Jewish University Students*, 49; GARF, fond 102, op. 76a, del. 2, d. 1934, ll. 28–29 (memo from Moscow City-Governor to the MVD, Dec. 18, 1900).

8. Engel, "V Zakharinke," 54–55. On the Bnei Moshe movement and Russian Jewish cultural nationalism in the 1880s and 1890s, see Zipperstein, *Elusive Prophet*, 21–66.
9. Slonimsky, *Perfect Pitch*, 96.
10. IR NBUV, fond 190, d. 263, ll. 6–6v, 7v (unpublished manuscript, "The First Evening of Jewish Music"); Engel, "V Zakharinke," 57–59; IR NBUV, fond 190, d. 266, l. 36 ("Jewish Folk Song: An Ethnographic Expedition, Summer 1912"); Levontin, *Shim'on Etsyoni*, 150–65.
11. Glushchenko, *Ocherki*, 100–101; Stupel, *Russkaia mysl*, 24; Nikolai Kashkin, "Russkoe muzykalnoe obshchestvo: III," *Moskovskii ezhenedelnik* 20 (1908), 54; Ravina, *Engel, hayyav ve-yetsirato*, 11. Engel's own perspective on Taneev's influence is recounted in Iu. D. Engel, "S. I. Taneev, kak uchitel," *Muzykalnyi sovremennik* 7 (1916), 42–73.
12. AV IV RAN, fond 85, op. 2, d. 301, l. 2v (Iu. D. Engel to D. S. Maggid, Nov. 19, 1909); *Internationale Musikgesellschaft, III*, 25. On Engel's music reference publications and translations, see S. G. Karpeshina, "K tvorcheskoi biografii Iu. D. Engelia," in Granovskii, *Evreiskaia muzyka*, 31–36. Riemann's influence on European musicology is analyzed in Rehding, *Hugo Riemann*.
13. A. Maslov, "Zadachi muzykalnoi etnografii," *RMG* 40, 45 (Oct. 3, Nov. 4, 1904), 872–73, 1046–48. The development of Russian ethnography is recounted in Nathaniel Knight, "Science, Empire, and Nationality: Ethnography in the Russian Geographical Society, 1845–1855," in Burbank and Ransel, *Imperial Russia*, 108–41; Hirsch, *Empire of Nations*, esp. 21–51; and Vera Tolz, "European, National, and (Anti-) Imperial: The Formation of Academic Oriental Studies in Late Tsarist and Early Soviet Russia," in David-Fox, Holquist, and Martin, *Orientalism*, 107–34. The specific history of Russian research on folk music is surveyed in Vulfius, *Russkaia mysl*. On nineteenth-century German anthropology, see Matti Bunzl and H. Glenn Penny, "Introduction: Rethinking German Anthropology, Colonialism, and Race," in Penny and Bunzl, *Worldly Provincialism*, 11–16.
14. The quotations are taken from the Russian-language version of the announcement, "O sobiranii evreiskikh narodnykh pesniakh (Pismo v redaktsiiu)," *Khronika voskhoda* 11 (Mar. 15, 1898), 388–89. See also *Ha-melits* 58 (Mar. 23, 1898), 1, and *Ha-tsefirah* 71 (Apr. 6, 1898), 411. On the collection's broader nationalist significance, see Bohlman, *Music of European Nationalism*, 56–57, 103–7.
15. GARF, fond 9533, d. 117, ll. 1–4 (P. S. Marek to Sh. M. Gintsburg, Oct. 16, 1897, Dec. 8, 1898, Oct. 26, 1899, and Apr. 27, 1900) and fond 9535, d. 21, l. 12. On Dubnow's positivist detachment from folklore, see Kiel, "Twice Lost Legacy," 399–400. For more on the distinction between ethnography and folklore and the latter discipline's philological model, see Azadovskii, *Istoriia russkoi folkloristiki*. On the influence of Herder on Russian ethnography in general and on the project in particular, see, respectively, Knight, "Constructing the Science," 52–53, and Gintsburg, *Amolike Peterburg*, 241–44.
16. I. V. Lipaev, "Eshche o narodnykh pesniakh evreev," *Khronika voskhoda* 13 (Mar. 29, 1898), 464; Leo Winz, "Starye voprosy i novye zadachi," *Voskhod* 10 (Oct. 1898), 1–2. For another critique of the project, see Bar-Ami, "Das Juedische Volkslied," *Die Welt* 4:3 (Mar. 1904), 149–60. On Lipaev's relationship with Engel, see Bernard Granovskii, "Ob evreiskoi muzyke v muzykalno-literaturnom nasledii I. V. Lipaeva," *Vestnik evreiskogo universiteta v Moskve* 2 (1993), 80–88.
17. GARF, fond 9533, d. 117, l. 4 (P. S. Marek to Sh. M. Gintsburg, Apr. 27, 1900); Gintsburg, *Amolike Peterburg*, 244; IR NBUV, fond 190, d. 139, ll. 1–17 (Engel's transcription notebook). For a detailed ethnomusicological analysis of this notebook, see Sholokhova, "Stanovlenie i razvitie," 40–47.

Meyer, "Two Persistent Tensions within *Wissenschaft des Judentums*," *Mod*-
4 (2004), 99–115. On the development of *Wissenschaft* musical and historical
Jewish-Christian musical links, see Judah Cohen, "Modes of Tradition? Nego-
Jewishness and Modernity in the Synagogue Music of Isadore Freed and Frederick
," *Jewish Culture and History* 5:2 (Winter 2002), 25–47; Peter Jeffery, "Werner's 'The
acred Bridge,' Volume 2: A Review Essay," *Jewish Quarterly Review* 77:4 (Apr. 1987), 283–
98; and Bohlman, *Jewish Music*, 73–105.

19. "Moisei Berlin," *Evreiskaia entsyklopediia*, vol. 4, cols. 271–72; Berlin, *Ocherk*, 42–44, 78. See also the 1877 study by the Russian philosemitic ethnographer Nikolai Leskov, which celebrates Ukrainian folk songs, denigrates Russian folk songs, and ignores Jewish folk songs altogether: Leskov, *Evrei v Rossii*, 36.

20. See Ilia Orshanskii, "O zamknutosti evreev," *Ha-karmel* 6:9 (June 10, 1866), 39–40, and 6:10 (June 17, 1866), 45–47; Orshanskii, "Prostonarodnye pesni russkikh evreev," *Ha-karmel* 6:31 (Jan. 20, 1867), 133–35, and 6:32 (Jan. 27, 1867), 137–39. The latter article is reprinted in Orshanskii, *Evrei v Rossii*, 391–401. See also Kiel, "Twice Lost Legacy," 124; Uri Finkel, "Der onheyber fun der yidisher folkloristik in Rusland," *Heymland* 6 (Aug. 1948), 121–27; Litvak, *Conscription*, 34–38; and Henekh Kon, "Yoyel Engel—Der Pionir," *Literarishe bleter* 20 (Aug. 29, 1924), 6.

21. IR NBUV, fond 190, d. 263, l. 10; IR NBUV, fond 190, d. 264, ll. 19–22 (unpublished manuscript, "On the Musical Characteristics of Jewish Song").

22. Iu. D. Engel, "Feleton: Pamiati A. G. Rubinshteina," *Khronika voskhoda* 27 (Dec. 7, 1904), 50.

23. Ravina, *Mikhtavim*, 59–62 (Iu. D. Engel to Leo Winz, Jan. 22, 1908).

24. IR NBUV, fond 190, d. 3, l. 1 (Iu. D. Engel to Aron Davidovich [1910]); IR NBUV, fond 190, d. 264, l. 22. For a concise description of Russian nationalist approaches to harmony, see Maes, *History of Russian Music*, 83–84.

25. For the program of this concert, see IR NBUV, fond 190, d. 297, l. 3 (concert programs of Iu. D. Engel, 1900–1927). On the concert's later influence, see IR NBUV, fond 190, d. 262, ll. 4–5; Braunzaft and Gorali, *Ha-eskolah ha-musikalit*, 13; Saminsky, *Ob evreiskoi muzyki*, 47–51; and Jacob Weinberg, "Joel Engel: A Pioneer in Jewish Musical Renaissance (Personal Recollections, 1902–1927)," *Jewish Music Forum* 7–8 (1946–47), 33–38.

26. Schwarz, *Music and Musical Life*, 5–6. On the role of musical ethnography and Engel in the Russian populist movement, see Engel, *Glazami*, esp. 166–68 and 500–501.

27. IR NBUV, fond 190, d. 263, ll. 9–9v, 17; I. V. Lipaev, "Eshche o narodnykh pesniakh evreev," *Khronika voskhoda* 13 (1898), 464.

28. IR NBUV, fond 190, d. 139, l. 13; Yo'el 'Engel, "Ha-neshef ha-rishon le-neginah 'ivrit," *Te'atron ve-omanut* 6–7 (Apr. 1926), 9; Moskovskaia Muzykalno-Etnograficheskaia Komissiia, *Opyty*, 239–40.

29. Gintsburg, *Amolike Peterburg*, 244–45.

30. V. V. Stasov, "Po povodu postroiki sinagogi v S.-Peterburge," *Evreiskaia biblioteka* 2 (1872), 435–36; "Dvadtsat piat let Russkogo iskusstvo: Nasha muzyka," *Vestnik Evropy* (1882–83), published in translation as "Twenty-Five Years of Russian Art: Our Music," in Stasov, *Selected Essays*, 66–116. Stasov's relationship to Jewish artists is explored in Seth L. Wolitz, "The Jewish National Art Renaissance in Russia," in Apter-Gabriel, *Tradition and Revolution*, 24–25.

31. Iu. D. Engel, "Pamiati V. V. Stasova," *RMG* 41 (Oct. 14, 1907), 896.

32. IR NBUV, fond 190, d. 265, ll. 24–25; Soltes, *Off the Willows*, 38–40.

33. Weinberg, "Joel Engel," 33–38; Jacob Weinberg, "Joel Engel, Champion of Jewish

Music," in Dawidowicz, *Golden Tradition*, 327–30; Gr. Prokofiev, "Moskovskie kontserty," *RMG* 8 (Feb. 21, 1910), 224.

34. "'Evreiskie narodnye pesni' (s notami) M. M. Varshavskago . . . [advertisement]," *Khronika voskhoda* 19:93 (Nov. 30, 1900), 26.

35. Sholem Aleichem, "A por verter tsu Varshavskis lider fun Sholem-Aleykhem," repr. in M. Varshavsky, *Yudishe folks-lieder*, 2nd ed. (New York: Maks. N. Maysel, 1918), v–viii.

36. Iu. D. Engel, "Feleton: Po povodu evreiskikh narodnykh pesen M. M. Varshavskogo," *Khronika voskhoda* 18 (Mar. 8, 1901), 19–22.

37. Mark Varshavskii, "Neskolko slov moemu retsenzentu," *Khronika voskhoda* 25 (Apr. 12, 1901), 20–22.

38. Sholem Aleichem, "A brief tsum H' Engel funem 'Voskhod,'" *Der yid* 24 (June 13, 1901), 14–16. The semantic ambiguities and shifting meanings of the Russian term *narod* are analyzed in Nathaniel Knight, "Ethnicity, Nationality and the Masses: *Narodnost* and Modernity in Imperial Russia," in Hoffman and Kotsonis, *Russian Modernity*, 41–64. On the Yiddish-language distinctions between *folkslid* and *folkstimlikher lid* (folk song and folkish song), see Kahan, *Shtudyes*, 194–201.

39. Yoel Engel, "A teshuvah dem hern 'Sholem Aleichem,'" *Der yid* 40 (Oct. 10, 1901), 15.

40. Peretz's comments are quoted in Y. Shatzky, "Perets-Shtudyes," *YIVO Bleter* 28 (1946), 63, and Mark Kiel, "Vox Populi, Vox Dei: The Centrality of Peretz in Jewish Folkloristics," *Polin* 7 (1992), 101–2.

41. See Kunin, "Muzykalno-kriticheskaia deiatelnost," 22–27, and Stupel, *Russkaia mysl*, 172–74; TsGMMK, fond 93, d. 536 ("Resolution of Moscow Composers and Musicians [Feb. 6, 1905]").

42. Taneev, *Dnevniki*, 3:271–72, 306–8, and 447; Engel-Roginskaia, "Iu. Engel," 499–500; Melgunov, *Vospominaniia*, 86–119; Balmuth, *Russian Bulletin*, 211–17.

43. IR NBUV, fond 190, d. 293, l. 52; Engel, *Narodnaia konservatoriia*, 3–5.

44. IR NBUV, fond 190, d. 263, ll. 6–18.

45. IR NBUV, fond 190, d. 296, ll. 1–37 (clippings notebook of reviews of Iu. Engel's concerts); Engel-Roginskaia, "Iu. Engel," 498; Kats, "*Raskat improvizatsii,*" 17–19, 134–39, and 153–56.

46. IR NBUV, fond 190, d. 266, l. 19; Ravina, *Mikhtavim*, 59–62 (Iu. D. Engel to L. Winz, Feb. 4, 1908); IR NBUV, fond 190, d. 3, l. 1.

47. Roskies, "S. Ansky and the Paradigm of Return," in Wertheimer, *Uses of Tradition*, 243–60; S. Anskii, "Evreiskoe narodnoe tvorchestvo," *Perezhitoe* 1 (1909), 276–314.

48. Ansky, *Yidishe etnografishe program*, 9. On Ansky's Russian and Jewish intellectual influences, see Safran and Zipperstein, *Worlds of S. An-sky*.

49. Roskies, "Introduction," *Dybbuk*, xxiii; Sh. Ansky, "Narodnye detskie pesni," *Evreiskaia starina* 3 (1910), 391–403, and "O evreiskikh narodnykh pesniakh," *Evreiskaia starina* 2 (1909), 56–70; TsGIA SPb, fond 1747, d. 20, l. 2 (concert program of the Society for Jewish Folk Music, Mar. 5, 1911).

50. Veniamin Lukin, "Ot narodnichestva k narodu (S. A. An-Skii—Etnograf vostochno-evropeiskovo Evreistva)," in Eliashevich, *Evrei v Rossii* (1995), 129.

51. Kann-Novikova, *Sobiratelnitsa*, 37, 62, and 74.

52. CAHJP, RU/11, 13–15, 22–25 (Protocols of the Jewish Historical-Ethnographic Society, Mar. 21–22, 1912).

53. For a good general account of the expedition, see Rekhtman, *Yidishe etnografie*. For an overview of the present-day archival holdings related to this expedition, see I. A. Ser-

geeva, "Etnograficheskie ekspeditsii Semena An-skogo v dokumentakh," *Paralleli* 2–3 (2003), 97–124, and I. A. Sergeeva, "'Khozhdenie v evreiskii narod': Etnograficheskie ekspeditsii Semena An-skogo v dokumentakh," *Ab imperio* 4 (2003), 395–473.

54. IR NBUV, fond 190, d. 266, ll. 10–16. On Yudovin's biography, see Apter-Gabriel, *Jewish Art*, v–xii, and V. Ia. Brodskii and Iurii Gerchuk, "Solomon Yudovin," *Paralleli* 2–3 (2003), 681–90.

55. GARF, fond 9535, d. 21, ll. 5–5v.

56. S. Anskii, "Pismo v redaktsii," *Evreiskaia starina* 12 (1915), 239–40. Engel's sound recordings have recently been reissued on a CD compilation from the Ukrainian Vernadsky National Library. See *Historic Collection of Jewish Music, 1912–1947*, vol. 1.

57. RIII, fond 8, razd. 7, d. 636, ll. 1–2 (Iu. D. Engel to A. N. Rimskii-Korsakov, Apr. 22, 1913). See also the treatment of this quotation in Kopytova, *Obshchestvo evreiskoi narodnoi muzyki*, 8.

58. Ravina, *Yo'el Engel, ḥayyav ve-yetsirato*, 35. For more on *The Dybbuk*, see Safran and Zipperstein, *Worlds of S. An-sky*.

Chapter 3. The Most Musical Nation

1. The translated Mussorgsky epigraph is found in Taruskin, *Musorgsky*, 380. All quotations from Isaac Babel are taken from Walter Morison's edition of *The Collected Stories*, 305–14. "Awakening" (*Probuzhdenie*) was originally published in *Molodaia gvardiia* 17–18 (1931).

2. *Materialy*, 16–22; TsGIA SPb, fond 361, op. 11, d. 595, l. 26 (IRMO St. Petersburg Branch internal memo [Dec. 23, 1914]), and fond 361, op. 11, d. 577, ll. 1–18 (IRMO and MVD memos and correspondence on Jewish residence rights [1911–12]); Mysh, *Rukovodstvo*, 18–20.

3. L. I. Saminsky, "Iubilei Peterburgskoi konservatorii i evrei (1862–1912)," in Saminsky, *Ob evreiskoi muzyke*, 75.

4. "Professor Leopold Auer Looks Backward," *American Hebrew* (Nov. 16, 1923), 7.

5. L. O. Kantor, "Pevtsy getto," *Perezhitoe* 2 (1910), 254–55; Gnesin, *Stati*, 154–55; Margarita E. Rittikh, "O nastavnike i druge," in Rittikh, *Elena Fabianovna*, 298.

6. RGALI, fond 2954, op. 1, d. 124, l. 84 (lecture typescript, "An Outline of the History of Jewish Music in Russia" [ca. 1929]).

7. Gnesin, *Stati*, 154–55; Kopytova, *Obshchestvo*, 23; RGALI, fond 2954, op. 1, d. 174, ll. 1–18 (M. Gnesin's memoirs).

8. RGALI, fond 2954, op. 1, d. 193, l. 28 (M. Gnesin's memoirs). For a similar account by another Jewish student at the time, see Shlomo Rosovsky, "Di gezelshaft far idishe folksmuzik in Peterburg (tsum 15 yorikn yubileum)," *Tealit* 5 (1924), 19.

9. RGALI, fond 2954, op. 1, d. 174, ll. 1–5, and d. 193, ll. 1–105; Saminsky, "Third Leonardo," 117–18, 136; Saminsky, "Iubilei," 78.

10. For more on Glazunov's philosemitism, see Rosowsky, "Great Musicians," 4, and Izaly Zemtsovsky, "Eine vergessene Kantate," in Kuhn et al., "*Samuel*" *Goldenberg*, 61–76. On quotas at conservatories, see *Materialy*, 16–22; TsGIA SPb, fond 361, op. 11, d. 595, ll. 2–2v and 26, and RGALI, fond 2954, op. 1, d. 191, ll. 33 and 47 (M. Gnesin's memoirs).

11. Kremlev, *Leningradskaia*, 96; Milstein, *From Russia*, 16–17; RGALI, fond 2954, op. 1, d. 124, l. 85, and fond 2954, op. 1, d. 191, l. 47; Kopytova, *Iasha Kheifets*, 91.

12. Elman, *Memoirs*, 65; RGALI, fond 2954, op. 1, d. 191, l. 30.

13. Rimskii-Korsakov, *N. A. Rimskii-Korsakov;* M. F. Gnesin, "N. A. Rimskii-Korsakov

v obshchenii so svoimi uchenikami," *Muzyka i revoliutsiia* 7–8 (July–Aug. 1928), 13–18; Gnesin, *Mysli*. For the formal Soviet canonization of Rimsky-Korsakov as the musical hero of 1905, see Iankovskii, *Rimskii-Korsakov*.

14. RGALI, fond 2954, op. 1, d. 124, l. 84; JTSA, Solomon Rosowsky Collection, box 2, folder 3/8, notebook 2, 26–27; TsGIA SPb, fond 361, op. 1, #4564, ll. 1–22 (conservatory records of Efraim Shkliar), and M. Rozumny, "Fuftsig yor muzikalishe tetikayt fun Efraim Shkliar," *Di shul un khazonim-velt* (Apr. 6/26, 1937), 15–19. On Balakirev's attitudes and public expressions of antisemitism, see Frolova-Walker, "Disowning," 19–60.

15. Saminsky, "Iubilei," 72–73, 78.

16. RGALI, fond 2954, op. 1, d. 12, l. 85. For evidence of the iconic status of this quotation, see Rosovsky, "Gezelshaft," 20; Weisser, *Modern Renaissance*, 44; Avraham Soltes, "The Hebrew Folk Song Society of Petersburg: The Historical Development," in Heskes and Wolfson, *Historic Contribution*, 20; Mendel Elkin, "A vikhtige kultur-date," *Idisher kemfer* 30:782 (1948), 9; and Engel-Roginskaia, "Iu. Engel," 497.

17. Rimskii-Korsakov, *Letopis*, 217, quoted in Ginzburg, *N. A. Rimskii-Korsakov*, 49; Gnesin, *Mysli*, 208; Boris Levenson, "How Rimsky-Korsakoff Taught," *Etude* 46:3 (Mar. 1928), 197–98.

18. Ginzburg, *N. A. Rimskii-Korsakov*, 51.

19. Taruksin, *Stravinsky*, 1:386–90; Kappeler, *Russian Empire*, 336–37; Rogger, *Jewish Policies;* Saminsky, "Third Leonardo," 69–76.

20. Weisser, *Modern Renaissance*, 45; "Evreiskaia zhizn'," *Razsvet* 10 (Mar. 8, 1908), 27; Rozumny, "Fuftsig yor," 19; Anatolii Drozdov, "1905 god v Leningradskoi konservatorii," *Muzyka i revoliutsiia* 1:1 (Jan. 1926), 10–14; "Raznye izvestiia," *RMG* 16–17 (Apr. 17–24, 1905), 491.

21. Dubnow, *Kniga zhizni*, 284–85; Frankel, *Jewish Politics*.

22. N. Romanova, "Kulturno-prosvetitelnye obshchestva Peterburga i vlast kontsa XVIII–XX vv. (K istorii vzaimootnoshenii)," in Eliashevich, *Evrei v Rossii* (1995), 46. Cf. Ivenina, *Kulturno-prosvetitelnye organizatsii*, esp. 34–38; Tumanova, *Obshchestvennye organizatsii;* and Jeffrey Veidlinger, "Jewish Cultural Associations in the Aftermath of 1905," in Mendelsohn and Hoffman, *Revolution of 1905*, 199–211.

23. On the response of Jewish political movements to the post-1905 cultural turn, see Gassenschmidt, *Jewish Liberal Politics;* Rabinovitch, "Alternative to Zion," 129–93; and Vladimir Levin, "The Jewish Socialist Parties in Russia in the Period of Reaction," in Mendelsohn and Hoffman, *Revolution of 1905*, 118–21.

24. Dubnow, *History of the Jews* 1:495; Horowitz, *Jewish Philanthropy*, 159–205. On 1905 as a turning point in a gradual process, see Fishman, *Rise of Modern Yiddish Culture*, 18–47, and Kenneth Moss, "1905 as a Jewish Cultural Revolution? Revolutionary and Evolutionary Dynamics in the East European Jewish Cultural Sphere, 1900–1914," in Mendelsohn and Hoffman, *Revolution of 1905*, 185–98.

25. Rosovsky, "Gezelshaft," 18, and JTSA, Solomon Rosowsky Collection, box 2, folder 3/8, notebook 2, 7–15, 25–35. Nesvizhskii later achieved fame as violinist Joseph Szigeti's accompanist before immigrating to Palestine in 1921. Bing, *Israeli Pacifist*, 5–6.

26. "Evreiskaia zhizn'," *Razsvet* 10 (Mar. 8, 1908), 27; RGALI, fond 2954, op. 1, d. 124, l. 85. On Gnesin's role in 1905, see Iankovskii, *Rimskii-Korsakov*, 34–35.

27. Saminsky, "Third Leonardo," 85, 127; TsGMMK, fond 93, d. 30, ll. 1–iv (autobiographical sketch by Lazare Saminsky [1913–14]). On Saminsky's life and work, see also Davidson, "Lazare Saminsky," and Weisser, "Jewish Music in Twentieth-Century United States."

28. "David Aronovich Chernomordikov," *Evreiskaia entsyklopediia*, vol. 15, col. 862, and Kopytova, *Obshchestvo*, 14.

29. Sliozberg, *Dela minuvshikh dnei*, repr. in Kelner, *Evrei v Rossii*, 249–51. On Sliozberg's other activities, see Nathans, *Beyond the Pale*, 325–39.

30. M. Nagen, "O evreiskoi muzyke," *Razsvet* 44 (Nov. 1, 1909), 6–7.

31. RGALI, fond 2954, op. 1, d. 124, l. 85.

32. Nisnevich, V. A. *Zolotarev*, 9–11, 15–16, and 204–11; "Khronika Sankt-Peterburgskie opera i kontserty," *RMG* 51–52 (Dec. 23–30, 1901), 1098–99; "Muzyka za granitsei," *RMG* 9 (Feb. 26, 1906), 259; YIVO RG 37, 1, 2/115–17 (concert program of the first musical evening of the Society for Jewish Folk Music, Jan. 21, 1909).

33. "K vecheru evreiskoi pesni," *Severnyi-zapadnyi golos* (Vilnius), Nov. 12, 1909; Nagen, "O evreiskoi muzyke," 3; Olenina-d'Algheim, *Le legs de Moussorgski*, 91–92; and Olenina-d'Algheim, *Zavety*, 42.

34. Quoted in Iu. D. Engel, "Zametki o evreiskoi muzyke," *Razsvet* 43 (Oct. 24, 1910), 13; Gilman, *Jewish Self-Hatred*, esp. 68–86 and 139–48.

35. Medtner's articles, written under the pseudonym "Volfing," were eventually anthologized in the 1912 book *Modernizm i muzyka*. Ivanov's comments are quoted (and contested) in "'Zhemchuzhiny' nashei muzykalnoi kritiki," *RMG* 5 (Feb. 2, 1913), 133–35. On the Russian modernist embrace of Wagner and musical antisemitism, see Bartlett, *Wagner and Russia*, 59–72 and 117–209; Bernice Glatzer Rosenthal, "Wagnerism in Russia," in Weber and Large, *Wagnerism*, 198–245; and Khaide Villikh-Lederbogen, "E. Metner, Ellis i R. Vagner (K postanovke problemy)" in Villikh-Lederbogen et al., *Rikhard Vagner*, 1:223–32.

36. Scriabin's remarks are recounted in Sabaneev, *Vospominaniia o Skriabine*, 281–82.

37. Ekaterina Vlasova, "Venera Milosskaia i printsipy 1789 goda: Propoved zhizni Mikhaila Gnesina," *Muzykalnaia akademiia* 3 (1993), 179–80.

38. RGALI, fond 2954, op. 1, d. 124, ll. 84–85; Marina Shemesh, "M. A. Milner: Kratkii biograficheskii ocherk," in Kopytova and Frenkel, *Iz istorii evreiskoi muzyki*, 37; L. I. Saminsky, "Glavnye linii istorii evreiskoi muzyki," in Saminsky, *Ob evreiskoi muzyke*, 15–17.

39. CAHJP RU/2 (Protocols of the Society for Jewish Folk Music, Mar. 15, 1910); M. F. Gnesin, "Vpechatleniia muzykanta: Kontsert evreiskoi dukhovnoi i narodnoi muzyki," *Evreiskii mir* 3 (1910), 55.

40. TsGMMK, fond 93, d. 428, l. 1 (charter of the Society for Jewish Folk Music); TsGIA SPb, fond 1747, op. 1, d. 1, ll. 1–1v, 6 (draft charters of the Society for Jewish Folk Music); "Vnutrenee obozrenie," *Evreiskii mir* 2 (1909), 12, 15–16; S. Ansky to H. N. Bialik (Feb. 26, 1912), quoted in Kiel, "Twice Lost Legacy," 402.

41. TsGIA SPb, fond 1747, op. 1, d. 7, ll. 128–29 (I. S. Okun to Iu. D. Engel, Oct. 28, 1915).

42. TsGIA SPb, fond 1747, op. 1, d. 1, ll. 1–54, and fond 1747, op. 1, d. 8, ll. 5, 9, 28 (official correspondence of the Society for Jewish Folk Music); Rosovsky, "Gezelshaft," 17.

43. "Evreiskaia zhizn," *Razsvet* 47 (Dec. 7, 1908), 24–25.

44. Barsova, *Iz istorii*, 53–55; TsGIA SPb, fond 408, d. 401, 1–1v (IRMO correspondence regarding the residence rights of I. S. Tomars); Stark, *Peterburgskaia opera*, 82–87; Herts, *Doyres bundistn*, 1:468–70.

45. TsGIA SPb, fond 361, op. 11, d. 595, ll. 26–26v; TsGIA SPb, fond 1747, op. 1, d. 8, l. 30; Imperatorskoe russkoe muzykalnoe obshchestvo, *Otchet I.R.M.O.*, 9–10.

46. "Teatr i muzyka," *Rech* 334 (Dec. 5, 1910), 5; TsGIA SPb, fond 1747, d. 8, ll 35, 44–45, 54, 75, and 84; Solomon, *A Woman's Way*, 31, 44. On gender, education, and the Russian musical profession, see Sargeant, "Middle Class Culture," 103–104 and 108–13. The revealing, analogous case of Jewish female medical students is examined in Carole B. Balin,

"The Call to Serve: Jewish Women Medical Students in Russia, 1872–1887," *Polin* 18 (2005), 132–52.

47. CAHJP RU/2 (Dec. 29, 1908; Mar. 29 and Oct. 13, 1909; and Jan. 18 and Mar. 15, 1910); TsGIA SPb, fond 1747, d. 8, l. 60.

48. YIVO RG37, 1, 2/115–17 and CAHJP RU/2 (Dec. 29, 1908).

49. "Khronika. S.-Peterburg," *RMG* 51–52 (Dec. 12–17, 1906), 1247.

50. Elman, *Memoirs*, 52–53; RNB, fond 183, op. 1014a, d. 187, ll. 1–19 (correspondence between Joseph Achron and Baron David Gintsburg [1905–8]; Kvartin, *Mayn lebn*, 312.

51. *Otchet obshchestva evreiskoi narodnoi muzyki za 1913 god*, 50–59. Further discussion of the new Jewish audiences in nineteenth-century Russian cultural life can be found in Zilberman and Smilianskaia, *Kievskaia simfoniia*, and Zipperstein, *Jews of Odessa*, 65–66.

52. JTSA, Solomon Rosowsky Collection, box 4, folder 12, 3.

53. "Teatr i muzyka," *Rech* 87 (Apr. 1, 1909), 5; IR NBUV, fond 190, d. 264, ll. 19–22, and fond 190, d. 265, ll. 24–34v; RIII, fond 4, op. 1, d. 179/1, ll. 1–2 (concert program, Apr. 12, 1909).

54. CAHJP RU/2 (Apr. 16, 1909); IR NBUV, fond 190, d. 296, l. 3v; M. Nagen, "Vecher evreiskoi narodnoi pesni," *Razsvet* 16 (Apr. 19, 1909), 12.

55. M. Nagen, "Vecher evreiskoi muzyki v Peterburge," *Razsvet* 3 (Jan. 17, 1910), 25; "In der 'gezelshaft far yudishe folks-muzik,'" *Der fraynd* 84 (Apr. 15, 1909), 3–4; Ivan Lipaev, "Kontserty," *RMG* 3 (Jan. 17, 1910), 81; "Yudishe khronik," *Der fraynd* 14 (Jan. 17, 1910), 2; Z. A. Kiselgof, "Kontsert o-va evreiskoi narodnoi muzyki," *Novyi voskhod* 2:10 (1911), 40.

56. Nagen, "Vecher evreiskoi muzyki," 25–26.

57. L. S. [L. I. Saminsky], "Kontsert khora Peterburgskoi sinagogi," *Razsvet* 20–21 (May 24–31, 1909), 27; TsGIA SPb, fond 1747, op. 1, d. 18, ll. 11–12, 61 (letters to the Society for Jewish Folk Music [1913]).

58. GARF, fond 9535, d. 21, l. 3v; Roskies, *Bridge of Longing*.

59. *Otchet obshchestva . . . za 1913 god*, 28; TsGIA SPb, fond 1747, d. 8, ll. 1–104; "Za nedeliu," *Novyi voskhod* 1:2 (Jan. 14, 1910), 22, and "Purishkevitshes brief," *Der fraynd* 14 (Jan. 17, 1910), 2. On Purishkevich's antisemitism, see Engelstein, *Keys to Happiness*, 312–13.

60. IR NBUV, fond 190, d. 262, ll. 4–5; RIII, fond 4, op. 1, d. 179/5, l. 2 (concert program, Dec. 12, 1913); YIVO RG37, 1, 7/526–37, 2 (concert program, Apr. 14, 1915); Buckler, *Literary Lorgnette*, 49. On the links between concert hall, classical music, and emerging modern social classes in nineteenth-century Europe, see Weber, *Music and the Middle Class*, and Johnson, *Listening in Paris*. The Russian case is analyzed in Sargeant, "Middle Class Culture"; Swift, *Popular Theater;* and Frame, *St. Petersburg Imperial Theaters*.

61. *Otchet obshchestva . . . za 1913 god*, 28–29; RIII, fond 4, op. 1, d. 179/1 and d. 179/2 (concert programs, Apr. 12, 1909, and Jan. 12, 1910); RIII, fond 96, op. 1, d. 61–62 (concert program with song text insert, Dec. 12, 1913); IR NBUV, fond 190, d. 297, ll. 5–6 (concert program with song text insert, Apr. 14, 1915); CAHJP RU/2 (Feb. 16, 1909, and Jan. 4, 1910); TsGIA SPb, fond 1747, op. 1, d. 20, ll. 2–2v (concert program, Mar. 5, 1911).

62. *Otchet obshchestva . . . za 1913 god*, 35.

63. YIVO RG37, 1, 7/526–37 (concert program, Apr. 14, 1915); RIII, fond 4, op. 1, d. 179/2 (concert program, Jan. 12, 1910); TsGIA SPb, fond 1747, op. 1, d. 20, ll. 1v, 17.

64. TsGIA SPb, fond 1747, op. 1, d. 18, ll. 7–62, and d. 11, ll. 1–2.

65. CAHJP RU/2 (May 13 and 24, Sept. 28, Oct. 18 and 25, 1910); "Literaturnaia-khudozhestvennaia khronika," *Evreiskaia nedelia* 11 (June 24, 1910), 18; *Otchet obshchestva . . . za 1913 god*, 15, 28–29; Rosowsky, "Society," 10.

66. Sargeant, "Middle Class Culture," 59–61.

Chapter 4. Frozen Folk Songs

1. Reprinted in N. Oyslender, "Tsu B. Slutskys 'Badkhonim-Shoyshpiler,'" *Tsaytshrift* 1 (1926), 261–62. See also the discussion of this text in Krasney, *Ha-badḥan*, 134–37, and Ariella Krasney, "The *Badkhn*: From Wedding Stage to Writing Desk," *Polin* 16 (2003), 7–28.

2. The role of print publishing in the emergence of modern Jewish culture in eastern Europe is discussed in Stein, *Making Jews Modern*, esp. 23–54. On Jewish book publishing in eastern Europe, see Kelner, *Ocherki po istorii;* Cohen, *Be-ḥanuto shel mokher;* and, more generally, Gries, *Book in the Jewish World*. For a broader overview of the Russian printing industry, see Steinberg, *Moral Communities*, 7–12.

3. Slobin, *Tenement Songs*.

4. For a suggestive discussion of this idea, see D. A. Eliashevich, "Russko-evreiskaia pechat i russko-evreiskaia kultura," in Eliashevich, *Evrei v Rossii*, 55–74. A good comparative perspective on the role of publishing and elite and popular culture involving Russian and Polish literature can be found in Holmgren, *Rewriting Capitalism*, esp. 1–13.

5. Fishman, *Rise of Modern Yiddish Culture*, 18–32; John Klier, "Exit, Pursued by a Bear": The Ban on Yiddish Theatre in Imperial Russia," in J. Berkowitz, *Yiddish Theatre*, 159–74; Yankev Shatzky, "Perets-shtudyes," *YIVO Bleter* 28 (1946), 56–58; Shaul Gintsburg, "Di 'Gezelshaft far yidisher folks-muzik,'" in Gintsburg, *Amolike Peterburg*, 245. On the legal status and political fate of Russian Jewish publishing in this period, see Eliashevich, *Pravitelstvennaia politika*, and Kelner, *Ocherki po istorii*.

6. Engel, *Uvy, nad bregom Iordana: Iz 'evreiskikh pesen' A. Maikova*, op. 9 (Moscow, ca. 1903); Engel, *Gazel, svobodna i legka: Iz 'evreiskikh melodii Bairona,'* op. 10, no. 1 (Moscow, ca. 1903); Ilia Sats, *Pesenka: Narodnye evreiskie napevy* (Moscow, ca. 1908); Engel, *Evreiskie narodnye pesni*.

7. Ḥayyim Leyb Fuks, "'Ha-zamir' bi-Lodz," *He-'avar* 23 (Sept. 1976), 114–17; A. L., "Vegen dem tsuzamenfohr fun di yudishe kunst-feraynen," *Der fraynd* 72 (Apr. 1, 1909), 2; M. Nagen, "O evreiskikh muzykalnykh obshchestvakh," *Razsvet* 48 (Nov. 29, 1909), 8.

8. Obshchestva evreiskoi narodnoi muzyki, *Ustav obshchestva evreiskogo narodnoi muzyki* (1910), 1; TsGIA SPb, fond 1747, op. 1, d. 1, l. 1 (charter draft); CAHJP RU/2 (Nov. 7, 1909, and Mar. 22, 1910).

9. IR NBUV, fond 190, d. 3, l. 1.

10. Kurt Schindler, "The Russian Jewish Folk-Song," *Menorah Journal* 3:3 (June 1917), 155; Heskes, *Passport to Jewish Music*, 203–4.

11. For the song's history and reception, see Bohlman, "Before Hebrew Song," 25–59, and Talila Eliram, "Shirei 'erets Yisr'a'el?" in Bartal, *Ha-'agalah ha-mele'ah*, 238–40.

12. Joseph Reider, "Secular Currents in the Synagogal Chant in America," *Jewish Forum* 1:10 (Dec. 1918), 583–94; David de Sola Pool, "The Music of the Synagogue," *Menorah Journal* 3:5 (Dec. 1917), 295–300; Arthur Friedlander, "Hatikvah ('The Hope'): The Zionists' National Song," *Musical Times* 61:928 (June 1, 1920), 415–16; Iu. D. Engel, "Evreiskie narodnye pesni: II," *Razsvet* 37 (Sept. 12, 1910), 9–10; and Gnesin, "Vpechatleniia muzykanta," 56–57.

13. For a thorough discussion of the compositional idiom and its relation to the Russian school, see Móricz, *Jewish Identities*, 26–91, and Eisenstein Baker and Nelson, *Leo Zeitlin*, xvi–xviii.

14. Solomon Rosowsky, "Yoysef Akhron," *Tsukunft* 56:6 (July–Aug. 1951), 277.

15. Joseph Achron, *Evreiskaia melodiia* (St. Petersburg: Obshchestvo evreiskoi narodnoi muzyki, 1914); Joseph Achron, "Notits vegn idisher muzik," *Bodn* 1:1 (1934), 57.

16. Rosowsky, "Yoysef Akhron," 278. On the ongoing debates over harmonization, see Rosovsky, "Gezelshaft," 18–19, and Joseph Yassar, "The Hebrew Folk Society of St. Petersburg: Ideology and Technique," in Heskes and Wolfson, *Historic Contribution*, 31–42.

17. Kopytova, *Iasha Kheifets*, 317–18 and 594–95; Bergmeier, Eisler, and Lotz, *Vorbei*, 389–91; Isadore Lhevinne, "On Wings of Song," *American Hebrew* (May 21, 1926), 35.

18. In 1916 a competition was even held by the newly established Jewish Society for the Support of Artists (Evreiskoe obshchestvo dlia pomoshchii khudozhnikov) to design the cover for the next group of publications. CAHJP, RU/2 (Mar. 22, 1910); "V 'Evreiskom obshchestve pooshchreniia khudozhestv'," *Evreiskaia nedelia* 4 (Jan. 24, 1916), 31. For further discussion of the visual iconography, see John Bowlt, "From the Pale of Settlement to the Reconstruction of the World," in Apter-Gabriel, *Tradition and Revolution*, 43–60.

19. TsGIA SPb, fond 1747, op. 1, d. 2, 11–11v (Protocols, Feb. 14, 1911). On language politics among the Russian Jewish intelligentsia, see Fishman, *Rise of Modern Yiddish Culture*, 33–47.

20. Engel, "Evreiskie narodnye pesni: II," 10.

21. Kugel, *Listia s dereva*, 22–23; *Otchet obshchestva . . . za 1913 god*, 2–6.

22. For contemporary evidence of these antisemitic stereotypes and Jewish responses, see Volfing, *Modernizm i muzyka*, 95–102 and 382–400; Khorkhe, "Prichiny upadka Russkoi chastnoi opery v provintsii," *RMG* 3 (Mar. 1897), 363–74; Kugel, *Listia s dereva*, 114–27; and Golinkin, *Me-hekhale Yefet*, 66–67. On the rise of musical entrepreneurs as a social phenomenon in pre–World War I Europe, see William Weber, "From the Self-Managing Musician to the Independent Concert Agent," in Weber, *Musician as Entrepreneur*, 105–29.

23. CAHJP, RU/2 (Mar. 1, 22, and 29, Apr. 6 and 22, May 24, and Sept. 28, 1910).

24. *Otchet obshchestva . . . za 1913 god*, 7; *Evreiskii mir* 10 (July 17, 1910), 25 [advertisement for sheet music publications].

25. *Otchet obshchestva . . . za 1913 god*, 2; TsGIA SPb, fond 1747, op. 1, d. 7, l. 129.

26. Pekka Gronow, "Ethnic Music and the Soviet Record Industry," *Ethnomusicology* 19 (1975), 90; Pekka Gronow, "The Record Industry Comes to the Orient," *Ethnomusicology* 25 (1981), 255–56; Michael Aylward, "Early Recordings of Jewish Music in Poland," *Polin* 16 (2003), 69; and Kvartin, *Mayn lebn*, 282–306.

27. TsGIA SPb, fond 1747, op. 1, d. 2, l. 66 (Oct. 7, 1913).

28. I. Kh., "Evreiskie pesni," *Grammofonnaia zhizn* 2:21 (Feb. 15, 1912), 7; TsGIA SPb, fond 1747, op. 1, d. 18, l. 31. "Khronika," *Grammofonnyi mir* 7 (Sept. 1, 1910), 11; "K desiati letiiu t-va 'Br. M. i V. Isserlin,'" *Grammofonnaia zhizn* 2:25 (Apr. 20, 1912), 7; "Grammofonnyi mir: Khronika," *Grammofonnyi mir* 5:8 (June 10, 1914), 10, and 5:9 (July 5, 1914), 13.

29. TsGIA SPb, fond 1747, op. 1, d. 18, ll. 32–34.

30. "Khronika," *Grammofonnyi mir* 3 (Apr. 22, 1910), 12, and Volkov-Lannit, *Iskusstvo*, 116–18; CAHJP, RU/2 (May 24, 1910).

31. Minkovskii, *Moderne liturgye*, 3–4; Kvartin, *Mayn lebn*, 132–35.

32. TsGIA SPb, fond 1747, op. 1, d. 18, ll. 31, 35; *Otchet obshchestva . . . za 1913 god*, 44. On the collapsing lines between secular and sacred, high and low in eastern European Jewish popular music, see Slobin, *Tenement Songs*, 36–47. On the broader issues of taste in contemporary European and Russian society, respectively, see Weber, *Music and the Middle Class*, esp. xii–xiv, and Holmgren, *Rewriting Capitalism*.

33. "Bi-'olamenu," *Ha-tsefirah*, Dec. 25, 1913; *Otchet obshchestva . . . za 1913 god*, 43–44; TsGIA SPb, fond 1747, op. 1, d. 18, ll. 14–22.

34. Moshe Gorali, "Shmu'el Alman—Autobiografiah," *Tatzlil* 5 (1966), 124–25.

35. TsGIA SPb, fond 1747, op. 1, d. 18, ll. 16–19 (A. Avshalomov to the Society for Jewish Folk Music, Nov. 12, 1913). Avshalomov went on to study briefly at the Zurich Con-

servatory, where he organized a Jewish musical club. In 1914 he immigrated to Shanghai and lived there on and off for decades, becoming one of the most important figures in precommunist Chinese classical music. His work *The Great Wall*, sponsored by Madame Sun Yat-Sen, drew wide acclaim as one of the first modern Chinese operas and a pioneering synthesis of Chinese and Western classical music. See Avshalomov and Avshalomov, *Avshalomovs' Winding Way*.

36. Israel Bartal, "The Ingathering of Traditions: Zionism's Anthology Projects," *Prooftexts* 17 (1993), 77–93, and Martina Urban, "The Jewish Library Reconfigured: Buber and the Zionist Anthology Discourse," in Zank, *New Perspectives*, 32–60.

37. CAHJP RU/2 (Apr. 16, Oct. 20, and Nov. 16, 1909); Dubnov-Erlich, *Life and Work of S. M. Dubnov*, 147–48.

38. *Otchet obshchestva . . . za 1912 god*, 2–4; *Otchet obshchestva . . . za 1913 god*, 1.

39. On the OPE's deliberations regarding modern Jewish education, see Zipperstein, *Imagining Russian Jewry*, 42–62, and Horowitz, *Jewish Philanthropy*, 95–158.

40. Gassenschmidt, *Jewish Liberal Politics*, 99–102; Rivesman, *Evreiskim detiam*. On the need for Jewish children's musical education, see S. Anskii, "Narodnye detskie pesni," *Evreiskaia starina* 2:3 (1910), 391–403, and I. E. Rubin, "Tvorchestvo evreiskikh detei i narodnaia pesnia," *Vestnik evreiskogo prosveshcheniia* 27 (Jan. 1914), 3–15.

41. IR NBUV, fond 190, d. 246, ll. 1–3 (autobiographical sketch of Z. A. Kiselgof) and RIII, fond 42, op. 1, d. 50, ll. 1, 8 (autobiographical sketch of M. A. Milner). For an evocative treatment of Kiselgof's life, see Beizer, *Jews*, 98–103. On the contents of Kiselgof's collection, see Lyudmila Sholokhova, "Kollektsiia Zinoviia Kiselgofa kak istochnik issledovanii po evreiskomu muzykalnomu folkloru," in Guralnik, *Iz istorii evreiskoi muzyki*, 67–86.

42. Kiselgof, *Sbornik pesen dlia evreiskoi shkoly i semi*, 4. The main statement of Kiselgof's views on Jewish folk songs can be found in his 1912 lithograph pamphlet, "Vegn yiddisher folks-muzik: Referat," also published in Russian and German translations by the Society for Jewish Folk Music.

43. Z. A. Kiselgof, "Kontsert obshchestva evreiskoi narodnoi muzyki," *Novyi voskhod* 2:10 (Mar. 10, 1911), 37–38.

44. Kiselgof, *Sbornik*, 14.

45. Shternshis, *Soviet and Kosher*, 108. For further discussion of this song, see Roskies, "Ideologies of the Yiddish Folk Song," 144–47.

46. Kiselgof, *Sbornik*, 4.

47. "Khronika i soobshcheniia," *Vestnik evreiskogo prosveshcheniia* 5 (Mar. 1911), 118; Kiselgof, *Sbornik*, 31. On the concept of German music as a universal form of art, with particular reference to Beethoven, see Applegate and Potter, "Germans as the 'People of Music,'" in Applegate and Potter, *Music and German National Identity*, 1–2.

48. Kiselgof, *Sbornik*, 4; Z. Kiselgof, "Vecher evreiskoi narodnoi muzyki," *Novyi voskhod* 3:42 (Oct. 18, 1912), 19–20.

49. "Sankt-Peterburgskaia letopis," *Khronika voskhoda* 46 (Nov. 13, 1894), 1222. For other examples, see Levenson, *V kontsertnoi zale*, 7–8, 145; Kipnis, *Velt-berimte yidishe muziker*, 65–71; Gintsburg, "Anton Rubinshteyn," 279–82; and Shor, *David Shor*, 173–81.

50. On the problem of Mendelssohn's Jewishness, see Sposato, *Price of Assimilation;* Leon Botstein, "Notes from the Editor: Mendelssohn and the Jews," *Musical Quarterly* 82 (1998), 210–19; and Michael P. Steinberg, "Mendelssohn's Music and German-Jewish Culture: An Intervention," *Musical Quarterly* 83 (1999), 31–44.

51. For a further exploration of this idea, see James Loeffler, "Richard Wagner's 'Jewish Music': Antisemitism and Aesthetics in Modern Jewish Culture," *Jewish Social Studies* 15:2 (Winter 2009), 2–36.

52. "Khronika i soobshcheniia," *Vestnik evreiskogo prosveshcheniia* 5 (Mar. 1911), 117; Kiselgof, *Sbornik*, 4.
53. TsGIA SPb, fond 1747, op. 1, d. 11, l. 17 (St. Petersburg branch to Kiev branch, Feb. 20, 1914); *Otchet obshchestva . . . za 1913 god*, 2, 7, and 19–22; YIVO RG 37, 1, 4/269 (Society for Jewish Folk Music Circular); YIVO RG 37, 1, 7/526-37.
54. Kiselgof, *Lider-zamelbukh far der yidishe shul un familye*, 2nd ed., 5. Peysakh Kaplan, "A lider-zamelbukh," *Der fraynd* 10:112 (May 18, 1912), 7–8; L. I. Saminsky, "Evreiskaia narodnaia pesnia v semi i v shkole," *Novyi voskhod* 3:14 (Apr. 5, 1912), 41–44; Iu. D. Engel, "Sbornik pesen dlia evreiskoi shkoly i semi," *Razsvet* 19–20 (May 18, 1912), 16–20.
55. TsGIA SPb, fond 1747, op. 1, d. 11, ll. 17, 20–20v.
56. AV IV RAN, fond 85, op. 2, d. 385, l. 37 (Society for Jewish Folk Music bulletin); TsGIA SPb, fond 1747, op. 1, d. 7, ll. 87, 94–95, 116, 129.
57. *Otchet obshchestva . . . za 1913 god*, 19, 25. TsGIA SPb, fond 1747, d. 11, ll. 4–32 (correspondence between Kiev and St. Petersburg branches); TsGIA SPb, fond 1747, d. 7, ll. 62–95 (correspondence between Moscow and St. Petersburg branches).
58. Rosovsky, "Gezelshaft," 19; "Der kontsert fun yudishen folks-muzik," *Der fraynd* 8:245 (Oct. 30, 1910), 3. On Peretz's obsession with Yiddish folk songs, see Hersh D. Nomberg, "Master of a Literary Generation," in Dawidowicz, *Golden Tradition*, 295–96.
59. Gintsburg, *Amolike Peterburg*, 192, 200–202; Mark Rivesman, "Vospominaniia i vstrechi," *Evreiskaia letopis* 3 (1924), 77–79. On the Polish Jewish tradition of folk song research and popularization, see Gottesman, *Defining the Yiddish Nation*, 3–74.

Chapter 5. The Neighbors' Melodies

1. The epigraph from Krein is quoted in Aleksandr Krein, "Problemy evreiskoi muzyki," *Novyi put* (June 1, 1918), 27–29. Sakketti, *Ocherk vseobshchei istorii muzyki*, 30; V. M[andel]., "Godovoe sobranie 'Obshchestva Evreiskoi Narodnoi Muzyki,'" *Novyi voskhod* 5:14–15 (Apr. 17, 1914), 32–34.
2. "Za nedeliu," *Novyi voskhod* 4:48 (Nov. 28, 1913), 13–17; "Za nedeliu," *Novyi voskhod* 6:1 (Jan. 8, 1915), 40.
3. TsGIA SPb, fond 1747, op. 1, d. 8, l. 66; "Literaturno-muzykalnyi vecher 6-go marta," *Novyi voskhod* 6:10–11 (Mar. 13, 1915), 50–51; "Literaturno-khudozhestvennaia khronika," *Evreiskaia nedelia* 1 (Jan. 4, 1915), 40; "Za nedeliu," *Novyi voskhod* 6:1 (Jan. 8, 1915), 40; "Za nedeliu," *Novyi voskhod* 6:12–13 (Apr. 3, 1915), 60–61; AV IV RAN, fond 85, op. 1, d. 385, l. 28 (Society for Jewish Folk Music circular); M. Bl., "V Petrograde," *Evreiskaia nedelia* 22 (May 23, 1916), 30–31. For broader overviews of the war's effects on Jewish communal life and cultural activity, respectively, see Steven Zipperstein, "The Politics of Relief: The Transformation of Russian Jewish Communal Life during the First World War," *Studies in Contemporary Jewry* 4 (1988), 22–40, and Aviel Roshwald, "Jewish Cultural Identity in Eastern and Central Europe during World War I," in Roshwald and Stites, *European Culture*, 88–116.
4. RGALI, fond 2954, op. 1, d. 875, ll. 24–25 (Society for Jewish Folk Music circular). On censorship, see Eliashevich, *Pravitelstvennaia politika*, 483, 488–89, and 506–8.
5. TsGIA SPb, fond 1747, d. 7, ll. 26–26v, 62–95, and 127–63 and d. 2, ll. 93–93v; TsGMMK, fond 93, d. 460, l. 1 (report on Moscow branch opening). On the biographies of Shor, Veinberg, and Krein, see, respectively, Shor, *David Shor*, 12–52, and Nina Segal Rudnik, "Evreistvo, Muzyka, Revoliutsiia: D. S. Shor," *Russica romana* 13 (2006), 87–113; Yaakov Veinberg, "Autobiografiiah," *Tatslil* 6:3 (1966), 68; and James Loeffler, "Alexander Krein," in Hundert, *YIVO Encyclopedia*, 1:941–42.

6. Saminsky, "Third Leonardo," 131.

7. L. I. Saminsky, "Khudozhestvennyi itog poslednikh rabot 'Obshchestva evreiskoi narodnoi muzyki,'" *Razsvet* 5 (Feb. 1, 1915), 27–28.

8. Iu. D. Engel, "Otkrytoe pismo L. I. Saminskomu," *Razsvet* 7 (Feb. 15, 1915), 17.

9. L. I. Saminsky, "O tsennosti bytovoi evreiskoi melodii (Otvet Iu. D. Engeliu)," *Razsvet* 9 (Mar. 1, 1915), 10–11.

10. For a musicological discussion of this mode, see Beregovski, *Jewish Instrumental Folk Music*, 15–19.

11. RGALI, fond 2435, op. 2, d. 184, l. 2 (L. I. Saminsky to A. A. Krein, Apr. 16, 1915); Kopytova, *Obshchestvo*, 57–58; Vl., "V Petrograde," 31.

12. Iu. D. Engel, "Evreiskaia bytovaia narodnaia pesnia," *Evreiskaia nedelia* 4 (Jan. 24, 1916), 46.

13. Engel, "Evreiskaia bytovaia narodnaia pesnia," 45.

14. L. I. Saminsky, "Spor o tsennosti bytovoi evreiskoi melodii (Otvet Iu. D. Engeliu)," *Evreiskaia nedelia* 12 (Mar. 20, 1916), 48.

15. Unicus [S. Ansky], "Vskolz: Vox profane," *Evreiskaia nedelia* 19 (May 8, 1916), 18. Saminsky later claimed erroneously that Engel gave up in defeat; see Saminsky, *Music of the Ghetto*, 247.

16. See the important, forceful reading of the Engel-Saminsky debate in Móricz, *Jewish Identities*, 65–91.

17. Saminsky, *Ob evreiskoi muzyke*, 55; Saminsky, "Spor o tsennosti," 48; Saminsky, "O tsennosti," 11; TsGMMK, fond 93, d. 30, l. 1; L. I. Saminsky, "Evreiskii otklik na iubilei Rikharda Vagnera," *Novyi Voskhod* 4:3 (Jan. 17, 1913), 39–40; Lazare Saminsky, "Ha-miḥadishim ('Al ha-'avodah ha-neginatit he-ḥadashah)," *Ha-ezrah* 1:3 (1919), 207–10. I address Idelsohn's model more closely in my article "Do Zionists Read Music from Right to Left? Avraham Zvi Idelsohn and the Invention of Israeli Music," *Jewish Quarterly Review* (forthcoming, 2010), as well as in "Richard Wagner's 'Jewish Music.'"

18. For examples of more politicized readings, see Zemtsovsky, "Muzykalnyi idishizm," 16–17, and Seth Wolitz, "Inscribing An-sky's *Dybbuk* in Russian and Jewish Letters," in Safran and Zipperstein, *Worlds of S. An-sky*, 181–82.

19. Saminsky, "Third Leonardo," 75. For related discussions of the politics of naming Jewishness in Russian Jewish culture, see Stanislawski, *Autobiographical Jews*, 93–97. The place of the Jew in the Russian antisemitic imagination is analyzed in Engelstein, *Keys to Happiness*, 299–333.

20. Saminsky, "Third Leonardo," 132. See Rosenthal, *Nietzsche*, 47–48.

21. Saminsky, "Third Leonardo," 139–40.

22. Saminsky, *Ob evreiskoi muzyke*, 5; L. I. Saminsky, "Istoricheskie dannye otnositelno bibleiskoi muzyki," *Novyi voskhod* 6:7 (Feb. 20, 1915), 42–47.

23. IR NBUV, fond 190, d. 267, ll. 55–56; Engel, *Glazami*, 476. For further discussion of these ideas, see James Loeffler, "Iulii Engel i razvitie evreiskogo muzykalnogo natsionalizma," in Kopytova and Frenkel, *Iz istorii evreiskoi muzyki*, 251–64, and Ludmila Sholokhova, "Iulii Engel i ego kontseptsiia sozdaniia evreiskoi natsionalnoi shkoly v muzyke," in *Evreiska istoriia ta kultura*, 225–27.

24. IR NBUV, fond 190, d. 267, l. 63; TsGMMK, fond 93, d. 430, ll. 1 and 7.

25. TsGIA SPb, fond 1747, op. 1, d. 6, ll. 3–3v (Petrograd branch to Kharkov branch, Feb. 12, 1916).

26. For a broader historical perspective on this type of nationalism, see Hutchinson, *Dynamics of Cultural Nationalism*.

27. IR NBUV, fond 190, d. 267, ll. 55-65 (typescript of lecture of opening remarks at Moscow branch concert, 1917).
28. IR NBUV, fond 190, d. 268, ll. 66-75 (typescript report on Moscow branch concert tour). Brackets are in the original.
29. On the overall fate of Jewish cultural projects during the Russian Revolution, see Moss, *Jewish Renaissance*.
30. Slonimsky, *Perfect Pitch*, 48-49; Nelson, *Music for the Revolution*, 13; Iu. Ia. Vainkon, "Kontsertnaia zhizn: Simfonicheskie i khorovye kontserty," in Bogdanov-Berezovskii, *Muzykalnaia kultura Leningrada*, 305.
31. TsGIA SPb, fond 1747, op. 1, d. 2, ll. 125-26.
32. Schwarz, *Music and Musical Life*, 18.
33. Ziva Galili, "Zionism in the Early Soviet State: Between Legality and Persecution," in Gitelman and Ro'i, *Revolution, Repression, and Revival*, 37-68; Gennadii Kostyrchenko, "Natsionalnyi vyzov sionistov i klassovyi otvet bolshevikov: Pervye shagi Sovetskoi vlasti v reshenii evreiskogo voprosa," in Budnitskii et al., *Mirovoi kriziz*, 215-30. For more on Bolshevik nationality policies, see the contrasting views presented in Martin, *Affirmative Action Empire*, and Hirsch, *Empire of Nations*.
34. V. Lebedeva-Kaplan, "Tri pisma iz 1919 g.," in Eliashevich, *Istoriia evreev*, 145; Beizer, *Evrei Leningrada*, 337-38; Binevich, *Evreiskii teatr*, 133-66. On the politics of music in Leningrad during the revolutionary years, see Haas, *Leningrad's Modernists*, 1-10, and Nelson, *Music for the Revolution*, 13-40. On Grinberg, see Beizer, *Evrei Leningrada*, 344-45, and Nemtsov, *Neue Jüdische Schule*, 78-80 and 132.
35. TsGMMK, fond 93, d. 433, ll. 1-6; Golinkin, *Me-hekhale Yefet*, 83; Aaron Oriman, "'Khram iskusstv' Mordekhaia Golinkina i Fedor Chaliapin: K istorii sozdaniia Izrailskoi oper," in Parkhomovskii, *Evrei*, 352-54; and Iosif Yasser, "Russkii orfei," *Novoe russkoe slovo* (Apr. 11, 1948), 3. Zimro traveled through Siberia and the Far East to the United States, where in New York in 1919 the group premiered a commissioned work by Sergei Prokofiev, his *Overture on Hebrew Themes* (op. 34). The next year, however, they disbanded when Bellison joined the New York Philharmonic as principal clarinetist. See Nelli Kravets, "Muzykalnaia deiatelnost kamernogo ansamblia 'Zimro' i 'Uvertiura na evreiskie temy' S. Prokofeva," in Kopytova and Frenkel, *Iz istorii evreiskoi muzyki*, 265-82.
36. TsGIA SPb, fond 1747, op. 1, d. 2, ll. 125-67; AV IV RAN, fond 85, op. 2, d. 263, l. 1 (S. B. Rosowsky to D. G. Maggid, Apr. 6, 1919). On the obstacles to private publishing, see Fitzpatrick, *Commissariat of Enlightenment*, 133, 262-65. For the definitive treatment of the Kultur-Lige, see Moss, *Jewish Renaissance*.
37. TsGIA SPb, fond 1747, op. 1, d. 2, ll. 144-49 (Apr. 10, 15, 21, 28, and May 18, 1919). On the cultural politics of the Kultur-Lige in Petrograd, see Lebedeva-Kaplan, "Tri pisma," 135-38. The general crisis in publishing in this period is outlined in Jeffrey Brooks, "The Breakdown in Production and Distribution of Printed Material, 1917-1927," in Gleason et al., *Bolshevik Culture*, 151-74.
38. YIVO RG 37, 11/940-42 (concert program, Mar. 28, 1919); TsGIA SPb, fond 1747, op. 1, d. 2, ll. 132-32v (Dec. 22, 1918), d. 7, ll. 22, 94, and d. 11, l. 28; Lebedeva-Kaplan, "Tri pisma," 140-43.
39. TsGIA SPb, fond 1747, op. 1, d. 2, ll. 150-67 (June 3, 1919-Apr. 7, 1920); JTSA, Solomon Rosowsky Collection, box 12, folder 11 (V. Mandel to S. Rosowsky, May 16-17, 1923), and box 12, folder 3 (contract between S. B. Rosowsky and M. L. Tsitron [ca. 1922]; Lebedeva-Kaplan, "Tri pisma," 141-42; Braun, *Jews and Jewish Elements*, 32; Bronfin, *Muzykalnaia kultura*, 32, 35; Levik, *Chetvert veka*, 100-103; Nemtsov, *Neue Jüdische Schule*, 78-

80, 131–35; Stepanova, *Muzykalnaia zhizn*, 49. On the attempts to revive the group in 1921 and 1922, see IR NBUV, fond 190, d. 246, l. 60 (I. S. Tomars and M. S. Rivesman to Z. A. Kiselgof [ca. 1921]), and Moddel, *Joseph Achron*, 55–56.

40. Hirshberg, *Music in the Jewish Community*, 78–92.

41. Sh. Rosovsky, "Der ershter prolog-akkord," *Di shul un khazonim-velt* 28 (June 8, 1937), 2; Ravina, *Yo'el 'Engel, hayyav ve-yetsirato*, 24–30; Izaly Zemtsovsky, "The Musical Strands of An-sky's Texts and Contexts," in Safran and Zipperstein, *Worlds of S. Ansky*, esp. 219–31.

42. RGALI, fond 2435, op. 2, d. 240, l. 43 (concert program of the Society for Jewish Music, May 11, 1918); TsGMMK, fond 93, d. 430, ll. 7v, 13–17v, and d. 449, 450, and 458 (Society for Jewish Music documents).

43. Stepanova, *Muzykalnaia zhizn*, 38, 40, and 123–24.

44. TsGMMK, fond 93, d. 534, l. 1; IR NBUV, fond 190, d. 1, l. 1 (Narkompros document about Engel's departure for Germany, Mar. 22, 1923), and d. 298, ll. 1–9 (Engel's Soviet passport and various publishing contracts); Iasha Nemtsov, "Moskovskoe otdelenie obshchestva evreiskoi narodnoi muzyki (1913–1922)," in Kopytova and Frenkel, *Iz istorii evreiskoi muzyki*, 233–50.

45. Fliegel, *Zavel Zilberts*, 71–72; Hirshberg, *Music in the Jewish Community*, 81 and 87; Ravina, *Yo'el Engel ve-hamusikah ha-yehudit*, 86–92; Seroussi and Regev, *Popular Music*, 15–19; Loeffler, "Do Zionists Read Music?" On the development of Israeli folk songs, or *shirei erets-yisra'el*, see Eliram, *Bo, shir 'Ivri*.

46. Yehude-Leyb Vohlman, "Nokh aron fun kompozitor Yoyel Engel," *Moment* 18:52 (Mar. 2, 1927), 4; RGALI, fond 2954, op. 1, d. 804, l. 4 (Joel Engel to Mikhail Gnesin, Mar. 29, 1925); Kohansky, *Hebrew Theatre*, 99–102; Halevy, *Darki 'ale bamot*, 113–20; IR NBUV, fond 190, d. 263, ll. 9–11; Yo'el 'Engel, "Li-neshef yetsirotav shel Y. Engel," *Haaretz* (Feb. 12, 1926), 5, quoted in translation in Hirshberg, *Music in the Jewish Community*, 245–46.

47. Ravina, *Yo'el 'Engel ve-hamusikah ha-yehudit*, 102; Yehoash Hirshberg, "Musikah be-Tel Aviv ha-katanah," in Yofeh, *'Esrim ha-shanim*, 147–49. Further information on Engel's final years in Tel Aviv can be found in Flomenboim, "Ha-eskolah ha-le'umit."

48. Saminsky, "Ha-mihadishim," 209; Lazare Saminsky, "Lazare Saminsky's Years in Russia and Palestine: Excerpts from an Unpublished Autobiography," *Musica Judaica* 2:1 (1977–78), 1–20.

49. JTSA, Solomon Rosowsky Collection, box 12, folder 18 (L. I. Saminsky to S. B. Rosowsky, Sept. 10, 1921); Lazare Saminsky, "Lazare Saminsky's Early Years in New York City (1920–1928): Excerpts from an Unpublished Biography," *Musica Judaica* 6:1 (1984), 21; Lazare Saminsky, "American Synagogue Music," *American Hebrew* (Feb. 17, 1928), 509, 521.

50. Saminsky, "Lazare Saminsky's Early Years," 10, 14. David Ewen, "Two Weeks of Symphony Society Concerts Featuring Interesting Compositions by Jews," *American Hebrew* (Nov. 18, 1927), 64. On Jews and American musical modernism, see Crumden, *Body and Soul*, 1–33, and Oja, *Making Music Modern*, esp. 11–24, 217–18, and 307–8.

51. Saminsky, *Music of Our Day*, 43; Saminsky, *Music of the Ghetto and Bible*, 8–9; Saminsky, *Living Music*, 119–27. For a thorough analysis of Saminsky's American-period ideas, see Schiller, *Bloch, Schoenberg and Bernstein*, 58–64.

52. Quoted in Gershon Ephros, "In Commemoration of Joseph Achron," *Jewish Music Forum* 10 (Jan. 1956), 17. On the broader experiences of these musicians in the United States in the 1920s, see Paula Eisenstein Baker, "Kompozitory obshchestva evreiskoi narodnoi

muyzki v Niu-Iorke v 1920-e gody," in Kopytova and Frenkl, *Iz istorii evreiskoi muzyki*, 283–308.

53. "The Jew of the Day: Jascha Heifetz," *Jewish Forum* 1:1 (Feb. 1918), 8; Osgood Caruthers, "Isaac Stern: Our Secret Weapon in the East-West Conflict," *Los Angeles Times* (June 26, 1966), B25.

54. Braun, *On Jewish Music*, 203–55; Dubinsky, *Stormy Applause*, esp. 3–33.

55. On the emergence of official Soviet Jewish culture, see Veidlinger, *Moscow State Yiddish Theater*, and Shneer, *Yiddish and the Creation of Soviet Jewish Culture*.

56. Galina Kopytova, "Opera M. A. Milnera 'Nebesa pylaiut,'" in Guralnik, *Iz istorii evreiskoi muzyki*, 87–100; Beregovskaia, *Arfy na verbakh*, 14–18; Beregovskii, *Evreiskie napevy*, 12–14.

57. On the role of Jews in Soviet musical culture, see Braun, *Jews and Jewish Elements;* Granovskii, *Evreiskaia muzyka;* and Nemtsov and Kuhn, *Jüdische Musik in Sowjetrussland.*

58. Gnesin, *Stati*, 7; Yehoash Hirshberg, "Ha-hitpathut ha-gufim ha-mivtsa'im ba-musikah," in Lissak, *Toldot ha-yishuv*, 1:266; Vlasova, "Venera Milosskaia," 180; Krivosheevoi and Konaeva, *Vs. Meierkhold i Mikh. Gnesin*.

59. RGALI, fond 2954, op. 1, d. 875, l. 32; Braun, *On Jewish Music*, 209–11; Rita Flomenboim, "The Fate of Two Jewish Operas in the Soviet Union during the 1920's and 1930's," in Braun et al., *Verfemte Musik*, 135–47; Nemtsov, *Neue Jüdische Schule*, 93–111. On Shor's simultaneous involvement in Zionist activities and Communist Party circles, see Galili, "Zionism in the Early Soviet State," 54–56. The Jibneh (Yibneh) Press issued more publications in the early 1920s in Berlin and later relocated to New York.

60. Nelson, *Music for the Revolution*, 20, 69–70.

61. Shneer, *Yiddish and Soviet Jewish Culture*, 50–51; Kostyrchenko, *Tainaia politika Stalina*, 178.

62. RGALI, fond 2954, op. 1, d. 884 (Protocols of the Moscow Society for Jewish Music, Oct. 8, 1923–Feb. 7, 1931). See also Nemtsov, *Neue Jüdische Schule*, 159–83.

63. V. V. Tropp, "Dom Gnesinykh," *Muzykalnaia zhizn* 11–12 (1994), 22.

64. Gnesin's letter to Stalin is published in Vlasova, "Venera Milosskaia," 182–85. On the details of this episode, see Marina Lobanova, "Michail Gnessin und die 'Proletarischen Musiker' (aus der Geschichte einer Konfrontation)," in Kuhn, Nemtsov, and Wehrmeyer, *"Samuel" Goldenberg und "Schmuyle,"* 105–18.

65. RGALI, fond 2954, op. 1, d. 867, ll. 1–66 (concert programs and lectures of M. F. Gnesin); Braun, *On Jewish Music*, 211–12.

66. M. Gnesin, *Trio dlia fortepiano, skripki i violincheli*, op. 63 (Moscow, 1947); RGALI, fond 2954, op. 1, d. 875, l. 66 (H. Smoliar to M. F. Gnesin, June 24, 1948).

67. RGALI, fond 2444, d. 137, ll. 117–78 (unpublished biography of A. M. Veprik [1967]); Tropp, "Dom Gnesinykh," 22; Rittikh, "O nastavnike i druge," 41–43; Bogdanova, *Muzyka i vlast*, 278–80; Vlasova, "Venera Milosskaia," 194. On the philosemitism of the Union of Composers, see Tomoff, *Creative Union*, 152–88, and Caroline Brooke, "Soviet Musicians and the Great Terror," *Europe-Asia Studies* 54:3 (May 2002), 397–413. The union's specific responses to incidents of antisemitism are also documented in Kostyrchenko, *Out of the Red Shadows*, 172, and Kostyrchenko, *Gosudarstvennyi antisemitizm*, 37–39, 346–48. The broader issues of music and Stalinist politics in the late 1920s and early 1930s are discussed in Nelson, *Music for the Revolution*, 207–46, and Fitzpatrick, *The Cultural Front*, 183–215.

68. RGALI, fond 2954, op. 1, d. 141, ll. 62–77 (lecture typescript, "Anton Rubinstein: On the Fortieth Anniversary of His Death" [1934]).

Conclusion

1. Mikhail Gnesin, "Antisemitizm i muzyka," *Priazovskii krai* 194 (July 24, 1916), 2; Volfing [E. Medtner], "Estrada," in Volfing, *Modernizm i muzyka*, 102–3, 117; Leonid Sabaneev, "Muzykalnye besedy: Muzyka i patriotism," *Muzyka* 107 (Dec. 8, 1912), 1044–51.
2. Gnesin, "Antisemitizm i muzyka," 2.
3. JTSA, Solomon Rosowsky Collection, box 1, folder 57 (Iu. D. Engel to S. B. Rosowsky, Feb. 25, 1924).
4. Schwarz, *Music and Musical Life*, 138; Melnik, "Novyi vzgliad," 194. At the Moscow Conservatory, authorities not only named the school after Tchaikovsky rather than its founder, Nikolai Rubinstein, they also removed Felix Mendelssohn's portrait from the Great Hall to be replaced with that of an ethnic Russian composer, Alexander Dargomyzhsky (though Richard Wagner's portrait reportedly remained); see Rapoport, *Na rubezhe*, 19–21.
5. Kostyrchenko, *Out of the Red Shadows*, 15–21, 194–97.
6. On Weinberg's biography, see James Loeffler, "Mieczsław Weinberg," in Hundert, *YIVO Encyclopedia*, 2:2012–13, and Per Skans, "Mieczsław Weinberg: Ein bescheidener Kollege," in Kuhn, Wehrmeyer, and Wolter, *Dmitri Schostakowitsch und das jüdische musikalische Erbe*, 298–324.
7. Per Skans, "Ein jüdischer Immigrant: Mieczsław Weinberg," in Kuhn, Nemtsov, and Wehrmeyer, *"Samuel" Goldenberg und "Schmuyle,"* 160–61; Vovsi-Mikhoels, *Moi otets*, 197–201; Kostyrchenko, *Tainaia politika Stalina*, 551–52.
8. Schwarz, *Music and Musical Life*, 365–69; Fay, *Shostakovich*, 228–35.
9. Fay, *Shostakovich*, 235–37.
10. Shostakovich's strong personal identification with the poem is attested to in his private correspondence. See Glikman, *Pisma k drugu*, 196.
11. Razhnikov, *Kirill Kondrashin rasskazyvaet*, 184–85.
12. Kvitko, *Geklibene verk*, 217–18; Kvitko, *Izbrannoe*, 180–81.
13. Avraam Ben-Eli, "'Evreiskaia skripka' Moshe Vainberga," *Menora* 25 (1984), 110–12. On Kvitko's arrest and execution, see Rubenstein and Naumov, *Stalin's Secret Pogrom*, 159–84. Lukonin's lyrics are quoted from the 1974 recording by the Moscow Philharmonic. Interestingly, the "official" printed version of Lukonin's poem leaves out references to both the United States and singing violins. Weinberg, Symphony No. 6 (recording), and Lukonin, *Stikhotvorenniia*, 189–90.
14. Tigranov, *Sovetskaia simfoniia*, 72–77.

Bibliography

Archival Collections

Arkhiv vostokovedeniia, Institut vostokovedeniia, Rossiiskaia akademiia nauk, Sankt-Peterburgskoe otdelenie (AV IV RAN) (St. Petersburg)
Fond 85   D. G. Maggid

Central Archives for the History of the Jewish People (CAHJP) (Jerusalem)
RU/2   Protocols of the Society for Jewish Folk Music
RU/11   Protocols of the Jewish Historical-Ethnographic Society

Gosudarstvennyi arkhiv rossiiskoi federatsii (GARF) (Moscow)
Fond 102   Departament politsii (MVD)
Fond 698   E. F. Raden
Fond 9532 L. E. Motylev
Fond 9533 P. S. Marek
Fond 9535 S. R. Kotsyna

Institut rukopisei, natsionalnaia biblioteka Ukrainy imeni V. I. Vernadskogo (IR NBUV) (Kiev)
Fond 190   Kabinet evreiskoi kultury AN USSR

Jewish Theological Seminary of America Archives (JTSA) (New York)
Solomon Rosowsky Collection

Otdel rukopisei, Rossiiskaia natsionalnaia biblioteka (OR RNB) (St. Petersburg)
Fond 183   D. G. Gintsburg
Fond 654   A. G. Rubinshtein

Otdel rukopisei biblioteky, Sankt-Peterburgskaia gosudarstvennaia konservatoriia (OR SPbGK) (St. Petersburg)
Fond Antona Grigorevicha Rubinshteina

Rossiiskii gosudarstvennyi arkhiv literatury i iskusstva (RGALI) (Moscow)
Fond 2435 A. A. Krein
Fond 2954 M. F. Gnesin

Rossiiskii institut istorii isskustv (RIII) (St. Petersburg)
Fond 4   Programmy kontsertov
Fond 8   N. N. Rimskaia-Korsakova

Fond 9 A. N. Rimskii-Korsakov
Fond 96 M. A. Bikhter

Tsentralnyi gosudarstvennyi arkhiv literatury i iskusstva, Sankt Petersburg (TsGALI SPb) (St. Petersburg)
Fond 493 L. A. Barenboim

Tsentralnyi gosudarstvennyi istoricheskii arkhiv Sankt-Peterburga (TsGIA SPb) (St. Petersburg)
Fond 361 Sankt-Petersburgskaia konservatoriia
Fond 408 Russkoe muzykalnoe obshchestvo
Fond 1747 Evreiskoe muzykalnoe obshchestvo

Tsentralnyi gosudarstvennyi muzei muzykalnoi kultury imeni Glinki, otdel rukopisei (TsGMMK) (Moscow)
Fond 50 A. K. Abramova
Fond 78 N. G. Rubinshtein
Fond 80 Moskovskaia konservatoriia
Fond 93 Iu. D. Engel
Fond 99 A. G. Rubinshtein
Fond 135 I. A. Sats
Fond 208 Ia. V. Veinberg
Fond 238 M. F. Gnesin

YIVO Institute for Jewish Research (YIVO) (New York)
RG37 Jewish Music Societies Collection

Published Primary Sources

Ansky, Sh. *Dos yidishe etnografishe program*. Petrograd: Evreiskaia etnograficheskaia ekspeditsiia imeni Barona G. O. Gintsburga, 1914.
Auer, Leopold. *My Long Life in Music*. New York: Frederick A. Stokes, 1923.
Avshalomov, Jacob and Aaron. *Avshalomovs' Winding Way: Composers out of China — A Chronicle*. [Philadelphia:] Xlibris, 2002.
Babel, Isaac. *The Collected Stories*. Ed. and trans. Walter Morison. New York: Meridian Fiction, 1955.
Babel, Nathalie, ed. *The Complete Works of Isaac Babel*. New York: W. W. Norton, 2002.
Badkhn, Peysakh-Eliyahu. *Kanaf renanim oder zeks folkslider*. Vilnius, 1871.
Beregovskaia, Eda, ed. *Arfy na verbakh: Prizvanie i sudba Moiseia Beregovskogo*. Moscow: Evreiskii universitet v Moskve; Jerusalem: Gesharim, 1994.
Beregovskii, Moisei. *Evreiskii muzykalnyi folklor*. Moscow: Gosudarstvennoe muzykalnoe izdatelstvo, 1934.
———. *Evreiskie napevy bez slov*. Moscow: "Kompozitor," 1999.
———. *Evreiskie narodnye pesni*. Ed. S. V. Aksiuk. Moscow: Sovetskii kompozitor, 1962.
———. *Jewish Instrumental Folk Music: The Collections and Writings of Moshe Beregovskii*. Ed. and trans. Mark Slobin, Robert Rothstein, and Michael Alpert. Syracuse: Syracuse University Press, 2001.
———. *Old Jewish Folk Music: The Collections and Writings of Moshe Beregovskii*. Ed. and trans. Mark Slobin. Philadelphia: University of Pennsylvania Press, 1982.
Berlin, Moisei. *Ocherk etnografii evreiskogo naseleniia v Rossii*. St. Petersburg: V. Bezobrazova, 1861.

Blagyi, D. D., ed. *A. V. Goldenveizer: Stati, materialy, vospominaniia*. Moscow: Muzyka, 1968.
Bogdanov, V. V. *Piatidesiatiletie imperatorskogo obshchestva liubitelei estestvoznaniia, antropologii i etnografii, 1863–1913*. Moscow: Tip. Tovarishchestva Riabushinskikh, 1914.
Chaikovskii, M. I. *Zhizn Petra Ilicha Chaikovskago*. 3 vols. Moscow: Jurgenson, 1900–1902.
Clark, Katerina, and Evgeny Dobrenko, with Andrei Artizov and Oleg Naumov, eds. *Soviet Culture and Power: A History in Documents, 1917–1953*. New Haven: Yale University Press, 2007.
Dubinsky, Rostislav. *Stormy Applause: Making Music in a Worker's State*. New York: Hill and Wang, 1989.
Dubnov, S. M. *History of the Jews in Russia and Poland*. 3 vols. Philadelphia: Jewish Publication Society of America, 1916–20.
———. *Kniga zhizni: Vospominaniia i razmyshleniia*. St. Petersburg: Peterburgskoe vostokovedenie, 1998.
———. *Ob izuchenii istorii russkikh evreev i ob uchrezhdenii russko-evreiskogo istoricheskogo obshchestva*. St. Petersburg: A. E. Landau, 1891.
Elman, Saul. *Memoirs of Mischa Elman's Father*. New York: S. Elman, 1933.
Engel, Iulii Dmitrevich. *Evreiskie detskie pesni dlia detskikh ochagov, shkol i semi: 50 nomerov dlia odnogo golosa i odnogolosnogo khora bez soprovozhdeniia*. Moscow: V. Grosse, 1916.
———. *Evreiskie narodnye pesni*. Vol. 1. Moscow: Jurgenson, 1909.
———. *Evreiskie narodnye pesni*. Vol. 2. Moscow: Iu. D. Engel, 1912.
———. *Gazel, svobodna i legka: Iz 'evreiskikh melodii Bairona,'* op. 10, no. 1. Moscow: Jurgenson, n.d.
———. *Glazami sovremennika: Izbrannye stati o russkoi muzyke, 1898–1918*. Ed. I. Kunin. Moscow: Sovetskii kompozitor, 1971.
———. *Kak poet evrei, tsygan, russkii*. Moscow: Jurgenson, 1900.
———. *Narodnaia konservatoriia*. Moscow: L. L. Levenson, 1908.
———. *Ocherki po istorii muzyki*. Moscow: N. N. Kluchkova, 1910.
———. *Uvy, nad bregom Iordana: Iz 'evreiskikh pesen' A. Maikova*, op. 9. Moscow: Jurgenson, n.d.
———. *V opere: Sbornik statei ob operakh i baletakh*. Moscow: Jurgenson, 1911.
Famintsyn, A. S. *Drevniaia indo-kitaiskaia gamma v Azii i Evrope*. St. Petersburg: Tip. Iu. Shtaufa, 1889.
Gintsburg, S. M. *Amolike Peterburg*. New York: Tsiko Bikher Farlag, 1944.
———. *Meshumodim in tsarishn Rusland*. New York: Tsiko Bikher Farlag, 1946.
Gintsburg, S. M., and P. S. Marek, eds. *Yiddish Folksongs in Russia*. 1901. Reprint, ed. Dov Noy. Ramat Gan: Bar-Ilan University, 1991.
Ginzburg, S. L., ed. *N. A. Rimskii-Korsakov i muzykalnoe obrazovanie: Stati i materialy*. Leningrad: Gosudarstvennoe muzykalnoe izdatelstvo, 1959.
Glikman, Isaak, ed. *Pisma k drugu: Dmitrii Shostakovich–Isaaku Glikmanu*. Moscow: Izdatelsvo "DSCH"; St. Petersburg: Izdatelstvo "Kompozitor," 1993.
Gnesin, M. F., ed. *Mysli i vospominaniia o N. A. Rimskom-Korsakove*. Moscow: Gosudarstvennoe muzykalnoe izdatelstvo, 1956.
———. *Stati, vospominaniia, materialy*. Ed. R. V. Glezer. Moscow: Sovetskii kompozitor, 1961.
Golinkin, Mordecai. *Me-hekhale Yefet le-ohole Shem (Zikhronot)*. Tel Aviv: Ha-Va'ad le-hotsa'at Sefer Zikhronot shel M. Golinkin, 1947.
Halevy, Moshe. *Darki 'ale bamot*. Tel Aviv: Hotsa'at Masadah, 1954.
Héritte-Viardot, Louise Pauline Marie. *Memories and Adventures*. Trans. and ed. E. S. Buchheim. New York: Da Capo Press, 1977.

Imperatorskoe russkoe muzykalnoe obshchestvo. *Otchet I.R.M.O. s 1 Sent. 1905 g. po 1 Sent. 1906 g.* St. Petersburg: IRMO, 1908.

Internationale Musikgesellschaft, III: Kongress der Internationalen Musik-Gesellschaft, Wien 25-29 mai 1909: Bericht vorgelegt vom Wiener Kongressausschuss. Vienna: [Im Selbstverlage des Festkomitees], 1909.

Kelner, V. E., ed. *Evrei v Rossii: XIX vek.* Moscow: Novoe literaturnoe obozrenie, 2000.

Kipnis, Menahem. *Di velt-berimte yidishe muziker.* Warsaw: Ha-Or, 1910.

Kiselgof, Z. A., ed. *Lider-zamelbukh far der yidishe shul un familye.* 2nd ed. St. Petersburg: Gezelshaft far Idisher Folks-Muzik in Peterburg, 1914.

———. *Sbornik pesen dlia evreiskoi shkoly i semi.* St. Petersburg–Berlin: Leo Winz, 1912.

———. "Vegn yiddisher folks-muzik: Referat." St. Petersburg: Gezelshaft far Idisher Folks-Muzik in Peterburg, 1912.

Kogut, A., ed. *Znamenitye evrei muzhchiny i zhenshchiny v istorii kultury chelovechestva.* 2nd ed. 4 vols. Odessa: M. S. Kosman, 1901–2.

Kugel, A. R. *Listia s dereva: Vospominaniia.* Leningrad: Izdatelstvo vremiia, 1923.

Kuprin, Alexander. *Gambrinus and Other Stories.* New York: Adelphi Company, 1925.

Kvartin, Zavel. *Mayn lebn.* Philadelphia: Gezelshaftlikher Komitet, 1952.

Kvitko, Lev. *Geklibene verk.* Moscow: Sovetskii pisatel, 1967.

———. *Izbrannoe: Stikhi, povest.* Moscow: Khudozhestvennaia literatura, 1990.

Lamzdorf, V. N. *Dnevnik V. N. Lamzdorfa (1886-1890).* Moscow: Academia, 1926.

Leskov, Nikolai. *Evrei v Rossii.* Moscow: Mosty kultury, 2003.

Levenson, O. Ia. *V kontsertnoi zale (Muzykalnye feletony), 1878-1880 gg.* Moscow: Tip. N. S. Skvortsova, 1880.

Levontin, Yeḥiel Yosef. *Shim'on Etsyoni: Roman me-reshit tekufat shenot ha-shemonim.* Warsaw: Tushiyah, 1899.

Lewinsky, Josef, ed. *Vor den Coulissen.* Vol. 2. Berlin: A. Hofmann, 1881.

Liapunova, A. S., ed. *Perepiska: M. A. Balakirev i V. V. Stasov.* 2 vols. Moscow: Muzyka, 1971–72.

Litvak, A. *Vos geven: Etyudn un zikhroynes.* Vilnius: B. Kletskin, 1925.

Lukonin, Mikhail. *Stikhotvoreniia i poemy.* Leningrad: Sovetskii pisatel, 1985.

M'Arthur, Alexander. *Anton Rubinstein: A Biographical Sketch.* Edinburgh: A. and C. Black, 1889.

Materialy po voprosu o prieme evreev v srednykh i vysshnykh uchebnykh zavedenii. St. Petersburg, 1908.

Melgunov, S. P. *Vospominaniia i dnevniki.* Paris: Sklag izd. "Les Éditeurs réunis," 1964.

Menkov, P. K. *Zapiski Petra Kononovicha Menkova.* 2 vols. St. Petersburg: V. A. Berezovskii, 1898.

Milstein, Nathan. *From Russia to the West.* New York: Henry Holt, 1990.

Minkovskii, Pinḥas. *Moderne liturgye in unzere sinagogen in Russland.* Odessa, 1910.

Moskovskaia Muzykalno-Etnograficheskaia Komissiia. *Opyty khudozhestvennoi obrabotki narodnykh pesen.* Moscow, 1912.

Mysh, M. I. *Rukovodstvo k russkim zakonam o evreiakh: Dopolnenie uzakoneniia i senatskie raziasneniia za 1903-1909 gody.* St. Petersburg, 1910.

Obshchestvo evreiskoi narodnoi muzyki. *Otchet obshchestva evreiskoi narodnoi muzyki za 1912 god.* St. Petersburg: O-vo evreiskoi narodnoi muzyki v S.-Peterburge, 1913.

———. *Otchet obshchestva evreiskoi narodnoi muzyki za 1913 god i ocherk deiatelnosti obshchestva za pervoe piatiletie (1909-1913 gg.).* Petrograd: O-vo evreiskoi narodnoi muzyki v S.-Peterburge, 1914.

———. *Ustav obshchestva evreiskogo narodnoi muzyki.* St. Petersburg: I. Fleitman, 1910.

Olenina-d'Algheim, M. *Le legs de Moussorgski.* Paris: E. Rey, 1896.
———. *Zavety M. P. Musorgskogo.* Moscow: Muzyka i zhizn, 1910.
Orshanskii, I. G. *Evrei v Rossii.* St. Petersburg: O. I. Bakst, 1877.
Pekelis, M., and A. Orlova, eds. M. P. *Musorgskii: Literaturnoe nasledie.* 2 vols. Moscow: Muzyka, 1971–72.
Peretz, Isaac Leib. *Ale verk.* New York: Tsiko Bikher Farlag, 1947.
Pobedonostsev, K. P. K. P. *Pobedonostsev i ego korrespondenty.* 2 vols. Moscow: Gosudarstvennoe izdatelstvo, 1923.
Rabinovitsh, Yisroel. *Muzik bay yidn.* Montreal: [Eagle Publishing], 1940.
Rapoport, Ia. L. *Na rubezhe dvukh epokh: Delo vrachei 1953 goda.* St. Petersburg: Izdatelstvo "Pushkinskogo fonda," 2003.
Ravina, Menashe, ed. *Mikhtavim 'al ha-musikah ha-yehudit.* Tel Aviv: Davar, 1941.
Razhnikov, Vladimir. *Kirill Kondrashin rasskazyvaet o muzyke i zhizni.* Moscow: Sovetskii kompozitor, 1989.
Rekhtman, Avraham. *Yidishe etnografie un folklor.* Buenos Aires: Yidishe Visnshaftlekher Institut, 1958.
Riemann, Hugo. *Muzykalnyi slovar.* Moscow: Jurgenson, 1901–4.
Rivesman, Mark. *Evreiskim detiam.* St. Petersburg: Tip. I. Lurie, 1908.
Rimskii-Korsakov, N. A. *Letopis moei muzykalnoi zhizni.* St. Petersburg: M. M. Stasiulevich, 1908.
———. *N. A. Rimskii-Korsakov: Muzykalnye stati i zametki.* Ed. A. N. Rimskii-Korsakov. St. Petersburg: M. M. Stasiulevich, 1911.
———. *Reminscences of Rimsky-Korsakov.* Ed. V. V. Iastrebtsev. New York: Columbia University Press, 1985.
Roth, Joseph. *Hiob: Roman eines einfachen mannes.* Berlin: G. Kiepenheuer, 1930.
Rubinstein. Anton. *Autobiography of Anton Rubinstein, 1829–1889.* Trans. Aline Delano. Boston: Little, Brown, 1903.
———. *Christus: Geistliche Oper in sieben Vorgängen nebst Prolog und Epilog.* Klavierauszug. Leipzig: Senff, n.d.
———. *Der Dämon: Phantastische Oper in drei Acten und sieben Bildern.* Klavierauszug. Leipzig: Senff, 1876.
———. *Dvenadtsat pesen na slova Mirza Shafi.* Moscow: Sovetskii kompozitor, 1960.
———. *Gedankenkorb.* 2nd ed. Leipzig: Senff, 1897.
———. *Kalaschnikoff, der Kaufmann von Moskau: Oper in drei Akten.* Klavierauszug. Leipzig: Senff, n.d.
———. *Korob myslei.* St. Petersburg: Olma-Press, 1999.
———. *Literaturnoe nasledie v trekh tomakh.* Ed. L. A. Barenboim. Moscow: Muzyka, 1983–86.
———. *Makkavei: Opera v trekh deistviakh.* Moscow: Jurgenson, 1891.
———. *Moses. Geistliche Oper in acht Bildern.* Partitur. Leipzig: Senff, n.d.
———. *Music and Its Masters.* Chicago: Charles H. Sergel, 1892.
———. *Muzyka i ee predstaviteli.* Moscow: Jurgenson, 1892.
———. *Piano music/Anton Rubinstein.* Ed. Joseph Banowetz. Mineola: Dover Publications, 2001.
———. *Sulamith: Ein biblisches Bühnenspiel in fünf Bildern.* Berlin: Bote and G. Bock, n.d.
Russkie vedomosti, 1863–1913: Sbornik statei. Moscow: Tipografiia "Russkikh vedomostei," 1913.
Sabaneev, L. L. *Evreiskaia natsionalnaia shkola v muzyke.* Moscow: Izdatelstvo obshchestva evreiskoi muzyki, 1924.

Sakketti, L. A. *Ocherk vseobshchei istorii muzyki.* St. Petersburg: V. Bessel, 1891.
Saminsky, Lazare. *Living Music of the Americas.* New York: Howell, Soskin and Crown, 1949.
———. *Music of Our Day: Essentials and Prophecies.* New York: Thomas Y. Crowell, 1932.
———. *Music of the Ghetto and Bible.* New York: Bloch, 1934.
———. *Ob evreiskoi muzyki: Sbornik statei.* Petrograd: Tip. "Sever," 1914.
Sats, Ilia. *Pesenka: Narodnye evreiskie napevy.* Moscow: Jurgenson, n.d.
Sbornik pamiati A. D. Idelsona. Berlin: Buchhandlung "jalkut," 1928.
Serov, A. N. *Kriticheskie stati.* 4 vols. St. Petersburg: Tip. Departamenta udielov, 1892–96.
Serova, Valentina. *Serovy, Aleksandr N. i Valentin A.: Vospominaniia.* St. Petersburg: Izd. "Shipovnik," 1914.
Sholom Aleichem. *From the Fair: The Autobiography of Sholom Aleichem.* Trans. and ed. Curt Leviant. New York: Viking, 1985.
Shor, David. *David Shor: Vospominaniia.* Ed. Iuliia Matveeva. Jerusalem–Moscow: Gesharim, 2001.
Shostakovitch: *Song Cycle from Jewish Folk Poetry; Alman: King Ahaz—Opera Excerpts.* London: Bnai Brith Recordings, BB0001, 1984.
Slonimsky, Nicholas. *Perfect Pitch: A Life Story.* New York: Oxford University Press, 1988.
Solomon, Flora, and Barnet Litvinoff. *A Woman's Way.* New York: Simon and Schuster, 1984.
Stasov, V. V. *Izbrannye sochineniia v troikh tomakh.* 3 vols. Moscow: Iskusstvo, 1949–52.
———. *Stati o muzyke.* 5 vols. Moscow: Muzyka, 1974–80.
———. *38 pisem An. K. Liadova i V.V. Stasova.* Petrograd: Tipografiia Sirius, 1916.
———. *Vladimir Vasilevich Stasov: Selected Essays on Music.* Trans. Florence Jonas. New York: Praeger, 1968.
Taneev, S. I. *Dnevniki v trekh knigah, 1894–1909.* Ed. L. Z. Korabelnikova. Moscow: Muzyka, 1985.
Tigranov, G. G., ed. *Leningradskaia konservatoriia v vospominaniiakh, 1862–1962.* Leningrad: Gosudarstvennoe muzykalnoe izdatelstvo, 1962.
Tiutcheva, Anna Fedorovna. *Pri dvore dvukh imperatorov: Vospominaniia, dnevnik, 1853–1882.* Cambridge: Oriental Research Partners, 1975.
Varshavsky, M. *Varshavskys yudishe folks-lieder.* 2nd ed. New York: Maks N. Maysel, 1918.
Voinskaia povinnost i konservatoriia. Odessa: Tip. O-va "Russkaia Rech," 1915.
Volfing [Emil Metner]. *Modernizm i muzyka: Stati, kriticheskie i polemicheskie (1907–1910).* Moscow, 1912.
Vovsi-Mikhoels, Nataliia. *Moi otets Solomon Mikhoels: Vospominaniia o zhizni i gibeli.* Moscow: Vozvrashchenie, 1997.
Vulfius, P. A., ed. *Iz istorii Leningradskoi konservatorii: Materialy i dokumenty, 1862–1917.* Leningrad: Muzyka, 1964.
———. *Russkaia mysl o muzykalnom folklore: Materialy i dokumenty.* Moscow: Muzyka, 1979.
Wagner, Richard. *Evreistvo v muzyke.* Moscow: Russkaia pravda, 2003.
———. *Evreistvo v muzyke.* St. Petersburg: S. E. Grozmani, 1908.
———. *Richard Wagner. Stories and Essays.* Ed. Charles Osborne. London: Owen, 1973.
Weinberg, Mieczsław. *Symphony No. 6 in A Minor.* Moscow Choir School Boys Choir and the Moscow Philharmonic Orchestra. Conducted by Kirill Kondrashin. [1974]. Recording, Olympia OCD 471, 1994.
Zolotarev, V. A. *Vospominaniia.* Moscow: Gosudarstvennoe muzykalnoe izdatelstvo, 1957.
Zunser, Eliokum. *Ha-menageyn.* Vilnius, 1873.

Secondary Sources

Adler, Israel, Bathya Bayer, and Eliyahu Schleifer, eds. *The Abraham Zvi Idelsohn Memorial Volume: Yuval 5*. Jerusalem: Magnes Press, 1986.
Altmann, Alexander. *Moses Mendelssohn: A Biographical Study*. Philadelphia: Jewish Publication Society of America, 1973.
Applegate, Celia, and Pamela Potter, eds. *Music and German National Identity*. Chicago: University of Chicago Press, 2002.
Apter-Gabriel, Ruth. *The Jewish Art of Solomon Yudovin (1892–1954): From Folk Art to Socialist Realism*. Jerusalem: Israel Museum, 1991.
———, ed. *Tradition and Revolution: The Jewish Renaissance in Russian Avant-Garde Art, 1912–1928*. Jerusalem: Israel Museum, 1987.
Ascheim, Steven. *In Times of Crisis: Essays on European Culture, Germans, and Jews*. Madison: University of Wisconsin Press, 2001.
Azadovskii, M. K. *Istoriia russkoi folkloristiki*. 2 vols. Moscow: Gosudarstvennoe uchebno-pedagogicheskoe izdatelstvo, 1958–63.
Balmuth, Daniel. *Censorship in Russia, 1865–1905*. Washington, D.C.: University Press of America, 1979.
———. *The Russian Bulletin, 1863–1917: A Liberal Voice in Tsarist Russia*. New York: Peter Lang, 2000.
Balzer, Harvey, ed. *Russia's Missing Middle Class: The Professions in Russian History*. Armonk: M. E. Sharpe, 1996.
Barenboim, L. A. *Anton Grigorevich Rubinshtein*. 2 vols. Leningrad: Gosudarstvennoe muzykalnoe izdatelstvo, 1957–62.
———. *Nikolai Grigorevich Rubinshtein: Istoriia zhizni i deiatelnosti*. Moscow: Izdatelstvo muzyka, 1982.
Barsova, Liudmila. *Iz istorii peterburgskoi vokalnoi shkoly*. St. Petersburg: Petrovskii fond, 1999.
Bartal, Israel, ed. *Ha-'agalah ha-mele'ah XX*. Jerusalem: Magnes Press, 2002.
Bartlett, Rosamund. *Wagner and Russia*. Cambridge: Cambridge University Press, 1995.
Bazunov, S. A. *A. N. Serov: Ego zhizn i muzykalnyi deiatelnost: Biograficheskii ocherk*. St. Petersburg: Ogshch. Polza, 1893.
Beizer, Mikhail. *Evrei Leningrada, 1917–1939: Natsionalnaia zhizn i sovetizatsiia*. Moscow: Mosty kultury, 1999.
———. *The Jews of St. Petersburg*. Philadelphia: Jewish Publication Society of America, 1989.
Beller, Steven. *Vienna and the Jews, 1867–1938: A Cultural History*. Cambridge: Cambridge University Press, 1989.
Bergmeier, Horst J. P., Ejal Jakob Eisler, and Rainer F. Lotz. *Vorbei . . . Beyond Recall: A Record of Jewish Musical Life in Nazi Berlin, 1933–1938*. Hambergen: Bear Family Records, 2001.
Berkowitz, Joel, ed. *Yiddish Theatre: New Approaches*. Oxford: Littman Library of Jewish Civilization, 2003.
Berkowitz, Michael, ed. *Nationalism, Zionism and Ethnic Mobilization of the Jews in 1900 and Beyond*. Leiden: Brill, 2004.
Bilski, Emily D., and Emily Braun, eds. *Jewish Women and Their Salons: The Power of Conversation*. New York: Jewish Museum under the auspices of the Jewish Theological Seminary of America; New Haven: Yale University Press, 2005.

Binevich, Evgenni. *Evreiskii teatr v Peterburge: Opyt istoricheskogo ocherka.* St. Petersburg: Evreiskii obshchynnyi tsentr Sankt-Peterburga, 2003.

Bing, Anthony. *Israeli Pacifist: The Life of Joseph Abileah.* Syracuse: Syracuse University Press, 1990.

Bogdanov-Berezovskii, V. M. *Muzykalnaia kultura Leningrada za 50 let: Muzykalno-istoricheskie ocherki.* Leningrad: Muzyka, 1967.

Bogdanova, Alla V. *Muzyka i vlast (poststalinskii period).* Moscow: Nasledie, 1995.

Bohlman, Philip V., ed. *Jewish Musical Modernism, Old and New.* Chicago: University of Chicago Press, 2008.

———. *Jewish Music and Modernity.* New York: Oxford University Press, 2008.

———. *Jüdische Volksmusik: Eine mitteleuropäische Geistesgeschichte.* Vienna: Böhlau, 2005.

———. *The Music of European Nationalism: Cultural Identity and Modern History.* Santa Barbara: ABC-CLIO, 2004.

Botstein, Leon. *Judentum und Modernität: Essays zur Rolle der Juden in der deutschen und österreichischen Kultur, 1848 bis 1938.* Vienna: Böhlau, 1991.

Botstein, Leon, and Werner Hanak, eds. *Vienna: Jews and the City of Music, 1870–1938.* Annandale-on-Hudson: Bard College; Hofheim: Wolke, 2004.

Bowen, Catherine Drinker. *Free Artist: The Story of Anton and Nicholas Rubinstein.* New York: Random House, [1939].

Braun, Joachim. *Jews and Jewish Elements in Soviet Music: A Study of a Socio-National Problem in Music.* Tel Aviv: Israeli Music Publications, 1978.

———. *On Jewish Music: Past and Present.* Frankfurt: Peter Lang, 2006.

Braun, Joachim, Heidi Tamar Hoffmann, and Vladimir Karbusicky, eds. *Verfemte Musik: Komponisten in den Diktaturen unseres Jahrhunderts: Dokumentation des Kolloquiums vom 9.–12. Januar 1993 in Dresden.* 2nd ed. Frankfurt: Peter Lang, 1997.

Braunzaft, Moshe. *Yo'el Engel.* Jerusalem: Kiryat Sefer, 1946.

Braunzaft, Moshe, and Moshe Gorali. *Ha-eskolah ha-musikalit ha-yehudit.* Jerusalem: Ever, 1940.

Bronfin, El. D. *Muzykalnaia kultura Petrograda pervogo poslerevoliutsionnogo piatiletiia, 1917–1922.* Leningrad: Sovetskii kompozitor, 1984.

Brown, Malcolm Hamrick, ed. *Musorgsky, in Memoriam, 1881–1981.* Ann Arbor: UMI Research Press, 1982.

Buckler, Julie. *The Literary Lorgnette: Attending Opera in Imperial Russia.* Palo Alto: Stanford University Press, 2000.

Budnitskii, O. V., O. V. Belova, V. E. Kelner, and V. V. Mochalova, eds. *Mirovoi krizis 1914–1920 godov i sudba vostochnoevropeiskogo evreistva.* Moscow: Rosspen, 2005.

Burbank, Jane, and David L. Ransel, eds. *Imperial Russia: New Histories for the Empire.* Bloomington: Indiana University Press, 1998.

Campbell, Stuart, ed. and trans. *Russians on Russian Music, 1830–1880: An Anthology.* Cambridge: Cambridge University Press, 1994.

Carlebach, Elisheva, John M. Efron, and David N. Myers, eds. *Jewish History and Jewish Memory: Essays in Honor of Yosef Hayim Yerushalmi.* Hanover: Brandeis University Press, 1998.

Cohen, Hagit. *Be-hanuto shel mokher ha-sefarim: Ḥanuyot sefarim yehudiot be-mizraḥ eiropa bamaḥatzit ha-shniya shel hame'ah ha-19.* Jerusalem: Magnes Press, 2006.

Crumden, Robert M. *Body and Soul: The Making of American Modernism.* New York: Basic Books, 2000.

Dahlhaus, Carl. *Between Romanticism and Modernism: Four Studies in the Music of the Later Nineteenth Century.* Trans. Mary Whittall. Berkeley: University of California Press, 1989.

David-Fox, Michael, Peter Holquist, and Alexander Martin, eds. *Orientalism and Empire in Russia. Kritika* Historical Studies 3. Bloomington: Slavica, 2006.

Dawidowicz, Lucy, ed. *The Golden Tradition: Jewish Life and Thought in Eastern Europe.* Boston: Beacon Press, 1967.

De Paoli, Domenico, ed. *Lazare Saminsky, Composer and Civic Worker.* New York: Bloch, 1930.

Dubnova-Erlich, Sophie. *The Life and Work of S. M. Dubnov: Diaspora Nationalism and Jewish History.* Trans. Judith Vowles and ed. Jeffrey Shandler. Bloomington: Indiana University Press, 1991.

Dudakov, Savelli. *Paradoksy i prigudy filosemitizma i antisemitizma v Rossii.* Moscow: Russian State Humanities University, 2000.

Eisenstein Baker, Paula, and Robert S. Nelson, eds. *Leo Zeitlin: Chamber Music. Recent Researches in the Music of the Nineteenth and Early Twentieth Centuries* 51. Middleton: A-R Editions, 2009.

Eliashevich, D. A., ed. *Evrei v Rossii: Istoriia i kultura: Sbornik nauchnykh trudov.* Seriia "Istoriia i etnografiia," vol. 3. St. Petersburg: Peterburgskii Evreiskii Universitet, 1995.

———. *Evrei v Rossii: Istoriia i kultura: Sbornik nauchnykh trudov.* Seriia "Istoriia i etnografiia," vol. 5. St. Petersburg: Peterburgskii Evreiskii Universitet, 1998.

———. *Istoriia evreev v Rossii: Problemy istochnikovedeniia i istoriiografii: Sbornik nauchnykh trudov.* St. Petersburg: Peterburgskii Evreiskii Universitet, 1993.

———. *Pravitelstvennaia politika i evreiskaia pechat v Rossii, 1797–1917.* Moscow: Mosty kultury; Jerusalem: Gesharim, 1999.

Eliram, Talila. *Bo, shir 'Ivri: Shirei Erets Yisra'el, hebetim muzikaliyim ve hevratiyim.* Haifa: University of Haifa Press, 2006.

Elon, Amos. *The Pity of It All: A History of Jews in Germany, 1743–1933.* New York: Metropolitan Books, 2002.

Endelman, Todd, ed. *Jewish Apostasy in the Modern World.* New York: Holmes and Meier, 1987.

Engelstein, Laura. *The Keys to Happiness: Sex and the Search for Modernity in Fin-de-Siècle Russia.* Ithaca: Cornell University Press, 1992.

Evreiska istoriia ta kultura v Ukraini: Materialy konferentsii, Kiev 8–9 grudnya 1994 r. Kiev: Institut iudaïki, 1995.

Fay, Laurel. *Shostakovich: A Life.* Oxford: Oxford University Press, 2000.

Findeizen, N. G. *A. G. Rubinshtein.* Moscow: Jurgenson, 1907.

Fishman, David. *The Rise of Modern Yiddish Culture.* Pittsburgh: University of Pittsburgh Press, 2005.

Fitzpatrick, Sheila. *The Commissariat of Enlightenment: Soviet Organization of Education and the Arts under Lunacharsky, October 1917–1921.* Cambridge: Cambridge University Press, 1970.

———. *The Cultural Front: Power and Culture in Revolutionary Russia.* Ithaca: Cornell University Press, 1992.

Flam, Gila, and Dov Noy, eds. *Hobn Mir a Nigndl: We Have a Little Tune: The Songs of the Yiddish "Troubadour" Nokhem Shternheim.* Jerusalem: Magnes Press, 2000.

Fliegel, Hyman. *Zavel Zilberts: His Life and Work.* New York: Shulsinger, 1971.

Frame, Murray. *The St. Petersburg Imperial Theaters: Stage and State in Revolutionary Russia, 1900–1920.* Jefferson: McFarland, 2000.

Frankel, Jonathan. *Jewish Politics and the Russian Revolution of 1905.* Tel Aviv: Tel Aviv University Press, 1982.

———. *Prophecy and Politics: Socialism, Nationalism, and the Russian Jews, 1862–1917.* Cambridge: Cambridge University Press, 1981.

Frankel, Jonathan, and Steven Zipperstein, eds. *Assimilation and Community: The Jews in Nineteenth-Century Europe.* Cambridge: Cambridge University Press, 1992.

Freeze, ChaeRan Y. *Jewish Marriage and Divorce in Imperial Russia.* Hanover: University Press of New England, 2002.

Friedman, Aron, ed. *Lebensbilder berühmter Kantoren.* 3 vols. Berlin: C. Boas, 1918–27.

Frumkin, Ia. G., G. Aronson, and A. A. Goldenveizer, eds. *Kniga o Russkom Evreistve.* 2 vols. Jerusalem: Gesharim; Moscow: Mosty kultury, 2002.

Frumkin, Jacob, Gregor Aronson, and Alexis Goldenweizer, eds. *Russian Jewry (1860–1917).* New York: Thomas Yoseloff, 1966.

Gassenschmidt, Christoph. *Jewish Liberal Politics in Tsarist Russia, 1900–14.* Oxford: Oxford University Press, 1995.

Gay, Peter. *Freud, Jews, and Other Germans: Master and Victims in Modernist Culture.* New York: Oxford University Press, 1978.

Geiger, F., ed. *Komponisten unter Stalin: Aleksandr Veprik (1899–1958) und die Neue Jüdische Schule.* Dresden: Hannah-Arendt-Institut für Totalitarismusforschung e. V. an der Technischen Universität Dresden, 2000.

Geraci, Robert, and Michael Khodarkovsky, eds. *Of Religion and Empire: Missions, Conversion, and Tolerance in Tsarist Russia.* Ithaca: Cornell University Press, 2001.

Gerasimov, I., S. Glebov, A. Kaplunovskii, M. Mogilner, and A. Semenov, eds. *Novaia imperskaia istoriia postsovetskogo prostranstva.* Kazan: Tsentr issledovanii natsionalizma i imperii, 2004.

Gilman, Sander. *Jewish Self-Hatred: Anti-Semitism and the Hidden Language of the Jews.* Baltimore: Johns Hopkins University Press, 1986.

Ginzburg, S. L. *K. Iu. Davydov: Glava iz istorii russkoi muzykalnoi kultury i metodicheskoi mysli.* Leningrad: Muzgiz, 1936.

Gitelman, Zvi, and Yaacov Ro'i, eds. *Revolution, Repression, and Revival: The Soviet Jewish Experience.* Lanham: Rowman and Littlefield, 2007.

Gleason, Abbott, Peter Kenez, and Richard Stites. *Bolshevik Culture: Experiment and Order in the Russian Revolution.* Bloomington: Indiana University Press, 1985.

Glebov, Igor [Boris Asafiev]. *Anton Grigorevich Rubinshtein, 1829–1929.* Moscow: Gosudarstvennoe muzykalnoe izdatelstvo, 1929.

Glushchenko, Georgii. *N. D. Kashkin.* Moscow: Muzyka, 1974.

———. *Ocherki po istorii russkoi muzykalnoi kritiki kontsa XIX–nachala XX v.* Minsk: Vysheishaia shkola, 1983.

Goldshtein, Mikhail. *Petr Stoliarskii.* Jerusalem: M. Sominskii, 1989.

Gonen, Rivka, ed. *Ba-hazarah la-'ayarah: An-ski ve-hamishlahat ha-etnografit ha-yehudit, 1912–1914: Me-osfe ha-muz'eon ha-mamlakhti le-etnografyah be-Sankt Petersburg.* Jerusalem: Israel Museum, 1994.

Gottesman, Itzik. *Defining the Yiddish Nation: The Jewish Folklorists of Poland.* Detroit: Wayne State University Press, 2003.

Granovskii, Bernard, ed. *Evreiskaia muzyka: Izuchenie i prepodavanie.* Moscow: Tsentr nauchnykh rabotnikov i prepodavatelei iudaiki v vuzakh 'Sefer,' 1998.

Gries, Zeev. *The Book in the Jewish World, 1700–1900.* London: Littman Library of Jewish Civilization, 2007.

Guralnik, Leonid, ed. *Iz istorii evreiskoi muzyki v Rossii.* Vol. 1. St. Petersburg: Evreiskii obshchinnyi tsentr Sankt-Peterburga, 2001.

Haas, David. *Leningrad's Modernists: Studies in Composition and Musical Thought, 1917–1932.* New York: Peter Lang, 1998.

Halevy, Zvi. *Jewish University Students and Professionals in Tsarist and Soviet Russia.* Tel Aviv: Diaspora Research Institute, 1976.
Harris, Hyman. *Toldot ha-neginah ve-hamusikah be-Yisra'el.* New York: Bitsaron, 1950.
Harshav, Benjamin. *Language in Time of Revolution.* Stanford: Stanford University Press, 1993.
———. *The Polyphony of Jewish Culture.* Stanford: Stanford University Press, 2007.
Herts, Y. Sh., ed. *Doyres bundistn.* 2 vols. New York: Unser Tsayt, 1956.
Heskes, Irene. *Passport to Jewish Music.* New York: Greenwood Press, 1994.
Heskes, Irene, and Arthur Wolfson, eds. *The Historic Contribution of Russian Jewry to Jewish Music.* New York: National Jewish Music Council, 1967.
Hirsch, Francine. *Empire of Nations: Ethnographic Knowledge and the Making of the Soviet Union.* Ithaca: Cornell University Press, 2005.
Hirshberg, Jehoash. *Music in the Jewish Community of Palestine, 1880–1948: A Social History.* Cambridge: Cambridge University Press, 1995.
Hoffman, David L., and Yanni Kotsonis, eds. *Russian Modernity: Politics, Knowledge, Practices.* New York: New York University Press, 2000.
Holmgren, Beth. *Rewriting Capitalism: Literature and the Market in Late Tsarist Russia and the Kingdom of Poland.* Pittsburgh: University of Pittsburgh Press, 1998.
Holtzman, Avner, ed. *Mikhah Yosef Berdits'evski: Meḥkarim u-te'udot.* Jerusalem: Mosad Bialik, 2002.
Horowitz, Brian. *Jewish Philanthropy and Enlightenment in Late-Tsarist Russia.* Seattle: University of Washington Press, 2009.
Hosking, Geoffrey. *Russia: People and Empire, 1552–1917.* Cambridge: Cambridge University Press, 1997.
Hundert, Gershon, ed. *The YIVO Encyclopedia of Jews in Eastern Europe.* 2 vols. New Haven: Yale University Press, 2008.
Hutchinson, John. *The Dynamics of Cultural Nationalism: The Gaelic Revival and the Creation of the Irish Nation State.* London: Allen and Unwin, 1987.
Iankovskii, M. O. *Rimskii-Korsakov i revoliutsiia 1905 goda.* Moscow: Muzgiz, 1950.
Iljine, Nicolas, ed. *Odessa Memories.* Seattle: University of Washington Press, 2003.
Iukhneva, N. V., ed. *Etnografiia Peterburga–Leningrada: Materialy ezhegodnykh nauchnykh chtenii.* Vol. 2. Leningrad: Nauka, 1988.
Ivanov, V. V. *Russkie sezony teatra Gabima.* Moscow: "Artist. Rezhisser. Teatr," 1999.
Ivenina, T. A. *Kulturno-prosvetitelnye organizatsii i uchrezhdeniia obshchestvennoi i chastnoi initsiativy v dorevoliutsionnoi Rossii (1900–1916 gg.).* Moscow: Moskovskii pedagogicheskii universitet, 2003.
Johnson, James H. *Listening in Paris: A Cultural History.* Berkeley: University of California Press, 1995.
Kahan, Y. L. *Shtudyes vegn Yidisher folksshafung.* New York: YIVO Institute for Jewish Research, 1952.
Kann-Novikova, E. *Sobiratelnitsa russkikh narodnykh pesen.* Moscow: Muzyka, 1952.
Kantsedikas, A. S., and I. A. Sergeeva. *Albom evreiskoi khudozhestvennoi stariny Semena Anskogo.* Moscow: Mosty kultury, 2001.
Kaplan, Marion. *The Making of the Jewish Middle Class: Women, Family, and Identity in Imperial Germany.* New York: Columbia University Press, 1991.
Kappeler, Andreas. *The Russian Empire: A Multi-Ethnic History.* Harlow: Longman, 2001.
Kashkin, N. D. *Ocherk istorii russkoi muzyki.* Moscow: Jurgenson, 1908.
Kassow, Samuel, James West, and Edith Clowes, eds. *Between Tsar and Society: Educated*

Society and the Quest for Public Identity in Late Imperial Russia. Princeton: Princeton University Press, 1991.
Kats, B. A. *"Raskat improvizatsii...": Muzyka v tvorchestve, sudbe i v dome Borisa Pasternaka.* Leningrad: Sovetskii kompozitor, Leningradskoe otdelenie, 1991.
Katz, Jacob. *The Darker Side of Genius: Richard Wagner's Anti-Semitism.* Cambridge: Harvard University Press, 1986.
———. *From Prejudice to Destruction: Anti-Semitism, 1700–1933.* Cambridge: Harvard University Press, 1980.
Kavos-Dekhtereva, S. T. *A. G. Rubinshtein: Biograficheskii ocherk, 1829–1894 g. i muzykalnye lekstsii (kurs fortepiannoi literatury), 1888–1889.* St. Petersburg: M. M. Stasiulevich, 1895.
Kazovskii, Gillel. *Khudozhniki kultur-ligi.* Moscow: Mosty kultury; Jerusalem: Gesharim, 2003.
Kelner, V. E. *Ocherki po istorii russko-evreiskogo knizhnogo dela vo vtoroi polovine XIX–nachale XX v.* St. Petersburg: Rossiiskaia natsionalnaia biblioteka, 2003.
Keren, Zvi. *Contemporary Israeli Music.* Ramat Gan: Bar-Ilan University Press, 1980.
Khoprova, T. A., ed. *Anton Grigorevich Rubinshtein: Sbornik statei.* St. Petersburg: Kanon, 1997.
Kleinmann, Yvonne. *Neue Orte—neue Menschen: Jüdische Lebensformen in St. Petersburg und Moskau im 19. Jahrhundert.* Göttingen: Vandenhoeck und Ruprecht, 2006.
Klier, John D. *Imperial Russia's Jewish Question, 1855–1881.* Cambridge: Cambridge University Press, 1995.
Kohansky, Mendel. *The Hebrew Theatre: Its First Fifty Years.* New York: KTAV, 1969.
Kopytova, Galina Viktorovna. *Iasha Kheifets v Rossii.* St. Petersburg: Kompozitor, 2004.
———. *Obshchestvo evreiskoi narodnoi muzyki v Peterburge-Petrograde.* St. Petersburg: Ezro, 1997.
Kopytova, Galina V., and Aleksandr Frenkel, eds. *Iz istorii evreiskoi muzyki v Rossii.* Vol. 2. St. Petersburg: Evreiskii obshchinnyi tsentr Sankt-Peterburga–Tsentr evreiskoi muzyki and Rossiiskii institut istorii istkusstv, 2006.
Korabelnikova, L. *S. I. Taneev v Moskovskoi konservatorii.* Moscow: Muzyka, 1974.
Kostyrchenko, Gennadi. *Out of the Red Shadows: Anti-Semitism in Stalin's Russia.* Amherst: Prometheus Books, 1995.
———. *Tainaia politika Stalina: Vlast i antisemitizm.* Moscow: Mezhdunarodnye otnosheniia, 2001.
———. *V plenu u krasnogo faraona.* Moscow: Mezhdunarodye otnosheniia, 1994.
———, ed. *Gosudarstvennyi antisemitizm v SSSR ot nachala do kulminatsii, 1938–1953.* Moscow: Materik, 2005.
Krasney, Ariella. *Ha-badhan.* Ramat Gan: Bar-Ilan University Press, 1998.
Kremlev, Iu. G. *Leningradskaia gosudarstvennaia konservatoriia, 1862–1937.* Leningrad: Muzgiz, 1938.
Krivosheevoi, I. V., and S. A. Konaeva, eds. *Vs. Meierkhold i Mikh. Gnesin: Sobranie dokumentov.* Moscow: Gitis, 2008.
Kugelmass, Jack. *Key Texts in American Jewish Culture.* New Brunswick: Rutgers University Press, 2003.
Kuhn, Ernst, J. Nemtsov, and A. Wehrmeyer, eds. *"Samuel" Goldenberg und "Schmuyle": Jüdisches und Antisemitisches in der Russischen Musikkultur.* Berlin: E. Kuhn, 2003.
Kuhn, Ernst, A. Wehrmeyer, and G. Wolter, eds. *Dmitri Schostakowitsch und das jüdische musikalische Erbe.* Berlin: E. Kuhn, 2001.
Lerski, Tomasz. *Syrena Record: Poland's First Recording Company, 1904–1939.* New York: Editions "Karin," 2004.

Levik, S. Iu. *Chervert veka v opere.* Moscow: Izdatelstvo "Isskustvo," 1970.
Liapunova, A. S., and E. E. Lazovitskaia. *Milii Alekseievich Balakirev: Letopis zhizni i tvorchestva.* Moscow: Muzyka, 1967.
Lisovskii, N. M. *Anton Grigorevich Rubinshtein: Piatdesiat let ego muzykalnoi deiatelnosti, 1839–1889.* St. Petersburg, 1889.
Lissak, Moshe, ed. *Toldot ha-yishuv ha-yehudi be-erets-yisra'el mi-az ha-'aliyah ha-rishonah.* 3 vols. Jerusalem: Mossad Bialik, 1998–2007.
Litvak, Olga. *Conscription and the Search for Modern Russian Jewry.* Bloomington: Indian University Press, 2006.
Ljunggren, Magnus. *The Russian Mephisto: A Study of the Life and Work of Emilii Medtner.* Stockholm: Almqvist and Wiksell International, 1994.
Maes, Francis. *A History of Russian Music: From Kamarinskaya to Babi Yar.* Berkeley: University of California Press, 2002.
Martin, Terry. *The Affirmative Action Empire: Nations and Nationalism in the Soviet Union, 1923–1939.* Ithaca: Cornell University Press, 2001.
McReynolds, Louise. *Russia at Play: Leisure Activities at the End of the Tsarist Era.* Ithaca: Cornell University Press, 2003.
Mendelsohn, Ezra. *Painting a People: Maurycy Gottlieb and Jewish Art.* Hanover: University Press of New England, 2002.
Mendelsohn, Ezra, and Stefani Hoffman, eds. *The Revolution of 1905 and Russia's Jews.* Philadelphia: University of Pennsylvania Press, 2008.
Mendes-Flohr, Paul. *German Jews: A Dual Identity.* New Haven: Yale University Press, 1999.
Mikhailov, M. A. K. *Liadov: Ocherk zhizni i tvorchestva.* Leningrad: Muzyka, 1961.
Moddel, Philip. *Joseph Achron.* Tel Aviv: Israeli Music Publications, 1966.
Móricz, Klára. *Jewish Identities: Nationalism, Racism, and Utopianism in Twentieth-Century Music.* Berkeley: University of California Press, 2008.
Moss, Kenneth B. *Jewish Renaissance in the Russian Revolution.* Cambridge: Harvard University Press, 2009.
Mosse, George L. *German Jews beyond Judaism.* Bloomington: Indiana University Press, 1985.
Nagler, A. M. *Hebbel und die Musik.* Cologne: J. P. Bachem, 1928.
Nathans, Benjamin. *Beyond the Pale: The Jewish Encounter with Late Imperial Russia.* Berkeley: University of California Press, 2002.
Nelson, Amy. *Music for the Revolution: Musicians and Power in Early Soviet Russia.* University Park: Pennsylvania State University Press, 2004.
Nemtsov, Jascha, ed. *Jüdische Kuntsmusik im. 20. Jahrhundert: Quellenlage, Entstehungsgeschichte, Stilanalysen.* Wiesbaden: Harrassowitz, 2006.
———. *Die neue Jüdische Schule in der Musik.* Wiesbaden: Harrassowitz, 2004.
Nemtsov, Jascha, and Ernst Kuhn, eds. *Jüdische Musik in Sowjetrussland: Die "Jüdische Nationale Schule" der zwanziger Jahre.* Berlin: E. Kuhn, 2002.
Nisnevich, S. G. *V. A. Zolotarev.* Moscow: Muzyka, 1964.
Oja, Carol J. *Making Music Modern: New York in the 1920s.* New York: Oxford University Press, 2000.
Ottens, Rita, and Joel Rubin. *Klezmer-Musik.* Kassel: Bärenreiter; Munich: Deutscher Taschenbuch, 1999.
Parkhomovskii, M., ed. *Evrei v kulture russkogo zarubezhia: Stati, publikatsii, memuary i esse.* Vol. 2. Jerusalem: M. Parkhomovskii, 1992.
Penny, H. Glenn, and Matti Bunzl, eds. *Worldly Provincialism: German Anthropology in the Age of Empire.* Ann Arbor: University of Michigan Press, 2003.

Petrovskii-Shtern, Iokhanan. *Evrei v russkoi armii, 1827–1914.* Moscow: Mosty kultury, 2003.

Puzyrevskii, A. I., and L. A. Sakketti. *Ocherk piatidesiatletie deiatelnost Sankt-Peterburgskoi konservatorii.* St. Petersburg: Tip. Glazunova, 1912.

Raaben, Lev Nikolaevich. *Zhizn zamechatelnykh skripachei: Biograficheskie ocherki.* Leningrad: Muzyka, 1967.

Rakitin, Vasilii, and Andrei Sarabianov, eds. *Semyon An-sky: The Jewish Artistic Heritage: An Album.* Moscow: "RA," 1994.

Ravina, Menashe. *Yo'el Engel, ḥayyav ve-yetsirato.* Jerusalem: Maḥleket ha-Tarbut shel ha-Va'ad ha-Leumi li-Keneset Yisra'el be-Erets-Yisra'el, 1937.

———. *Yo'el 'Engel ve-hamusikah ha-yehudit.* Tel Aviv: Ha-Mosad le-Musikah, 1947.

Rehding, Alexander. *Hugo Riemann and the Birth of Modern Musical Thought.* Cambridge: Harvard University Press, 2003.

Ridenour, Robert C. *Nationalism, Modernism, and Personal Rivalry in Nineteenth-Century Russian Music.* Ann Arbor: UMI Research Press, 1981.

Rittikh, Margarita E., ed. *Elena Fabianovna Gnesina: Vospominaniia sovremennikov.* Moscow: Praktika, 2003.

Rogger, Hans. *Jewish Policies and Right-Wing Politics in Imperial Russia.* Berkeley: University of California Press, 1986.

Ro'i, Yaacov, ed. *Jews and Jewish Life in Russia and the Soviet Union.* Ilford, Essex, UK: Frank Cass, 1995.

Ro'i, Yaacov, and Avi Beker, eds. *Jewish Culture and Identity in the Soviet Union.* New York: New York University Press, 1991.

Rosenthal, Bernice Glatzer, ed. *Nietzsche in Russia.* Princeton: Princeton University Press, 1986.

Roshwald, Aviel, and Richard Stites, eds. *European Culture in the Great War.* Cambridge: Cambridge University Press, 1999.

Roskies, David G. *A Bridge of Longing: The Lost Art of Yiddish Storytelling.* Cambridge: Harvard University Press, 1995.

———, ed. *The Dybbuk and Other Writings by S. Ansky.* New York: Schocken Press, 1992.

Ruane, Christine. *Gender, Class, and the Professionalization of Russian City Teachers, 1860–1914.* Pittsburgh: University of Pittsburgh Press, 1994.

Rubenstein, Joshua, and Vladimir P. Naumov, eds. *Stalin's Secret Pogrom: The Postwar Inquisition of the Jewish Anti-Fascist Committee.* New Haven: Yale University Press, 2001.

Ryszhkova, V. P., ed. *Gnesinskii istoricheskii sbornik k 60-letiiu RAM im. Gnesinykh: Zapiski memoralnogo muzeia-kvartiry El. F. Gnesinoi.* Moscow: RAM im. Gnesinykh, 2004.

Safran, Gabriella. *Rewriting the Jew: Assimilation Narratives in the Russian Empire.* Stanford: Stanford University Press, 2000.

Safran, Gabriella, and Steven J. Zipperstein, eds. *The Worlds of S. An-sky: A Russian Jewish Intellectual at the Turn of the Century.* Stanford: Stanford University Press, 2006.

Sats, Ilia. *Ilia Sats.* Moscow–Petrograd: Gosudarstvennoe izdatelstvo, 1923.

Sats, N. I., ed. *Ilia Sats: Iz zapisnykh knizhek: Vospominaniia sovremennikov.* Moscow: Sovetskii kompozitor, 1968.

Schiller, David. *Bloch, Schoenberg and Bernstein: Assimilating Jewish Music.* Oxford: Oxford University Press, 2003.

Schröder-Nauenburg, Beate. *"Der Eintritt der Jüdischen in die Welt der Kuntsmusik": Die Anfänge der Neuen Jüdischen Schule: Werkanalytische Studien.* Wiesbaden: Harrassowitz, 2007.

Schwarz, Boris. *Music and Musical Life in Soviet Russia, 1917–1981.* Enlarged ed. Bloomington: Indiana University Press, 1983.

Seroussi, Edwin, and Motti Regev. *Popular Music and National Culture in Israel.* Berkeley: University of California Press, 2004.
Shneer, David. *Yiddish and the Creation of Soviet Jewish Culture, 1918–1930.* New York: Cambridge University Press, 2004.
Shternshis, Anya. *Soviet and Kosher: Jewish Popular Culture in the Soviet Union, 1923–1939.* Bloomington: Indiana University Press, 2006.
Sitsky, Larry. *Anton Rubinstein: An Annotated Catalog of Piano Works and Biography.* Westport: Greenwood, 1998.
Slezkine, Yuri. *The Jewish Century.* Princeton: Princeton University Press, 2004.
Slobin, Mark. *Tenement Songs: The Popular Music of the Jewish Immigrants.* Urbana-Champaign: University of Illinois Press, 1982.
Soltes, Avraham. *Off the Willows: The Rebirth of Modern Jewish Music.* New York: Bloch, 1970.
Soroker, Y. L. *Rossiiskie muzykanty, evrei: Bio-bibliograficheskii leksikon.* 2 vols. Jerusalem: Y. Soroker, 1992.
Sposato, Jeffrey S. *The Price of Assimilation: Felix Mendelssohn and the Nineteenth-Century Anti-Semitic Tradition.* Oxford: Oxford University Press, 2005.
Stanislawski, Michael. *Autobiographical Jews: Essays in Jewish Self-Fashioning.* Seattle: University of Washington Press, 2004.
———. *Tsar Nicholas I and the Jews: The Transformation of Jewish Society in Russia, 1825–1855.* Philadelphia: Jewish Publication Society of America, 1983.
———. *Zionism and the Fin de Siècle: Cosmopolitanism and Nationalism from Nordau to Jabotinsky.* Berkeley: University of California Press, 2001.
Stargardt-Wolff, Edith. *Wegbereiter grosser Musiker.* Berlin–Wiesbaden: Bote and G. Bock, 1954.
Stark, E. A. *Peterburgskaia opera i ee mastera, 1890–1910.* Leningrad: Izdatelstvo "Isskustvo," 1940.
Stein, Leon. *The Racial Thinking of Richard Wagner.* New York: Philosophical Library, 1950.
Stein, Sarah Abrevaya. *Making Jews Modern: The Yiddish and Ladino Press in the Russian and Ottoman Empires.* Bloomington: Indiana University Press, 2005.
Steinberg, Mark. *Moral Communities: The Culture of Class Relations in the Russian Printing Industry, 1867–1907.* Berkeley: University of California Press, 1992.
Steinberg, Michael P. *Judaism Musical and Unmusical.* Chicago: University of Chicago Press, 2008.
———. *Listening to Reason: Culture, Subjectivity, and Nineteenth-Century Music.* Princeton: Princeton University Press, 2004.
Stepanova, Svetlana R., ed. *Muzykalnaia zhizn Moskvy v pervye gody posle oktiabria.* Moscow: Sovetskii kompozitor, 1972.
Stevens, Lewis. *Composers of Classical Music of Jewish Descent.* London: Vallentine Mitchell, 2003.
100 [Sto] let leningradskoi konservatorii, 1862–1962: Istoricheskii ocherk. Leningrad: Gosudarstvennoe muzykalnoe izdatelstvo, 1962.
Stupel, A. M. *Russkaia mysl o muzyke, 1895–1917: Ocherk istorii russkoi muzykalnoi kritiki.* Leningrad: Muzyka, 1980.
Swift, E. Anthony. *Popular Theater and Society in Tsarist Russia.* Berkeley: University of California Press, 2002.
Taruskin, Richard. *Defining Russia Musically.* Princeton: Princeton University Press, 1997.
———. *Musorgsky: Eight Essays and an Epilogue.* Princeton: Princeton University Press, 1993.

———. *On Russian Music*. Berkeley: University of California Press, 2009.
———. *Opera and Drama in Russia as Preached and Practiced in the 1860s*. Rochester: University of Rochester Press, 1993.
———. *Stravinsky and the Russian Traditions: A Biography of the Works through "Mavra."* 2 vols. Oxford: Oxford University Press, 1996.
Täuschel, Annakatrin. *Anton Rubinstein als Opernkomponist*. Berlin: E. Kuhn, 2001.
Taylor, Philip S. *Anton Rubinstein: A Life in Music*. Bloomington: Indiana University Press, 2007.
Tewes, Henning, and Jonathan Wright, eds. *Liberalism, Anti-Semitism, and Democracy: Essays in Honour of Peter Pulzer*. Oxford: Oxford University Press, 2001.
Tigranov, Georgii Grigorevich, ed. *Sovetskaia simfoniia za 50 let*. Leningrad: Muzyka, 1967.
Tokarev, S. A. *Istoriia russkoi etnografii*. Moscow: Nauka, 1966.
Tomoff, Kiril. *Creative Union: The Professional Organization of Soviet Composers, 1939–1953*. Ithaca: Cornell University Press, 2006.
Tumanov, Aleksandr. *The Life and Artistry of Maria Olenina-d'Alheim*. Trans. Christopher Barnes. Edmonton: University of Alberta Press, 2000.
———. *Ona i muzyka, i slovo: Zhizn i tvorchestvo M. A. Oleninoi-d'Algeim*. Moscow: Muzyka, 1995.
Tumanova, A. S. *Obshchestvennye organizatsii i russkaia publika v nachale XX veka*. Moscow: Novyi khronograf, 2008.
Valter, V. G., S. M. Gorodetskii, and I. I. Vitol, eds. *An. K. Liadov*. Petrograd: Izd. popechitelnago sovieta dlia pooshchreniia russkikh kompozitorov i muzykantov, 1916.
Veidlinger, Jeffrey. *Jewish Public Culture in the Late Russian Empire*. Bloomington: Indiana University Press, 2009.
———. *The Moscow State Yiddish Theater: Jewish Culture on the Soviet Stage*. Bloomington: Indiana University Press, 2000.
Vernadsky National Library of Ukraine. *The Historic Collection of Jewish Music, 1912–1947*, vol. 1: *Materials of the J. Engel Ethnographic Expedition, 1912*. Kiev: Vernadsky National Library of Ukraine, 2001.
———. *The Historical Collection of Jewish Musical Folklore 1912–1947*, vol. 2: *Materials from the Zinoviy Kiselgof Collection: Religious Songs*. Kiev: Vernadsky National Library of Ukraine, 2004.
———. *The Historical Collection of Jewish Musical Folklore 1912–1947*, vol. 3: *Materials from the Zinoviy Kiselgof Collection: Jewish Folk Music and Theater*. Kiev: Vernadsky National Library of Ukraine, 2004.
Vigoda, Samuel. *Legendary Voices*. New York: M. P. Press, 1981.
Villiers, Douglas, ed. *Next Year in Jerusalem: Portraits of the Jew in the Twentieth Century*. New York: Viking Press, 1976.
Villikh-Lederbogen, Khaide, V. B. Kataeva, and R.-D. Kluge, eds. *Rikhard Vagner v Rossii: Izbrannye trudy uchastnikov russko-nemetskoi konferentsii v Marte 1997 goda v Moskve*. Tübingen: Slavisches Seminar der Universität, 2001.
Volkov, Shulamit, ed. *Deutsche Juden und die Moderne*. Munich: Oldenbourg, 1994.
Volkov-Lannit, L. F. *Iskusstvo zapechatlennogo zvuka*. Moscow: Iskusstvo, 1964.
Wallace, Robert K. *A Century of Music-Making: The Lives of Josef and Rosina Lhevinne*. Bloomington: Indiana University Press, 1976.
Weber, William. *Music and the Middle Class: The Social Structure of Concert Life in London, Paris and Vienna between 1830 and 1848*. 2nd ed. Aldershot: Ashgate, 2004.
———, ed. *The Musician as Entrepreneur, 1700–1914: Managers, Charlatans, and Idealists*. Bloomington: Indiana University Press, 2004.

Weber, William, and David Large, eds. *Wagnerism in European Culture and Politics*. Ithaca: Cornell University Press, 1984.

Weeks, Theodore. *Nation and State in Late Imperial Russia: Nationalism and Russification on the Western Frontier, 1863–1914*. DeKalb: Northern Illinois University, 1996.

Weiner, Marc A. *Richard Wagner and the Anti-Semitic Imagination*. Lincoln: University of Nebraska Press, 1995.

Weisser, Albert. *The Modern Renaissance of Jewish Music*. New York: Bloch, 1954.

Wertheimer, Jack, ed. *The Uses of Tradition: Jewish Continuity in the Modern Era*. New York: Jewish Theological Seminary of America, 1992.

White, Harry, and Michael Murphy, eds. *Musical Constructions of Nationalism: Essays on the History and Ideology of European Musical Culture, 1800–1945*. Cork: Cork University Press, 2001.

Wirtschafter, Elise Kimerling. *Social Identity in Imperial Russia*. DeKalb: Northern Illinois University, 1997.

Yofeh, A. B., ed. *'Esrim ha-shanim ha-rishonot: Sifrut ve-omanut bi-Tel Aviv ha-katanah, 1909–1929*. Tel Aviv: Ha-Kibbutz Ha-Meuḥad, 1979.

Zalkind, N. G. *Moskovskaia shkola antropologov v razvitii otechestvennoi nauki o cheloveke*. Moscow: Nauka, 1974.

Zank, Michael, ed. *New Perspectives on Martin Buber*. Tübingen: Mohr Siebeck, 2006.

Zaporozhets, N. A. K. *Liadov: Zhizn i tvorchestvo*. Moscow: Gosudarstvennoe muzykalnoe izdatelstvo, 1954.

Zilberman, Iurii, and Iuliia Smilianskaia. *Kievskaia simfoniia Vladimira Gorovitsa*. Kiev: Zadruga, 2002.

Zipperstein, Steven. *Elusive Prophet: Ahad Ha'am and the Origins of Zionism*. Berkeley: University of California Press, 1999.

———. *Imagining Russian Jewry: Memory, History, Identity*. Seattle: University of Washington Press, 1999.

———. *The Jews of Odessa: A Cultural History, 1794–1881*. Stanford: Stanford University Press, 1986.

Principal Periodicals Consulted

Baian
Evreiskaia nedelia
Evreiskaia starina
Evreiskaia zhizn
Evreiskii mir
Der fraynd
Grammofonnaia zhizn
Grammofonnyi mir
Grazhdanin
Jewish Forum
Jewish Music Forum
Ha-melits
Menorah Journal
Der moment
Moskovskie vedomosti
Nedelnaia khronika voskhoda

Novoe vremia
Novyi voskhod
Nuvellist
Perezhitoe
Razsvet
Russkaia muzykalnaia gazeta
Russkaia starina
Russkii evrei
Russkoe slovo
Ha-shiloah
Di shul un khazonim-velt
Te'atron ve-omanut
Ha-tsefirah
Voskhod
Der yid

Doctoral Dissertations and Other Unpublished Sources

Avrutin, Eugene. "A Legible People: Identification Politics and Jewish Accommodation in Tsarist Russia." PhD diss., University of Michigan, 2004.
Davidson, Charles. "Lazare Saminsky (1882–): A Preliminary Study of the Man and His Works." MSM thesis, Jewish Theological Seminary of America, 1957.
Flomenboim, Rita. "Ha-eskolah ha-le'umit shel ha-musikah ha-yehudit-omanutit: Yo'el Engel (1868–1927) ve-Mikha'il Gnesin (1883–1957)." PhD diss., Bar-Ilan University, 1996.
Kiel, Mark. "A Twice Lost Legacy: Ideology, Culture and the Pursuit of Jewish Folklore in Russia until Stalinization (1930–1931)." PhD diss., Jewish Theological Seminary of America, 1991.
Knight, Nathaniel. "Constructing the Science of Nationality: Ethnography in Mid-Nineteenth Century Russia." PhD diss., Columbia University, 1995.
Kosloski, Gary. "The Teaching and Influence of Leopold Auer." PhD diss., Indiana University School of Music, 1977.
Kruk, Michael. "Voices of Odessa: David Nowakowsky, Pinchas Minkowsky, Jacob Bachmann, Aron Dunajewsky." MSM thesis, Hebrew Union College–Jewish Institute of Religion, 1993.
Powell, Jonathan. "After Scriabin: Six Composers and the Development of Russian Music." DPhil diss., King's College, Cambridge University, 1999.
Quint, Alyssa. "The Botched Kiss: Abraham Goldfaden and the Literary Origins of the Yiddish Theatre." PhD diss., Harvard University, 2002.
Rabinovitch, Simon. "Alternative to Zion: The Jewish Autonomist Movement in Late Imperial and Revolutionary Russia." PhD diss., Brandeis University, 2007.
Saminsky, Lazare. "Third Leonardo: Illusions of a Warrior of Civilization." Unpublished manuscript.
Sargeant, Lynn. "Middle Class Culture: Music and Identity in Late Imperial Russia." PhD diss., Indiana University, 2001.
Sholokhova, L. V. "Stanovlenie i razvitie evreiskoi muzykalnoi folkloristiki v Rossiiskoi imperii v nachale XX st." Kandidat diss., Ukrainian National Musical Academy, 2000.
Weisser, Albert. "Jewish Music in Twentieth-Century United States: Four Representative Figures." DSM thesis, Jewish Theological Seminary of America, 1980.

Index

Achron, Joseph, 1, 142, 143 fig.11, 144, 200; "Evreiskaia melodiia" (Hebrew Melody) by, 144, 145 fig. 12, 146, 146–47 ex. 7, 148, 150 fig. 13
Aeolian mode, 77, 164, 180, 180 ex. 9, 181
Aḥad Ha'am. *See* Gintsburg, Asher
Aisberg, Ilia, 104, 122
Aleichem, Sholem, 9, 11, 13–14, 75–76, 77–79; "Tevye" stories, 13–14
Alexander II (tsar), 28, 44
Alexander III (tsar), 44, 51, 52–53
Alkan, Charles-Valentin, 9
All-Russian Jewish Congress, 189
Alman, Samuel, 156–57; *King Aḥaz* (opera), 156, 157
altered Dorian mode ("mi shebeyrakh"), 144
altered Phrygian mode ("pan-Oriental"), 179–80, 180 ex. 9, 181
Ansky, S.: ethnographic expedition and, 12, 82, 83–85, 87, 88 fig. 3, 89, 91–92, 118, 180, 201; and Jewish cultural activities, 64, 120, 123, 128, 158; as Jewish cultural populist, 182–83
Ansky, S., writings: *The Dybbuk* (play), 93, 193; *Jewish Ethnographic Program*, 83
"anticosmopolitanism" campaign, Soviet-era, 207, 215, 244n4
antisemitism: in Europe, 3, 8, 24, 31, 102, 104, 114, 117, 142, 168, 183, 185; Gnesin's essay on, 210–11; Marxist-Leninist, 201–2; and philosemitism, 3, 12, 98, 104–105, 106, 108, 114, 116, 117, 210–12, 221n2, 226n49; Rubinstein's response to, 25–26, 31, 42, 43, 49–54, 95; in Russia, 1, 3, 11, 12, 30–31, 32, 37, 44, 45–53, 67, 80, 84, 92, 95, 96, 98, 100, 102, 104, 106, 107–8, 109, 116, 117, 118, 127–28, 152, 154, 155, 185, 201, 207, 210, 212, 214, 226n47, 234n35; in Soviet Union, 216, 217, 244n4; in the U.S., 140. *See also* Wagner, Richard

Antokolskii, Mark, 73
Arensky, Anton, 49
art music: commercial recordings and, 153–54, 155, 156; concert hall decorum and, 128; Eastern *vs.* Western civilizations and, 35–36, 167–68; European, 3, 8, 20–21, 167–68; folk songs and, 35, 69–70, 118, 123, 125, 130, 148, 171–72, 186; Jewish aesthetic in, 214, 219; Jewish "national school" of, 173–74; Jewish national spirit and, 11, 12, 114–15, 122, 127, 131–32, 139, 171–72; Jewish liturgical melodies in, 178–80, 181, 185; "nationality" in, 106–7, 148; and popular culture, 135, 172; sheet music publication and, 138–39, 144, 145 fig. 12, 146–47 ex. 7, 148–49, 150 fig. 13; in *Songbook* anthology, 162, 165–69, 170. *See also* Society for Jewish Folk Music
arts. *See* graphic arts, Jewish; music; opera; theater, Yiddish
Ashkenazim: musical traditions of, 7–8, 9, 11, 12, 37, 66, 68, 94, 127, 139, 180, 182; traditional culture of, 4, 5, 8, 57, 163. *See also* Hasidic Jews; Jews, German; Jews, Russian; Yiddish language
Auer, Leopold: as convert to Christianity, 118; performances by, 148; and Russian classical music, 200; violin students of, 1, 94, 98, 103, 144, 200
augmented second interval: as Jewish musical marker, 37, 68, 71, 168, 181; as "Oriental" musical idiom, 36, 37, 68, 71, 168, 179, 181
Avshalomov, Aaron, 157; in China, 237–38n35; *Esther* (overture), 157; *The Great Wall* (opera), 237–38n35
"Awake and Rise Up, Working People" (song), 194
Azeff, Evno, 184

Babel, Isaac, 10, 94, 95, 133; "Awakening," 94–95
Babus, Elizaveta (Leah), 121
Bachman, Jacob, 33–34
badkhn (wedding jester), 8, 56, 130, 161
Badkhn, Peysakh-Eliyahu, 134, 135–36, 137; *Kanaf renanim oder zeks folkslider* (Songbird, or Six Folk Songs), 134
Balakirev, Mily, 36, 47, 52, 94, 104, 106, 119, 212
Balfour Declaration, 192. *See also* Palestine; Zionism
Balmont, Konstantin, 204
Beethoven, Ludwig van, 15, 22, 107, 166–67, 168
Bellison, Simeon, 118, 191, 241n35
Benenson, Grigorii, 121, 123
Benenson, Sophie, 121
Berdichev (Ukraine), 18–19, 22, 24, 33, 45
Beregovskii, Moisei Ia., 201, 202
Beria, Lavrenty, 216
Berlin, Jewish émigrés in, 193, 195
Berlin, Moisei, 66–67
Berlioz, Hector, 107
Bessel (music publishing house), 138
Bialik, Ḥaim Naḥman, 64, 118, 201
biblical chant (*trop*), 162, 169, 179, 180, 181
Bloch, Ernest, 199
Blok, Alexander, 204
Bnei Moshe (Zionist organization), 60
Bolshevik Revolution of 1917: as musical theme, 204; socio-cultural impact of, 175, 188–93, 194–95, 201–2
Bolshevism, 111
Borodin, Alexander, 47
bourgeoisie, Russian Jewish: cultural heritage and, 126–28, 137, 213; as musical amateurs, 9, 19, 46; musical ambitions and, 94–95, 104; and public culture, 81, 121, 123; salons and, 20
Bramson, Leon, 61, 123, 192
Bruch, Max, 213; *Kol Nidre* by, 213
Buber, Martin, 64, 158
Bülow, Hans von, 24
Bundists, 108, 109, 113, 120, 159–60, 163, 183, 187, 188, 190, 191
Byron, lord (George Gordon), 36, 37; *Hebrew Melodies*, 36, 37

Carnegie Hall, 148, 200
Catherine the Great, 7
Caucasus: Jewish communities in, 178; Saminsky's vision of, 185, 186

censorship, of Yiddish-language publications, 137–38
Chagall, Marc, 14, 195, 196 fig. 15
Chaliapin, Fyodor, 80, 191
Chamberlain, Houston Stewart, 116
Chekuanova, Vera Aleksandrovna, 34–35
Chernomordikov, David A., 111, 120, 204; *Pervyi sbornik revoliutsionnykh pesen* (First Collection of Revolutionary Songs), 111
Chlenov, Yeḥiel, 61
Chopin, Frédéric, 20
Communism, Soviet, 6, 217. *See also* Soviet Union
composers, Russian Jewish: in China, 237–38n35; as émigrés to the United States, 199–200; "national music" and, 7, 106–7, 117, 167–68, 174; in Palestine, 193, 195, 197–98; preferred terms for, 117–18, 167; in Society for Jewish Folk Music, 121–22, 139, 177; in Soviet Union, 12, 201–9, 215–16, 217–19. *See also* names of individuals
conservatories, Russian: anonymous article attacking, 47–48; as avenues of Jewish opportunity, 10, 18, 43–45, 95, 100; classical music traditions in, 203–4, 205; prominent graduates of, 49, 94–95; Rubinstein's defense of, 48–52; Soviet-era, 203; as state institutions, 51–52; symbolic importance of, 127, 132. *See also* Moscow Conservatory; St Petersburg Conservatory
Constitutional Democratic Party (Kadets), 80, 113
conversion, of Jews to Christianity: in Germany, 3, 9, 20, 22, 102, 104, 115; in Russia, 2, 10, 17, 18–19, 24, 26, 28, 31, 43, 98, 100, 118, 138, 167, 168; in medieval Spain, 41
Copland, Aaron, 199
copyright law, U.S., 140
cultural nationalism, Jewish, 7, 11–13, 39, 41, 55, 56–57, 58, 59, 60, 61, 71, 73, 81, 82–83, 93, 95–96, 114, 117, 133, 158, 186–87, 188, 189, 204, 213; impact of modernist ideologies on, 175–76, 177–88, 208–9. *See also* Diaspora nationalism; nationalism, folk-oriented; nationalism, Jewish; Society for Jewish Folk Music
cultural synthesis, Russian-Jewish, 132–33, 199, 212–13

Daniel Deronda (Eliot), 10
Dargomyzhsky, Alexander, 244n4
Davydov, Alexander M., 120, 154–55
Davydov, Karl, 43, 44

INDEX   265

Diaspora nationalism, 108, 113, 156–57, 183, 184, 187
Dobroven, Issay, 174
Dorian mode, 77
Drachevskii, Daniil V., 119
Dubnow, Simon, 56–57, 64, 82, 83, 85, 108, 109, 183; "On the Study of the History of the Russian Jews and the Creation of a Russian-Jewish Historical Society," 56
Dzimitrovsky, Abraham I., 191

Education, tsarist Ministry of, 28, 45, 97
Efron, Ilia, 123
Elena Pavlovna (grand duchess), 23, 27, 28, 31, 33
Eliot, George: *Daniel Deronda*, 10
Elman, Mischa, 1, 2, 94, 140, 148, 200
emancipation, Jewish: cultural nationalism and, 187; and modern study of Jewish music, 65–67; music as means of, 17–18, 32–33, 55, 67, 95, 211; political-legal strategies for, 98, 100, 113; political resistance to, 81; Russian Revolution of 1905 and, 108–9; Russian Revolution of 1917 and, 4, 188. *See also* liberalism
emigration, of Russian Jewish musicians, 172, 174–75, 176, 192–93, 195, 197–200, 208, 233n25, 237–38n35, 241n35
Engel, Ada, 79
Engel, Joel: career paths of, 3, 11–12, 57–58, 62–63, 72, 96; as emigrant to Palestine, 193, 195, 197–98; folk songs arranged by, 81–82, 125, 130, 138, 139, 191, 197; "Ha-tikva" and, 142; hybrid cultural identity of, 58–59, 92–93, 127; at Malakhovka Colony, 195, 196 fig. 15; as musical ethnographer, 11, 68, 71–72, 82–85, 86 fig.2, 87, 88 fig.3, 89, 90 fig. 4, 91–92, 107, 161, 162, 180, 197, 201, 212; as musical populist, 56, 175, 177–82, 183–84, 186, 187, 194, 197; music composed by, 93, 138, 197; in polemic with Saminsky, 175, 177–82, 183–86, 197, 198, 208, 240n15; in Revolution of 1905, 79–80; Revolutions of 1917 and, 188, 193–95; Rimsky-Korsakov and, 106; and Russian-Jewish cultural synthesis, 212–13, 215–16; and Society for Jewish Folk Music, 123, 125, 177, 188; on Society for Russian Folk Music, 213; Stasov and, 73–75; Warshavsky's songs and, 75–79; as young musician, 59–62
Engel, Joel, compositions: *Dybbuk Suite*, 193, 194 ex. 10; *Esther* (operetta), 61
Engel, Joel, songs arranged by: *Evreiskie narodnye pesni* (Jewish Folk Songs), 81–82, 138; "A Ḥabadisher nigun" (A Ḥabad Melody), 125; "Shloyf, mayn kind" (Sleep, My Child), 125, 153; "Vi er zingt" (How He Sings), 71–72, 72 ex. 5
Engel, Joel, writings: "Jewish Domestic Folk Song," 181
Engel, Vera, 79
Enlightenment, Jewish. *See* Haskalah
"ethnographic concerts," 67–72, 123
ethnography, in Russia, 12, 56, 63, 65, 84, 201, 230n19. *See also* Jewish Historical-Ethnographic Expedition; musical ethnography
European culture, Jews and, 3, 142, 159, 168, 174, 183, 187. *See also* modernism, European
evrei (positive term for Jew), 37, 67, 184, 226n49. *See also* Hebrews, ancient
evrei-muzykanty (Jew-musicians), as negative term, 117–18
Evreiskaia entsyklopediia (Jewish Encyclopedia), 111
Evreiskaia narodnaia gruppa, 108
evreiskie kompozitory (Jewish composers), as professional designation, 117–18
Evreiskoe obshchestvo dlia pomoshchii khudozhnikov (Jewish Society for the Support of Artists), 237n18

Fayfer, Shayke, 98
February Revolution of 1917. *See* Bolshevik Revolution of 1917
Feramors (Rubinstein), 37–38
Fiddler on the Roof (musical and film), 13–14
Findeizen, Nikolai, 226n49
folklore, Jewish: Ansky's views on, 83, 84
folk music, Jewish. *See* folk songs; klezmer; *nigunim*
folk-oriented nationalism. *See* nationalism, folk-oriented
folk songs, Jewish: Engel and, 61, 69–70; "frozen," 12–13, 171–72; IOLEAE and, 63; Jewish "national spirit" and, 84; musical national character and, 107, 114, 230n19; Olenina-D'Alheim and, 115–16; published collections of, 81–82, 125, 130, 138, 139, 158–59, 161–70, 176, 181, 182, 191; in Yiddish, 56–57, 64–65, 66, 67, 68, 69, 125, 130, 138. *See also* Jewish Historical-Ethnographic Expedition; Society for Jewish Folk Music
folk songs, Russian, 35, 63, 71–72, 74, 76, 85, 153, 155, 181, 230n19

folk songs, Ukrainian: ethnographic study of, 230n19; in Jewish repertoire, 48; recordings of, 85, 153, 155; as similar to Jewish music, 77, 142, 178, 181, 182
Folks-Partey, 108, 183, 190
Free Artist status (*svobodnyi kudoshnik*), for musicians, 18, 27–28, 29, 31–32, 79–80, 95
Frug, Shimon, 123, 128
Funeral Ode in Memory of Lenin (Krein), 204

Gablits, Karl I., 31
Gabrilowitsch, Ossip, 94, 95
Gay, Peter, 6
"geistliche Oper" (spiritual opera), 41–43
Georgii Aleksandrovich (grand duke), 144
German Jews. *See* Jews, German
Gershuni, Grigorii, 184
Gershwin, George, 199
Gertsenshtein, Mikhail, 80
Gilels, Emil, 200
Gintsburg, Asher (Ahad Ḥa'am), 60, 157–58, 183
Gintsburg, David (baron), 108
Gintsburg, Evzel (baron), 33
Gintsburg, Horace (baron), 106, 113, 123
Gintsburg, Shaul: at Ethnographic Expedition conference, 83; *Evreiskie narodnye pesni v Rossii* (Jewish Folk Songs in Russia), 64, 81, 83, 84, 159; at OPE, 33; on St. Petersburg Jewish acculturation, 126–27; *Voskhod* by, 138; and Yiddish folk song project, 64–65, 67, 73, 76, 77, 81, 84, 138, 159, 162
Gintsburg, Vladimir, 83
Glazunov, Alexander, 100, 101 fig. 6, 102–4, 105 fig. 7, 203, 212; *Tsar Iudeiskii*, 103
Glinka, Mikhail, 35, 36, 106, 107, 119, 133, 167, 170; "Evreiskaia pesnia" (Hebrew Melody), 170; "Persian Chorus," 167; *Ruslan and Lyudmila*, 167
Gnesin, Bella, 98
Gnesin, Fabian, 98, 100, 203, 207
Gnesin, Grigorii, 205
Gnesin, Mikhail F.: "Antisemitism and Music" essay by, 210–11; family background of, 98, 100; on Jewish musical harmony, 142; Palestine and, 193, 197; portrait of, 99 fig. 5; Society for Jewish Folk Music and, 110, 114, 117, 161; Soviet-era career of, 201, 202–8, 215; at St. Petersburg Conservatory, 100, 101 fig. 6, 102–4, 105 fig. 7, 106, 108
Gnesin, Mikhail, compositions: Piano Trio (op. 63), "In Memory of Our Murdered Children," 205–7, 206 ex. 11
Gnesin Musical Institute, 100, 203, 204, 207
Goldfaden, Avrom, 130; "Feryomert, ferlogt" (In Grief, In Despair), 139; "Shtey oyf, mayn folk" (Arise, My People), 139
Golem legend, 25
Gordon, Judah Leyb, 73
graphic arts, Jewish: in music publishing, 150 fig. 13, 237n18; for program covers, 124 fig. 9, 128, 129 fig. 10
Grinberg, Zerach, 191, 192
Guzikov, Yeḥiel Mikhl, 9

Ha'am, Aḥad. *See* Gintsburg, Asher
Habimah Theater (Moscow), 193, 204–5
Halévy, Jacques Fromental, 9, 119
Halkin, Shmuel, 217
Hall of the Nobility, Jewish concert at, 126, 127–28
Harshav, Benjamin, 5, 6
Hasidic Jews, 87, 134, 137; music of, 7–8, 37, 57, 66, 69 ex. 4, 71, 113, 195
Haskalah (Jewish Enlightenment), 11, 60, 65–66, 98, 136, 137, 168
Ha-tikvah (musical group), 108, 110
Hebbel, Friedrich, 25
Hebrew language: cultural Zionism and, 183, 187, 195, 197; opera in, 203; songs in, 130, 153, 162–63, 166, 167, 191, 197; theater productions in, 193, 204–5
Hebrew Melodies (Byron), 36, 37
Hebrews, ancient (*evrei*), 36–37, 67, 183, 184
Heifitz, Jascha, 2, 94, 95, 98, 148, 174, 200
Herder, Johann Gottfried, 64
Hofshteyn, Dovid, 195
Holocaust, 4, 117, 207, 216
Horowitz, Vladimir, 2

Idelsohn, Avraham Tsvi, 141, 183
Idelson, Abram D., 60–61, 110
Ilish, Robert F., 39–41
Imber, Naftali Herts, 140
Imperatorskoe obshchestvo liubitelei estestvoznaniia, antropologii i etnografii (Imperial Society of Lovers of Natural History, Anthropology, and Ethnography) (IOLEAE), 63, 67, 70–71
Imperial Academy of Arts, 28, 29, 51
Imperial Court, Ministry of, 31, 45, 97
Imperial Russian Music Society (IRMO): as conservatories' parent body, 44, 45, 50, 51,

52, 59, 96–97, 121, 156; founding of, 15; and Jewish art music concert, 115
Imperial Theater: Jews and, 48, 120, 154; opera at, 117, 128, 154; Rubinstein and, 22–23, 27, 28, 51
Imperial Theater School, 47
"indigenization" (*korenizatsiia*) policy, toward Soviet national minorities, 201
Internal Affairs, Ministry of (MVD), 43, 97, 103, 154
"Internationale" (song), 111, 194
Internationale Musikgesellschaft, 62
IOLEAE. See *Imperatorskoe obshchestvo liubitelei estestvoznaniia, antropologii i etnografii* (Imperial Society of Lovers of Natural History, Anthropology, and Ethnography) (IOLEAE)
Iollos, Grigorii, 80
IRMO (Imperial Russian Music Society). See Imperial Russian Music Society (IRMO)
Israel, ancient: Russian identification with, 36–37; music of, 183, 184
Israel, modern: 6, 197, 198, 208, 228n5. See also Palestine; Tel Aviv; Zionism
Isserlin, Wolf, 154, 155–56
Itelson, Grigorii, 25–26
Iunost Avraama (Gnesin), 203
Ivanov, Mikhail M., 116
Ivanov, Viacheslav, 204

Jabotinsky, Vladimir, 165
Jewish cultural nationalism. See cultural nationalism, Jewish; national culture, Jewish
Jewish culture, modern: changing nature of, 178; complex influences within, 56–59, 132, 135–36, 183–84
Jewish Historical-Ethnographic Expedition, 12, 82, 83–85, 86 fig.2, 87, 88 fig. 3, 89, 90 fig. 4, 91–92, 118, 180
Jewish Historical-Ethnographic Society, 82, 83, 109, 120
Jewish Literary Society, 152, 158, 171
Jewishness: in "Babi Yar" symphony, 217; difficulty of defining, 211; as Russian identity, 217
"Jewish scale," in music, 68. See also augmented second interval
Jewish Society for the Support of Artists (*Evreiskoe obshchestvo dlia pomoshchii khudozhnikov*), 237n18
Jews, Central Asian, 178, 180
Jews, German: and cultural modernism, 6;

fluid cultural identity of, 3–4, 212; music and, 3, 8–9, 12, 121; prejudices against, 8, 116. See also names of individuals; *Wissenschaft des Judentums*
Jews, medieval Spanish, 41
Jews, Russian: as arts patrons, 33, 123; complex cultural identity of, 2, 4–5, 6–7, 11, 12, 13, 14, 15, 17, 23–26, 33, 37, 41, 53, 55, 58–59, 93, 95, 96, 98, 100, 110, 111, 113, 126–27, 132–33, 171–72, 184, 187, 199, 211, 212–13, 218, 219; contradictory images of, 184, 210; cultural history sources on, 56–57; emancipation and, 4, 17–18, 32–33, 55, 65, 66, 67, 81, 95, 96, 98, 100, 108–9, 113, 188; ethnographic research on, 56–57; European modernism and, 175, 185–86, 192–93, 199, 202, 203, 204; folk songs of, 56–57, 64, 66, 67, 68, 69, 74; literature and, 6–7, 171; "national music" and, 114, 117, 126, 167; pogroms against, 1, 41; as political activists, 79–80, 96, 108–9, 184; resistance to "assimilation" of, 83, 84, 111, 123; in Russian music conservatories, 1, 2, 10, 11, 30, 32, 33, 43–50, 94–95, 211–12; Russian terms for, 26, 37, 67, 80, 94; socio-legal status of, 1, 17, 21–22, 28, 32; Soviet repression of, 215, 216. See also Ashkenazim; bourgeoisie, Russian Jewish; conversion, of Jews to Christianity; European culture, Jews and; *evrei*; Hasidic Jews; Haskalah; names of individuals; *zhid*
Jibneh Press, 203
Joachim, Joseph, 20
Judaism, Science of. See *Wissenschaft des Judentums*
Jurgenson (music publishing house), 138

"Kaddish of Rebbe Levi-Yitzhok of Berdichev," 91
Kaplan, I.: "Numo Feraḥ" (Sleep, Flower), arrangement by, 153
Kashkin, Nikolai, 62, 63, 80
Khachaturian, Aram, 207
Kharkov, University of, Jewish students at, 59–60
khazn (cantor): in concert, 34, 122; conservatory training and, 33, 104, 110, 120, 183; cultural role of, 8; ethnographic research and, 87, 123, 183; musical talent and, 67; opera and, 9, 34, 156–57, 179; recorded music and, 155; and study of Jewish music, 66

Kheifits, Antonina K., 62
Khrennikov, Tikhon, 207
Kiev, University of, Jewish students at, 59–60
Kinor tsion (musical group), 108, 110
Kirche der Kunst (sacred musical theater), 42
Kiselgof, Zisman, 91, 159–60, 160 fig. 14, 161–63, 165–70, 179, 180, 192, 201, 205
Kissin, Evgeny, 2
Klausner, Joseph, 157–58
klezmer (instrumental Ashkenazi folk music), 7, 8; art music and, 69, 115, 138, 216; cultural roles of, 9, 57; musical ethnographers and, 61, 69, 91, 115, 130, 161; Saminsky and, 178, 179; *Wissenschaft* view of, 66–67
klezmer musicians (Ashkenazi folk musicians), 8, 9, 201; as intuitive musicians, 9, 66–67; Koussevitzky and, 61; musical ethnographers and, 115, 161; popular images of, 13–14, 218
Knorozovskii, Isai, 120, 151–52
Kogan, Leonid, 200
Kol Nidre (Bruch), 213
Kol Nidre prayer, 40–41
Koussevitsky, Serge, 2, 61, 118, 152
Krehbiel, Henry, 85
Krein, Alexander A., 173, 174, 177, 180, 194, 201, 203, 204–5
Krein, David, 118
Kreinin, Miron, 123
Kultur-Lige (League for Culture), 191
Kuprin, Alexander, 10
Kvartin, Zavel, 155
Kvitko, Leyb, 217, 218; "Dos fidele" (*Skripka* / The Little Violin), 218

League of Composers, 199
Leningrad Conservatory, renaming of, 215
Lermontov, Mikhail, 36, 185; *Hadji Abrek*, 23
Leskov, Nikolai, 230n19
Levenshteyn, Ḥayyah, 19
Levontin, Yeḥiel Yosef, 61; *Shim'on Etsyoni*, 61
Lewandowski, Louis, 130
Lhevinne, Isadore, 148
Liadov, Anatoly, 49, 100, 102–3, 212
Liberalism: ethnographic concerts and, 71; in Europe, 22; Glazunof and, 103–4; Rubinstein and, 46, 49, 51–52, 53, 55; Russian Jews and, 6, 67, 79–80, 96, 108–9, 113, 159, 188, 190; Stasov and, 73. *See also* emancipation, Jewish
Lifshits, A. D., "Numo Feraḥ" (Sleep, Flower) (poem), 153
Lineva, Evgeniia, 85

Lipaev, Ivan, 65, 71
Liszt, Franz, 10, 15, 20, 22, 23
literature, Jewish, 5, 7, 114, 157–58, 171
Loew, Judah (rabbi of Prague), 25
Lourié, Arthur, 189
Lukonin, Mikhail, 217; "Sleep, People" (poem), 218, 244n4
Lunts, Mikhail, 61, 79
Lvov, Peysakh (Pavel) R., 104, 120, 126, 162, 163, 164

Maggid, David, 83, 123
Maharal, The. *See* Loew, Judah (rabbi of Prague)
Mahler, Gustav, 116
Maimon, Moses, 149
Malakhovka Colony, 195, 196 fig. 15
Mandel, Benjamin, 174
Marek, Peysakh: and ethnographic expedition plans, 83–85; *Evreiskie narodnye pesni v Rossii* (Jewish Folk Songs in Russia), 64, 81, 83, 84, 159; and Yiddish folk song project, 56, 64–65, 67, 73, 76, 77, 81, 159, 162; in Zakharinka circle, 61, 63; Markon, Isaak, 123
Maria Fedorovna (tsarina), 144
Marranos (medieval Spanish Jewish converts), 41
Marxism, 172, 201–2, 204, 205; cultural policies of, 214
Medtner, Emil, 116; *Modernizm i muzyke*, 234n35
Medvedev, Alexander, 132
Mendelssohn, Felix: hybrid identity of, 3, 168, 211; as "musical Jew," 9, 22, 102, 115, 167, 169, 244n4; Rubinstein and, 20; Wagner and, 104
Mendelssohn, Moses, 8, 168
Meshcherskii, Vladimir P., 52
Meyerbeer, Giacomo, 9, 20, 115, 119, 213
Meyerhold, Vsevolod, 202, 205
Mikhail Aleksandrovich (grand duke), 189
Mikhoels, Solomon, 216
Milner, Mikhail (Moisei) A., 104, 117, 120, 202; *Di himlen brennen* (opera), 202
Milstein, Nathan, 103, 148, 200
Minkovskii, Pinhas, 56, 123, 155
Mixolydian mode, 77
modal theories of music, 179–80, 181
modernism, European: Jewish role in, 2, 3, 5–6, 185–86; Russian engagement in, 62, 184; salons and, 20–21
modernism, in music: internationalist, 199,

203, 204, 205; Russian, 116, 130, 185–86, 234n35
"Modern Jewish Revolution, The" (Harshav), 5
Moniuszko, Stanisław, 98
Moscow: anti-Jewish policies in, 60; musical culture in, 10, 19, 193; music publishing in, 138, 177; as postrevolutionary capital, 193; Society for Jewish Folk Music branch in, 177
Moscow Conservatory: Engel and, 11, 59–60, 61–62, 81, 194; founding of, 24; Gnesin and, 100, 204; Jewish student enrollment at, 43, 60, 100, 102; Jewish works in concerts at, 132, 201; People's Conservatory and, 80; renaming of, 244n4; and Society for Jewish Folk Music, 177
Moscow Musical-Ethnographic Commission, 63, 67, 70, 72, 80, 85, 107
Moscow Society for Jewish Music, 194, 195, 203, 204, 205
Mozart, W. A., 26, 167, 168
music: "nationality" in, 106–7; as transformative power, 55, 94, 95
music, European: Jewish presence in, 2, 3–4, 8–9, 142; salons and, 20–21
music, Gypsy, 48, 71, 155
music, Jewish: Ashkenazi, 7–8, 9, 11, 12, 37, 57, 66, 68, 94, 127, 139, 144; biblical chant as, 162, 169, 180; broad appeal of, 213–14; commercialization of, 12–13, 135–72; cultural nationalism and, 7, 11–13, 39, 41, 56–57, 58, 59, 61, 71, 81, 82–83, 93, 95–96, 114, 117, 133, 158, 171–72, 183; as cultural synthesis, 219; distinctive qualities of, 68–69, 71, 77, 106, 141, 142, 144, 168, 178–82; efforts to define, 114–15, 132, 162–63, 168, 177, 178–87; in "ethnographic concerts," 67–72; ethnographic recording of, 85, 86 fig. 2, 87, 89, 90 fig. 4, 91, 92, 160 fig. 14, 161; foreign influences on, 178–79; liturgical, 33, 34–35, 40–41, 57, 66–67, 73, 114, 120, 123, 126, 130, 142, 153, 155, 161, 162–63, 168, 170, 174, 176, 178–80, 181; modal theory of, 179–80, 181, 182; modern meanings of, 172, 216; modern study of, 65–79; "national," 7, 114–16, 171–72, 177, 178, 179, 182, 185; "national school" in, 174; non-Jewish musicians and, 114–15, 130, 166; nostalgic appeal of, 14, 40–41, 93, 126–27, 163–65; scholarly recognition for, 173–74; Soviet modernist idiom in, 218; Soviet repression of, 215; Soviet suppression of, 217; supposed absence of, 7. See also composers, Russian Jewish; folk songs, Jewish; musicians, Russian Jewish; opera; Society for Jewish Folk Music
music, Russian: cultural nationalism in, 47, 50, 51, 106, 139; distinctive qualities of, 71, 139; folk-oriented nationalism in, 31, 35, 36; Jewish elements in, 35–36, 37, 59, 73–74, 115, 119, 215–19; Jewish predominance in, 1–2, 7, 43–46, 48, 97–98, 103, 113–14, 200–201, 210, 212; liturgical, 73–74; modernism in, 116, 130, 185–86, 192–93; nationalism in, 2, 31, 35–37, 47, 49, 50, 70–72, 75; Russian-Jewish symbiosis in, 215; Soviet-era politicization of, 203–4; *vostochnyi* in, 36, 37, 106, 167–68
musical ethnography, 11, 57, 63–79, 82, 135, 139, 144, 161, 179, 201. *See also* Jewish Historical-Ethnographic Expedition; nationalism, folk-oriented
musical history, Jewish: Saminsky's theory of, 178
musicality, Jewish reputation for, 7, 66–67, 83, 96, 98, 102, 103–4, 113–14, 116–17, 210–11, 215
music criticism, in Russia, 57–58, 62
musicians, Russian Jewish: in American concert careers, 200; in Ashkenazi communities, 9; Bolshevik Revolution impact on, 188–95, 200–205; contrasting images of, 167–68; and creation of modern Jewish music, 12–13, 14; cultural redefinition of, 27–28, 96; emigration and, 172, 174–75, 176, 192–93, 195, 197–200, 208, 233n25; Jewish community demand for, 131–32; from Odessa, 9–10, 94–95, 200; sociocultural dilemmas of, 114, 201; Stalinist era and, 202, 205–8; statistical overrepresentation of, 1–2, 7, 43–46, 48, 97–98, 103, 113–14, 200–201, 210, 212. *See also* composers, Russian Jewish; Free Artist status; klezmer musicians; Moscow Conservatory; names of individuals; Society for Jewish Folk Music; St. Petersburg Conservatory
musicology, as academic discipline, 62, 66, 179
music publishing, cultural implications of, 135–36, 171–72; graphic arts and, 81, 150 fig. 13, 237n18
Mussorgsky, Modest: Jewish themes and, 36, 37, 38 ex. 1a–1b, 115–16, 119, 148, 167; on Jews and music, 94
Mussorgsky, Modest, compositions: "Evreiskaia pesnia" (Hebrew Songs), 37, 38 ex. 1a; *Iisus Navin* (*Joshua* cantata), 37, 119,

INDEX

Mussorgsky, Modest (continued)
167; *Pictures at an Exhibition*, 37, 38 ex. 1b, 226n47
Myaskovsky, Nikolai, 201
Mysh, Mikhail, 123

"Nagen, M." (pseud.), 114, 125, 126, 138
Narkompros (People's Commissariat for Enlightenment), 189, 190–91, 192, 194, 201
Narodnaia konservatoriia (People's Conservatory), 80–81
Narodnyi universitet (People's University), 81
narodovedeniia (science of nationality), 63, 64
Nathans, Benjamin, 32
national culture, Jewish: organizations promoting, 109–11, 113, 114, 117–22, 171–72, 237n18; in Palestine, 193; Soviet policies toward, 190–91, 192, 201–5, 208, 209. *See also* names of cultural organizations
national culture, Russian: broad definition of, 211. *See also* music, Russian
national identity, Jewish: and attachment to Russian culture, 212; and folk music, 213; in musical character, 106–7, 179–83; and Russian imperial ethos, 4, 12, 59, 70–71, 92, 132, 185, 197; twentieth century redefinition of, 2–3
nationalism, Jewish: cultural, 11, 41, 55, 60, 61, 73, 77–79, 81, 84, 95–96, 109–10, 111, 113, 117, 157, 159, 193, 214, 219; Dubnow's ideas on, 56–57, 64, 108; Engel's conflicted role in, 57–59, 91–93; folk-oriented, 13, 55, 56, 64, 84, 171; liberals and, 108, 113; musical, 91, 95–96, 108, 111, 114, 117, 118; political, 175; in songbook for schools, 161–69. *See also* music, Jewish; Zionism
nationalism, Russian: conservative, 73, 95, 104, 212; ethnic distinctions and, 107; musical, 59, 63, 70–72, 75, 107; reactionary, 109; Soviet regime and, 214–15
Naumborg, Samuel, 66
Nesvizhskii, Lev (Arieh Abileah), 110, 111, 120, 125, 193, 233n25
New York: Russian émigrés in, 198–200, 241n35; Yiddish theater in, 140
Nicholas I (tsar), 28, 138
Nicholas II (tsar), 80
nigunim (Hasidic melodies), 7–8, 37, 57, 66, 69 ex. 4, 71, 113, 125, 130, 144, 161, 162, 169, 178, 179, 182, 195
Nister, Der (Pinhas Kahanovich), 195
Novoe Vremia (New Time), 45, 47, 48, 51, 52, 116

Obshchestvo dlia rastropranenii proveshcheniia mezhdu evreiami v Rossii (Society for the Promotion of Enlightenment among the Jews of Russia) (OPE), 32–33, 52, 113, 119–20, 152, 159, 161, 169
Ocherk etnografii evreiskogo naseleniia v Rossii (Ethnographic Outline of the Jewish Population of Russia) (Berlin), 66–67
October Manifesto of 1905, 80
October Revolution of 1917: impact on Jews of, 189–92, 193–95
Odessa (Ukraine): Jewish musical culture in, 9–10, 34, 67, 119, 131, 158, 176; prodigies from, 46, 94–95, 103, 111, 123, 200; Rubinstein family in, 24, 53; Zionist Committee in, 202
Offenbach, Jacques, 9
Oistrakh, David, 2, 200
Okun, Israel S., 120, 155, 187
Olenina-d'Alheim, Maria, 115–16
OPE. *See Obshchestvo dlia rastropranenii proveshcheniia mezhdu evreiami v Rossii* (Society for the Promotion of Enlightenment among the Jews of Russia) (OPE)
opera: Jews and, 9–10, 23, 34, 37–38, 41–43, 98, 115, 120, 123, 154–55, 156–57, 179, 202, 203, 237–38n35; as universal art form, 35; Wagnerism, 117
Orientalism, in music, 36, 107, 195. *See also* augmented second interval; "pan-Oriental" mode; *vostochnost/vostchnyi* (easternness)
Orshanskii, Ilia, 67
"Our Conservatories" (anonymous attack on Rubinstein), 47–48
"Oyfn pripetshik" (Warshavsky), 163, 164–65, 164 ex. 8

Pale of Settlement, 1, 5, 9, 10, 12, 15, 32, 33, 43, 57, 59–60, 64, 65, 75, 77, 82, 84, 95, 97, 108, 115, 131, 153, 169, 171, 186; abolition in 1917 of, 188; cultural changes within, 134–35; ethnographic recordings in, 160 fig. 14, 161, 169, 180; impact of World War I on, 175, 176, 177. *See also* Jewish Historical-Ethnographic Expedition
Palestine: Jewish national culture and, 193; plans for opera and conservatory in, 191, 195; Russian Jews in, 131, 176, 193, 195, 197–98, 202, 203, 207, 233n25. *See also* Israel, modern; Tel Aviv; Zionism
"pan-Oriental" mode, 179–80, 180 ex. 9, 181
pan-Slavism, 31. *See also* music, Russian
Pasternak, Boris, 81

Pasternak, Leonid, 81
People's Conservatory (Narodnaia konservatoriia), 80–81
People's University (Narodnyi universitet), 81
Peretz, Isaac Leybush, 12–13, 64, 82, 128, 138, 171–72, 173, 197
Petrograd. *See* St. Petersburg
philosemitism, 73–75, 96, 97, 100, 102, 103–4, 115, 167; and antisemitism, 3, 12, 98, 104, 106–8, 114, 116, 117, 210–12, 221n2, 226n49, 230n19; in characterization of Jewish musicians, 210; as distorted view of Jews, 211
phonograph recordings. *See* recordings, of Jewish music
Poland, Ashkenazi music in, 7–8
Poliakin, Miron, 174
political activism, Russian Jewish, 79–80, 96, 108–9
political songs, Jewish, 140–42
populism, Jewish cultural: 68, 75–79, 82–84, 161, 182–83, 186, 197, 204
pravo zhitelstva (right of residence), 1, 21–22, 32, 46, 95, 103, 106, 121
Prokofiev, Sergei, 201; *Overture on Hebrew Themes* (op. 34), 241n35
Purishkevich, Vladimir, 128, 154
Pushkin, Alexander, 185

quotas: for Jewish student populations, 1, 45, 60, 97–99, 100, 117, 207

Rabinovich, Sholem. *See* Aleichem, Sholem
Rachmaninov, Sergei, 80
Raden, Edith F., 28
Radziwiłł family, 19
Razsvet (Dawn), 110, 113, 125, 138, 149, 177, 178, 179, 180
"Reb Naḥman's Nigun" (Reb Naḥman's Melody) (arr. Zeitlin), 153
recordings, of Jewish music: commercial, 13, 136, 140, 153–56; ethnographic, 12–13, 85, 86 fig. 2, 89, 90 fig. 4, 91, 160 fig. 14, 201; opposition to, 155
Revolution of 1848 (Germany), 21
Riemann, Hugo: *Musik-Lexicon*, 63
right of residence (*pravo zhitelstva*), in Russia, 1, 21–22, 32, 46, 95, 103, 106, 121
Rimsky-Korsakov, Andrei, 92
Rimsky-Korsakov, Nikolai: as conservatory faculty member, 1, 7, 79, 100, 101 fig. 6, 104, 105 fig. 7, 106–8, 110, 115, 120, 133,

174, 203, 204, 212, 215; Engel and, 92, 106; Oriental musical motifs and, 36, 106, 119
Rivesman, Mark, 120, 128, 159, 163, 166
Rodenberg, Julius, 25, 37, 42
Romanticism, 219; cultural influence of, 20–21, 22, 29, 30, 31, 35, 48, 55, 64, 70, 74, 83, 84, 106–7, 184, 186; in musical style, 130, 139, 203, 209; nationalism and, 114
Roskies, David, 165
Rosowsky, Borukh Leyb, 33, 110
Rosowsky, Solomon, 104, 105 fig. 7, 110, 111, 113, 119, 120, 123, 168, 171, 192, 193, 198, 200, 216; on Society for Jewish Folk Music, 213
rossiiskii (Russian). *See* "Russianness"
Rubinshteyn, Reuven. *See* Rubinstein, Roman Ivanovich
Rubinstein, Alexander, 53
Rubinstein, Anton, 2, 10–11, 15–55, 224n25; Balakirev and, 47, 52, 104, 106; as conservatory director, 2, 15, 31–32, 33–34, 41, 43, 44–53, 120, 215; collection of thoughts by, 54–55; cultural legacy of, 219; hybrid identity of, 53, 55, 58–59, 119, 167, 168, 208, 211, 226n49; Jewish musical idioms and, 37–39, 39 ex. 2, 40–41, 115, 119; jubilee celebration for, 47, 48, 52–53; manifesto on artist's status by, 29–30; musical criticism by, 35–36; as musical prodigy, 95; music of, 211, 213; operas and, 23, 25–26, 37, 39, 41–43, 53, 170, 179, 192; Oriental musical color and, 37–38, 167–68, 179; portrait of, 16 fig. 1, 103
Rubinstein, Anton, compositions: "Evreiskaia melodiia" (Hebrew Melody), 37, 39 ex. 2; *Persian Songs*, 37–38
Rubinstein, Anton, operas: *Cain*, 42; *Christ* (op. 117), 42; *Demon*, 37–38; *Dmitri Donskoi* (*The Battle of Kulikovo*), 23; *Feramors*, 37–38; *Fomka Durachok* (Fomka the Fool), 23; *Job*, 42; *The Maccabees*, 37, 39, 170, 192; *Mest* (Vengeance), 23; *Moses* (op. 112), 42; *Sibirskie okhotniki* (The Siberian Hunters), 23; *Sulamith*, 37, 42; *The Tower of Babel* (op. 80), 42, 167
Rubinstein, Anton, writings: *Anton Rubinstein's Gedankenkorb*, 54–55; "On Music in Russia," 29–30
Rubinstein, Grigorii Romanovich, 19
Rubinstein, Jacob (Iakov), 21–22
Rubinstein, Kaleriia Khristoforovna, 19, 22, 24, 26, 223n1, 223–24n11
Rubinstein, Liubov, 223–24n11

Rubinstein, Nikolai, 20, 21–22, 24, 54, 244n4
Rubinstein, Roman Ivanovich, 18–19, 21, 24
Rubinstein, Sophia, 22, 24, 80
Rubinstein, Vera Aleksandrovna Chekuanova, 34–35
Russia, Imperial: censorship in, 137–38; conservative nationalism in, 48, 50, 53, 152; culturally inclusive ideal for, 212–13; easternness as cultural theme in, 73, 167, 185; Jewish patriotism toward, 59, 111; liberal reform efforts in, 17–18, 28, 29–30; as multi-ethnic empire, 212–13; multi-ethnic ideal of, 70–72, 73, 107, 119; musical culture in, 2, 22, 29, 30, 152, 176, 184; musical education system in, 15; national identity and, 2, 4–5, 23–24, 29–30, 36; national minorities and, 118–19, 158, 185, 190; professional status for musicians in, 27–28, 29; social unrest in, 1, 12, 108–9; socio-legal estate system in, 21–22, 26–27, 31, 32. *See also* music, Russian
Russia, post-Soviet: Engel's reputation in, 58
Russia, Soviet. *See* Soviet Union (USSR)
"Russian Composers" (Rubinstein), 35–36
Russian Jews. *See* evrei; composers, Russian Jewish; Jews, Russian; musicians, Russian Jewish; zhid
Russian language, in Jewish culture, 159
Russian Musical Society, 28–29, 31
"Russianness": as citizenship *vs.* ethnicity, 2, 4–5, 23–24, 29–30, 48, 49, 50, 51, 107, 227n67; in Soviet culture, 214, 215
Russian Revolution of 1905, 79–80, 96, 103, 104, 108, 109, 138, 155, 159, 185
Russian Revolution of 1917. *See* Bolshevik Revolution of 1917; October Revolution of 1917
Russkie vedomosti (Russian Bulletin), 57, 62, 80
Russification, cultural, 4, 24, 33, 132
russkii (Russian). *See* "Russianness"
Ruzhin, Tsaddik of, 87

Sabaneev, Leonid, 117, 210
Sacchetti, Libero, 173–74; *Lectures on the History of Music*, 173–74
salons: in European culture, 20–21; in St. Petersburg, 23, 121
Saminsky, Lazare I.: as émigré to the United States, 198–200; in polemic with Engel, 175, 177–82, 183–86, 195, 197, 198, 208, 240n15; portrait of, 112 fig. 8; and Society for Jewish Folk Music, 111, 117, 120, 122, 126, 139, 161, 170; at St. Petersburg Conservatory,

104; "Unter Soreles vigele" (Under Little Sarah's Cradle), arranged by, 139
Saminsky, Lazare I., writings: "Artistic Achievement in the Recent Work of the Society for Jewish Folk Music," 177; *Music of Our Day: Essentials and Prophecies*, 199; *Music of the Ghetto and Bible*, 199; *Ob evreiskoi muzyke* (On Jewish Music), 170, 178, 186
Sandler, Peretz, 130; "Eili, Eili" (My God, My God), 140
Sargeant, Lynn, 44
Sats, Ilia, 138
Schiller, Friedrich: "Ode to Joy," 166–67
Schindler's List (film), 165
Schir Iwri (film), 148
Schoenberg, Arnold, 3, 191, 199, 200
Schumann, Clara, 20
Science of Judaism. *See Wissenschaft des Judentums*
Scriabin, Alexander, 62, 116–17, 185
secular (*svetskaia*) music, Jewish: "national" character and, 74, 114, 162–63, 175, 177–82, 183–84, 186, 187. *See also* folk songs, Jewish
Serov, Alexander, 30–31
Shalyt, Mordechai, 140
Sheftel, Mikhail, 123
Shkliar, Efraim: as Jewish nationalist, 111; and Society for Jewish Folk Music, 110, 120, 122, 139, 148; at St. Petersburg Conservatory, 104, 106, 108
Shkliar, Efraim, songs arranged by: "Di alte kashe" (The Old Question), 139; "Di gildene pave" (The Golden Peacock), 139; "Ha-tikvah," 140–41, 141 ex. 6, 142
Shor, David, 61, 80, 177, 193, 202, 203
Shostakovich, Dmitri, 12, 215–17, 218, 219; First Violin Concerto, 218; Thirteenth Symphony, "Babi Yar," 216–17
Shteinberg, Maksimilian O., 101 fig. 6, 107
Shternberg, Lev, 84, 85
Shtreilker, Liubov, 174, 185
shund (Jewish popular music), 154, 155, 174
Sibelius, Jean, 110
Sibirskie okhotniki (opera), 23
Silver Age (*Serebrianyi vek*), Russian, 62, 184
Singer, Josef, 66
Sirota, Gershon, 122, 155
Slavophilism, 31. *See also* music, Russian
Slezkine, Yuri: *The Jewish Century*, 5–6
slianie (fusion, rapprochement), 53
Sliozberg, Genrikh B., 113, 120

Slonimsky, Nicholas, 189
Smetana, Bedrich: *The Moldau*, 141, 142
Social Democratic Party, 111, 113, 188
socialism, and Russian Jewish culture of, 175, 208
Socialist Revolutionary movement, 183
Society for Jewish Folk Music: anticommercial mandate of, 149, 151, 156, 157, 170, 172; breakup of, 13, 192, 203, 213, 215; commercial sound recordings and, 136, 153–56; concerts sponsored by, 115, 122–23, 125–28, 130–32, 135, 161, 171, 173, 174, 176, 191–92; cultural agendas of, 3, 12, 13, 91, 95–96, 109, 114, 117–18, 119, 121–22, 125, 127–28, 130–31, 132–33, 135, 138–39, 155, 156, 157, 158, 171–72, 176–77, 213; cultural objectives of, 213; founding of, 137, 161; membership of, 3, 12, 91, 104, 110, 111, 113, 117, 118, 120, 121–22, 123, 151, 158, 161, 169, 170–71, 176, 177, 190, 191, 199–200, 202, 203; musical anthology sponsored by, 157–59, 161–70, 176; as music publisher, 138–42, 144, 145 fig.12, 146, 148–49, 150 fig. 13, 151–53, 155, 157, 169, 170, 172, 176, 186, 191, 203; opera prize offered by, 155–56; pre-concert lectures for, 125, 128, 161; printed concert programs for, 124 fig. 9, 128, 129 fig. 10, 130; and Revolution of 1917, 188, 189–90, 191–92, 193–94; under Soviet rule, 175; World War I activities of, 176–77
Society for the Promotion of Enlightenment among the Jews of Russia. *See Obshchestvo dlia rastropranenii proveshcheniia mezhdu evreiami v Rossii* (Society for the Promotion of Enlightenment among the Jews of Russia) (OPE)
Solov'ev, Nikolai, 49
Songbook for the Jewish School and Family, 158–59, 161–70, 176, 181, 182, 191
soslovie (socio-legal estate system), 21, 27, 32. *See also* right of residence
Soviet Union (USSR): Engel's reputation in, 58; Jewish music and, 175, 200–205, 208–9, 210–19; Russian Jewish experience in, 6, 214; Stalinist era in, 202, 205–9
Spendiarov, Alexander, 107
spiritual opera ("geistliche Oper"), 41–43
Stalin, Joseph, 205, 207, 215, 216
Stasov, Vladimir, 11, 30, 31, 36, 47, 73–75; "Twenty-Five Years of Russian Art," 36
Stern, Isaac, 200
Stoliarskii, Petr, 94
Stolypin, Petr, 103, 158

St. Petersburg: Jewish elite of, 121, 123, 125, 126–27, 158; Jewish music publishing in, 136–42, 144, 146, 148–49, 151, 178; musical culture in, 10, 21, 22, 23, 114, 117, 123, 131, 171 (*See also* Society for Jewish Folk Music); postrevolutionary conditions in, 189–92
St. Petersburg Conservatory: antisemitic attacks on, 45–53, 95, 98; crisis of 1905 at, 79, 103, 108; faculty of, 1, 173–74; female students at, 29, 31, 46, 105 fig 7, 120–21; founding of, 10, 11, 15, 18, 28–30, 31, 32, 96–97; hundredth anniversary of, 219; Jewish music concerts at, 122–23, 127, 128, 132, 191–92; Jewish students at, 1, 10, 11, 12, 30, 32, 33, 43–45, 50, 94, 97–98, 100, 101 fig. 6, 102–4, 105 fig. 7, 106, 107–8, 111, 119, 120–21, 127; as means of Jewish emancipation, 211; scholarships at, 52, 106. *See also* Free Artist status (*svobodnyi khudoshnik*)
Strauss, Richard, 110
Stravinsky, Igor, 62, 183, 199, 201
Sulzer, Salomon, 130
Suvorin, Aleksei S., 52
symbolist movement, in Russia, 116
Symphonic Monument to 1905–1917 (Gnesin), 204
Syrkin, M. G., 192
Szigeti, Joseph, 233n25

Taneev, Sergei, 62, 63, 70, 80, 186, 212
Taruskin, Richard, 226n47
Tchaikovsky, Peter, 33, 49, 59, 244n4
Tchernichowsky, Saul, 166, 167
Tel Aviv: Engel composition prize in, 58; Russian Jewish émigrés in, 175, 193, 195, 197–98
Temple Emanu-El (New York), 198–99
theater, Yiddish: in New York, 140; in Russia, 5, 130, 137, 139, 140, 153, 154, 156, 201, 204–5
Thesaurus of Hebrew-Oriental Melodies (Idelsohn), 183
Tolstoy, Lev, 185
Tomars, Joseph (Iosif) S., 120, 192
trop (biblical chant), 162, 169, 180

Ukraine. *See* Berdichev; folk songs, Ukrainian; Odessa
Union of Composers, 207
Union of Russian People, 80, 119
United States: Jewish community in, 198–99; postrevolutionary émigrés in, 193, 198–200; Russian Jewish émigré experience in, 214

"Unter Soreles vigele" (folk song, arr. Saminsky), 139
USSR—Shock Brigade of the World Proletariat, The (Krein), 204

Vaisenberg, Fania, 121
Varshavskii, Mark, 123
Vazeh, Mirza-Shafi, 37
Veinberg, Jacob, 174, 177, 193, 200
Veisberg, Iuliia L., 105 fig. 7, 107, 174
Veprik, Alexander, 201
"Vi er zingt" (How He Sings) (folk song, arr. Engel), 71–72, 72 ex. 5
Vinaver, Maksim, 83, 123
Volkonsky, Vladimir, 103
vostochnost/vostochnyi (easternness), as cultural theme, 36, 37, 73, 106, 167–68, 185

Wagner, Richard: antisemitism and, 3, 31, 42, 102, 104, 116, 117, 142, 183, 184, 234n35, 244n4; as "German" composer, 107, 110; "Judaism in Music," 102, 117, 221n2; *Ring* cycle by, 117; rumored Jewish background of, 211
Warsaw, Jewish culture in, 171
Warsaw Ghetto Uprising, fifth anniversary of, 207
Warshavsky, Mark, 75–77, 78, 79, 163, 164–65; *Evreiskie narodnye pesni* (Jewish Folk Songs), 75; "Di mezinke oysgegeben" (The Youngest Daughter Married Off), 75; "Oyfn pripetshik" (On the Hearth)/"Der alef beys" (The Alphabet), 75, 163, 164 ex. 8, 164–65
Weinberg, Moisei (Mieczsław), 12, 215–16, 217–19; Sixth Symphony, "Jewish Violin," 218–19, 244n4
Weintraub, Hirsh, 66
Weissenberg, Samuel, 83–84
Winz, Leo, 65, 153, 169
Wissenschaft des Judentums (science of Judaism), 11, 66, 67, 74
Wolff, Hermann, 54
women: as arts sponsors, 19–20, 23, 121; ethnographic expedition and, 91; as music conservatory students, 29, 31, 46, 47, 105 fig 7, 120–21; as professional musicians, 98, 100, 115–16, 174. *See also* names of individuals
World War I: Jewish relief activities and, 176; onset of, 171, 172; and violence against Jews, 175, 176

Yesenin, Sergei A., 204
Yevtushenko, Yevgeny, 216, 217
Yiddish language: Bolshevik support for, 201; folk songs in, 7, 56–57, 64, 66, 67, 68, 69, 125, 130, 138, 139, 153, 161, 162, 163, 178, 179, 181, 183, 204; Jewish culture and, 8, 11–12, 58, 60, 61, 77–78, 87, 88, 162, 187, 191, 195, 197; Jewish literature in, 5, 136, 171; mass printing techniques and, 136; in modern Jewish music, 216; opera in, 157, 192, 202; origins of, 7; poetry in, 218; poets, 217; popular songs composed in, 10, 75–77, 78, 79, 134–35, 139, 140, 163, 164–65, 164 ex. 8; prevalence in Russia of, 4, 5; sheet music published in, 136–37; song lyrics translated into, 166; theater in, 5, 130, 137, 139, 140, 153, 154, 156, 201, 204–5; tsarist censorship and, 137–38
Yudina, Maria, 174
Yudovin, Solomon, 87, 88 fig. 3, 89

Zakharin, Grigorii A., 60
Zakharinka circle, 60–61, 63, 65, 69
Zeitlin, Leo, 200; "Reb Nahmans nigun" (Reb Nahman's Melody) arranged by, 153
zhid (negative term for Jew), 37, 67, 80, 94, 127–28, 184, 226n49
Zhitomirsky, Alexander M., 104, 120, 162, 163
Ziloti, Alexander, 102
Zimbalist, Efrem, 1, 2, 94, 95, 105 fig. 7, 148, 200
Zimro Ensemble, 191, 241n35
Zionism: activists in, 6, 60, 61, 108, 109, 177, 191, 202; Jewish identity and, 4, 54, 56, 58, 208–9, 214; music and, 113, 140–42, 165, 183, 184–85, 186, 187, 188, 193, 195, 197–98, 202; opponents of, 109, 110, 111, 183; organizations promoting, 110, 131, 191; publication projects and, 157–58. *See also* Israel, modern; Palestine; Tel Aviv
zmires (Sabbath table songs), 33, 113
"Zog zhe rebeynu" (Tell Me Rabbi) (folk song), 153
Zolotarev, Vasilii A., 115; *Evreiskaia rapsodiia* (Jewish Rhapsody), 115
Zunser, Eliokum, 134, 137

Printed in the USA
CPSIA information can be obtained
at www.ICGtesting.com
JSHW081339031123
51320JS00012B/157